Histories of the Normal and the Abnormal

Each culture and historic period has its specific ways of defining what we would nowadays refer to as the 'normal'. Until the middle of the nineteenth century, the term 'normal' was defined in English dictionaries simply in a formalistic way as 'standing at right angles', while the first edition of the *Dictionnaire de l'Académie française* of 1694 does not even carry a definition for 'normal'. Where we now would use the term 'normal', pre-modern definitions referred to the 'natural'. The change from a religiously ordained natural order to a scientifically grounded secular framework, and the emergence of the normal/abnormal dichotomy in preference to the earlier polarisation of natural/unnatural, encapsulate an important shift, with the emergence of modern science bringing issues of norms and normativity into sharp focus.

The essays in this collection engage with the concepts of the normal and the abnormal from a variety of different academic disciplines, including the history of art, the social history of medicine and cultural anthropology. The internationally respected contributors use as their conceptual anchors the works of moral and political philosophers (Foucault, Canguilhem and Hacking), sociologists (Durkheim, Goffman) and anthropologists (Benedict, Douglas and Mead). Major themes covered include the way norms are constructed and reinforced; how the abnormal is streamlined or excluded; how the abnormal serves to reassert norms and normality; and the representations of the abnormal as spectacle and wonder.

Waltraud Ernst is Reader in History at the University of Southampton.

Routledge studies in the social history of medicine
Edited by Joseph Melling
University of Exeter
and
Anne Borsay
University of Wales, Swansea, UK

The Society for the Social History of Medicine was founded in 1969, and exists to promote research into all aspects of the field, without regard to limitations of either time or place. In addition to this book series, the Society also organises a regular programme of conferences, and publishes an internationally recognised journal, *Social History of Medicine*. The Society offers a range of benefits, including reduced-price admission to conferences and discounts on SSHM books, to its members. Individuals wishing to learn more about the Society are invited to contact the series editors through the publisher.

The Society took the decision to launch 'Studies in the Social History of Medicine', in association with Routledge, in 1989, in order to provide an outlet for some of the latest research in the field. Since that time, the series has expanded significantly under a number of series editors, and now includes both edited collections and monographs. Individuals wishing to submit proposals are invited to contact the series editors in the first instance.

1 **Nutrition in Britain**
Science, scientists and politics in the twentieth century
Edited by David F. Smith

2 **Migrants, Minorities and Health**
Historical and contemporary studies
Edited by Lara Marks and Michael Worboys

3 **From Idiocy to Mental Deficiency**
Historical perspectives on people with learning disabilities
Edited by David Wright and Anne Digby

4 **Midwives, Society and Childbirth**
Debates and controversies in the modern period
Edited by Hilary Marland and Anne Marie Rafferty

5 **Illness and Healing Alternatives in Western Europe**
Edited by Marijke Gijswit-Hofstra, Hilary Maarland and Has de Waardt

6 **Health Care and Poor Relief in Protestant Europe 1500–1700**
Edited by Ole Peter Grell and Andrew Cunningham

7 **The Locus of Care**
Families, communities, institutions, and the provision of welfare since antiquity
Edited by Peregrine Horden and Richard Smith

8 **Race, Science and Medicine, 1700–1960**
Edited by Waltraud Ernst and Bernard Harris

9 **Insanity, Institutions and Society, 1800–1914**
Edited by Bill Forsythe and Joseph Melling

10 **Food, Science, Policy and Regulation in the Twentieth Century**
International and comparative perspectives
Edited by David F. Smith and Jim Phillips

11 **Sex, Sin and Suffering**
Venereal disease and European society since 1870
Edited by Roger Davidson and Lesley A. Hall

12 **The Spanish Influenza Pandemic of 1918–19**
New perspectives
Edited by Howard Phillips and David Killingray

13 **Plural Medicine, Tradition and Modernity, 1800–2000**
Edited by Waltraud Ernst

14 **Innovations in Health and Medicine**
Diffusion and resistance in the twentieth century
Edited by Jenny Stanton

15 **Contagion**
Historical and cultural studies
Edited by Alison Bashford and Claire Hooker

16 **Medicine, Health and the Public Sphere in Britain, 1600–2000**
Edited by Steve Sturdy

17 **Medicine and Colonial Identity**
Edited by Mary P. Sutphen and Bridie Andrews

18 **New Directions in Nursing History**
Edited by Barbara E. Mortimer and Susan McGann

19 **Medicine, the Market and Mass Media**
Producing health in the twentieth century
Edited by Virginia Berridge and Kelly Loughlin

20 **The Politics of Madness**
The state, insanity and society in England, 1845–1914
Joseph Melling and Bill Forsythe

21 **The Risks of Medical Innovation**
Risk perception and assessment in historical context
Edited by Thomas Schlich and Ulrich Tröhler

22 **Mental Illness and Learning Disability since 1850**
Finding a place for mental disorder in the United Kingdom
Edited by Pamela Dale and Joseph Melling

23 **Britain and the 1918–19 Influenza Pandemic**
A dark epilogue
Niall Johnson

24 **Financing Medicine**
The British experience since 1750
Edited by Martin Gorsky and Sally Sheard

25 **Social Histories of Disability and Deformity**
Edited by David M. Turner and Kevin Stagg

26 **Histories of the Normal and the Abnormal**
Social and cultural histories of norms and normativity
Edited by Waltraud Ernst

Also available in the Routledge Studies in the Social History of Medicine series:

Reassessing Foucault
Power, medicine and the body
Edited by Colin Jones and Roy Porter

Histories of the Normal and the Abnormal

Social and cultural histories of norms and normativity

Edited by Waltraud Ernst

LONDON AND NEW YORK

First published 2006
by Routledge
2 Park Square, Milton Park, Abingdon, Oxon OX14 4RN

Simultaneously published in the USA and Canada
by Routledge
711 Third Avenue, New York, NY 10017

Routledge is an imprint of the Taylor & Francis Group, an informa business

First issued in paperback 2012

© 2006 Selection and editorial matter, Waltraud Ernst; individual
chapters, contributors

Typeset in Garamond by Wearset Ltd, Boldon, Tyne and Wear

All rights reserved. No part of this book may be reprinted or
reproduced or utilised in any form or by any electronic, mechanical,
or other means, now known or hereafter invented, including
photocopying and recording, or in any information storage or
retrieval system, without permission in writing from the publishers.

British Library Cataloguing in Publication Data
A catalogue record for this book is available from the British Library

Library of Congress Cataloging in Publication Data
A catalog record for this book has been requested

ISBN13: 978-0-415-36843-8 (hbk)
ISBN13: 978-0-415-64832-5 (pbk)
ISBN13: 978-0-203-02825-4 (ebk)

Contents

List of figures	ix
List of contributors	xi
Acknowledgements	xiv

1 **The normal and the abnormal: reflections on norms and normativity**   1
WALTRAUD ERNST

2 **Invisible friends: questioning the representation of the court dwarf in Hapsburg Spain**   26
JANET RAVENSCROFT

3 **From 'monstrous' to 'abnormal': the case of conjoined twins in the nineteenth century**   53
SARAH MITCHELL

4 **Eccentric lives: character, characters and curiosities in Britain, *c.*1760–1900**   73
JAMES GREGORY

5 **Constructing the common type: physiognomic norms and the notion of 'civic usefulness', from Lavater to Galton**   101
LUCY HARTLEY

6 **Norms and violations: ugliness and abnormality in caricatures of Monsieur Mayeux**   122
NICOLA COTTON

viii *Contents*

7 Made to measure? Tailoring and the 'normal' body in
   nineteenth-century France   142
   ALISON MATTHEWS DAVID

8 'A masculine mythology suppressing and distorting all
   the facts': British women contesting the concept of the
   male-as-norm, 1870–1930   165
   LESLEY A. HALL

9 Interpreting abnormal psychology in the late nineteenth
   century: William James's spiritual crisis   183
   FRANCIS NEARY

10 Can kinship be designed and still be normal? The
   curious case of child adoption   205
   ELLEN HERMAN

11 Flexible norms? From patients' values to physicians'
   standards   225
   CHRISTIANE SINDING

12 A matter of degree: the normalisation of hypertension,
   *c.*1940–2000   245
   CARSTEN TIMMERMANN

13 Deviant roles, normal lives: why every piazza needs its
   own 'madman'   262
   SARA BERGSTRESSER

   Subject index   282
   Name index   285

Figures

2.1	*Cardinal Granvelle's Dwarf* (Anthonis Mor, *c.*1550)	37
2.2	*Infanta Isabel Clara Eugenia and Magdalena Ruiz* (Alonso Sánchez Coello, *c.*1585–8)	41
2.3	*Las Meninas* (Diego Velázquez, 1656)	45
3.1	Chang and Eng, the original Siamese Twins, represented in an idealised Oriental landscape	57
4.1	'Chevalier Desseasau', from *The Book of Wonderful Characters*	75
4.2	Title page of *The Book of Wonderful Characters, Memoirs and Anecdotes of Remarkable and Eccentric Persons in All Ages and Countries*	79
5.1	Illustration from Johann Caspar Lavater, 'On the Harmony between Moral and Corporeal Beauty'	107
5.2	Frontispiece from Francis Galton, *Inquiries into Human Faculty and Its Development*	114
6.1	'Mr Mayeux, a life drawing by Hippolyte Robillard'	129
6.2	'The famous Mayeux: not stuffed, but alive. You will see him tie his shoelaces without bending down. Go in and see, come and see, come up and see, you will see . . .'	130
6.3	'Yes Mrs Mayeux, I received the votes of my fellow citizens, I have been elected . . . I bloody deserved it too!'	131
6.4	'Out of the question, my dear. I'm on duty now . . . Later perhaps . . .'	132
6.5	'Bloody hell, I think those sly young rascals are making fun of me and drawing a caricature of me!'	134
6.6	'Vous n'êtes pas grand, mon cher!'	135
7.1	The interior of an eighteenth-century tailor's workshop	145
7.2	Illustration from George Delas, *Le Somatomètre*	149
7.3	Honoré Daumier, 'The Military Review Board'	154
7.4	Illustration from Alexis Lavigne, *Méthode du tailleur* (Tailoring Method)	155

x *List of figures*

13.1 Advertisement for a festival sponsored by a cooperative of
ex-psychiatric patients, Bergamo, June 2000   263
13.2 A spray-painted homage to Carlos, the Basque juggler, after
his death, located in the area where he would most often
appear to perform his juggling act for passers-by   271

Contributors

Sara Bergstresser is a Postdoctoral Research Fellow in Mental Health Care Policy at Harvard Medical School, Boston, USA. She is currently working on a book manuscript based on her doctoral research: 'Therapies of the Mundane: Community Mental Health Care and Everyday Life in an Italian Town'. Future research directions include continuing research within the fields of medical anthropology, mental health policy, and science and technology studies.

Nicola Cotton teaches in the Department of French at the University of Bristol and is also a Visiting Lecturer in the Department of Visual Culture at the Faculty of Art, Media and Design at the University of the West of England. She completed her PhD on representations and theories of ugliness in modern French culture at University College London in 2000, and has since published articles on monsters, physiognomy and nineteenth-century French caricature. In 2002 she co-curated an exhibition of contemporary art, 'Nausea: Encounters with Ugliness', which showed in Nottingham and London. She is currently working on a book based on her doctoral thesis while also looking at the issue of ugliness in women's writing in French from the 1960s to the present, and at the links between nineteenth-century French aesthetics and twentieth- and twenty-first-century art.

Waltraud Ernst is Reader in History at the University of Southampton. Her publications include *Mad Tales from the Raj: The European Insane in British India* (1991); *Race, Science and Medicine* (edited together with B. J. Harris, 1999); and *Plural Medicine, Tradition and Modernity* (ed., 2002). She is a member of the editorial board of *History of Psychiatry*, and co-editor of *Social History of Medicine* and *Asian Medicine, Tradition and Modernity*. She is currently the President of the International Association for the Study of Traditional Asian Medicine (website: www.iastam.org).

James Gregory has taught Modern British History at the Universities of Durham and Southampton. His doctoral research was on the British vegetarian movement in the Victorian period, and he has published articles

xii *List of contributors*

and biographical studies on this topic. His recent research has focused on 'eccentricity' in nineteenth-century British culture, with several monographs published or forthcoming on the place of the 'eccentric' or 'character' in the northeast of England and in relation to wider British identities. His ongoing research on Victorian moral and social reform is organised around a study of the public careers and private lives of William Cowper-Temple, Lord Mount Temple, and his second wife, Georgina.

Lesley A. Hall, FRHistS, is Senior Archivist, Wellcome Library for the History and Understanding of Medicine London, and Honorary Lecturer in History of Medicine, University of London. She has published extensively on subjects to do with sexuality and gender in Britain during the nineteenth and twentieth centuries. Her edited anthology, *Outspoken Women: British Women Writing about Sex, 1870–1969*, was published by Routledge in 2005. Her website is www.lesleyahall.net.

Lucy Hartley is a Senior Lecturer in English at the University of Southampton, who specialises in the cultural and intellectual history of the nineteenth century. Her first book, *Physiognomy and the Meaning of Expression in Nineteenth-Century Culture*, was published by Cambridge University Press in 2001; and she is currently completing a book entitled 'The Democracy of the Beautiful, 1843–1893'.

Ellen Herman teaches history at the University of Oregon, USA. She is the author of *The Romance of American Psychology: Political Culture in the Age of Experts* (1993) and is working on a book, 'Kinship by Design', about the history of child adoption in the United States during the twentieth century. She maintains a website, The Adoption History Project: www.uoregon.edu/~adoption.

Alison Matthews David is Assistant Professor in the Faculty of Design and Communication, Ryerson University, Toronto, Canada. Her area of research is nineteenth- and early twentieth-century dress and textiles, and she was awarded her doctorate in 2002 for a thesis on tailoring and gender in nineteenth-century Paris. She has published on synthetic dyes, military uniforms and footwear, and Victorian horsewomen. Her current research areas include a project on camouflage and fashion during the First World War as well as a book on the medical hazards of dress entitled 'Fashion Victims: Death by Clothing', to be published by Berg Press in 2007.

Sarah Mitchell is currently completing her dissertation, entitled 'Entering the "Secret Workroom of Nature": Medical Treatment, Scientific Theories and Exhibition of Double Monsters in the Nineteenth Century', in History at the University of Southampton. She is also working as a Visiting Assistant Professor in the History Department at Virginia Tech, Blacksburg, Virginia.

List of contributors   xiii

Francis Neary is a Research Associate at the Centre for the History of Science, Technology and Medicine, University of Manchester. He works on late nineteenth-century psychology and psychiatry, particularly studies of human consciousness and scientific biography. He has also done some recent work on twentieth-century medical technologies with special reference to joint replacement.

Janet Ravenscroft is working on a PhD thesis entitled 'Invisible Friends: Questioning the Representation of the Court Dwarf in Early Modern Spain' at Birkbeck College, University of London. In her other life she is the Senior Commissioning Editor of adults' and children's books for a small, independent book packager.

Christiane Sinding is Director of Research at the Centre de Recherche Médecine, Sciences, Santé et Société (CERMES) in France. She is the author of *Le Clinicien et le chercheur. Des grandes maladies de carence à la médecine moléculaire, 1880–1980* (Presses Universitaires de France, 1991) and co-editor of *Dictionnaire de la pensée médicale* (Presses Universitaires de Frances, 2004). She is currently working on a book on the history of insulin.

Carsten Timmermann worked as a biochemist before he turned to the history of science and medicine in 1995. He holds an MA and a PhD from the University of Manchester, where he still works as a Wellcome Research Fellow. After writing on the history of hypertension treatments, he is now researching the history of lung cancer, as part of a larger project on the history of cancer research and cancer services in Britain since the Second World War.

Acknowledgements

The editor's academic interest in notions of the normal and abnormal was first roused when asked to contribute a historical essay on personality disorders to *A History of Clinical Psychiatry* (edited by G. E. Berrios and Roy Porter). This led to an engagement with medical and social norms, in particular in relation to psychopathic and antisocial behaviour disorders. At the time, few historians of medicine focused on the wider conceptual challenges posed by psychiatric categorisations and normative statements. Dr Chandak Sengoopta, now at Birkbeck College London, was a notable exception. He lectured on 'The normal and the abnormal in the history of psychiatry' at the Wellcome Centre for the History of Medicine and subsequently at Manchester University. He joined the editor in organising a conference entitled 'Historical Perspectives on the Normal and the Abnormal', held in 2002 at the Wellcome Unit for the History of Medicine and Centre for the History of Science, Technology and Medicine (CHSTM) at Manchester. Many thanks are due to him for his friendly support during the organisation of the event and for applying his intellectual rigour and supportive criticism to the selection of papers to be presented, making it possible for this volume to become a viable project following on from the meeting. Thanks are also due to the other staff at Manchester, and in particular the directors at the Wellcome Unit/CHSTM, Mick Worboys (from 2002) and John Pickstone (until 2002), who not only provided a congenial atmosphere for the meeting, but also offered much intellectual stimulation and constructive critique.

Some of the contributors originally presented their papers at Manchester (Bergstresser, Hartley, Herman, Mitchell, Ravenscroft, Timmermann). Thanks are due to them for exhibiting the kind of patience, trust and goodwill needed during the various stages of a book project of this kind. The remaining authors joined the book project at a later stage (Cotton, Gregory, Hall, Matthews David, Neary, Sinding). Thanks are due to them for further enhancing and complementing the perspectives employed in this volume and for agreeing to submit their essays within a tight timeframe.

Last but not least, many thanks to The Wellcome Trust and the Society for the Social History of Medicine for sponsoring the conference; to the Routledge Commissioning Editor, Terry Clague, for his interest in the topic and his efficiency; and in particular to the SSHM/Routledge Series Editor, Anne Borsay, for her supportive and helpful comments.

1 The normal and the abnormal
Reflections on norms and normativity

Waltraud Ernst

This book engages with the concepts of the normal and the abnormal from the perspectives of a variety of academic disciplines – ranging from art history to the social history of medicine, literature and science studies to sociology and cultural anthropology. The contributors use as their conceptual anchors the works of moral and political philosophers (Canguilhem, Foucault, Hacking), as well as the ideas put forward by sociologists (Durkheim, Goffman) and anthropologists (Benedict, Douglas, Mead). Such a plurality of approaches and diversity of theoretical background requires clarification of terms, not least because the issues of norms, normalisation and normativity are contested, and subject-specific methodologies and conceptual points of reference necessarily imbue terms with varied meanings.

Diversity of subject-specific methodologies and conceptual points of reference has the potential to harbour conceptual imprecision and confusion. Alternatively, it can constitute a fertile ground for conceptual refinement through interdisciplinary engagement. The ethnologist and psychoanalyst Georges Devereux suggested the latter in his *The Normal and the Abnormal*: 'A truly interdisciplinary science is the product of cross-fertilisation between the various key concepts of the involved disciplines.'[1] It is within such a framework of disciplinary exchange that the contributions to this volume need to be set.

Devereux does not only invite us to look over the often all too narrowly conceived rim of disciplinary boundaries. He also seems to imply that the terms 'normal' and 'abnormal' originated from the discipline of psychiatry.[2] Other scholars in contrast see Foucault and, increasingly, Canguilhem as the originators of these terms.[3] Sociologists in turn consider Durkheim, one of the founding fathers of their discipline, as their major fount of wisdom and inspiration in regard to social norms, while anthropologists refer to Boas's work.[4] Philosophers in contrast will place concerns about norms within the realm of ethics, because reflections on what 'is' and what 'ought' to be – on what is to be considered a given (or 'fact') in contrast to what is being prescribed or put forward as a normative suggestion – have been part and parcel of metaphysics and ethics respectively throughout the history of moral philosophy in the West.[5]

2 *Waltraud Ernst*

Such varied and competing foundation histories (and myths) and attempts to trace the origins of our key terms may rightly be seen as indicative of the fragmentation of, or − to put a slightly more positive construction on it − the increasing specialisation in, what have become the 'social sciences'. Given such fecundity, it is perhaps not surprising that a number of definitions of the nature, scope and meaning of norms − and of their assumed counterpart, variously labelled 'the abnormal' or 'the pathological' − should prevail, leading to some confusion, imprecision, and conflation of terms. Although any attempt at a definite answer to the question of the original source and single most authoritative meaning of our key terms is likely to be a moot point, a brief outline of major conceptual and linguistic shifts may aid clarification of terms and concepts, and provide the wider historiographic context within which specific case studies need to be set. In a similar vein, and as suggested by the moral philosopher Alasdair MacIntyre, the historical and cultural specificity of the key terms needs to be considered in order to avoid ungrounded generalisation and anachronism.[6] Further elucidation of key terms will of course also be undertaken in relation to and within the particular contexts of the specific historical and empirical evidence put forward in the individual case studies assembled in this volume.

The normal and abnormal in historical and cultural context

Until about the middle of the nineteenth century the term 'normal' was defined in English dictionaries simply in a formalistic way as 'standing at right angles'. Yet although no moral prescription appears to be inherent in this seemingly purely mathematical definition, the seed of evaluation and prescription can be discerned: the notion of measurement and measuring, of imposing a standard against which things and people are measured. A norm in this sense of 'running the rule' over someone or 'getting the measure of them' points us to the norm as a standard, a rule, or principle to be complied with. This leads to the modern, nineteenth- and twentieth-century meaning of the term: the norm as signifying expected forms of social behaviour, based on sets of more or less implicit social rules that exist independently of individuals and exercise a coercive influence, with breaches of the norm being subject to sanctions. This definition of norms as *social* norms that refer to conventions of behaviour and standards of value is taken as the starting point of analysis by thinkers such as Durkheim, Foucault and Canguilhem alike. This understanding fits in also with philosophical conventions, which are careful to differentiate between prescriptive and evaluative ('normative') statements (i.e. what 'ought' to be) on the one hand, and mere descriptions or statements of matters of fact (i.e. what 'is') on the other. It is the realm of the former that has been at the core of moral philosophy.

One important distinction that further exemplifies the 'ought'–'is' dichotomy needs to be made: the distinction between social norms and what could be called statistical norms. While the former signify a standard, rule, principle used to judge or direct human conduct as something to be complied with, the latter refer to an average or usual level of attainment or performance, which is nowadays frequently calculated by means of statistical procedures. The best-known statistical procedure involves the Gaussian or 'normal distribution', which has received particular attention recently following heated debates about the process of statistical racialisation alleged to have been inherent in the work by Richard Herrnstein and Charles Murray on the bell curve.[7] When a number of objects or persons are measured (heights, or the intelligence of African-Americans, for example, as in the case of Herrnstein and Murray's work), most measurements will cluster around some central point, with progressively fewer data points as one moves away from that centre, thus creating the shape of what looks like a bell. The dangerous temptation is to take the core set of data at the centre of a normal distribution as that which also provides a standard of what *ought* to be the social norm – a procedure that implies moving from descriptive data of what 'is' to prescriptive statements. With the upsurge of statistics in the modern period, the conflation of statistical norms and social norms has become a focus of analysis, as in Ian Hacking's work on the 'taming of chance', and David Armstrong's Foucauldean critique of the modern type of a 'surveillance medicine', which works by deriving normative guidelines for control and intervention from statistical averages and probabilities.[8] Hacking even suggests that the word 'normal' became 'the most powerful ideological tool of the twentieth century'.[9]

One of the issues that is at stake in what Hacking considers to be a new style of scientific reasoning, namely the 'probabilisation' of the Western world, is the move from what is 'normal' to what is 'normative' – that is, from a statistical average to a prescriptive statement. Yet even in a non-statistical sense, 'normal' and 'normative' are importantly distinct, as it is not the case that what is normal necessarily represents a standard or value to be complied with. Crucially, therefore, any statement that proceeds from a description of the 'normal' to a prescriptive assertion of standards or norm needs to be probed carefully. In philosophy this slippage from a statement on what 'is' to one of 'ought' is known as a manifestation of a 'naturalistic fallacy', namely any inference that purports to derive a normative conclusion from purely factual premises. The title of Frankfurt School philosopher Habermas's only recently translated work, *Between Facts and Norms*, gives away the starting point of his analysis of norms in the development of contemporary democracies.[10] Similar issues are involved in debates about concepts of the 'natural' and 'unnatural' being used as a standard or in a normative sense.[11]

It is tempting to conceive of the terms 'natural' and 'unnatural' as the mere predecessors of the modern binary of 'normal' and 'abnormal'. To a certain extent it is indeed valid to suggest that what we nowadays refer to as 'normal' had its equivalent in the pre-modern term 'natural'. However, the

4   Waltraud Ernst

change from a religiously ordained natural order to a scientifically grounded secular framework and the emergence of the normal/abnormal dichotomy in preference to the earlier binary of natural/unnatural needs to be seen to encapsulate an important shift in kind and semantics and not merely one of magnitude and terminology – unless we subscribe to a notion of history as the unfolding of a linear process. The socio-political contexts within which notions of the natural and unnatural were embedded were highly different from those of later periods, so that it is necessary, as we will see in two contributions to this book (Ravenscroft, Chapter 2; Mitchell, Chapter 3), to differentiate between modern interpretations of pre-modern phenomena (which use as their point of reference the familiar ab/normal binary), and what would have been the contemporary understanding (which would be based on quite different social and political cosmologies, of which the un/natural couplet is but one dimension).

Reference to the natural and unnatural is of course still common nowadays, leading to further conflation of terms in day-to-day parlance and conceptual imprecision among scholars. Homosexuality, for example, has throughout the nineteenth century and by some even up until recently been morally condemned as 'unnatural', despite the fact that the notion of it as a disease and 'abnormality' had been mooted from the late nineteenth century onwards.[12] This shows that earlier terms such as the natural and unnatural have penetrated well into the modern area, existing alongside newer ones such as the normal and the abnormal. What is more, the way the earlier binary has been used still retains its earlier flaws, namely the potential conflation of 'is' and 'ought', as was the case in pre-modern Western societies that were based on a religiously ordained order that collapsed the natural (what 'is') into the ethical (what 'ought' to be). In other words, pre-modern and current appeals to nature in pursuit of guidance on moral behaviour and standards conflate the distinction between descriptive statement and moral prescription. Although the 'is'–'ought' distinction emerged as part of the Enlightenment emancipation from religious prescription (so that what 'is', as scientifically discovered, is more clearly independent from what 'ought' to be), arguments on issues such as homosexuality, for example, are still infused with moral appeals to what is supposed to be a biological given.[13] The justification of moral standards through biology or 'nature' is particularly common in regard to gender and race issues, when a statement on biological difference (what 'is') is turned into an argument about what is 'unnatural' or 'abnormal'.[14] In classical ethics, in contrast, the appeal to the natural in pursuit of guidance on the ethical would have been rejected, as the ancient Greeks and their Roman followers have usually seen nature as something devoid of morals and therefore requiring reason to impose on it the ethical.[15]

The 'rise of reason' and the privileging of rationality in the Western world have of course been heavily contested, not only during the recent era (or fashion) of post-modernity, but right from the inception of Enlightenment thinking and the emergence of 'objective' science.[16] One major point of contention has been the question to what extent scientific description of what 'is' can be entirely devoid of value judgements, and whether therefore the qualitative distinction between value judgements and moral standards on the one hand and objective, value-free description and facts on the other is indeed valid.[17] The emergence of modern science therefore has brought issues of normativity and objectivity into sharp focus, in particular in the fields of science-based medicine and affiliated sciences, which mainly concern the contributors to this book as they assess the application of norms on the physical body and, by implication, the moral body and body politic. The slippage from 'scientific' to 'moral' (as in the biologisation of race and gender, for example) and from 'moral' to 'scientific' (as in the moralisation of homosexuality, for example) has recently undergone much scrutiny and is one major theme discussed in a number of essays in this volume.

In the field of science studies, scholars such as Barnes, Bloor, Collins and Latour have taken a step further the issue of whether the validity of scientific knowledge transcends its specific cultural origins, suggesting instead that the core criteria of science (objectivity, rationality, description of 'is') are subject to the same rules as govern other social and cultural phenomena.[18] Debates on the social construction of scientific knowledge and methodologies, and on how we discover what 'is', have flourished in the past two decades in particular and stimulated further probing into the status of norms and values. These epistemological debates on whether science on account of its supposedly inherent objectivity is indeed the best way to inquire into what 'is' or whether it is itself value laden and prescriptive have had much to contribute to a more critical understanding of the status of science in the modern world. However, the distinction between 'is' and 'ought' (ontological) is not necessarily undermined by debates on the social construction of science (epistemology). In other words, even if values are embedded in a description, it is an additional step to arrive at a normative statement. This is an issue that has been most succinctly formulated by Hume.[19]

Most philosophers would agree on the importance of differentiating ontological statement (descriptions of what exists) from epistemological deliberations (normative reflections on the nature of knowledge), and descriptive from prescriptive reflections. However, the suggested conceptually strict boundaries between the latter in particular are not necessarily manifest as clearly in the empirical world. Whereas stipulations of what is supposed to count as 'normal' in contrast to the 'abnormal' can be more or less clearly delimited in scientific theories and models, what can actually be observed in the real world is much more likely to be located on a continuum. Statistical approaches to the definition of the normal and the abnormal provide a particularly good example of abnormality being defined as a matter of degree rather than an absolute entity. As is evidenced in some of the essays in this volume (Sinding, Chapter 11; Timmermann, Chapter 12), the normal/abnormal binary as a guiding theoretical model can exist side by side

6   *Waltraud Ernst*

with ideas on the normal and the abnormal being part of a measurable spectrum.

Reflections on norms have a long history, but it is during the Enlightenment period that moral norms in particular came into sharp focus, as in the theories put forward in the eighteenth and nineteenth centuries on moral sense, for example.[20] Since then, discussion has partly focused on the question of whether norms and differentiation between what is to be considered normal and abnormal are a 'good thing' or problematic, constructive and vital or oppressive. The former contention has been accentuated by Durkheim and Habermas, who contend that norms (if they are built on consensus) are necessary for democratic societies, as restrictions on individuals' possibly destructive socially harmful behaviours and inclinations need to be employed in order to guarantee social cohesion and a good life for the majority of people. Hobbes's well-known dictum that, if left unrestricted (i.e. in its natural state), life would be full of 'continual fear, and danger of violent death; and the life of man, solitary, poor, nasty, brutish and short' encapsulates this.[21] Hobbes developed his reflections in the aftermath of the English Civil War, which in his view resulted in the above state. Durkheim's theories of the necessity of social norms emerged from a highly different, late nineteenth-century political context that had seen other kinds of social unrest and revolution, but enunciated similar concerns. In the aftermath of the Islamist fundamentalists' terror attacks of 9/11, 3/11 and 7/7 in New York, Madrid and London, discussions on the necessity of norms have gained renewed urgency, with references to the importance of restrictive laws, punitive actions and military intervention in order to guarantee 'our way of life' reverberating an earlier contention that 'covenants without the sword are but words'.[22]

On the other hand, there exists a body of thought that puts emphasis on the negative and oppressive aspects of social norms and focuses on the restrictive measures imposed by modern states on groups and individuals, through medico-legal discourse in particular. In this view, which links up with earlier conceptions of natural states being characterised by gentle innocence rather than brutishness, norms are intrinsically oppressive and have the tendency to subjugate that which is considered abnormal.[23] In Foucault's view this is achieved through the process of 'normalisation', which in his reading aims at the integration and incorporation (rather than exclusion) of the abnormal or pathological into the normal. One of Foucault's mentors, Canguilhem, focuses on similar concerns, yet puts emphasis not so much on the process of normalisation as on 'normativity'. The latter term becomes a concept imbued with very specific meaning in Canguilhem's medically focused philosophical work: being 'healthy', he argues, 'means being not only normal in a given situation but also normative in this and other eventual situations'.[24] The normal and normativity are therefore intrinsically linked in the sense that the concept of the 'normal' always implies a moral code that sets a normative standard; medical norms are both the result and the cause of social norms.

Canguilhem's concept cuts across the more common conception of the distinction between the normal and the normative, which stipulates that the normal does not necessarily represent a standard to be complied with. In a similar divergence from a more common reading of a specific term, Goffman's concept of the 'normal deviant' and Durkheim's idea of the abnormal as a normal phenomenon within a healthy society suggest that the abnormal, pathological or deviant is necessary for the functioning and progressive development of a society built on consensus.[25]

In the face of such diverse readings of the key terms, it is important to consider the case studies presented in this volume as always closely linked with particular theories and conceptual specifications, and situated within specific contexts, challenging the reader to engage with a variety of alternative interpretations. The application of different terms that are used as synonymous with or in contradistinction to the 'abnormal' – such as the 'pathological' and the 'deviant' – further highlights the fact that a variety of academic disciplines have contributed to discussions about norms and abnormality, with medically focused thinkers preferring the term 'pathology', and sociologists 'deviance'.

Key themes and concepts

A number of themes emerge in the contributions to this book. In the opening chapter, Janet Ravenscroft contrasts modern reactions to portraiture from the 1550s to 1650s in terms of their enunciations of the normal/abnormal, with early modern perceptions framed in the contemporary terms of the natural and unnatural. She focuses on three oil paintings of dwarfs by the famous artists Anthonis Mor, Alonso Sánchez Coello and Diego Velázquez that had been commissioned by the Hapsburg court in Spain. She points out that although the ideal body was then imagined as well balanced and proportioned, constrained and neat, court dwarfs were represented as both out of the ordinary, or 'monstrous' in contemporary terms, and part of God's scheme of nature. As Ravenscroft shows, twentieth-century art critics and viewers of paintings of 'monsters' find it more difficult to reconcile with each other the multiple connotations that were evoked for early modern audiences who engaged with dwarfs with both admiration and horror, seeing them as both marvels and monsters. The modern problem with 'ambivalence', which has been identified most succinctly and eloquently by postcolonial critiques, seems to have led many an art critic to make anachronistic statements on the supposed inferior status and grotesque nature of the dwarf paintings.[26] By translating any trace of what had earlier been referred to as the 'unnatural' (i.e. 'monstrous' in the sense of unusual yet still part of nature) into the modern 'abnormal', they also fail to appreciate the humanness and integrity of the people depicted.

Ravenscroft shows that allusion to the alleged abnormality of the dwarfs as represented in the court paintings engenders an absolute distance between 'normal' viewer and 'abnormal' subject, while from an early modern perspective the 'monstrous' would have been conceived of as different in degree only from 'ideal man', reminding us of the importance of historically contextualising visual representations. Drawing on Canguilhem's distinction between quantitative differences (augmentation, diminution) and qualitative ones (alteration), she shows that the early modern focus on the former enabled viewers still to appreciate monsters as individual persons, even if those monsters might also have been instrumental in letting the king shine in contrast to them.

Ravenscroft investigates also how 'normals', or those who do not depart negatively from the particular expectations at issue, relate to those they stigmatise as 'abnormal'. This is an important issue not only in the world of art criticism but also in any sphere where we confront difference as represented in 'other' bodies and 'other' minds. Goffman refers to the kinds of situations where normals and stigmatised find themselves in the same context as 'mixed contacts'. Ravenscroft uses this notion and Stuart Hall's ideas about stereotyping and representations to explore how readers or viewers at different historical periods are, for the duration of their analysis, part and parcel of the 'contact zone', rather than being mere innocent bystanders. Fittingly, therefore, Ravenscroft's essay not only ends with reflections on how dwarfs could contribute to the normalisation of the Hapsburg court, but also, perhaps more importantly, problematises the role of the viewer (or reader) in this process. The latter is an invitation to reflect on the implicit normalisation that occurs when a 'normal modern reader/viewer' (who, in Hall's reading, is conceived to be white, male and middle class; and young and healthy, one would perhaps need to add) confronts someone who is considered different, deviant, unnatural, abnormal.[27] As becomes clear from Ravenscroft's analysis, it is not only art critics who need to consider the impact on their object of study of 'The "I" of the Beholder'.[28] The issue of reflexivity and the necessity of assuming a critical meta-perspective on the subjects at hand is vital, especially when we deal with norms and processes of stigmatisation and normalisation.[29]

The extent to which the cultural context and social agenda of modern observers have had a bearing on the way they interpreted particular phenomena is particularly evident in the national stereotyping, quasi-animalisation and racialisation of the two different kinds of dwarfs in some twentieth-century appraisals of the court paintings (i.e. proportionate or hypopituitaristic dwarfs and achondroplastic dwarfs). These issues are discussed also in Sarah Mitchell's essay on conjoined or 'Siamese' twins. Mitchell shows that although conjoined twins were not uncommon prior to the nineteenth century, they enjoyed particular attention during that period, partly because of the great fame achieved by a pair of brothers from Thailand (Siam) who were exhibited to a wide public in Britain and the United States. Cheng and Eng were different and 'other' not only because they were connected by a band of flesh at the chest and abdomen, but also because of their race.

Mitchell points out that disease and unusual bodily states were easily linked up with other nations that were conceived as strange, peculiar and inferior (as in the case of Siam, which was imaged in the West as a place ruled by a cruel despot and inhabited by barbarous people). In the nineteenth century, disease and what would previously have been considered 'monstrous' states were no longer considered as 'natural' but as aberrations from a healthy state. Ideas and representations of race and disease easily went hand in hand, as racial science and medical science began to flourish in tandem, and conjoined twins constituted an object of interest on account of both their bodily and their racial otherness. Disturbingly, the label of 'Siamese twins' for all conjoined twins has maintained some currency in popular parlance until the present day.[30]

To European and North American audiences the twins from Siam were awesomely different and 'other', and paying to gaze at them constituted good value for money, as two spectacular abnormalities could be had for one ticket at a freak show. However, as Mitchell shows, conjoined twins also became a focus of interest for medical professionals who would probe and test and experiment on them, and soon spread medical norms and views of the human body into wider society. This gradual medicalisation of the phenomenon of conjoined twins contributed to their reconceptualisation, from 'monsters' and both beguilingly and repulsively unusual parts of the natural world whose appearance can entertain as well as educate about the fecundity of nature, to an abnormality that required normalisation through separation. Separation as reconstitution of the 'normal' – that is, mono-bodied – person was of course not an option until quite recently, concomitant on the development of surgical techniques and affiliated procedures. What is more, for a time separation was seen as not only practically impossible but also undesirable, as it would render the two resulting individual bodies abnormal owing to the physical deficiencies that had previously been compensated for by shared physiological functioning. The medicalisation of conjointment and, ironically, well-meaning humanists' and philanthropists' campaigns to make conjoined twins the subject of medical, scientific experts' gaze rather than subjecting them to the gawping of the wider public, led to its pathologisation as a medical condition that required 'fixing' in order to effect a 'normal' anatomy, even at the cost of deficits in the resulting individual physiological functioning and subsequent death.

The nineteenth-century shift from monstrosity to abnormality appears to suggest a move towards a clear-cut dichotomy between what was to be considered a normal body and the abnormal body. Although Mitchell provides evidence that this was the case, she also highlights that at the same time the definition of clear boundaries between normal and abnormal, and different kinds and degrees of abnormality, constituted problems. This became more acute from the end of the nineteenth century onwards when a greater number of cases of conjoined twins had been accumulated in medical records and attempts at providing guidelines to midwives and non-specialist doctors

10   *Waltraud Ernst*

were made as to how to deal with different types of conjoined twins during delivery. The themes of the abnormal as an absolute and discrete category, in contradistinction to the normal, and of the abnormal as a 'matter of degree', located on a continuum, are focused on also by several other contributors to this volume. As is the case in Mitchell's account, these themes coexist alongside each other and inform public and medical discourses alike, even when precedence appears to be given to bifurcated definitions.

In his chapter on eccentricity (Chapter 4), James Gregory, too, substantiates the contention that what is 'off centre' can be conceived of simultaneously as a discrete state (that reassures the 'normals' of their own perfection) and a matter of degree (providing comfort to those whose own condition is not located squarely in the centre of normality). In the genre of 'eccentric biographies', which enjoyed immense popularity in Britain from the late eighteenth to the end of the nineteenth century, a wide range of marvels are presented to both entertain and inform the reader about the peculiar variations in Nature. As in the modern Murdoch press – arguably its successor not only in regard to the high level of commercialisation – superlatives and shock-horror headings prevail, as in the example of the *New Wonderful Magazine* in 1793, which encompassed 'extraordinary productions, events, and occurrences, in providence, nature, and art', and 'such curious matters as come under the denominations of miraculous! queer! odd! strange! supernatural! whimsical! absurd! out of the way! and unaccountable!'.[31] Then, as now, the eager readers' gawping at crime, cruelty and the wide spectrum of the unusual was rationalised as grounded in scientific interest, public concern and the teaching of morals, be it only the comfort derived from the knowledge that individuals manage to cope and live even under the most extraordinary of circumstances.

The eccentricities favoured in biographies were not restricted to shocking and supposedly inferior or disadvantaged physical and behavioural variations from the familiar and common norm. They embraced also superior qualities and abilities: 'the WONDERFUL and the *ridiculous*', including biographies of 'many very eccentric Characters famous for Long Life, Courage, Extraordinary Strength, Avarice, astonishing Fortitude, as well as genuine Narratives of Giants, Dwarfs, Misers, Impostors, singular Vices and Virtues'.[32] How particular samples of such diverse life stories were evaluated at the time was subject to considerable variation. As Gregory points out in regard to perceived transgressions of the received social order (for example, in the case of the peculiarly(!) 'intelligent pauper'), interpretations and the morals derived from them could encompass benevolent views that focused on the remarkable nature of the case; hostile reflections that remarked on the reprehensible nature of social deviation that defied social definition, and ridiculed or satirised it; as well as a mixture of admiration and abhorrence. Gregory shows that the scope and range of biographies decreased steadily over the period, in particular in regard to the inclusion of a medley of physical as well as behavioural abnormalities, as attitudes towards physical disabilities

The normal and the abnormal   11

shifted, leading to what has more recently been framed as a more sensitive attitude towards the 'physically challenged'.

An important theme highlighted by Gregory is how behavioural eccentricity was valued as a positive phenomenon, to the extent that it was seen as socially and politically desirable precisely on account of its deviant non-conformity. It signified strength of character and the possibility of individual freedom, values that had been promulgated by Enlightenment-influenced thinkers such as John Stuart Mill. This implied that originality of character was seen as a virtue, just as the 'mad genius' had been. Human singularities and peculiarities were considered central to the realisation of the freedom to be individual. This emphasis on the role of the individual resonated with the political message inherent in Enlightenment and Romantic thought, and also chimed in with the national stereotypes and self-perceptions of the English. Abnormality became seen as a virtue, or, as John Stuart Mill proclaimed in 1859 in his reflections on liberty, 'In this age, the mere example of nonconformity, the mere refusal to bend the knee to custom, is itself a service.'[33]

This positive perspective on that which is non-standard within society was later taken up by Durkheim. His suggestion that the abnormal was a necessary part of the normal, and that abnormal phenomena such as crime (even if socially undesirable) are still necessary to maintain social cohesion and facilitate social change and progress of society as a whole, provides the conceptual framework also for Lucy Hartley's essay on nineteenth-century constructions of physical and moral norms (Chapter 5). Hartley elaborates on the conceptual overlap between Foucault's and Durkheim's ideas on the positive, integrative reading of the process of normalisation in modern societies: where Durkheim focuses on the 'normal abnormal' as part of a healthy society, Foucault highlights the integrative, inclusivist response to abnormalities such as the plague (in contrast to earlier exclusivist measures of expelling the 'impure', such as the leper, from the society of the pure). This arguably distinctly modern way of dealing with the undesirable and abnormal by means of assimilation and integration relies on a power that exerts continued control and is involved in the constant assessment or surveillance of individuals and social groupings to ensure they conform to the desired norms. The important contribution of physiognomic typologies and eugenic guidelines derived from them to this process of normalisation is the focus of Hartley's analysis.

Hartley takes the work of Johann Caspar Lavater on physiognomy and Frances Galton's eugenicist ideas as prominent historical exemplars of a still widespread kind of cultural stereotyping that relies on the supposed correlation between external bodily features and a person's character or inclinations. In the Western world, physiognomy originated in the classics, and experienced a renaissance during the eighteenth and nineteenth centuries, when questions of humankind's place in nature were major concerns. As Hartley shows, Lavater perfected physiognomy into an art, while Galton's

12   *Waltraud Ernst*

ambition was to place it firmly within the realm of science and provide clear guidelines of social intervention for the newly emerging field of eugenics. Lavater's classification scheme was based on the delineation of 'natural' types from 'unnatural deviations', while Galton conceived of different types in terms of 'the degraded', 'the ordinary' and 'the exceptional', which were central to his attempts not only to measure human/social development but also to indicate which ones among these groupings contain the 'best specimens' to meet the criteria of 'civic usefulness'. The legacy of this moralisation of body types that was sparked off by Lavater's correlation between idealised body types and ideal moral types, and reconfigured into a normative typology that highlighted the desirable central type and warned against the socially disadvantaged degraded and degenerate types, has been identified in its newly politicised form in current modern discourse. Drawing on Sander Gilman's suggestion that health, beauty, the erotic and the good have become aligned with the 'normal', and illness, ugliness, the repulsive and the evil with the 'abnormal', Hartley highlights the continuity of the conceptualisation of the 'normal' in terms of a physical principle anchored in the human body (in contrast to earlier abstract standards or patterns, derived from geometry, for example), from the late nineteenth century onwards. Rather as in Galton's scheme, in current discourse, too, the 'good citizen' is equated with the desirable physico-moral type, nowadays the healthy and beautiful, thus accentuating the political dimension inherent to the moralisation of bodily types.

Nicola Cotton's essay (Chapter 6) is one of two that focuses on norms within the context of France during the post-revolutionary period. Her analysis of the popular caricatures of Monsieur Mayeux that featured in French newspapers and on the stage during the early nineteenth century reflects on the aesthetics of the 'ugly' and the way in which caricature as a genre is based on the violation of the norm. In contrast to Gilman's and Hartley's proposition that the 'ugly' and the 'beautiful' are binary notions, she suggests that norms relating to ugliness are subject to an 'aesthetics of a different order', following Kant's suggestion that aesthetic judgements are by definition judgements about beauty only.[34] Judgements about the ugly and perceptions of caricature are, in Cotton's view, analogous to views on dirt, as postulated by Mary Douglas.[35] They concern the relationship between observer and observed, between subject and object, whereby the latter is perceived by the former to be 'out of place' or 'in the wrong place' – that is, they violate the expected norm within a particular context. This refutation of the beauty–ugliness binary has an important impact on the ways Cotton applies the concepts of the normal and the abnormal, as here the abnormal is not a deviation from the norm, and possibly a matter of degree, but a violation of the norm itself, and therefore something qualitatively different. This conceptual framework enunciates the political and cultural context of early nineteenth-century France, where a 'new order' was seen to constitute not simply yet another variation of the old order, but a

The normal and the abnormal   13

new kind of order in itself – that is, a violation of rather than a variation from the ancient regime.

Following Foucault, Cotton highlights the importance of normalising measures and the preoccupation with the identification of social types within a post-revolutionary France that, in the absence of sovereign power, had to rely on new techniques of control. These drew on the normalising powers of medical and scientific knowledge and judicial authority – impersonal norms that are willed collectively. That this process of the tyranny of a new collective, impersonal, normative order did not occur smoothly and unchallenged is evidenced, in the cultural sphere, by the popularity of caricature. As the example chosen by Cotton shows, the pretentious Mr Mayeux, the embodiment of middle-class physical and moral imperfections, is represented as ugly and abnormal, and as such ridiculed, but exposed the pretensions of the aspired petty-bourgeois normality of the new regime. As Cotton puts it, 'Through his failure to realise existing norms physically, morally and politically, Mayeux made those norms visible and . . . presented the bourgeois public with images of its own imperfections in a palatable, entertaining way' (p. 136). The revulsion induced by the ugly and abnormal assumed a positive function, as it enabled the post-revolutionary public to experience quasi-second-hand the flaws and excesses of its collective aspirations.

In Alison Matthews David's account of tailoring in nineteenth-century France (Chapter 7), 'average man' and the newly standardised procedures of measuring his body are at the centre of analysis. The impact of statistical measurements on conceptions of the male body, and the concomitant changes in perception that no longer saw bodily variation merely as 'personal quirks' but as deviations from a standard size or absolute norm, are well evidenced in the development of tailoring during the course of the nineteenth century. Where tailors previously took individual measures from their customers, they would now use the kind of standard sizes so familiar to today's average consumer, who purchases an L or XL off the hook in retail outlets. As Matthews David shows, this process can be seen as evidence of the 'hegemony' of statistical measurement as a mode of scientific and social investigation, as suggested by Ian Hacking, and the newly emerging tyranny of size M. It can also be interpreted as a move towards democratisation and the egalitarian treatment of every body, as argued by the statistician Quetelet, who quantified physical measurements of populations to arrive at mathematical averages or norms. Quetelet explicitly attacked the classics' and their Renaissance admirers' geometry-based abstract principles of the 'ideal' man (such as da Vinci's Vitruvian Man), promulgating instead the notion of 'real man' whose proportions were derived from statistical calculations of the average type in a given population of real people. The tension between the Enlightenment ideals of individuality on the one hand and universality on the other is encapsulated here. Matthews David observes, 'The tensions between democratic yet normative principles of sartorial uniformity and more personal needs for individual

14   *Waltraud Ernst*

identity informed the heated debates over tailoring in the nineteenth century' (p. 143).

As is evident also in other contributions to this volume, the wider context of nineteenth-century typological analyses of bodies, and what Matthews David calls 'a quasi-scientific taxonomy of physical conformations' (p. 156), determined a variety of newly emerging specialisms, ranging from anthropometry, ethnography and the study of racial types, to orthopaedics, anatomy and tailoring. Importantly, individual and collective conformity to the desirable norms arrived at by means of statistics and other scientific procedures became a signifier of the stage of development in the great Western scheme of civilisation. Western man as a superior type was located at the pinnacle of racial hierarchies, in contrast to the inferior types who occupied their bottom rungs and were construed as savages – naked savages. Civilised average man was well clothed, even if at times uncomfortably squeezed into a standard-size suit. Correspondingly, the tailor's mission was no longer to provide garments for a selective few in the land, as had been the case in 'less enlightened' times, but to clothe the majority of a civilised nation.

The physical norm of the 'average male' not only confined men's physical idiosyncrasies and bodily quirks and bulges, but also had in its non-physical constructions an impact on the construction of the female as the other sex. As Lesley Hall argues (in Chapter 8), the male-as-norm in Britain was predicated on the representation of the female-as-abnormal. In her contribution to this volume she shows how a number of well-educated and vocal women in the late nineteenth and early twentieth centuries contested a 'masculine mythology' that in their view suppressed and distorted the expression of female sexuality. Hall shows that anatomy books during this period set the male body as the standard or default, so that not only did female anatomical characteristics appear as variants of the male norm, but their functioning could also best be explained in relation to and dependent on male functioning.

Drawing on sources ranging from polemic essays and advice to parents, to marriage manuals and social observations, Hall provides evidence of women's resistance to two of the widespread male-focused assumptions that appeared to be substantiated by anatomical and physiological norms: first, while men's sexual needs ought to be catered for, women's expression of their sexuality was undesirable and abnormal; second, female desire was derivative from the male norm. The passing of the 1860s Communicable Diseases Acts was crucial in the confirmation of male-focused ideas about women's sexual activities, as they enshrined the complementary principles that 'vice' was a necessity for men while women and their sexual behaviour had to be controlled to guarantee that men could engage in vice in a healthy and male-focused way.

Women's responses were, as Hall highlights, not uniform, but fuelled by different perspectives, as they included women from Christian, conservative and radical freethinking backgrounds. The moral double standard that

The normal and the abnormal   15

allowed men to enjoy their sexuality outside marriage, while women were supposed to satisfy their needs only within, was more easily challenged – at least on a rhetorical level. The difficult issue to contend with for women from such a variety of ideological contexts was the question of the nature of female sexuality and the extent to which it was a mere reflection of, or response to, male desires, or of a different quality altogether. As Hall points out (p. 179), the legacy of the construction of male sexual functioning as the norm is still felt today:

> Recent discussions about a 'female Viagra' point up the extent to which ideas of female sexuality are still modelled on the assumption that the male model can simply be extended to women, or that women need to be fixed to conform to male specifications.

Ellen Herman, in Chapter 10, deals with the question of what constitutes a 'normal family' and how its common equation with shared biological features had an adverse impact on adoption in early to mid-twentieth-century North America. Herman shows that the common conflation of the 'normal' with the 'natural' (i.e. blood ties) made adoption appear 'abnormal' and caused agencies to develop new criteria in attempts to normalise it. She grounds her analysis in the work of cultural anthropologists such as Franz Boas, Margaret Mead and Ruth Benedict, whose notion of the cultural specificity of normative statements and perceptions also had an impact on discussions about the normalisation of adoption during the early twentieth century. Benedict's suggestion in 1934 that 'the concept of the normal is properly a variant of the concept of the good' resonated with government agencies keen on ensuring that potential adoptees – who by definition lacked the attribute of being a prospective family's 'natural' children – were at least 'good' candidates, and that aspiring parents, too, had the potential to make a 'good' and therefore by implication 'normal' family. The criteria on the basis of which decisions about a child's and an adoptive couple's potential to become a 'good' family were made came increasingly to rely on seemingly objective statistical data and scientific methods of testing.

The contentious issue was for a time of course the question of whether social and scientific procedures could adequately substitute for natural processes, and the related concern about whether kinship can be 'designed' yet still be normal. For most of the first part of the twentieth century the common view was that adoption was indeed abnormal, with both adoptive children and parents being perceived as strange and abnormal, if not criminal and degenerate. However, once psychological testing and population screening became more refined and prominent, and family-making, too, began to be subjected to scientific regulation and standardisation, adoption became more popular. It came to be acceptable to assume that even if a child was not a couple's natural offspring, it could still become part of a normal family, as long as normalising procedures were adhered to prior to

16 *Waltraud Ernst*

family-making. The trust in nature as guarantor for a good family was complemented by a trust in science as a safeguard for successful 'kinship by design'. Official adoption agencies were to ensure standards and provide safeguards in order to make adoption safe and as close to normal as possible.

The underlying assumption still remained what it had been in earlier decades, namely that adoption was abnormal by default, and needed scientific intervention such as screening, testing and therapeutic support and scientifically trained experts' assessment to detect hidden psychogenic factors in order to normalise it. Herman concludes, 'Choice – typically lauded as an exemplary value in a liberal, individualistic culture such as the United States – was precisely what made adoption appear weak and distant from the kind of permanent and unchosen kinship that nature made' (p. 218). Although the advent of new reproductive technologies has more recently indicated that appeals to nature as the ultimate norm are fraught with problems, 'its allure as a source of legitimation for family-making persists undiminished' (p. 218). Rather than looking at adoption as simply a different way to have a family, the common perception still appears to be that '[k]inship could not be designed and, at the same time, be entirely normal' (p. 218).

Scientific norms and procedures are at the centre of Christiane Sinding's essay, too (Chapter 11). Here, medical norms in relation to the chronic condition of diabetes mellitus are focused on alongside patients' values about how to lead a good life. Basing her analysis on the sociological distinction between norms as rules of action and behaviour that are shared by specific groups on the one hand, and values as the expression of desires and choices of individuals on the other, Sinding shows that doctors' medical norms and patients' values may be identical, but are not necessarily so. She looks closely at how doctors' ideas on the correct long-term treatment and day-to-day management of diabetes met at times with non-compliance or failure to implement the ordered medical regime on the part of patients set on pursuing their own agenda and making their personal lifestyle choices. Sinding identifies different stages in the relationship between doctors and their patients, and a gradual change towards a more patient-focused treatment approach. Combining Canguilhem's conceptual focus on patients' capacity to create their own norms that are congruent with their individual ambitions ('normativity') with Foucault's emphasis on medical norms propagated by medical experts backed up by institutions and their role in the control of patients' values and experiences through the medical gaze ('normalisation'), she disentangles the various components prevalent in the construction of norms at different periods of time.

At the beginning of the twentieth century, doctors involved in the treatment of diabetes patients insisted that patients' autonomy was counterproductive as it frequently led to a deterioration of the condition. As dietary intake is an important variable in diabetes, patients' impact on treatment outcomes was particularly pronounced, because their cooperation in the pursuit of specific food regimes was vital. Doctors were quick to blame

The normal and the abnormal 17

negative treatment outcomes on patients' bending of the dietary rules. This was so especially when 'starvation diets' were imposed and the strict monitoring of urine, and glycosuria and glycaemia levels was pursued by a particular group of experts whom Sinding calls 'disciplinarians', echoing Foucault's analysis in *Discipline and Punish*.[36] Although they used a moralising language that was resonant of religious preaching, the rationale for these doctors' disciplining approach was invariably based on scientific arguments (involving better control of the condition itself and of concurrent infections, and increased life expectancy). Here, doctors' norms and patients' values and inclinations clearly were not in harmony.

Sinding concludes that until well into the 1950s this kind of disciplining, authoritarian regime held sway, mirroring Parsons's view of the patient–doctor relationship as being characterised by the patient assuming a 'passive role' in the face of the doctors' active demeanour and control over the person in their charge.[37] Subsequently, techno-scientific changes, combined with the emergence of a more critical patient-as-consumer culture, played a major role in the modification of this relationship. Control over patients became relaxed as the application of insulin, for example, allowed for the treatment to be adapted to the patients' normal lifestyles rather than the other way round, as had previously been the case.

Sinding is, however, careful to avoid a homogenising view of doctors' construction of the 'good' and the 'bad' patient, pointing out also disagreements between experts and the extent to which new technologies and scientific findings influenced doctors' diagnostic and treatment regimes in different ways. This had been the case in the early twentieth century, as Sinding shows, as well as in the later period, when a new measuring technique in the 1980s would be used by some doctors as a detective technique to find out patients' compliance rates. In contrast to what was the case in earlier decades, moralising came now to be embodied in technical devices rather than in doctors' preaching. Overall, Sinding discerns a positive move towards a plurality of flexible norms that tend to validate patients' values. Following Canguilhem, she welcomes the development of a more 'individualised medicine' that is 'an evolving sum of applied knowledge, constantly reconstituted for each patient in view of a specific therapeutic project' (p. 241).

Carsten Timmermann frames his analysis of the normalisation of high blood pressure in the mid- to late twentieth century (Chapter 12) also in relation to Canguilhem's ideas. He focuses in particular on the notions of the normal and the abnormal, in relation to the pathological, and further investigates how statistical approaches came to be seen as suitable for judging individual patients' health. While the distinction between normal and pathological states may be clear in relation to individual patients, the boundary between the normal and the pathological is not clearly discernible on the level of whole populations – even if statistical procedures tend to identify the range of the abnormal. This is so, according to Canguilhem,

18 *Waltraud Ernst*

because the opposite of the normal is the abnormal, and *not* the pathological. Therefore, a (statistically identified) anomaly does not automatically lead to illness, but might merely constitute a variation, and even be potentially useful. Physiological markers such as blood pressure are the basis for medico-statistical techniques, but they do not necessarily provide information on a particular patient's pathology, as high blood pressure may, for example, be an individual's quite healthy attempt to adapt to a specific situation. As Canguilhem equates health with an individual's potential to adapt to the environment by adopting new norms (what he terms 'normativity'), measurements gained in laboratory conditions and through statistical procedures fail to provide guidelines as to the relative health or pathology of any one individual, leading to seemingly paradoxical descriptions such as 'the healthy cancer patient'. As far as individual patients are concerned, true illness occurs when they are no longer able to adapt (i.e. realise their 'normativity').

Timmermann looks at the controversy between two British clinicians about the nature of hypertension. He aims at charting the institutional and research network parameters that shaped the developing notion of high blood pressure as a 'quantitative disease' that can best be understood, studied and treated as a quantitative variation of health. He shows that the institutional context within which two main protagonists – Platt and Pickering – worked, and their very different professional experiences and patient populations, engendered highly different perspectives on hypertension. While the former combined clinical practice and research, focusing mainly on ill patients whose ability to be normative was already severely constrained, as they were subjected to the narrow norms imposed on them by disease, the latter specialised in research and studied the blood pressure of apparently healthy people. Consequently, Platt favoured the suggestion that hypertension was restricted to a distinct group of hypertensives who suffered from a specific disease that was not present in the normal majority of people – that is, hypertensitivity was akin to a gene that you either had or did not have. Pickering in contrast favoured the position that hypertension was a 'quantitative disease' in which deviation from the norm was one of degree and not of kind – that is, blood pressure, like intelligence and height, was distributed on a continuum, whereby hypertensives were located on the upper end of the statistical bell curve. Platt eventually conceded that his assumption of a high blood pressure gene was unfounded. The development towards what Armstrong described as a new kind of 'surveillance medicine' (no longer based on the treatment of individual, ill bodies in hospitals, but on the continual assessment of seemingly normal and healthy populations, and the treatment of risk factors prior to the onset of a specific pathology/illness) blurred the distinction between discrete states of illness and normal states of absolute health even further. Treatment came to be applied prior to the identification of a distinct pathology, and expected success of treatment came to define diagnosis. The normalising gaze pene-

The normal and the abnormal 19

trated a whole population and no longer only particular groups, such as an institutionalised and 'abnormal' section.

In contrast to Sinding's cautiously optimistic and positive ending to the story of diabetes, in which she sees the experience of the patient eventually shine through, Timmermann's account ends with the potentially detrimental effect that the strategy of risk factor assessment and the treatment of 'risk' rather than illness has on patients' identity and how it affects individuals' capacity for 'normativity' (as when a patient who had been happy, content and apparently healthy hears that he may not be as healthy as he had felt). Timmermann also points out the divergence of meanings of the normal and the pathological within the different realms of clinical science, medical practice and health administration. In regard to the latter, the rising cost of modern health-care systems occasions a politicisation of risk factors and provides an incentive to turn physiological into political norms, impacting detrimentally on patients' experience of well-being, and restricting their freedom of choice and their capacity for 'normativity'.

The late nineteenth-century psychologist and philosopher William James is considered by many as a paragon of American intellectual culture and central to debates in the field of 'abnormal psychology'.[38] He is well known for his attempt to integrate normal and abnormal phenomena within the same explanatory framework; in his psychological and philosophical work, religious experience, spiritualism as well as new sciences such as Darwinism are embraced equally. Francis Neary looks, in Chapter 9, at the different ways in which a particular episode in James's life has been interpreted by a range of twentieth-century scholars from different academic disciplines, and discusses how James's own experience of abnormality informed and was informed by his writing about psychology. Like Timmermann, he alerts us to the determining role of academic networks, of scholars' disciplinary background and personal experiences, in their varied analyses and conceptual schema.

As Neary shows, interpretations of James's situation in the 1870s have focused on this period as years of 'crisis' or breakdown, even suggestive of an abnormality. The causes attributed to this crisis were variously seen to have been of a physical, mental, philosophical, experiential or personal nature. Despite such diversity in interpretation, all commentators agree that this episode in James's life was distinctly different from his 'normal' state – that is, they have constructed it as an abnormal episode. As Neary suggests, James himself, if he followed his own line of thinking as espoused in his psychological notion of 'the stream of thought', would have expected nothing but a range of diverse and possibly even contradictory interpretations. In James's view, individuals harbour unique interests that lead them to assess the various parameters involved in particular situations (such as a 'crisis') in very specific ways, leading to each individual producing internally coherent accounts of the world that differ from others' accounts. In contrast to his various biographers, James is also unlikely to have seen his

20 *Waltraud Ernst*

life-experience in the 1870s as an abnormal state that was clearly disjointed from his earlier and later 'normal' condition. For James, normal and abnormal phenomena were located on a continuum, rather than constituting discrete states. Yet even if James had conceived of his alleged 'crisis' as one characterised by an abnormal state, he would have looked at it in intrinsically positive terms. As in Durkheim's work, so too in James's, the abnormal has a positive role to play, as it produces progress and change, and ultimately is part of the normal. In reference to Comte's suggestions of two possible approaches to the normal, Neary concludes that James supported the view of the normal as only average and to be improved on, rather than as the average, correct state of being. On the basis of this positive and dynamic reading of the abnormal, one would also need to conclude that the majority of interpretations of James's alleged 'crisis' tell us more about their authors' idiosyncratic streams of thought and the ways in which twentieth-century scholars reconstruct James's ideas on abnormal psychology, than about the nature of James's condition.

In the concluding essay in this volume (Chapter 13), Sara Bergstresser draws on Goffman's notion of the 'normal deviant', which enables her to highlight the normalising role of mentally ill people within particular community settings. As she shows in relation to the 'piazza madman', notions of their deviance and abnormality persist, yet the predictable presence of the madman in the piazza provides a sense of normality to a specific community to the extent that 'if the familiar "madman" were to fail to appear one day, local residents would notice his absence, and the piazza would take on a sense of unfamiliarity' (p. 262).

Bergstresser notes that the role of the piazza madman became available to mentally ill people only recently when psychiatric hospitals were closed down and their inmates sent to live within the community in the wake of the Italian anti-psychiatry movement and subsequent mental health reforms in the 1970s. Previously, institutionalised patients had to find themselves new, socially acceptable roles within the wider landscape of normality. This constituted a problem, as the common identification of the normal with the desirable seemed to reserve only stigma or hilarity and contempt for the mentally ill. Yet the folk memory of fools and madmen inhabiting the centre of villages and towns in a distant, nostalgically construed past lent itself to providing an allegedly 'traditional', and therefore acceptable, normal role to formerly institutionalised patients.

The role of the 'traditional' piazza madman became particularly salient on account of the benefit derived from it by the local community, as the person performing the role of the 'deviant' defined, and thereby contained, a potentially threatening abnormality in a reassuringly predictable manner. Once established and accepted by the community, the role of the normalised deviant – of the individual who had contested the notion of homogenised public behaviour without being expelled or suffering detrimental consequences – would also serve to reassure the community of the potential acceptability of difference. As Bergstresser shows, the notions of 'locality' and 'place' are of central importance in the construction of the piazza madman as an acceptable and even desirable role. In Italian life the term *territorio* evokes not only a sense of place but also a shared history and feelings of belonging. Perceptions of a particular place are therefore imbued with expectations of continuity and permanence – expectations that had been threatened in the wake of post-war modernisation and migration in the region. The appearance of the madman as a regular feature on the piazza helped Italians to reconnect with nearly lost values and sentiments. This explains the relative ease with which at least some ex-psychiatric patients could slip into a socially acceptable role of contained deviance. Bergstresser concludes (p. 278) that

> the maintenance of locality not only depends on the repetition of local norms, but also necessitates periodic reminders of what constitutes locally salient abnormal action. Local distinction is achieved through deviance as effectively as it is defined through consistency or reiteration of norms. In this way, it is not only possible but also necessary for some individuals to construct normal lives based on abnormal roles.

Epilogue

In an academic world in which distinct mission statements, clearly discernible corporate labelling of scholarly products, and crisply formulated and easily remembered key terms and take-home messages have become important, this book may be a mixed blessing for some. The catchy terms of its title suggest a clearly focused content and deep engagement with, and resolution of, notions that enjoy wide usage. The editor and the contributors indeed hope that readers will appreciate specific contributions this way, as they are self-contained and stringently focused on particular issues and concepts. Those who have the time, tenacity and leisure to read the book from cover to cover – something that few among today's hard-pressed scholars, apart from the occasional book reviewer, can do – may, however, find that in the volume as a whole more questions are raised than answered. Those inclined to expect unequivocal statements and clear conclusions may regret this. Alternatively, it might be seen as a good feature by those who believe that academic research is relevant not only in cases when it produces nicely packaged answers, but also when it highlights unresolved questions and stimulates further research. The editor for one appreciated the opportunity to travel along on the various discursive paths taken by the contributors to the book, and valued the intellectual challenge these posed, fuelling further reflection on contentious issues.

22 Waltraud Ernst

Notes

1 Translated from the German: 'Die wirklich interdisziplinären Wissenschaften sind Produkte eines wechselseitigen Fruchtbarmachens der jeder der beteiligten Wissenschaften zugrunde liegenden Schlüsselkonzepte.' G. Devereux, *Normal und anormal. Aufsätze zur allgemeinen Ethnopsychiatrie* (translation of *Essai d'ethnopsychiatrique général*, Paris, 1970), Frankfurt, Suhrkamp, 1982, pp. 7–8. See also G. Devereux, *Basic Problems of Ethnopsychiatry*, trans. B. M. Gulati and G. Devereux, Chicago, University of Chicago Press, 1979.

2 'Das Grundbegriffspaar der Psychiatrie bilden das "Normale" und das "Anormale".' Devereux, *Normal and anormal*, p. 7.

3 Michel Foucault, *Les Anormaux: cours au Collège de France, 1974–1975* (ed. François Ewald and Alessandro Fontana, Paris, Seuil et Gallimard, 1999; Georges Canguilhem, 'Le Normal et le pathologique', in *La Connaissance de la vie*, Paris, Vrin, 1980 [1952]; Georges Canguilhem, *The Normal and the Pathological*, New York, Zone Books, 1991; G. Canguilhem, *Études d'histoire et de philosophie des sciences*, Paris, Vrin, 1983. For appraisals of Foucault's and Canguilhem's work on norms, see Gary Gutting, *Michel Foucault's Archaeology of Scientific Reason*, Cambridge, Cambridge University Press, 1989; Malcolm Nicolson, 'The Social and the Cognitive: Resources for the Sociology of Scientific Knowledge', *Studies in the History and Philosophy of Science*, 1991, 22, pp. 347–69; C. Jones and R. Porter, eds, *Reassessing Foucault: Power, Medicine and the Body*, London, Routledge, 1994; Mary Tiles, 'The Normal and Pathological: The Concept of a Scientific Medicine', *British Journal for the Philosophy of Science*, 1993, 44, pp. 729–42; J. D. Marshall, *Michel Foucault: Personal Autonomy and Education*, Dordrecht, Kluwer, 1996; Christiane Sinding, 'The Power of Norms: Georges Canguilhem, Michel Foucault, and the History of Medicine', in Frank Huisman and John Harley Warner, eds, *Locating Medical History: The Stories and their Meanings*, Baltimore, Johns Hopkins University Press, 2004, 262–84; Special Issues on Canguilhem, *Economy and Society*, 1998, 27, 2 and 3, pp. 151–331); G. Renard, *L'épistemologie chez Georges Canguilhem*, Paris, Nathan, 1996; P. Mackery, 'La Philosophie de la science de Georges Canguilhem', *La Pensée*, 1964, 113, pp. 50–74; and E. Balibar, M. Cardot, F. Duroux, M. Fichant, D. Lecourt and J. Roubaud, *Georges Canguilhem: philosophe, historien des sciences*, Paris, Albin Michel, 1993.

4 Emile Durkheim, 'The Normal and the Pathological', *Social Deviance: Readings in Theory and Research*, ed. Henry N. Pontell, Englewood Cliffs, NJ, Prentice-Hall, 1993; E. Durkheim, 'The Normal and the Pathological', in M. Wolfgang, L. Savitz and N. Johnston, eds, *The Sociology of Crime and Delinquency*, London, Wiley, 1970; Emile Durkheim, *The Rules of Sociological Method*, trans. S. A. Solovay and J. H. Mueller, Chicago, University of Chicago Press, 1938 [1895]; Franz Boas, *Anthropology and Modern Life*, London, George Allen and Unwin, 1929.

5 A. Reath, B. Herman and C. M. Korsgaard, eds, *Reclaiming the History of Ethics: Essays for John Rawls*, Cambridge, Cambridge University Press, 1997; L. D. Katz, ed., *Evolutionary Origins of Morality: Cross-disciplinary Perspectives*, Thorverton, Imprint Academic, 2000; P. A. Railton, *Facts, Values, and Norms: Essays toward a Morality of Consequences*, Cambridge, Cambridge University Press, 2003; D. Copp, *Morality, Normativity and Society*, Oxford, Oxford University Press, 2001.

6 Alasdair MacIntyre, *A Short History of Ethics*, London, Routledge & Kegan Paul, 1967 [1966]; Alasdair MacIntyre, *After Virtue: A Study in Moral Theory*, London, Duckworth, 1981; John Horton and Susan Mendus, eds, *After MacIntyre: Critical Perspectives on the Work of Alasdair MacIntyre*, Oxford, Polity Press, 1994.

The normal and the abnormal   23

7 Richard J. Herrnstein and Charles Murray, *The Bell Curve: Intelligence and Class Structure in American Life*, New York, Free Press, 1994. For discussion surrounding the 'bell curve', see S. Fraser, ed., *The Bell Curve Wars: Race, Intelligence and the Future of America*, New York, Basic Books, 1995; S. Jones, *In the Blood: God, Genes and Destiny*, London, HarperCollins, 1996; and D. Nelkin, 'The Politics of Predisposition: The Social Meaning of Predictive Biology', in A. Heller and S. Puntscher Riekmann, eds, *Biopolitics: The Politics of the Body, Race and Nature*, Aldershot, UK, Avebury, 1996, pp. 133–43.
8 Ian Hacking, *The Taming of Chance*, Cambridge, Cambridge University Press, 1990; David Armstrong, 'The Rise of Surveillance Medicine', *Sociology of Health and Illness*, 1995, 17, pp. 393–404; David Armstrong, *Political Anatomy of the Body: Medical Knowledge in Britain in the Twentieth Century*, Cambridge, Cambridge University Press, 1983. See also Theodore M. Porter, *Trust in Numbers: The Pursuit of Objectivity in Science and Public Life*, Princeton, NJ, Princeton University Press, 1995, and M. L. Taper and S. R. Lele, eds, *The Nature of Scientific Evidence: Statistical, Philosophical, and Empirical Considerations*, Chicago, University of Chicago Press, 2004.
9 Hacking, *Taming of Chance*, 1990, p. 169.
10 Jürgen Habermas, *Between Facts and Norms: Contributions to a Discourse Theory of Law and Democracy*, Cambridge, Polity, 1996; Jürgen Habermas, *Faktizität und Geltung*, Frankfurt, Suhrkamp, 1992.
11 G. Hatfield, *The Natural and the Normative*, Cambridge, MA, MIT Press, 1989; S. Horigan, *Nature and Culture in Western Discourses*, London, Routledge, 1988.
12 For literature on homosexuality, see, for example, Chris White, ed., *Nineteenth-Century Writings on Homosexuality: A Sourcebook*, London, Routledge, 1999; Jeffrey Weeks, *Making Sexual History*, Cambridge, Polity, 2000; Vernon A. Rosario, ed., *Science and Homosexualities*, New York, Routledge, 1997; and Netta M. Goldsmith, *The Worst of Crimes: Homosexuality and the Law in Eighteenth-Century London*, Aldershot, UK, Ashgate, 1998.
13 For appeals to biology in regard to 'race', see W. Ernst and B. J. Harris, eds, *Race, Science and Medicine*, London, Routledge, 1999, and S. Harding, ed., *The 'Racial' Economy of Science: Toward a Democratic Future*, Bloomington and Indianapolis, Indiana University Press, 1993.
14 For appeals to biology in regard to gender, see, J. W. Scott, 'Universalism and the History of Feminism', *Difference: A Journal of Feminist Cultural Studies*, 1995, 7:1, pp. 1–14; G. Fraisse, *Reason's Muse: Sexual Difference and the Birth of Democracy*, Chicago, University of Chicago Press, 1994; N. L. Stepan, 'Race and Gender: The Role of Analogy in Science', in D. T. Goldberg, ed., *Anatomy of Racism*, Minneapolis, Minnesota University Press, 1990, pp. 38–57; Joanna de Groot, ' "Sex" and "Race": The Construction of Language and Image in the Nineteenth Century', in Susan Mendus and Jane Rendall, eds, *Sexuality and Subordination*, London, Routledge, 1989; and Londa Schiebinger, *Nature's Body: Gender in the Making of Modern Science*, Boston, 1993.
15 Malcolm Schofield and Gisela Striker, eds, *The Norms of Nature: Studies in Hellenistic Ethics*, Cambridge, Cambridge University Press, 1986; Christopher Gill, *Greek Thought*, Oxford, Oxford University Press, 1995; William J. Prior, *Virtue and Knowledge: An Introduction to Ancient Greek Ethics*, London, Routledge, 1991.
16 Roy Porter and Mikulas Teich, eds, *The Scientific Revolution in National Context*, Cambridge, Cambridge University Press, 1992; R. Olson, *Science Deified and Science Defied: The Historical Significance of Science in Western Culture*, Berkeley, University of California Press, 1990; Steven Shapin, *The Scientific Revolution*, Chicago, Chicago University Press, 1996; John Harley Warner, 'The Idea of Science in English Medicine: The "Decline of Science" and the Rhetoric of Reform, 1815–45', in Roger French and Andrew Wear, eds, *British Medicine in*

24 *Waltraud Ernst*

an Age of Reform, London, Routledge, 1991; Steve Sturdy and Roger Cooter, 'Science, Scientific Management, and the Transformation of Medicine in Britain, c.1870–1950', *History of Science*, 1988, 26, pp. 421–66.

17 See, for example, Jürgen Habermas, *On the Logic of the Social Sciences*, Oxford, Polity, 1988; M. J. Smith, ed., *Philosophy and Methodology of the Social Sciences*, London, Sage, 2005; and R. Bhaskar, *The Possibility of Naturalism*, Hemel Hempstead, UK, Harvester, 1989.

18 Bruno Latour and Steven Woolgar, *Laboratory Life: The Social Construction of Scientific Facts*, Princeton, NJ, Princeton University Press, 1986; Harry Collins and Trevor Pinch, *The Golem: What Everyone Should Know about Science*, Cambridge, Cambridge University Press, 1994; Barry Barnes and David Bloor, *Scientific Knowledge: A Sociological Analysis*, Chicago, University of Chicago Press, 1996. See also Roy Bhaskar, *A Realist Theory of Science*, London, Verso, 1997.

19 David Hume, *Essays Moral, Political and Literary*, ed. E. F. Miller, Indianapolis, Liberty Fund, 1987 [1742–52]; David Hume, *A Treatise of Human Nature*, ed. D. F. Norton and M. J. Norton, Oxford, Oxford University Press, 2000 [1739–40]; J. Fieser, ed., *Early Responses to Hume's Moral, Literary and Political Writings*, Bristol, Thoemmes, 2005.

20 On moral sense, see, for example, F. Hutcheson, *An Essay on the Nature and Conduct of the Passions and Affections: With Illustrations on the Moral Sense*, London, W. Innys *et al.*, 1754; A. Broadie, ed., *The Cambridge Companion to the Scottish Enlightenment*, Cambridge, Cambridge University Press, 2003; and J. L. Mackie, *Hume's Moral Theory*, London, Routledge & Kegan Paul, 1980.

21 Thomas Hobbes, *Leviathan*, ed. C. B. Macpherson, Harmondsworth, UK, Penguin, 1968 [1651], I, xiii, 9; Q. Skinner, *Reason and Rhetoric in the Philosophy of Hobbes*, Cambridge, Cambridge University Press, 1996.

22 'Covenants without the Sword, are but Words, and of no Strength to secure a Man at all'. Hobbes, *Leviathan*, 1968 [1651], II, xvii, 223.

23 R. Porter and M. Teich, eds, *Romanticism in National Context*, Cambridge, Cambridge University Press, 1988; G. W. Stocking, ed., *Romantic Motives: Essays on Anthropological Sensibility*, Madison, University of Wisconsin Press, 1989; M. Halliwell, *Romantic Science and the Experience of Self: Transatlantic Crosscurrents from William James to Oliver Sacks*, Aldershot, UK, Ashgate, 1999; D. F. Kress, *Contagion: Sexuality, Disease, and Death in German Idealism and Romanticism*, Bloomington, Indiana University Press, 1998; A. Cunningham and N. Jardine, eds, *Romanticism and the Sciences*, Cambridge, Cambridge University Press, 1990; D. P. Haney, *The Challenge of Coleridge: Ethics and Interpretation in Romanticism and Modern Philosophy*, University Park, Pennsylvania State University Press, 2001; A. Richardson, *British Romanticism and the Science of the Mind*, Cambridge, Cambridge University Press, 2001.

24 Canguilhem, *The Normal and the Pathological*, 1991, p. 34.

25 Emile Durkheim, 'The Normal and the Pathological', *Social Deviance: Readings in Theory and Research*, ed. Henry N. Pontell, Englewood Cliffs, NJ, Prentice Hall, 1993; E. Goffman, *Stigma: Notes on the Management of Spoiled Identity*, New York, Simon & Schuster, 1963.

26 On the post-colonial reading of ambivalence, see H. K. Bhabha, 'Of Mimicry and Man: The Ambivalence of Colonial Discourse', *October*, 1984, p. 28 (reprinted in H. K. Bhabha, *The Location of Culture*, London, Routledge, 1994); R. J. C. Young, *Colonial Desire: Hybridity in Theory, Culture and Race*, London, Routledge, 1995.

27 S. Hall, *Representation: Cultural Representations and Signifying Practices*, London, Sage, 1997; C. Hall, *White, Male and Middle-Class: Explorations in Feminism and History*, Cambridge, Polity, 1992.

The normal and the abnormal 25

28 D. Shuger, 'The "I" of the Beholder', in P. Fumerton and S. Hunt, eds, *Renaissance Culture and the Everyday*, Philadelphia, University of Pennsylvania Press, 1999.

29 S. Woolgar, ed., *Knowledge and Reflexivity: New Frontiers in the Sociology of Knowledge*, London, Sage, 1988; H. Lawson, *Reflexivity: The Post-modern Predicament*, Hutchinson, 1985; R. J. Bogdan, *Minding Minds: Evolving a Reflexive Mind by Interpreting Others*, Cambridge, MA, MIT Press, 2003; U. Neisser, ed., *The Perceived Self: Ecological and Interpersonal Sources of Self-Knowledge*, Cambridge, Cambridge University Press, 1993; R. Hertz, ed., *Reflexivity and Voice*, London, Sage, 1997.

30 For the link between 'race' and Down's syndrome, see M. Jackson, 'Changing Depictions of Disease: Race, Representation and the History of "Mongolism"', in W. Ernst and B. J. Harris, eds, *Race, Science and Medicine, 1700–1960*, London, Routledge, 1999, pp. 167–89.

31 *The New Wonderful Magazine and Marvellous Chronicle*, London, C. Johnson, 1793, 'Preface', p. 4. See James Gregory's chapter in this volume, p. 76.

32 Title page, *The New Wonderful Museum and Extraordinary Magazine*, London, A. Hogg, 1804. See James Gregory's chapter in this volume, p. 76.

33 J. S. Mill, *On Liberty*, London, 1859, ch. 3: 'Of Individuality, as one of the elements of well-being', OUP World Classic edition, 1991, pp. 82–3. See James Gregory's essay in this volume, p. 84.

34 I. Kant, *The Critique of Judgement*, transl. J. C. Meredith, Oxford, Clarendon Press, 1973 [1790]; P. Guyer, ed., *Kant's Critique of the Power of Judgment: Critical Essays*, Lanham, MD, Rowman & Littlefield, 2003; H. E. Allison, *Kant's Theory of Taste: A Reading of the* Critique of Aesthetic Judgment, Cambridge, Cambridge University Press, 2001. A. Savile, *Kantian Aesthetics Pursued*, Edinburgh, Edinburgh University Press, 1993.

35 Mary Douglas, *Purity and Danger: An Analysis of the Concept of Pollution and Taboo*, London, Routledge, 2002 [1966].

36 M. Foucault, *Discipline and Punish: The Birth of the Prison*, London, Allen Lane, 1977 (translation of *Surveiller et Punir*, Paris, Gallimard, 1975).

37 T. Parsons, *The Social System*, New York, Free Press, 1951.

38 W. James, *The Principles of Psychology*, Cambridge, MA: Harvard University Press, 1981 [1890]; W. James, *The Varieties of Religious Experience: A Study in Human Nature*, New York, Modern Library, 1994; W. James, *The Will to Believe and Other Essays in Popular Philosophy*, London, Longman's, Green, 1899; M. Knight, ed., *William James: A Selection of His Writings on Psychology*, Harmondsworth, UK, Penguin, 1950.

2 Invisible friends

Questioning the representation of the court dwarf in Hapsburg Spain

Janet Ravenscroft

In this essay I examine representations of court dwarfs who lived in the Spanish Hapsburg court between the early 1550s and the late 1650s. I look at three categories of painting: the portrait of a dwarf and dog; a double portrait of a dwarf and her average-sized mistress; and a group painting that includes individuals with different types of dwarfism. Although other 'marvels', such as conjoined twins and bearded ladies, were occasionally brought to court and captured on canvas, only dwarfs were painted alongside members of the royal family.[1] In order to understand why this was the case, it is important to be aware of how dwarfs were perceived in early modern Spain. Therefore, I present some contemporary descriptions of the 'monstrous' figure of the dwarf that reveal how discussions were framed within the discourse of the 'natural' and the 'unnatural'. My aim in studying the visual and textual evidence is to achieve what Ivan Gaskell has defined as 'historical understanding':

> One of the conditions of the creation of art objects is that, however they might have been understood and used by their makers and their competent contemporaries, they will inevitably be subject to different uses and understandings thereafter . . . original meaning as such must remain inaccessible. Yet to regard the changes in the world between the original circumstances of the art object and the present time as a screen or obstacle that prevents us from addressing the question of what an original significance might have been is equally mistaken. We might profitably think in terms of historical *understanding* rather than art-historical retrieval.[2]

In this chapter I will review modern critical reactions to the paintings to see what the language used can tell us about the authors' ideas about the ab/normal body, as well as early modern perceptions. As we will see, in the period under scrutiny the ideal body was regular in all its parts – a body that was neither too tall nor too short; too fat nor too thin. The 'normal' body, then, was constructed as a rarely realisable ideal. I will argue that the dwarfs were involved in the construction of the ideal body and, more specifically, the royal body.

The situation of the dwarf was complex. The dwarf's body made him or her a figure of fun. Paradoxically, however, it was these same uncommon bodies that made the dwarfs worthy of a place at court and memorialisation on canvas. In the first Renaissance treatise on the portrait, the Portuguese court painter Francisco de Holanda (1517–84) argued that 'only princes and people of exceptional merit had the right to be portrayed'.[3] Although prescriptive texts such as Holanda's should always be treated with caution, I would contend that the dwarfs portrayed were deemed to be of sufficient merit for reasons other than their anomalous bodies. In other words, modern critical views about the aesthetic and moral worth of the court dwarfs should not blind us to the fact that these individuals were considered worthy of being painted by the most esteemed painters of their day and hung alongside images of the ruling elite. This situation is an example of what Richard Brilliant has noted: 'Portraits make value judgements not just about the specific individuals portrayed but about the general worth of individuals as a category.'[4]

Modern critiques demonstrate how concepts of the ab/normal have shifted since the paintings were created, demonstrating Roy Porter's point that 'the history of bodies must incorporate the history of their perceptions'.[5] As I hope to demonstrate, there was a shift from an inclusive view of the dwarf in which the 'monstrous' was evidence of God's fecundity as demonstrated through the workings of nature, to the construction of the dwarf as 'other', and therefore separate and distinct from 'us' – a group constructed as the 'normal' majority.

The monster defined

In sixteenth- and seventeenth-century Europe the figure of the dwarf theoretically belonged to a very broad category that embraced 'monsters', 'marvels' and 'prodigies' – all terms that denoted something or someone who was out of the ordinary but included in God's great scheme. Discussions of the monstrous were framed by ideas about what was natural and unnatural. A key text on the subject was French surgeon Ambroise Paré's (1510–90) treatise *Des monstres et prodiges* (1573). Paré was writing as a medical practitioner, and his discussion of monstrous births demonstrates that he saw the monstrous as both a natural and a medical issue.

Dwarfs appeared in chapter XIII of Paré's *Des monstres et prodiges* as '[e]xamples of monsters caused by hereditary illness'. Paré explained that 'where the father and mother are small, the children are often born as dwarfs, with no other deformity, so long as the father and mother have no congenital malformation'.[6] His words seem to suggest that to be born a dwarf is not a grave kind of deformity. The dwarf's only anomaly is to be small. In her illuminating preface to a 1996 edition of the treatise, Gisèle Mathieu-Castellani noted Paré's use of the Aristotelian analogy of man as a microcosm of the cosmos, arguing: 'The analogy allows one to understand

28 *Janet Ravenscroft*

the production of monstrous forms, which are the reflection in miniature . . . of phenomena observable in the universe.'[7] Thus, even 'that which seems to go *against* or *beyond* the ordinary course of nature is only the sign of "prodigious" fecundity of nature'. In this model the extraordinary still respects the laws of nature.

In his highly influential work of 1977, *La Nature et les prodiges: l'insolite au XVIe siècle, en France*, which focuses on the work of Paré, Jean Céard argued for an understanding of contemporary uses of words that had multiple meanings, which perhaps seem contradictory to us nowadays. A failure to come to grips with the positive connotations of the word 'monstrous' lies behind many twentieth-century historians' misinterpretation of images of dwarfs. Although Céard's work is on France, and French and Latin terminology, his arguments can be applied to sixteenth- and seventeenth-century Spanish texts: '[I]n the sixteenth century, *marvellous* often means both "admirable" and "terrifying", as *horrifying* or *terrifying* are not devoid of all sense of admiration; or again, *miracle* has shades of terror or even of repulsion, while *monster* can indicate admiration.'[8]

As Céard explained in the preface to the 1996 edition of his book, readers of the first edition, believing monsters to be evil, vainly looked for a chapter on the 'diabolical monster'. However, as he explains, 'for a sixteenth-century mind the effect of a lodestone is no less rare than that of a comet or a Cyclops'.[9] It is anachronistic to ascribe twentieth-century ideas to early modern minds. As Céard says, 'it is towards God and Nature, His servant, that a monster directs the eyes of man in the Renaissance'.[10]

The first dictionary of the Castilian language was published in 1611. To define 'monster', cleric and lexicographer Sebastián de Covarrubias (1539–1613) used the example of conjoined twins, explaining that a monster is 'any birth that goes against natural order, such as a man being born with two heads, four arms and four legs'.[11] Dwarfs are not mentioned here. In the entry for 'dwarf', Covarrubias made it clear that although nature might have made the physical frame monstrous, the essence of the person was untouched. The head – the site of rational thought – was unaffected:

> The dwarf has much about him that is monstrous. Because nature wanted to make dwarfs into playthings, like other monsters, she gave them a lump in the spine, twisted their legs and arms like bows, and shortened the whole body, with the exception of the brain, leaving the head alone in its proper proportions.[12]

According to Covarrubias, that princes should support 'monsters' in order to satisfy their curiosity and to be entertained by them is 'truly a disgusting thing and abominable to any right-thinking man'. However, perhaps in an attempt to excuse his patron Philip III and the king's forebears from such abominable behaviour, he then cites a reference to a proportionate dwarf of whom the Roman statesman Brutus was very fond, saying:

The court dwarf 29

It could be that this [dwarf] was smooth and well proportioned in all his limbs, like Estanislao, one of Philip II's dwarfs – may he rest in peace – and like the dwarf that our King Philip III has – may God protect him – who is called Bonamí.[13]

Thus, Covarrubias uses Roman precedent and Greek terminology to validate his support of these important members of the court. (We will return to the case of Estanislao later.) He also makes a distinction between the achondroplastic dwarf ('characterized by an average-size trunk, short arms and legs, and a slightly enlarged head and prominent forehead'[14]) and the proportionate dwarf ('a short-stature condition in which a person's head, trunk and limbs are in the same proportion as an average-size person's'[15]) that is not explicit in the Spanish language: the word *enano* is used for both types of little person. Covarrubias's reference to the smoothness of the man's limbs is also interesting. George Canguilhem, in his classic work on the normal and the pathological, reminds us that the word ' "[a]nomaly" comes from the Greek *anomalia* which means unevenness, asperity; *omalos* in Greek means that which is level, even, smooth, hence "anomaly" is, etymologically, *an-omalos*, that which is uneven, rough, irregular'.[16]

The moral and theoretical debate continued in Spain's dominions. In 1695, José de Rivilla Bonet y Pueyo – who was a doctor and surgeon to the governor of Lima – wrote *Desvios de la naturaleza o tratado del origen de los monstruos*. Rivilla gave as one of his 27 meanings of the word 'monster', 'anything that exceeds common limits'.[17] The monster, therefore, is something or someone that breaks the rules. He later defined the monster as anomalous because it does not quite fit into the natural order of things.[18] This late seventeenth-century reading, then, continues to discuss monsters in terms of where they fit in the natural world; it is an inclusive view. There is an implicit desire in Rivilla's text to fit the monster into the great scheme of things, rather than to reject him completely.

Rivilla divides monstrous births into various categories, one of which is 'magnitude'. A monster of magnitude might be disproportionately large or small or have one or more disproportionate body parts.[19] The proportionate dwarf is presented as the archetypal example of a monster of magnitude. Elsewhere, Rivilla excludes proportionate dwarfs from the category 'monster' altogether in those cases where the mother's uterus is too small. In such cases 'exceedingly small children are born, like dwarfs, but their limbs are not out of proportion'.[20] These words reflect the extreme importance of proportion in early modern constructions of the ideal body.

Constructing the elite body

In sixteenth-century treatises and conduct books, the 'normal' body was constructed as an ideal that very few people could ever achieve without the help of artificial aids, such as cosmetics and fine clothes. This is an example of

30   Janet Ravenscroft

what Erving Goffman has noted: '[T]here are other norms, such as those associated with physical comeliness, which take the form of ideals and constitute standards against which almost everyone falls short at some stage in his life.'[21] Goffman differentiates these norms from those achieved by the majority of the population, 'such as sightedness and literacy'. Following this suggestion, the king and courtiers can be seen as separated from the dwarfs by degrees of difference, not by absolutes. The inclusion of dwarfs in portraits of the royal family enabled them to construct counterposing, 'ideal' images of themselves. In his critique of the works of nineteenth-century medical theoreticians, Georges Canguilhem defined a quantitative difference as one involving augmentation and diminution, and a qualitative difference as one involving alteration.[22] Early modern constructions of ideal and anomalous bodies seem to involve quantitative differences, in Canguilhem's terms.

The ideal body was ordered, neat and constrained, bringing to mind what Mikhail Bakhtin described as the 'completed, self-sufficient' classical body in his ground-breaking work on the political power of carnival.[23] The most influential early modern treatise on the elite body is perhaps Baltasar Castiglione's (1478–1529) *The Book of the Courtier*, first published in 1528. According to Virginia Cox (an editor of Sir Thomas Hoby's 1561 English translation), '*The Courtier*'s reception in Europe was rapid and enthusiastic.'[24] A Castilian translation of *The Courtier* made by Juan Boscán (1493–1542) was published in 1540. In *The Courtier*, Baltasar Castiglione (writing as 'Count Lodovico') constructs the body of the courtier by explaining what it should *not* be like. The courtier

> should be neither too small nor too big, since either of these two conditions causes a certain contemptuous wonder and men built in this way are stared at as if they were monsters. . . . So I wish our courtier to be well built, with finely proportioned members.[25]

In a similar vein, Fadrique Furió Ceriol (died 1592) in his 1559 treatise (dedicated to Philip II) discussed the ideal age (not over 30), the ideal temperament (not melancholic or phlegmatic), and the ideal body of the king's counsellor. Like Castiglione before him, Ceriol constructed this body by a series of oppositions. He noted that all philosophers and astrologers had proven that any extreme suggests an immoderate character, so the counsellor must be of 'medium height and weight, as any extreme in this part looks bad, and takes authority away from the Counsellor'.[26] The counsellor must have no more and no fewer limbs than necessary, as, according to Ceriol, the wrong number 'would offend the sight of whoever looks at him. Good proportion in all parts of the body is an ordinary convention, as it is that the head should be neither larger nor smaller than the body needs'.[27] At the period, ideas about proportion were based on the Aristotelian notion of man as a microcosm, 'reflecting the structure of the cosmos in his own body'.[28] 'Natural proportion' was linked to goodness and godliness.

Castiglione believed tall men were 'thick-headed' and 'unsuited for sport and recreation'.[29] Ceriol agreed that very short men had fewer faults than very tall men, though for different reasons. Tall men, he argued, are 'violent, presumptuous, and people laugh at them and hold them in low esteem, which is natural but that is no excuse and one cannot excuse it'.[30] For the same reason, the king should get rid of very fat and very thin men, as one cannot help laughing at them either. In other words, the prince's dignity could be undermined by the presence of disproportionate individuals in his entourage. The importance of proportion raises interesting questions when we consider the position of dwarfs in the royal household. Would achondroplastic dwarfs have been perceived as furthest from the ideal because of the evident lack of harmony or proportion in their limbs? Or would they have been of particular value because of their 'ridiculous', anomalous bodies?

Castiglione (through his character Bernado Bibbieno) argued that 'the source of the ridiculous is to be found in a kind of deformity; for we laugh only at things that contain some elements of incongruity and seem disagreeable though they are not really so'.[31] Thus, that the anomalous body should cause laughter was seen as 'natural' if not entirely laudable. I believe that Castiglione's presentation of how a courtier should inspire laughter provides a clue as to how court entertainers behaved. The courtier was advised to avoid 'contorting the face or person grotesquely':

> In this kind of imitation one must eschew satire that is too cruel, especially as regards facial or physical deformities; for physical defects often provide splendid material for laughter if one exploits them discreetly, but to be too savage in doing this is the work not only of a clown but of an enemy.[32]

At that time, the classical notion that a capacity for laughter was one of the characteristics that separated humankind from animals was still accepted. Laughter at the right time (and always in moderation) was deemed to be good for health.[33] Covarrubias expressed the view that too much laughter indicated a lack of reason and a frivolous spirit.[34] The elite (including royalty) had to know when to laugh, how much, and in front of whom.[35] There was a danger that by laughing too uproariously, the courtier could turn himself into a figure of fun, as Castiglione explained, using the example of cretins:[36]

> [W]henever you see someone staring too intently, with blank eyes like an idiot, or laughing stupidly like those goitered mutes of the mountains of Bergamo, even though he doesn't say or do anything else, don't you take him for a great oaf?[37]

The dwarf at court

The situation in the Hapsburg court highlights what Erving Goffman has termed 'the issue of "mixed contacts" – the moments when stigmatised and normal are in the same "social situation", that is, in one another's immediate physical presence'.[38] Just as Emile Durkheim has argued that 'crime is normal because a society exempt from it is utterly impossible', so the presence of dwarfs at the notoriously formal Hapsburg court was entirely normal.[39] As Andrés de Villamanrique argued in 1675, 'the extraordinary rarity of the dwarf's deformity is what renders him precious and makes him worthy of esteem'.[40] According to Villamanrique, 'the deformity of these imperfect figures makes the perfect figure shine more'.[41] One of the dwarf's most important roles, then, was to affirm a lesser degree of aberration from the idealised body in their masters by their own physical imperfections.

As a young man, the future Philip II (1527–98) was criticised by his father, the emperor Charles V, for spending too much time with the *gente de placer* (jesters, dwarfs and other entertainers), but he continued to enjoy their company throughout his life.[42] Although Philip II disliked the theatre, and plays were never presented at court, according to Sánchez Belén, 'he enjoyed the company (as his correspondence to his daughters Isabel Clara Eugenia and Catalina Micaela proves) of fools, dwarfs and monsters, characters who also delighted Philip IV and his second wife, Mariana of Austria'.[43]

The starting point for anyone interested in the lives of Spanish court dwarfs is the catalogue of 1939 compiled by José Moreno Villa (1887–1955), who scoured the palace archives for evidence of the numbers and living conditions of – as the title of his book has it – 'Madmen, dwarfs, blacks, and court children' resident at court between the years 1563 and 1700.[44] Moreno Villa's task was a difficult one because, as he explains, to be a dwarf or a 'mad person' was not an official role with a starting date and regular monetary payments. He noted a lack of clarity in the palace papers: the scribes often made no distinction between dwarfs and mad people, describing them as 'So and So (madman or dwarf)', perhaps suggesting that they were of equal rank as far as the administrators were concerned.[45] Also, court dwarfs were often given 'pet' names or named after their masters in the manner of slaves, which added to Moreno Villa's difficulty in identifying individuals with any accuracy.[46] All the entertainers were paid in kind by different departments, so the evidence was gleaned from the accounts of the bakers, shoemakers, tailors, cap-makers and the like.[47]

Moreno Villa gave the names and, in most cases, some details from the lives of over 175 individuals. Of these, some 74 (the largest single category) were catalogued as dwarfs. They held a variety of roles in the royal household. As Glyn Redworth and Fernando Checa have argued in relation to the influential role of steward (*mayordomo mayor*), 'Household office, and the princely favour that its possession indicated, could thus trump the proudest grandee.'[48] Gonzalo Fernández de Oviedo (1478–1557), who wrote an

The court dwarf 33

account of court life between 1490 and 1548, was of the opinion that the slightly inferior role of royal chamberlain (*camarero mayor*) was the best job in the royal household because it gave 'the most access and familiarity to the person of the prince'.[49] According to the household accounts, many dwarfs held the position of valet (*ayuda de cámara*), the next rank down from chamberlain.[50] Only one individual in Moreno Villa's list is catalogued as 'dwarf and jester', which raises a fascinating question: were the dwarfs not expected to be funny, or was their ridiculous quality so obvious to everyone that there was no need to mention it?[51]

It was not until 1991 that a fuller account of the lives of dwarfs and court entertainers appeared, written by Spanish social historian Fernando Bouza Álvarez. According to Bouza, stories about extraordinary people and events, 'giants and dwarfs, very old people and precocious children, strong women and cowardly knights, monstrous births and identical twins, hermaphrodites and bearded ladies, unexpected inheritances and unfortunate deaths' were immensely popular in the sixteenth and seventeenth centuries.[52] People who appeared anomalous, then, were appreciated by the commonality, but, as Bouza says, only royal and noble families could consider keeping 'the most varied, strange and sad individuals' in their own homes.[53] Bouza argued that the entertainers were united by the function they had at court, which was to be funny and to bear the brunt of courtiers' taunts.[54] Although the records suggest that the dwarfs played a greater and more varied role than this, their anomalous bodies no doubt provoked laughter.

All the court entertainers came in for criticism in early modern Spain because they were believed to be lazy and to earn a good living immorally – that is, without working. Jesters or 'false fools' (variously known as *locos fingidos*, *bufones*, *truhanes* or *chocarreros*) were able-bodied and therefore capable of earning a more honourable living. Dwarfs and genuine 'fools' (i.e. people with a physical or mental handicap) were made that way by God, and so were not to be blamed for their monstrous condition. Genuine fools (and children) were also valued at court because they were believed to tell the truth.[55]

Some critics in the twentieth century emphasised what they considered to be the physically grotesque in the images of dwarfs. Likewise, the monarchs who commissioned these paintings were pilloried for allowing such inappropriate individuals into their household. For example, in 1955 José Deleito y Piñuela expressed outrage that Philip IV should allow members of his family to be painted alongside such 'freaks': 'The king had no scruples about having himself and his children portrayed in extraordinary promiscuity with those hideous monsters.'[56] He goes on to say that the dwarfs and jesters

> were like part of the family, and the king, not happy with constantly seeing their pathetic shapes, desired that his painter [Velázquez] should reproduce the images of those poor beings, in order to decorate the walls of the royal rooms, along with portraits of himself, of his wives, his children and his siblings.[57]

34 *Janet Ravenscroft*

In 1986 the Prado in Madrid held an exhibition of 'monsters, dwarfs, madmen, buffoons, "entertainers" [*hombres de placer*] and, as they said in those days, "palace vermin"'. The then-director of the Prado, Alfonso Pérez Sánchez, opened his introduction to the exhibition catalogue with an apology that stereotypes the entertainers as a deformed mass with no individuality:

> It might seem surprising, or even in bad taste, to dedicate an exhibition to the certainly disagreeable and painful world of the physically and psychologically deformed beings who swarmed around the European courts and most particularly in those of the Spanish Hapsburgs and others related to it, up until the very dawn of the eighteenth century.[58]

Reactions such as these by Deleito y Piñuela and Pérez Sánchez echo early modern criticisms of the court, and can be also read for clues about attitudes towards disability within 1950s and 1980s Spain. In modern discussions, then, the dwarf is often perceived as the 'other' – as fundamentally different to 'us', from whom he is totally separate. As Stuart Hall explained, stereotyping 'is part of the maintenance of social and symbolic order. It sets up a symbolic frontier between the "normal" and the "deviant"'.[59] In other words, it is a method of control used by the 'normal' majority in any given arena. Pioneering sociologist Erving Goffman defined 'normals' as '[w]e and those who do not depart negatively from the particular expectations at issue', making plain his view that normal and abnormal are cultural constructs.[60] He argued that we '*normals*'

> believe the person with a stigma is not quite human. . . . We construct a stigma theory, an ideology to explain his inferiority and account for the danger he represents, sometimes rationalizing an animosity based on other differences, such as those of social class.[61]

Dwarfs and 'midgets'

As I have shown, early modern texts suggest that the hypopituitaristic or proportionate dwarf was valued differently to the individual with achondroplasia. Critics of the paintings also tend to privilege the proportionate dwarf for reasons that are seldom articulated, but that seem to be inextricably linked to notions of what is normal and acceptable.[62] Until quite recently, a proportionate dwarf would have been described as a 'midget', which the *Oxford English Dictionary* gives as a late nineteenth-century term for 'an extremely small person; *spec.* such a person publicly exhibited as a curiosity'. This distinction is also apparent in discussions of dwarfs in other areas. For example, in his 1978 social history of 'freaks', Leslie Fiedler still described dwarfs as 'grotesque':

The court dwarf 35

[I]n England and America we distinguish ['Dwarf'] from 'Midget', using the former for little people long in the trunk, big in the head, short in the legs, and finally grotesque, and preserving the latter for those perfectly proportioned and beautiful.[63]

As recently as 1997, Rosamond Purcell, who curated an exhibition on what were termed 'natural anomalies', contrasted the *abnormal* dwarf with the *normal* midget: 'Anatomically, a dwarf has a genetically inherited condition that, generally speaking, shortens the limbs and enlarges the head, while a midget is diminutive in size with normally proportioned limbs.'[64]

John Southworth – a historian of the fool and jester in England – used the terms 'normal' and 'abnormal' when summarising the two broad categories of dwarf. They were described as

> *pituitary* or 'proportionate' dwarfs, . . . who have normal proportions of limbs and trunk and are without obvious deformity, and those who are subject to *achondroplasia* (the commonest form) in whom arms and legs are abnormally short and the head somewhat large in relation to the rest of the body.[65]

Southworth also noted the 'other-worldly' quality that has traditionally been ascribed to dwarfs in legend:

> [D]warfs were distinguished throughout the whole of their early [medieval] history by a certain 'liminal' quality. Everywhere they are seen as belonging to, or having links with, that 'other' world that in the universal experience of humanity is felt to lie beyond the edges of what is ordinarily perceptible.[66]

Susan Stewart noted this same characteristic in the language used in an English eighteenth-century handbill advertising the showing of 'the Black Prince' and his wife, 'the Fairy Queen', who is described as being as 'straight and proportionable as any woman in the land':

> Here is the contrast between dwarf and midget, between the grotesque and the model, which has made quite different the reception of these two varieties of anomaly. The dwarf is assigned to the domain of the grotesque and the underworld, the midget to the world of the fairy – a world of the natural, not in nature's gigantic aspects, but in its attention to the perfection of detail.[67]

Elsewhere, John Southworth describes proportionate dwarfs as being 'like the pygmies of Africa . . . near-perfect replicas of full-sized men'.[68] In other words, the proportionate dwarf is a facsimile of the 'normal' man against whom he is judged and found wanting.[69] David Williams used 'pygmy' and

36 *Janet Ravenscroft*

'dwarf' as synonyms when he argued that 'the pygmy, or dwarf, fails to achieve the norm through atrophy and becomes a figure of deprivation'.[70] I am unconvinced by Williams's argument that the abnormal is 'absolute' and that it is this – the abnormal – that defines the 'normal':

> In the deforming of bodily size, we see most clearly the way in which the abnormal engenders the normal and transgression precedes limits. The grotesquerie of the minuscule exists only in relation to some norm; how small is small enough to constitute monstrosity? The range of the normal is great, indeed, while there exists no range for the abnormal. The normal is, therefore, relative, the abnormal absolute. . . . It is not in measuring some suspected deviant against an established, absolute norm that the abnormal is derived from the normal; prior to that measurement there must have occurred a comparison of beings of a range of sizes against extremes of large and small, the maximum and the minimum, for the norm to have come into existence. In this way, the abnormal always precedes the normal, making possible the definition of the normal.[71]

Williams's binary model fails to take into account the fact that monsters slip into and out of sight depending on who is doing the viewing. Early modern texts show that monstrous individuals were seen as different in degree from the ideal man, whereas modern criticism tends to envisage an absolute distance between the 'normal' viewer and the 'abnormal' subject. The distinction does not appear to have been so clear-cut in the Hapsburg court. Thus, as Susan Stewart has argued in relation to participants in eighteenth-century freak shows:

> Often referred to as a 'freak of nature', the freak, it must be emphasized, is a freak of culture. His or her anomalous status is articulated by the process of the spectacle as it distances the viewer, and thereby it 'normalizes' the viewer as much as it marks the freak as an aberration.[72]

The paintings

In this section I shall use paintings and critical reactions to them as evidence of what Roy Porter has noted: '[E]very picture [of a body] tells its story and incorporates a value-system.'[73] The first portrait is of an unknown man with a dog: *Cardinal Granvelle's Dwarf* (Anthonis Mor, *c.*1550, Louvre, Paris). This, the earliest surviving painting of a dwarf in Spanish art, was created by Utrecht-born Anthonis Mor (1516–76) during the reign of Charles V (1550–8). Antoine Perrenot de Granvelle (1517–86) was Anthonis Mor's patron and would become Philip II's Chief Minister in the Netherlands. Mor later became court painter to Philip II, who assumed control of Spain and its territories on the abdication of his father in 1556.[74] Mor was immensely important in Spanish art, as he was largely responsible for setting the conventions of portraiture that would be followed in Europe for the next 200 years.[75]

The second painting is the double portrait of Philip II's eldest daughter and a female dwarf: *Isabel Clara Eugenia with Magdalena Ruiz* (Alonso Sánchez Coello, c.1585–8, Prado, Madrid). Sánchez Coello took over the role

Figure 2.1 Cardinal Granvelle's Dwarf (Anthonis Mor, c.1550). Louvre, Paris.

38   *Janet Ravenscroft*

of court painter from Mor in 1562. Like Mor, he is barely known today despite the appearance in the past ten years of some excellent studies of his work.[76] The final example is *Las Meninas*, in which a male and a female dwarf appear with the family of Philip IV (1605–65) of Spain (Diego Velázquez, 1656, Prado, Madrid). In the eyes of the clear majority of art historians, Velázquez was the pre-eminent painter of the seventeenth-century Hapsburg court. His portraits of dwarfs are the standard against which other, earlier paintings are measured.[77]

The man in Anthonis Mor's painting is shown full length. The standing pose is significant, because '[r]oyal personages are shown for the most part standing, while commoners and their ladies are seated'.[78] His body is in the three-quarters pose conventionally used for court portraiture, and he looks confidently out at the viewer. It is generally agreed that the composition was based on a painting of the Emperor Charles V with a dog created by Seisenegger (1532) and copied by Titian (1533). The man is finely dressed in a suit and cap of green – traditionally the colour of hunting outfits and the colour of suits worn by entertainers in Spanish courts since at least 1499. It was also associated with everything natural and with madness.[79] The cloak is edged with gold braid and has gold tassels up the front.[80] The man wears a heavy gold chain around his neck and carries a very fine sword.[81] In his right hand he carries a staff; his left hand rests on the shoulders of a hunting hound. The beautifully rendered dog wears Granvelle's arms on his collar.

The painting has been the subject of some harsh criticism. For example, Narciso Sentenach, in a book about 'Spain's great portrait painters' (1914), blamed Anthonis Mor's painting for 'inaugurating ... this series of ridiculous deformed figures in our art' – words that suggest such images sullied Spanish art as a whole.[82]

The dwarf was infantilised in the Louvre's 1953 catalogue entry, in which Edouard Michel described the human sitter as having a 'bulging, furrowed, swollen, over-sized head' supported by the deformed body of this 'stunted man with the legs of a child'. Thus, the person in the portrait – despite being a proportionate dwarf – was seen as both physically abnormal and childlike. Michel further made clear his opinion on the abnormality of the dwarf by asserting that Mor was 'particularly interested in these dregs of humanity'. He backed up this assertion with references to a portrait of another proportionate dwarf and that of an entertainer of average height.[83]

Erica Tietze-Conrat (1957), in a book about the role of the court fool, suggested, 'There may have been some inward analogy between this and Titian's portrait of Charles V and his dog on the lines of the "king and fool" motifs.' She found evidence in the composition of the dog being master of the dwarf, who 'however he may puff himself up in his fine clothes, needs a strong chain to keep the dog under control'. Had Tietze-Conrat looked at the original painting, she would have seen that the dog is not tethered.[84] In 1990 Lorne Campbell used the painting as an example of how '[c]ertain poses became conventional enough to be burlesqued in portraits of children,

The court dwarf 39

jesters and freaks'.[85] It is not clear in which category Campbell seeks to place the dwarf – child, jester or freak – but this is an example of the de-individualisation of the dwarf. While the pairing of a dwarf and a large dog was used again,[86] to judge by those paintings that survive, paintings of members of the royal family with hunting hounds were more common.[87] The very existence of these subsequent paintings also calls into question Campbell's assertion that the pose is a burlesque.

Comments about the dog reveal critics' views on the exact status of the man. In 1910 Henri Hymans argued that the purpose of the dog was to highlight the moral deficiencies of the human sitter. He described the man as 'grotesque' and a 'deplorable specimen of humanity', contrasting him with the 'noble' dog that is tall enough to 'serve him as a mount', words that surely conjure up the image of a freak show, such as those popular when Hymans's catalogue was compiled.[88] Hymans adopts the role of 'normal' observer, his distance from the dwarf represented as much by moral and physical difference as by time. It might also be the case that Anthonis Mor used the dog to establish scale because, were it not for the dog's presence, it would be difficult to ascertain the man's height, as Eduardo Chamorro has pointed out.[89]

Critics of the painting do not make use of the abundant evidence about a dwarf who was renowned as a skilled huntsman. This was Estanislao, whom Covarrubias cited as an example of an acceptable dwarf, one who was 'smooth and well proportioned in all his limbs' – in other words, a proportionate dwarf like the man in the painting.[90] Moreno Villa believed that the sitter in Mor's portrait was Estanislao, but there is no hard evidence to back this up.[91] Estanislao might have been a gift to Charles V (Philip II's father) from Sigismond of Poland, a country that was a traditional source of dwarfs.[92] 'It seems that the emperor valued him highly for his wit and good manners.'[93] According to an account written a few years after his death in 1579, Estanislao 'decorated the door to his apartment at court with hunting trophies that he obtained "as he crept amongst the bushes, concealed by his small size, dressed in green"'.[94] This is the only reference that draws attention to Estanislao's height. Philip II referred to Estanislao's hunting prowess some seven years after the dwarf's death.[95] Philip II, like his father, had a passion for hunting, which could explain why Estanislao was held in high regard and memorialised on canvas and in print.[96]

There were several portraits of a dwarf named Estanislao, all of which are now lost. Philip II (when still a prince) had a portrait of Estanislao in his rooms in 1553;[97] in 1562 his son Don Carlos (then heir to the throne) had 'a lifesize portrait of Estanislao' that he kept in his private chambers.[98] When Philip II created Spain's first royal portrait gallery at the country palace of El Pardo in 1563, he placed in it two portraits of Estanislao by the Venetian artist Titian.[99] These – the only representations of dwarfs or entertainers in the gallery – were hung beneath 45 portraits of Philip and members of this family.[100] When a fire destroyed the gallery in 1604, the portraits of

40   *Janet Ravenscroft*

Estanislao and the 'landscapes and battle scenes' that hung beside them were the only paintings to survive the blaze.[101] Sadly, one of the two portraits had disappeared by the time the paintings were inventoried again ten years later. Since then, that too has disappeared.[102]

As Miguel Falomir Faus has said, the most remarkable thing about Philip II's collection of portraits 'was its heterogeneity, as next to members of the family were courtiers ... enemies and self-portraits by Titian and Anthonis Mor'.[103] Why were these paintings of Estanislao kept separate from 'various portraits of dwarfs and grotesque characters by Mor' found in other rooms?[104] As Ivan Gaskell has said, 'that no object is perceived in isolation and that how any given object is perceived is vitally affected by its juxtaposition to other objects is a truism of curatorial practice'.[105] How might these lost portraits of Estanislao and of the man catalogued as *Cardinal Granvelle's Dwarf* have been perceived by a sixteenth-century audience?

There is no doubt that a man of such diminutive stature who was also a skilled huntsman would have been seen as monstrous in the early modern sense of exceptional and marvellous. The fact that Philip II and Don Carlos had portraits of Estanislao in their private apartments, and that there were two paintings of him at El Pardo suggests that this man was remarkable in some way. Joanna Woodall tells us that from the end of the fifteenth century, 'collections of exemplary portraits included both members of the hereditary nobility and the non-noble elites. ... As exemplars, they all signified admired qualities or achievements which rendered them worthy of immortalisation in paint and inclusion within an honorific archive'.[106]

Modern assessments of the dwarf's abnormality fail to take into account contemporary notions of the anomalous. We do not know who the man in Mor's painting is, but there is no sense that the artist intended to convey mockery of his subject; nor is there any suggestion in the dwarf's gravity and composure that his role was to amuse. While being a dwarf and a great hunter might have made him 'monstrous' and 'unnatural' in early modern terms, there is no evidence in the painting of the deformed, childlike monster that modern critics have identified.

The next painting is a double portrait of Philip II's eldest daughter, the Infanta Isabel Clara Eugenia, with her companion, Magdalena Ruiz. The Infanta stands on a carpet in front of a rich wall-hanging; her companion is placed in a darker area of the painting, in front of a pillar.[107] The Infanta displays a cameo featuring the head of Philip II in her right hand; her left hand rests on Magdalena's head in a pose previously used to portray Philip's sister and a black child or dwarf.[108] Magdalena kneels at the Infanta's side and gazes up at her mistress in a pose conventionally used for a supplicant at the feet of a saint.[109] She is portrayed as a woman of advancing years, and wears the black dress and white cowl of a widow, not the entertainer's livery of green. Magdalena also holds a cameo, but it has been painted in a deliberately blurred way that makes it impossible to make out whom it shows. Some critics have argued that it shows Philip II.[110] More recently, Maria

Figure 2.2 Infanta Isabel Clara Eugenia and Magdalena Ruiz (Alonso Sánchez Coello, c.1585–8). Prado, Madrid.

42   Janet Ravenscroft

Kusche suggested that it depicts Magdalena's deceased husband.[111] Leticia Ruiz has made the more general point that a medallion on a chain was 'a jewel frequently used at the time to recognise services given and loyalty tested'.[112]

Magdalena holds two monkeys: the monkey on the left is tethered around its hindquarters; the other animal does not appear to be tethered in any way. I shall focus on critical reactions to these animals, which are fascinating for what they reveal about the writers' views of the dwarf's status. In a catalogue entry of 1986, Manuela B. Mena Marqués suggested that they served to indicate Magdalena's position between 'the monkeys and the best of humankind, here represented by the beautiful Infanta'.[113] Maria Kusche argued that the monkeys serve to underscore Magdalena's role as an object of ridicule and to contrast the dwarf's liveliness with the elite, immobile body of the Infanta.[114] It has also been suggested that 'the red coral necklace worn by Magdalena and the two long-haired Asiatic monkeys that she holds in her arms are souvenirs of Portugal' and add a trace of 'exoticism' to the painting.[115]

Might it not also be that the monkeys were inserted because they were linked to ideas about mimicry? In her history of the mirror, Sabine Melchior-Bonnet noted that 'A common iconographical image of the mirror from the Middle Ages to the Renaissance is that of a monkey who copies and ridicules everything he sees.'[116] Covarrubias wrote that someone who tried and failed to be like his or her betters was referred to as a 'monkey', and his late sixteenth-century book of emblems showed an 'abominable and ugly' monkey looking into a mirror and finding herself beautiful.[117] I believe that the monkeys are playing with something that either is – or serves as – a mirror, and that the artist has included the viewer in an interplay of gazes.

According to Debora Shuger, 'most Renaissance mirrors resemble miniatures: small oval or circular, worn as an ornament – usually on a ribbon attached to one's waist'.[118] The animal on the right (who looks out of the picture at the viewer) presents a blank, grey oval to the other monkey. This creature holds the oval with its left paw, and looks up at Magdalena, who in turn looks up at the Infanta – who looks out at us. Are we being asked to consider where we stand between the animals, the 'anomalous', yet highly privileged, servant, and the Infanta?

Magdalena has also been discussed in relation to dogs. In 1986 Mena Marquez claimed that by putting Magdalena in the compositional role of the 'favourite dog' in paintings such as Titian's *Charles V*, the artist places Magdalena Ruíz 'in the exact position' that she occupied at court.[119] In 1999 David Davies agreed that 'this class of representation . . . seems to have its remote origin in *Emperor Charles V with a Dog* by Titian', but argued that the pose 'revealed not only an intention to elevate the master, but also to indicate reciprocal affection'. While one can argue that the artist wanted to suggest the bond between mistress and servant, I would question Davies's conclusion that 'the princess treats the dwarf with obvious affection: almost

The court dwarf 43

like a pet!'[120] There is a denial here of Magdalena's individuality. To confuse the compositional role of the dog/woman dehumanises the person portrayed and makes her into a non-specific, stereotyped 'other'. I would contend that there are other ways to read the painting that subtly reinforce Magdalena Ruiz's status, rather than diminish it. These readings might also bring us closer to contemporary ways of interpreting the image.

The hand-on-head pose was first used in Spanish court painting by Sánchez Coello's teacher and predecessor, Anthonis Mor. In Mor's painting, Doña Juana of Portugal (Philip II's younger sister), rests her right hand on the head of a black child. Both she and the fan held by Juana in the painting were references to Portugal's overseas colonies. The painting was made in 1551, just before Juana left Spain to marry Prince João of Portugal.[121] Magdalena Ruiz was servant to Juana in the 1550s. The hand-on-head pose used by Sánchez Coello in the painting of Infanta Isabel Clara Eugenia therefore contains references both to Magdalena's time with the Infanta's aunt, Doña Juana, and to Portugal, of which more later.

There is no doubt that Magdalena may have been included in the painting to enhance the idealised image of the Infanta. As Roy Porter noted, height was once tied to health and prestige, which I believe might be one reason why members of the elite were only ever portrayed next to dwarfs and never by the sides of entertainers of average height.[122]

The height of Isabel Clara Eugenia and her sister is a topic that crops up several times in their father's letters.[123] In line with the fashion of the day, the princess would have worn *chapines*, shoes with 'very high cork soles, that obliged women to walk with tiny steps so that they looked as though they were gliding'.[124] Alonso Sánchez Coello painted a shadow under the Infanta's dress so that she looks as though she is floating, in direct contrast to the earth-bound figure beside her. But if Magdalena was a dwarf, why is she kneeling? This fact, plus the size of her hands, indicate that if she stood up, she probably would not be much shorter than the Infanta Isabel Clara Eugenia. It is likely that the artist painted her kneeling to emphasise the contrast in height between the two women, and to place Magdalena in the conventional, subordinate role.[125]

We know something about Magdalena's life thanks to the letters that Philip II wrote from Portugal to his daughters in Madrid.[126] The king never intended these personal, handwritten letters to be seen by anyone other than their recipients, who were nearly 14 and 15 years old when the correspondence began in April 1581.[127] We can, therefore, read them as family letters first and foremost.[128] In among the family news are reports of the health and activities of Magdalena and the other *gente de placer*. The king frequently reports that Magdalena was bad-tempered with him and members of the royal household, in this case Luis Tristán:

Magdalena has been cross with me since I last wrote to you, because I didn't reprimand Luis Tristán for a dispute that they had in front of my

44 Janet Ravenscroft

nephew. . . . She was very cross with me, saying that she wanted to leave . . . but I think that she will have forgotten about it in the morning.[129]

Philip never criticises Magdalena; her behaviour is presented as quite normal – though plainly noteworthy – perhaps because being outrageous in speech and deed was what made her an entertaining companion.[130] Although Moreno Villa catalogued Magdalena as *enana y loca* (dwarf and madwoman), as Juan Miguel Serrera has rightly pointed out, 'to judge by her will and the correspondence maintained between Philip II and his daughters, [Magdalena Ruiz] doesn't seem to be as mad as the palace accounts and inventories say'.[131] The fact that Magdalena left a will also proves that she was sane in the eyes of the law.[132]

Magdalena also wrote to the princesses, though, sadly, none of her letters survives.[133] She wrote somewhat irregularly, to judge by the frequency with which Philip tells his daughters that Magdalena has been too busy to write to them or was not in the right mood. He often adds his own commentary to Magdalena's words, as when he sends a message from her, 'excusing herself for not having written today; and I believe it is due to having visitors, as she spends days at her window watching the blacks dancing'.[134] One gets the impression from reports such as these that Magdalena had considerable liberty to do as she chose, no doubt because she was under the protection of royalty.

The visual and textual evidence raises questions about the nature of Magdalena's alleged madness and her status as a dwarf. She was catalogued by Moreno Villa as a 'dwarf and a mad woman' but, as we saw earlier, he made the point that record-keepers used the terms interchangeably.[135] There is also the question of terminology. Sebastián de Covarrubias gives a number of definitions of someone defined as mad, including 'a man who is in his right mind, but who is very talkative', or again, someone who 'is mischievous and plays the fool'.[136] In other words, a person who behaved in an inappropriate way could be defined as *loco* (mad). As Philip II's letter suggested, Magdalena's behaviour was inappropriate by early modern standards of decorum, but normal and natural for someone in her position.

What about her monstrosity? If she was indeed a dwarf, then she was monstrous by early modern definitions. But evidence from the painting suggests that she was perhaps not much shorter than the Infanta Isabel. Her role as eccentric companion could be suggested by the inclusion of the monkeys, which, along with the coral necklace, link her to the king (whose image appears in the Infanta's cameo) and make reference to her first mistress, Doña Juana of Portugal, whom she had served three decades before this painting was created.[137] I would therefore contend that, rather than being marginalised and treated 'like a pet', Magdalena was an integral part of the royal family – normal in the sense of familiar.

The final painting serves in many ways as a fitting conclusion, as it draws together two of the strands already discussed: the situation of the dwarf at

Figure 2.3 Las Meninas (Diego Velázquez, 1656). Prado, Madrid.

court and the comparative status of the achondroplastic and proportionate dwarf. It is one of the most written-about Spanish paintings of the period, but no one has yet remarked upon the fact that this was the first time in Spanish court painting that two people with different types of dwarfism were portrayed together. *Las Meninas* ('The Ladies in Waiting') was known as 'the Family of Philip IV' or just 'the Family' until 1843.[138] Covarrubias defined 'family' as 'people whom a lord sustains within his house'.[139] Fernando Marías, editor of a ground-breaking collection of essays on Diego Velázquez's most famous painting, argued that *Las Meninas* 'can be interpreted as a family portrait in the broadest sense'.[140] It is a painting that

46 Janet Ravenscroft

represents 'mixed contacts' in Erving Goffman's terms: a scene at court in which members of the royal family (the central figure of the Infanta Margarita María, and Philip IV and Mariana of Austria, who appear in a mirror on the back wall), able-bodied attendants and two dwarfs are in close proximity.

Modern descriptions of these individuals shed light on the authors' ideas about the differing status of the achondroplastic and the proportionate dwarf: Mari-Bárbola Asquín and Nicolasito Pertusato. Writing in 1955, José Deleito y Piñuela (whose dislike of the dwarf portraits we have already seen) described Mari-Bárbola as a 'horrible and big-headed dwarf', and argued that her figure contrasts 'with the grace of the other feminine figures'.[141] In other words, her anomalous body makes her unfeminine. Eduardo Chamorro also focused on Mari-Bárbola's body, discussing her in terms of Rabelaisian physicality, bringing to mind the traditional notion of the grotesque achondroplastic dwarf as contrasted with the perfect, proportionate dwarf, here represented in the Ariel-like form of Pertusato:

> In a canvas in which everything is delicate . . . Maribarbola is a gigantic dwarf, a wall of flesh topped by a face in which the features are folds of fat, and next to her Nicolasito Pertusato is a delicate and mischievous child.[142]

José Maria Gudiol used national stereotypes when he described the pair as 'Mari-Barbola, a deformed, almost monstrous German woman, and the Italian Nicolo de Pertusata, both dwarfs'.[143] Although they are 'both dwarfs', Gudiol's language makes clear that there is a vital difference in their physical acceptability. While Mari-Bárbola's appearance is worthy of comment, Nicolasito's is not, perhaps suggesting that Gudiol perceives Nicolasito as the less abnormal of the two. Maribarbola, then, is all grotesque Bahktinian excess: 'a body in the act of becoming . . . never finished, never completed',[144] her very body threatening to overflow and swamp the fairy-like man-child beside her. Hers is perceived as an excessive figure whereas his is delicate and childlike. Neither of these people is treated as fully adult or as entirely 'normal'.

It is noteworthy that in this painting the artist portrayed Mari-Bárbola as taller than the Infanta; conventionally, the dwarf's head is always placed on a lower plane than his or her companion's. The relation of the dwarf and her mistress in the previous painting (*Isabel Clara Eugenia and Magdalena Ruiz*) is a good example of this. Mari-Bárbola is not actively serving the young princess, but rather stands and gazes confidently out at the viewer. Instead, a lady-in-waiting of average height fills the position traditionally filled by a dwarf. She kneels beside the Infanta Margarita offering a jug in a composition first used by Alonso Sánchez Coello.[145] I would contend that by painting Nicolasito with his foot nudging the resting hound, Velázquez is referring back to those paintings that feature a dwarf and a dog, such as *Car-*

dinal Granvelle's Dwarf. Here, there is no question about the superior position of the man, small though he may be.

As we saw earlier, Philip II's letters demonstrated that the royal family and their entertainers were constantly in each other's company. It can be argued that in *Las Meninas* Velázquez created a picture of 'normal' court life in which the court's elite and 'monstrous' members lived side by side. There is no hint in the painting that Velázquez sought to criticise this situation: indeed, it would have been inconceivable for an artist to criticise his patron in this way. Philip IV was evidently pleased with the painting, which hung in his private office at the Alcázar palace.

Conclusion

In this chapter I have raised questions about how dwarfs may have been perceived in the Spanish Hapsburg court by drawing on both visual evidence and early modern texts in order to achieve a 'historical understanding' of the anomalous body. I believe that the evidence suggests that achondroplastic and proportionate dwarfs were categorised differently in the early modern period. The reactions of modern critics suggest that they are not fully aware of this distinction, even though some of them treat the proportionate dwarf as less 'abnormal' than his or her achondroplastic cousin.

The situation of the dwarf was complex and paradoxical. Dwarfs' anomalous bodies made them valuable at court, where they were involved in the construction of the idealised royal body. I believe that rather than being marginalised, the dwarfs were central to life at court. By failing to take into account the social and historical context in which these paintings were produced, modern critics have sometimes arrived at anachronistic conclusions. Nonetheless, an examination of modern critical reactions helps to illuminate some of the ways in which concepts of the ab/normal have shifted since the paintings were created.

Notes

1 F. Bouza, *Locos, enanos y hombres de placer en la corte de los Austrias: oficio de burlas*, Madrid, Ediciones Temas de Hoy, 1996, p. 58.
2 I. Gaskell, *Vermeer's Wager: Speculations on Art History, Theory and Art Museums*, London, Reaktion Books, 2000, pp. 230–1.
3 Francisco de Holanda, *Do tirar polo natural*, 1549. Translated into Spanish in 1563 by Manuel Denis. See M. Falomir Faus, 'Imágenes de poder y evocaciones de la memoria. Usos y funciones del retrato en la Corte de Felipe II', in Sociedad Estatal para la Conmemoración de los Centenarios de Felipe II y Carlos V, *Felipe II, Un monarca y su epoca: un príncipe del Renacimiento*, Madrid, Museo Nacional del Prado, 1999, p. 204.
4 R. Brilliant, *Portraiture*, London, Reaktion Books, 1991, p. 14.
5 R. Porter, 'History of the Body', in P. Burke, ed., *New Perspectives in Historical Writing*, Cambridge, Polity, 1991, p. 208.
6 A. Paré, *Des monstres et prodiges*, preface by G. Mathieu-Castellani, Paris and Geneva, Éditions Slatkine, 1996, p. 109.

48   *Janet Ravenscroft*

7   Ibid., p. 13.
8   J. Céard, *La Nature et les prodiges: l'insolite au XVIe siècle, en France*, Geneva, Librairie Droz, 1996 [1977], p. ix.
9   Ibid., Preface, p. 5.
10 Ibid., Preface, p. 7.
11 S. de Covarrubias, *Tesoro de la lengua castellana o española*, ed. M. de Riquier, Barcelona, Editorial Alta Fulla, 1998 (1st edition 1943), p. 812.
12 Ibid., p. 250, 510–11; E. M. W. Tillyard, *The Elizabethan World Picture*, London, Pelican, 1981, p. 77.
13 Covarrubias, *Tesoro*, p. 511.
14 www.lpaonline.org/resources_dwarftypes.html (accessed 16 August 2004).
15 Ibid.
16 G. Canguilhem, *The Normal and the Pathological*, trans. Carolyn R. Fawcett, New York, Zone Books, 1991, p. 131.
17 J. de Rivilla Bonet y Pueyo, *Desvios de la naturaleza o tratado del origen de los monstruos*, Lima, 1695, folio 2, v.
18 Ibid., folio 11, r.
19 Ibid., folio 18, v.
20 Ibid., folio 47, v.
21 E. Goffman, *Stigma: Notes on the Management of Spoiled Identity*, London, Penguin, 1990, p. 153.
22 Canguilhem, *The Normal*, p. 62.
23 M. Bakhtin, *Rabelais and his World*, trans. Hélène Iswolsky, Bloomington, Indiana University Press, 1984, p. 29.
24 B. Castiglione, *The Book of the Courtier*, ed. V. Cox, London, J. M. Dent, 1994, p. 409.
25 B. Castiglione, *The Book of the Courtier*, trans. G. Bull, Harmondsworth, UK, Penguin, 1967, p. 61.
26 F. Furió Ceriol, *Concejo y consejeros del principe*, Antwerp, 1559, folio 60, v.
27 Ibid., folio 61, v.
28 M. Clayton, *Leonardo da Vinci: The Divine and the Grotesque*, London, Royal Collection, 2002, p. 21
29 Castiglione, *The Book of the Courtier*, p. 61.
30 Furió Ceriol, *Concejo*, folio 60, v.
31 Castiglione, *The Book of the Courtier*, p. 155.
32 Ibid., p. 160.
33 Bouza, *Locos*, pp. 90–1.
34 Covarrubias, *Tesoro*, p. 901.
35 Bouza, *Locos*, p. 94.
36 According to Leroi, '"neurological" cretins ... are mentally defective, have severe motor-neuron problems and tend to be deaf-mute'. A. M. Leroi, *Mutants: On the Form, Varieties and Errors of the Human Body*, London, HarperCollins, 2003, p. 194.
37 Castiglione, *The Book of the Courtier*, p. 137.
38 Goffman, *Stigma*, p. 23.
39 Emile Durkheim, 'The Normal and the Pathological', in M. Wolfgang *et al.*, eds, *The Sociology of Crime and Delinquency*, New York, John Wiley & Sons, Inc., 1970 (2nd edn), p. 12. J. H. Elliott, *Spain and Its World, 1500–1700*, New Haven, CT, Yale University Press, 1989, pp. 149–50.
40 Cited in F. J. B. Alvarez, 'La cosmovisión del Siglo de Oro. Ideas y supersticiones', in J. N. Alcalá-Zamora, ed., *La vida cotidiana en la España de Velázquez*, Madrid, Temas de Hoy Historia, 1999, p. 218.
41 Bouza, *Locos*, p. 23.
42 Ibid., p. 74.
43 J. A. Sánchez Belén, ' "La patria de todos". La Corte de la España barroca', in

Arte y saber: la cultura en tiempo de Felipe III y Felipe IV, Valladolid, Ministerio de Educación y Cultura, 1999, p. 222.
44 Moreno Villa, *Locos, enanos, negros y niños paleciegos siglos XVI y XVII*, Mexico City, Casa de España en México, 1937.
45 Ibid., p. 37.
46 Bouza, *Locos*, p. 141.
47 Villa, *Locos*, p. 16.
48 G. Redworth and F. Checa, 'The Kingdoms of Spain: The Courts of the Spanish Habsburgs, 1500–1700', in J. Adamson, ed., *The Princely Courts of Europe: Ritual, Politics and Culture under the Ancien Régime, 1500–1750*, London, Weidenfeld & Nicolson, 1999, p. 45.
49 Gonzalo Fernández de Oviedo, *Libro de la cámara real del Principe Don Juan e officios de su casa e serucio ordinario* (Madrid, 1870, pp. 8–10), cited in Redworth and Checa, 'The Kingdoms of Spain', p. 45.
50 Villa, *Locos*, pp. 55–150.
51 Ibid., pp. 51, 106.
52 Bouza, *Locos*, p. 12.
53 Ibid., p. 13.
54 Ibid., pp. 13–14.
55 Ibid., p. 81.
56 J. Deleito y Piñuela, *El Rey se divierte: recuerdos de hace tres siglos*, Madrid, Espasa-Calpe, 1955, p. 128.
57 Ibid., p. 128.
58 A. E. Pérez Sánchez, 'Monstruos, enanos y bufones', in *Monstruos, enanos y bufones en la Corte de los Austrias (A propósito del 'Retrato de enano' de Juan Van der Hamen)*, Madrid, Amigos del Museo Nacional del Prado, 1986, p. 9.
59 S. Hall, ed., *Representation: Cultural Representations and Signifying Practices*, London, Sage, 2003, p. 258.
60 Goffman, *Stigma*, p. 15.
61 Ibid., p. 15.
62 'Normal' did not appear in a Spanish dictionary until 1869, when it was still framed in relation to ideas about the natural: 'That which finds itself in its natural state. // That which serves as a norm or rule.' *Diccionario de la lengua castellana por la Real Academia Española*, 11th edn, Madrid, 1869, p. 540.
63 L. Fiedler, *Freaks: Myths and Images of the Secret Self*, New York, Simon & Schuster, 1978, p. 43.
64 R. Purcell, *Special Cases: Natural Anomalies and Historical Monsters*, San Francisco, Chronicle Books, 1997, p. 96.
65 J. Southworth, *Fools and Jesters at the English Court*, Stroud, UK, Sutton Publishing, 2003, p. 229, n. 13.
66 Ibid., pp. 21–2.
67 S. Stewart, *On Longing: Narratives of the Miniature, the Gigantic, the Souvenir, and the Collection*, Durham, NC, Duke University Press, 1993, p. 111.
68 Southworth, *Fools*, p. 18.
69 In 1991 Anne Lake Prescott also used 'pygmy' as a synonym for dwarf. See J. J. Cohen, ed., *Monster Theory*, Minneapolis, University of Minnesota Press, 1996, p. 75.
70 D. Williams, *Deformed Discourse: The Function of the Monstrous in Mediaeval Thought and Literature*, Exeter, University of Exeter Press, 1996, p. 111.
71 Ibid., p. 113.
72 Stewart, *On Longing*, p. 109.
73 Porter, 'History of the Body', p. 223.
74 E. Michel, *Musée National du Louvre, Catalogue raisonné des peintures du*

50 *Janet Ravenscroft*

Moyen-Age, de la Renaissance et des temps modernes: peintures flamandes du XVe et du XVIe siècle, Paris, Editions des Musées Nationaux, 1953, p. 222.

75 Pérez Sánchez, 'Monstruos, enanos y bufones', p. 18.

76 Most recently, Maria Kusche's excellent *Retratos y retradadores: Alonso Sánchez Coello y sus competidores Sofonisba Anguissola, Jorge de la Rúa y Rolán Moys*, Madrid, Fundación de Apoyo a la Historia del Arte Hispánico, 2003.

77 Diego Velázquez created the following paintings of dwarfs: *Baltasar Carlos with Dwarf, c.*1632; *Baltasar Carlos in the Riding School, c.*1636 (two versions); *Francisco Lezcano, c.*1636–8, *Don Diego de Acedo, c.*1636–8; *Sebastián de Morra, c.*1643–9.

78 M. Friedlander, *Early Netherlandish Painting*, Vol. 13: *Antonis Mor and His Contemporaries*, Leydon, A. W. Sijthoff, and Brussels, La Connaissance, 1975, p. 69.

79 A. Sánchez Ortíz, 'Juegos cromáticos de aparencia y poder en las cortes europeas medievales', *Goya*, March–April 2003, 293, p. 100; Bouza, *Locos*, pp. 109–10.

80 According to A. R. Jones and P. Stallybrass, the kind of gold braid seen in the painting 'was made by spinning gold or silver wire around a core of silk thread'. *Renaissance Clothing and the Materials of Memory*, Cambridge, Cambridge University Press, 2000, p. 25.

81 As only *caballeros* (knights) had the right to bear arms, the presence of the sword is intriguing. Sadly, there is not space to explore the potential significance of this here.

82 N. Sentenach, *Los grandes retratistas en España*, Madrid, Bola, 1914, p. 28.

83 Michel, *Musée National du Louvre*, pp. 222–3.

84 E. Tietze-Conrat, *Dwarfs and Jesters in Art*, London, Phaidon, 1957, p. 33.

85 L. Campbell, *Renaissance Portraits: European Portrait-Painting in the 14th, 15th and 16th Centuries*, New Haven, CT, Yale University Press, 1990, p. 104.

86 For example, those by the studio of Diego Velázquez (*Portrait of a Dwarf with a Dog*, no. 1203, Museo del Prado, Madrid) and José Ribera (*Dwarf with a Dog, c.*1643, lost).

87 Portraits of royal sitters with dogs are more numerous than those of dwarfs with dogs. Among them are Philip II's younger sister, Doña Juana de Portugal (*Juana of Portugal*, no. 3127, Vienna, Kunsthistorisches Museum, 1557), and the Archduke Alberto (*Archduke Albert*, Innsbruck, Ambras Castle, no. 9699, 1574), who would go on to marry Philip II's daughter, Isabel Clara Eugenia.

88 H. Hymans, *Antonio Moro: son œuvre et son temps*, Brussels, G. Van Oest, 1910, p. 129.

89 E. Chamorro, *El enano del Rey (una visión del Barroco a través de sus cortesanos más diminutos)*, Madrid, Editorial Planeta (Colección Memoria de la Historia), 1991, p. 159.

90 Covarrubias, *Tesoro*, p. 511.

91 Villa, *Locos*, p. 95. The author confuses the Mor painting with the lost portraits by Titian.

92 Villa, *Locos*, p. 95; Bouza, *Locos*, p. 53.

93 Villa, *Locos*, p. 95.

94 Argote de Molina, *Discurso sobre el libro de la montería*, cited in Bouza, *Locos*, p. 55.

95 Letter XLIX, in F. Bouza, ed., *Cartas de Felipe II a sus hijas*, Madrid, Ediciones Akal, 1998, p. 136.

96 Ibid., p. 136. See also Bouza, *Locos*, p. 55.

97 Bouza, *Locos*, p. 55.

98 Ibid., p. 189, n. 98.

99 Falomir Faus, 'Imágenes de poder y evocaciones de la memoria', pp. 215–16.

The court dwarf   51

100 M. Kusche, 'La antigua galería de retratos del Pardo: su importancia para la obra de Tiziano, Moro, Sánchez Coello y Sofonisba Anguissola y su significado para Felipe II, su fundador', *Archivo Español de Arte*, 1992, 65, pp. 1–36 at p. 6.

101 M. Kusche, 'La antigua galería de retratos del Pardo: su reconstrucción arquitectónica y el órden de colocación de los cuadros', *Archivo Español de Arte*, 1991, 64, pp. 1–28 at p. 1.

102 Kusche, 'La antigua galería de retratos del Pardo', 1992, p. 6.

103 Falomir Faus, 'Imágenes de poder y evocaciones de la memoria', p. 218.

104 F. Collar de Cáceres, 'Las aficiones, residencias y colecciones del monarca', in *El Mundo de Carlos V. De la España medieval al Siglo de Oro*, Madrid, Sociedad Estatal para la Conmemoración de los Centenarios de Felipe II y Carlos V, 2001, p. 93.

105 Gaskell, *Vermeer's Wager*, p. 86.

106 J. Woodall, ed., *Portraiture: Facing the Subject*, Manchester, Manchester University Press, 1997, p. 15.

107 This is the first appearance of a carpet in a Spanish court portrait, according to Kusche, *Retratos*, p. 440.

108 *Doña Juana de Portugal* by Cristobál de Morales, *c.*1552, Musées Royaux de Bruxelles.

109 Kusche, *Retratos*, p. 443.

110 See, for example, L. Roblot-Delondre, *Portraits d'infantes*, Paris, Librairie Nationale d'Art, 1913, p. 136; F. Bouza, *Locos*, p. 118; E. Valdivieso, '"El Niño de Vallecas": consideraciones sobre los enanos en la pintura española', in Fundación Amigos del Museo del Prado, *Velázquez*, Barcelona, Galaxia Gutenberg, 1999, p. 390.

111 Kusche, *Retratos*, p. 443.

112 L. Ruiz (no. 8.4), in *El linaje del emperador*, Cáceres, Sociedad Estatal para la Conmemoración de los Centenarios de Felipe II y Carlos V, 2000, pp. 372–3.

113 M. Mena Marqués (no. 16), in *Monstruos, enanos y bufones en la corte de los Austrias (A propósito del 'Retrato de enano' de Juan Van der Hamen)*, Madrid, Amigos del Museo Nacional del Prado, 1986, p. 64. In the same catalogue, Pérez Sánchez stated as a fact that dwarfs 'are friends of animals':, 'Monstruos, enanos y bufones', p. 11.

114 Kusche, *Retratos*, p. 443.

115 A. Jordan (no. I), in *El arte en la Corte de los Archiduques Alberto de Austria e Isabel Clara Eugenia (1598–1633): un reino imaginado*, Madrid, Sociedad Estatal para la Conmemoración de los Centenarios de Felipe II y Carlos V, 2000, p. 140.

116 S. Melchior-Bonnet, *The Mirror: A History*, trans. Katherine H. Jewett, London, Routledge, 2002, p. 192.

117 Covarrubias, *Tesoro*, p. 811, and *Emblemas Morales, Emblemas Morales de Don S. de Covarrubias Orozco*, Madrid, Luis Sanchez, 1589, p. 98.

118 D. Shuger, 'The "I" of the Beholder', in P. Fumerton and S. Hunt, eds, *Renaissance Culture and the Everyday*, Philadelphia, University of Pennsylvania Press, 1999, p. 21.

119 Mena Marqués (no. 16), in *Monstruos*, p. 64.

120 D. Davies, 'El Primo', in *Velázquez*, Fundación Amigos del Museo del Prado, Barcelona, Galaxia Gutenberg, 1999, pp. 176–7.

121 *Doña Juana de Portugal* by Anthonis Mor, *c.*1551, Musées Royaux de Bruxelles; Kusche, *Retratos*, p. 82.

122 Porter, 'History of the Body', p. 210.

123 Bouza, *Cartas*, Letters XV, XVI, XVII.

124 C. Bernis, 'La moda en la España de Felipe II a través del retrato de corte', in S.

52 *Janet Ravenscroft*

Saavedra, ed., *Alonso Sánchez Coello y el retrato en la corte de Felipe II*, Madrid, Museo del Prado, 1990, p. 87.

125 When the painting was catalogued in 1600, Magdalena Ruiz was not listed as either a dwarf or a madwoman. See Kusche, *Retratos*, p. 439.

126 The first edition of Philip's letters was compiled in French by Louis Prosper Gachard in 1884. There have been three Spanish editions, the first of which was compiled in 1943 and the last in 1998. There is still no English edition.

127 Bouza, *Cartas*, pp. 12, 6–7.

128 This is not to ignore the fact that any letters dealing with the health of royal children and the future of the dynasty must inevitably have a political component.

129 Ibid., Letter IX.

130 Elliott, *Spain*, p. 154.

131 Moreno Villa, *Locos*, p. 43 (there are only three individuals in this category); J. M. Serrera, 'Alonso Sánchez Coello y la mecánica del retrato de corte', in S. Saavedra, ed., *Alonso Sánchez Coello y el retrato en la corte de Felipe II*, Madrid, Museo del Prado, 1990, p. 39.

132 Bouza, *Cartas*, pp. 39–40, n. 22.

133 A letter survives that she wrote to Fernando Álvarez de Toledo, third Duke of Alba from the house of Don Diego de Córdoba (a great friend of Philip II) in 1568. See Bouza, *Locos*, p. 29.

134 Ibid., Letter XXI.

135 Villa, *Locos*, p. 37.

136 Covarrubias, *Tesoro*, p. 770.

137 Bouza, *Locos*, p. 202, n. 12.

138 The painting was catalogued as *Las Meninas* by Pedro de Madrazo in his *Catálogo de los cuadros del real museo de pintura y escultura*, Madrid, 1843.

139 Covarrubias, *Tesoro*, p. 584. The painting was created by Diego Velázquez in 1656, and hangs at the Museo del Prado, Madrid.

140 F. Marías, 'El género de *Las Meninas*: los servicios de la familia', in F. Marías, ed., *Otras Meninas*, Madrid, Ediciones Siruela, 1995, p. 256.

141 Deleito y Piñuela, *El Rey*, p. 129.

142 Chamorro, *El enano*, p. 187.

143 J. M. Gudiol, *Velázquez: 1599–1660. Historia de su vida, catálogo de su obra, estudio de la evolución de su técnica*, Barcelona, Ediciones Poligrafa, 1973, p. 288.

144 Bakhtin, *Rabelais*, p. 317.

145 The traditional identification of the model for this composition is *Juana de Mendoza, La Duquesa de Béjar with Her Dwarf* by Alonso Sánchez Coello, *c.*1585 (private collection). (See, for example, J. Camón Aznar, *Summa artis: historia general del arte*, Vol. XXIV: *La pintura española del siglo XVI*, Madrid, Espasa-Calpe, 1970, p. 500. i.) Recently, Kusche has suggested a different attribution and model. See *Retratos*, pp. 259–60.

3 From 'monstrous' to 'abnormal'

The case of conjoined twins in the nineteenth century

Sarah Mitchell

In the nineteenth century, twins born joined to each other were considered 'monstrosities', and often referred to in the medical literature as 'double monsters'. They were rare, and the majority of them were stillborn or died shortly after birth. Medical men speculated about what caused the condition and described to their colleagues in medical society meetings in minute detail exactly how they were joined and how their parts appeared to function. They marvelled at the capacity of nature to allow such births to occur. Very rarely, if ever, did they mention the possibility of surgically separating them. Double monsters were expected to live out the course of their natural lives and it was assumed by doctors that the death of one would necessitate the death of the other. At the time of their deaths, the expected role of double monsters was to become the subject of medical dissection for the benefit of scientific knowledge.

In the early twenty-first century, twins born joined to each other are typically called 'conjoined twins' and their condition is considered both an 'abnormality' and a disability.[1] They are still rare, occurring approximately once in every 50,000–100,000 births.[2] They are perhaps even rarer than in the nineteenth century, because of fetal monitoring technologies that allow early diagnosis of the condition and the option for therapeutic abortions. Physicians no longer spend much time speculating as to the cause, as there are accepted theories to which they subscribe. They do not give 'nature' a chance to accommodate their delivery for, as in most cases of twins, they are delivered by Caesarean section. Virtually always, particularly since the 1950s, when the first 'cluster' of separation surgeries was performed, the question of surgical separation is addressed.[3] Separation is viewed as vital to 'normalise' the infants physically, enabling them to lead 'normal' lives. A 2003 *New York Times* headline concisely expresses the goal of separation surgery: 'Two Boys, Joined Skulls, One Goal: Two Lives.'[4]

Throughout the nineteenth century, monstrosity was a contested site on which medical men, the public, showmen, human 'monstrosities' and their representatives all grappled with issues pertaining to the interpretation, exhibition, medical status and even physical ownership of monstrous bodies. My aim in this chapter is to explore the medical transition from viewing conjoined twins as 'monstrous' to perceiving them as 'abnormal'. I argue that this shift represented a change in the medical approach to monstrosity, closely related to the changing professional identity of medical men, who were enjoying increased status and authority. The status of medicine as authority today is taken for granted and its origin is rarely questioned.[5] According to philosopher Mary Tiles, medical men (and women) today arrive at their 'conception of the norm from three sources – from physiology, as the science of normal man, from clinical experience, and from the representation of the norm which is dominant in the society within which [they are] working'.[6] Medical men succeeded in carving new territory for themselves and expanding their areas of expertise in part by 'medicalising' or framing what had previously been regarded simply as variations of behaviour, sins, or natural biological processes into medical conditions or diseases requiring medical supervision and intervention.[7] Medical men were on the cutting edge of the nineteenth-century preoccupation with establishing norms. Science and medicine, broadly defined, as 'ways of knowing', were privileged and accorded medical and cultural authority.[8] Once established in medicine, the concept 'normal' spread to many other fields and increasingly to everyday life.[9]

First, I focus on the ways in which medical men attempted to make sense of monstrosity throughout most of the nineteenth century. In their descriptions of and explanations for cases they encountered, medical men linked bodily anomaly to a larger body of contemporary scientific inquiry – for example, the study of 'race' as a category of difference. Second, as the study of monstrosity became subject to scientific methodologies, medical men tended to downplay individual differences among monstrosities such as 'race' and emphasised other attributes that allowed them to classify monstrosities into increasingly specific categories. Monstrosity did not disappear, but it became articulated differently, as its hybrid nature was increasingly bifurcated into the categories 'normal' and 'abnormal'.

The 'Siamese Twins' and race

As an example of how race was used as a lens through which to view 'monstrosity' in the early to mid-nineteenth century, I refer to the case of Chang and Eng, arguably the most famous of double monsters. This case study begins in London in early 1830. On 1 April 1830 Dr George Buckley Bolton read a report to the assembled members of the Royal College of Surgeons about the pair of brothers. He began his physical description of the youths born in Siam (now Thailand) by comparing them to their European counterparts in terms of size. At 'five feet two inches' with a 'united weight ... [of] one hundred and eighty pounds', he stated, 'they are much shorter, and appear less advanced in puberty than youths of this country at the age of eighteen years; but the average stature of their countrymen is less than that of Europeans'.[10] It is not surprising that Bolton used this comparative

Conjoined twins 55

approach, as many of his scientific contemporaries followed the conventions of the French palaeontologist Georges Cuvier (1769–1832), the British geologist Charles Lyell (1797–1875), the French medical anatomist Étienne Serres (1793–1860) and the German physiologist J. F. Blumenbach (1752–1840), to name a few, in assigning different races and ethnicities to a graded scale.[11] Comparing the young men to Europeans was a reflection of this tendency, as was equating them with the Chinese, specifically in terms of complexion and physiognomy.[12] Bolton addressed this by saying that 'they have not the broad and flat forehead so characteristic of the Chinese race, but resemble the lower class of the people of Canton in the colour of their skins, and in the forms of their noses, lips, eyes, and ears'.[13] An American doctor attributed their appearance to the fact that they were 'three-quarters Chinese' and thus did not possess the 'bright gamboge-yellow like colour' that typified the 'pure Siamese'.[14]

Although the topic of race and comparative anatomy was a common one for meetings of bodies such as the Royal Society, Chang and Eng were of interest for another reason. They also happened to be joined to each other at the chest and abdomen by a band of flesh, which had drawn the attention of Robert Hunter, the British merchant who had 'discovered' Chang and Eng in their native Siam in 1824.[15]

Bolton was uniquely qualified to provide his report because for the four months preceding the meeting he had been the personal medical attendant of these unusual twins. They were not ill, but their unusual formation was sufficient to warrant close medical supervision. In fact, the previous November, within days of their arrival in London, Chang and Eng had been the featured attraction at a by-invitation-only event, attended by 'the most distinguished persons of the medical faculty, and a considerable body of literary and scientific gentlemen', the number in attendance reaching several hundred 'gentlemen of science'.[16] Because of their unusual anatomy, they were noticed, pursued, acquired and taken from their home country first to the United States, then to Britain, for the purpose of being displayed widely to the public for a profit. A secondary purpose was to make them available to representatives of the medical profession. The latter was seen to be a mutually beneficial arrangement: Chang and Eng's promoters could use the statements provided by medical men assuring the public that the brothers were legitimate monstrosities and the physicians, in turn, were given permission to examine them.

For example, Joshua Brooks (1761–1833), leading London anatomist, examined Chang and Eng at a 'private levee' in 1829. He wrote out a certificate that was then signed by several other eminent medical men, confirming 'that the twins were a great natural curiosity, and that there was no deception'.[17] Whether it was necessary to have a medical man verify a deformity or not, the fact that such men's word was accepted as proof is an indication of the cultural authority they possessed.

Bolton's ten-page address included a detailed physical description of the

56   Sarah Mitchell

brothers, medical data concerning their mother's previous experience with childbirth, and the results of experiments performed on the youths designed to determine at what point, if any, they experienced common sensation. Bolton's report contained descriptions of their eating habits, past illnesses, differences from each other, their remarkable strength, relationship with each other, and observations about how they moved, ran, walked, played and generally manoeuvred their world.

To a modern audience it may be striking that it was only after this description that Bolton finally arrived at the issue of where and how they were joined:

> The band of union is formed in the following manner. At the lowest part of the sternum of each boy, the ensiform cartilage is bent upwards and forwards, meeting the other in the middle of the upper part of the band ... the entire band is covered with common integument; and when the boys face each other, its length at the upper edge is one inch and three quarters, and at the lower, not quite three inches.[18]

Bolton's description emphasised Chang and Eng's status as monstrous in form, but he also placed them in relation to Europeans of the same age and within what he considered their closest ethnographic category. He also referred to the contemporary theory of acclimatisation in favour at the time in his offhand comment that 'their bodies are much paler now than they were on their first arrival in England'.[19] Bolton, in addition to his medical and physiological observations, included ethnographic information about where they came from.[20] His and other early descriptions seem to conflate China and Siam, a land unfamiliar to the majority of Westerners. Chang and Eng's promoters often represented them in an idealised 'Oriental' setting, although the artists never actually saw them in their home country. Instead, artists relied on stereotypes of Siam as exotic and its inhabitants as 'other'. In early images, Chang and Eng are portrayed with exaggerated Asian features and darker skin that they do not have in later representations. They appear dressed in 'native' garb with hairstyles to match, wearing 'the costume of their country'.[21] This emphasis on exotic 'Oriental' qualities is consistent with medical and scientific interest in the customs and practices of other cultures.

Historians writing about Chang and Eng have tended to concentrate on their conjoined bodies and have paid less attention to their race.[22] This omission is striking, because of the importance of views of race at the time they were first being introduced to Western audiences. In Britain, especially, debates were ongoing concerning whether or not British subjects who relocated to tropical colonies would eventually adapt to the unhealthy and unfamiliar climate.[23] As cultural historians tell us, however, the 'past is a foreign country', and it is important to understand the differences in the ways race and disability were viewed by Chang and Eng's contemporaries. They were

Conjoined twins 57

Figure 3.1 Chang and Eng, the original Siamese Twins, represented in an idealised Oriental landscape. Wellcome Library, London.

not seen apart from their race. This was made explicit in newspaper accounts, which frequently described them as resembling the Chinese. In November 1829, four months before Bolton's address to the Royal Society, *The Times* reported that

> in the colour of their skin, in the form of the nose, lips, and eyes, they resemble the Chinese, whom our readers may probably have seen occasionally about the streets of London, but they have not the broad and flat face which is characteristic of the Mingol [*sic*] race. Their foreheads are higher and narrower than those of the majority of their countrymen.[24]

58   *Sarah Mitchell*

It seems that Chang and Eng's racial characteristics and their conjoined bodies were both so strange to viewers that it was difficult to consider one without the other, and they became conflated in the eyes of many, hence the emergence of 'Siamese twins' as a common term of reference for conjoined twins generally. One woman who visited Chang and Eng in their early days of exhibition recalled that when she first saw

> the Siamese Twins, their strange foreign features, and the few sentences spoken for my entertainment in the harsh dialect of their country, made as strong an impression on my childish fancy as the freak of Nature which had united them so closely.[25]

Several months before Chang and Eng's arrival, on 5 March 1829, Bransby Blake Cooper (1792–1853), Surgeon at Guy's Hospital in London, presented to the Royal Society a detailed report on the dissection of the foot of a Chinese woman who had practised foot-binding. After her body was discovered floating in the river at Canton, the foot was removed, transported to England and presented to the surgeon and anatomist Sir Astley Cooper (1768–1841). In his report to the society, Cooper did not provide details about who had removed or transported the curious artefact. He speculated that, owing to the circumstances under which the body was discovered, 'it was one of the lower orders'. His assumption that 'we should naturally expect to find the most perfect specimens among those of the highest rank' led him to the conclusion that 'the measured proportions of the foot are therefore to be considered somewhat above the more successful results of this cruel act when completed on the feet of those in more exalted stations of life'.[26] Cooper concluded his report by explaining why he chose to share this report with the society, describing it as curious and of interest to scientific men. The practice of foot-binding which created the foot in question had apparently been a topic of discussion by this scientific body in the past, which further encouraged him to write the report. Perceptions of 'Oriental' practices such as foot-binding and suspicion of the alleged cruelty of the Siamese king went hand in hand and combined to seemingly justify the commonly held view that Chang and Eng were far better off in their new lives in the Western world than they had been in their homeland.

Throughout the nineteenth century, non-Westerners employed as 'freaks' were displayed in 'native' garb, conflating their racial otherness with their unusual physical anatomy in a seemingly irresistible combination.[27] Promotional brochures sold at Chang and Eng's appearances contained basic information about Siam, such as its location, as well as a more subjective portrayal of Siam's perceived exotic qualities, such as its houses, 'chiefly built upon rafts, composed of bamboos'.[28] Another popular representation focused on Siam's supposedly unenlightened and cruel king: 'The government of Siam is probably one of the most despotic and cruel in the world.'[29] Visitors to Siam, such as John Crawfurd (1783–1868), a Scottish medical doctor employed by the East India Company and elected president of the Ethnological Society in 1861, described the country and its inhabitants as 'half-naked and enslaved barbarians'.[30] His ethnographic observations opined that although the Siamese are

> certainly a handsomer people than either the Chinese or Indian islanders, beauty, according to our notions of it, is a stranger to them. The physiognomy of the Siamese . . . conveys rather a gloomy, cheerless, and sullen air, and their gait is slow, sluggish, and ungraceful.[31]

He criticised other aspects of Siamese appearance as well, saying that their 'mode of dressing the head is singular and grotesque', they 'permit the nails of their hands to grow to an unnatural and inconvenient length' and 'have the same prejudice against white teeth with many other Eastern people, and at an early age they stain them with an indelible black'.[32]

In spite of these disparaging observations, Crawfurd saw the Siamese as one of 'the most civilized and leading nations' in that part of the world.[33] One wonders what this says about his views of Siam's neighbours! Overall, though, he painted an unflattering picture and confirmed 'what has been often asserted of the Siamese by European writers, that they are servile, rapacious, slothful, disingenuous, pusillanimous, and extravagantly vain'.[34] This is consistent with an unspoken assumption of Western superiority. The extent to which denigrating statements such as these may have influenced the medical view of Chang and Eng is unknown. However, association with the Chinese race may have further 'othered' them since, as Sander Gilman argues, from the 1820s, 'Western contempt for all things Chinese began to manifest itself in Europe and the Americas'.[35]

Chang and Eng cannot be viewed solely as representative of their race however, when their physical configuration set them apart not only from the majority of Europeans, but from the majority of other Siamese and Chinese as well. Chang and Eng were brought to the West because of their conjoinmen, but, once there, could not be seen apart from their race. In their case, perceptions of their race became conflated with perceptions of their monstrosity. The term 'Siamese' twins was one of the terms originally applied to Chang and Eng and has become perhaps the most commonly used, although 'conjoined' is now considered the most appropriate term. Gradually throughout the nineteenth century, 'Siamese' began to be used to refer to other pairs of conjoined twins, no matter what their nationality, and has become synonymous with the condition of conjoined twinning itself.[36] This is in large part due to the extreme fame that Chang and Eng experienced. They were exhibited and their appearances promoted extensively in the early 1830s. After they retired and settled down in North Carolina to farm, marry and raise families, they continued to appear in the news from time to time, and even exhibited themselves for brief stints later in life, ensuring that they never disappeared completely from the collective memory.[37]

60 *Sarah Mitchell*

Although the term 'Siamese' no longer refers to an Asian state, as Siam became Thailand in 1939, exotic cultural references arguably still linger on in the term 'Siamese twins' to the present day. Knowledge of 'Siam' itself among Westerners was often limited to what they knew of the 'Siamese Twins'.[38] Equating non-white races with persons with disabilities, according to historian Douglas Baynton, was a connection routinely made in the nineteenth century.[39] Perhaps the most intriguing example of this is the case of Down's syndrome, originally known by the racially charged term 'mongolism',[40] because of superficial similarities between the faces of those diagnosed as having the condition and stereotype of the facial characteristics of Mongolians. In fact, this association of anomalies with the 'other', and with people and places seen as exotic, led some to speculate that monstrosities were indeed more common in Asia. Not long after Chang and Eng arrived, another pair of twins, joined in a similar fashion, caused one doctor to comment that

> the union of twins by a corporeal band, as in the example of the two Siamese youths now exhibiting in the metropolis, is a phenomenon not unparalleled, especially in the East, where *lusus naturae* [freaks of nature] are, perhaps, more frequent than in other parts of the world.[41]

Another example was reported in the *British Medical Journal* in a 'case of parasitic fetus' in 1888.[42] It concerned an Indian child named Laloo who had a sibling attached. The author of the article commented that Laloo's mother was 25 years old when the child was born and had given birth to a normal son the previous year. 'This excludes any theory in the present case of early Oriental marriages as a cause of monstrosity.'[43] Although this type of explanation for monstrosity was not widely supported, reference to it points to the existence of such associations among medical professionals. The notion that monstrosity was more prevalent among non-Europeans continued into the late nineteenth century. In 1884, after teaching anatomy and supervising the dissection of almost 300 subjects for nine years, an American doctor, Francis J. Shepherd (1851–1929) remarked that he had 'found variations to occur more frequently in negro and Indian subjects than in those of European descent'.[44]

Medical interest in Chang and Eng paralleled the preoccupation among medical men and scientists with racial classification and ethnography. Their acquisition from Siam made them part of a larger tradition of voyages of exploration and discovery in which exotic curiosities deemed of scientific interest and as potentially valuable commodities were actively sought. The results of these gathering expeditions ended up in museums, zoological gardens, private collections, and at anatomical schools.[45] These collections figured in the developing scientific disciplines and classificatory schemes being constructed at the time. Medicine relied on specimens and data acquired during expeditions, and medical men based much of their claim to authority on their knowledge of anatomy and other subjects gained through examination of specimens.[46]

Meanings of monstrosity

The rich historiography of monstrosity shows that it has long been a subject of fascination and curiosity, and one whose interpretation is imbued with cultural meaning.[47] By the early nineteenth century, cultural meanings of the 'monstrous' had already undergone a number of changes and were no longer viewed as 'prodigies', 'marvels' or 'freaks of nature'. Although their cause was not understood, the development of monstrosities was presumed to be subject to the same rules of nature as other beings. This was the principle upon which the French zoologist Isidore Geoffroy Saint-Hilaire (1805–61) founded teratology, the scientific study of monsters. The anatomist Richard Owen (1804–92) reiterated this sentiment in 1837 when he stressed in one of a series of lectures that 'monsters are, like the Beings called Normal, subject to constant rules'.[48] In 1854 an American physician, H. V. N. Miller, concurred when he wrote that 'extended observation has shown that they do not occur by chance or from the mere caprice of nature, but are under the influence of certain fixed laws of organization which they never transcend'.[49] Further proof of the universal nature of laws governing monstrous development was the observation that every form of monstrosity met with among humans had also 'been observed in other animals, showing the universal operation of those laws of organization to which they owe their origin and in accordance with which they attain their development'.[50] The frequency with which they appeared in humans, along with their universal appearance in other species, also lent an assumption of order and a certain amount of predictability to double monstrosity. H. V. N. Miller wrote in 1854 that

> the order which prevails even in the production of monsters is strikingly manifested by the definite number in which they occur, being in Paris about 1 to 3,000 births ... some are so common as to be scarcely worthy of note ... while others, from their infrequency, are in themselves in the highest degree interesting.[51]

In this category of most interesting he included, not surprisingly, double monstrosity.

Knowledge of the laws of development gave medical men the special ability to 'at once distinguish between true cases of monstrosity and those which are alleged to have been met with, but which really never occurred'.[52] Dr John North lectured to medical students in 1840 at the Middlesex Hospital Medical School that 'we can distinguish between the fabulous monsters of bygone days, and those which really existed. Many cases of monstrosity recorded in former times were mere fables. . . . The law regarding the formation of double monstrosities is universal and invariable'.[53]

62 Sarah Mitchell

A cursory title search of the medical periodical literature in the United States and Britain between 1800 and 1910 reveals that forms of the term 'monster' were used frequently throughout the period. The greatest use occurred between 1870 and 1890.[54] A number of other, descriptive terms, such as *lusus naturae* and variations on the phrases 'united twins', 'joined twins', 'double' or 'duplex twins' as well as 'Siamese twins', were used synonymously. At first the latter term was used specifically to refer to Chang and Eng, the 'original' Siamese twins; later it was frequently applied to other pairs of twins joined in a similar manner, although it never replaced variations of the word 'monstrosity'.[55] The first reference to 'conjoined twins' that I have found appeared in 1861, with the term 'abnormal' following in 1875.[56] In the 1880s, terms that denoted increasing scientific classification, including location and degree of connection, began to appear regularly. Several of these end with the Greek suffix *pagus* which means 'fastened', and are still used today. The prefix refers to the manner in which they were fastened. 'Pygopagus' twins, for example, were joined at the coccyx and sacrum. 'Ischiopagus' twins were joined at the backbone and sacrum. This new level of detail is indicative of the efforts of the medical profession to bring order, through increasingly specific classificatory terms, to their understanding of unusual anatomies. According to the American doctor J. W. Ballantyne, this change in naming ways demonstrated the extent to which by the turn from the nineteenth to the twentieth century teratology as a science had become international in scope. However, he conceded that these terms were 'uncouth and unfamiliar to the eye and ear of the English-speaking medical man' and that 'it would be easier to give the various monstrosities English names', thus enabling people to 'speak of a double-headed twin monster, or of a brainless fetus, or of a one-eyed monstrosity'.[57] These 'designations', he asserted, would

> be more easily understood by us than such names as dicephalus, anencephalus . . . but to scientists of other nationalities their meaning might not be plain. So it has come about, for the sake of international convenience, Greek words have been made use of to found a teratological nomenclature.[58]

The variety of terms available simultaneously suggests that understanding of conjoined twins was in flux. It is also due to the fact that medical men from a variety of backgrounds, levels of education, and region all contributed to the literature. In addition, interest in monstrosity crossed a variety of disciplines and was not confined to teratology. Rather, it was set within the larger context of other newly emerging scientific disciplines such as anthropology, ethnology, biology, pathological anatomy as well as teratology, whose discourses contributed to the conversations taking place among doctors attempting to make sense of 'double monsters'. A focus of many of these disciplines was to identify and explain difference among and between human populations.[59] Differences were measured and classified, providing 'scientific', hence 'objective', data with which to delineate different kinds of human populations.

Medical and scientific professions alike saw the proliferation of organised growth including societies and specialist training institutions being formed, and new journals published.[60] These new venues permitted the diffusion of scientific knowledge and contributed to bringing the study of difference under the purview of professional scientific expertise. The medical journal, one of the main venues through which medical men shared their cases and ideas, was a major repository of details of monstrosities. In many cases a physician wrote to his colleagues through the medium of the journal, to share his experience in assisting the delivery of a monstrosity. Traditionally only present during childbirth in the case of difficult deliveries, medical men gained increasing acceptance as attendants in uncomplicated births as well, with their claims to provide safer and less painful deliveries.[61] Because they were present at more deliveries, medical men were also more likely to observe the births of monstrous children, or children with a wide variety of birth defects that might not otherwise have come to their attention. Medical men saw their experiences with monstrosity as relevant to their professional development and identity. Although not all cases of monstrous birth were complicated, medical men needed to be able to decide correctly when to let nature take its course and when to interfere.

The American physician James Pendleton, lecturer on midwifery and diseases of women and children, was one of a number of contributors to the medical literature who tried to convince their colleagues of the importance of the study of monstrosities. For too long, he proclaimed in 1826, it had been seen as a subject 'of mere idle curiosity, and offering nothing of interest but the gratification of our natural appetite for what is marvelous and unnatural'.[62] Instead, he argued that

> a knowledge of it is indispensable to the practitioner of midwifery, and that if ignorant of such cases, the symptoms and phenomena by which they are devoted, he may allow the mother to fall a sacrifice to his ignorance, or unnecessarily destroy the child.[63]

Decades later, in 1853, the British doctor W. F. Montgomery (1797–1859) used the same argument when he wrote that a knowledge of 'the circumstances attending the birth of these monstrous productions . . . may . . . tend to assist some of us in practice, should such anomalous cases present themselves for our management'.[64]

Although the medical literature, according to Pendleton, contained plenty of descriptions of deformed children at birth, it rarely offered practical information that could help in an actual delivery. There was a strong minority opinion, in fact, that knowledge of monstrosity would not necessarily help the practitioner when confronted with one at a delivery.

64 *Sarah Mitchell*

One doctor dismissed the subject of monsters and obstetrics by saying that monsters are not usually carried full-term, so their delivery should not cause problems in the first place and that in the event of a 'full-sized double-headed monstrosity', teaching would be of little help anyway.[65] Another expressed the pessimistic viewpoint that 'the impossibility of diagnosing such a condition in the ordinary stages of labour makes general directions as to treatment worthless'.[66] From the case he had attended, the only thing he felt was worth discussing was 'when the attachment of the children was discovered – whether to sever them at the uniting part, or to attempt delivery as they were'.[67]

Once a delivery was complete, the first concern of most medical men was, if the children were alive, to examine them as closely as the parents would allow and describe them in great detail in the subsequent report to the profession. If the child/ren were not alive, which was more common, medical men endeavoured to persuade the parents to allow dissection of the newborn/s and, if possible, possession of the 'specimen'. This was such a pressing issue for them that it was often included in reports to the profession. Dr R. W. O'Donovan wrote in 1851 that he was 'unable to obtain permission to make an anatomical examination' of a particular 'monster, which presented an excellent example of complete duplicity'. He commented on the parents' refusal – in this case, he explained, due to 'the prejudice that exists amongst the lower orders in this country [Ireland]'.[68] Medical men such as O'Donovan clearly saw themselves as representatives of the authority of science. Not to be willing to comply with their scientific requests was to demonstrate one's superstition, ignorance and/or other non-scientific traits.

Influenced by the rise of pathological anatomy, doctors sought privileged access to bodies for the purposes of dissection and often exhibition within a medical community. In some cases medical men went to great lengths to procure specimens. Access to bodies was both limited and quite controversial in the 1820s and 1830s, amid public debate over the value and propriety of dissection. Limited legal venues to acquiring bodies led some medical students to somewhat unorthodox methods to secure them (such as body-snatching or grave-robbing). These actions, although often tacitly condoned by medical schools, incurred the wrath and distrust of the public. Any body was valued for this purpose; however, monstrous bodies were of particular interest to anatomists and as commodities were worth the most.[69]

Degrees of monstrosity

Whether referred to as 'double monsters' or 'conjoined twins', children born joined to one another always constitute an exceptional birth.[70] However, for a better understanding of double monsters in the nineteenth century, it is useful to view them in context as one type of monstrosity, along a graded scale with many others.[71] There was discussion among medical men as to

Conjoined twins 65

what exactly constituted a monstrosity. According to Saint-Hilaire, every genus and species of animal had a specific type. This specific type encompassed size, shape, structure and the arrangement of the individual's internal organs. Every deviation from this specific type, from the most trivial to the most severe, constituted an anomaly, or monstrosity.[72] This definition was far too broad for some, who preferred to reserve the term 'monster' for only the most extraordinary and obvious anomalies. Too inclusive a definition might erroneously sweep mere effects of disease or simple varieties under the carpet of monstrosity. According to the British obstetrician Francis Ramsbotham (1801–68) in his 1841 popular textbook, the term 'monsters' should be used

> in instances in which some great deviation from normal structure is observed, either as the result of original natural formation, confusion of the organs of two separate children, or irregular or diseased action of a specific kind, such as can only exist in, and influence the organization of, the fetus in utero.[73]

Ramsbotham also promoted the French naturalist Georges Buffon's (1707–88) classification as the simplest and most natural. Buffon allows for four varieties: 'those in which there is a deficiency of parts', 'those which are redundant in organs', those 'where the parts are misshapen' and those 'where, although the organs may be naturally formed, they are misplaced'.[74] The Dutch physician Willem Vrolik (1801–63) situated double monsters on a scale, or 'continued series', on which the 'lowest degree of duplicity', he wrote in 1853, was 'that of a single part of the body; for example, a double or supernumerary finger, as the highest, a complete double monster, with two heads, four upper and four lower limbs, and two trunks, such as the Siamese twins. And between these two extremes', he continued, 'there are different forms of duplicity, which gradually run into the other'.[75]

Somewhere between the two extremes articulated by Vrolik was the case of Josephine Myrtle Corban, born in Tennessee in 1868. In June of that year she was described by Professors Joseph Jones and Paul F. Eve of the University of Nashville as having 'four legs and two distinct external female organs of generation'.[76] In spite of the 'curious manifestation of the powers of nature in abnormal productions', this infant was also said to possess 'the head and trunk ... of a living, well-developed, healthy, active infant of about five weeks'. They speculated that should she 'reach maturity and the generative organs be double, there [was] nothing to prevent conception on both sides'.[77]

In these borderline cases, medical men claimed that they possessed specialised training that would allow them to diagnose certain monstrous conditions that might not be as obvious as, for example, conjoined twins. In this they saw a role for the teratologist:

One task of the systematic teratologist is to endeavour to encourage the practical obstetrician to be on the look-out for rare varieties of monster. There is little fear that an anencephalous fetus may be overlooked. Its hideous aspect and its bulk strike the attention of the most ignorant midwife, nor can it escape the notice of the overworked practitioner.[78]

But there were less obvious cases that could be missed – so the utmost vigilance was required of the practitioner. In other words, presence of monstrosity was not always obvious and it might take a professional to diagnose certain cases accurately.

Ballantyne addressed this as well, in his 1904 compendium, *Manual of Antenatal Pathology and Hygiene*. 'It might appear at first that a line could easily be drawn between double and single monsters,' he begins.

Between the Siamese Twins and an anencephalic fetus there is all the difference possible, for the one is so obviously two united individuals, and the other is nothing more than a single defective fetus; but there are double monsters which show almost no external signs of duplicity at all.

'Such cases', he cautions,

illustrate very well the disturbing effect of these intermediate varieties upon classifications; but they have at least served the useful purpose of demonstrating that in Teratology we have to do, not so much with a series of clearly differentiated types, as with an almost interminable number of kinds of monstrous forms related more or less intimately to each other, and shading off each other by almost imperceptible degrees.[79]

It was this possibility of not recognising a monstrosity when it presented itself that contributed to the later drive for more and more specific, discrete definitions in classification systems. As knowledge of more cases was recorded and disseminated, it became ever more apparent that monstrosities could indeed be categorised. Medical men compared and contrasted 'cases' of united twins in order to assess the relative rarity or frequency with which their particular type occurred.

Although not the first, Isidore Geoffroy Saint-Hilaire's classification system for human monstrosities quickly became the standard system cited in the literature and was widely accepted and quoted. The American doctor J. W. Ballantyne saw it as 'nothing less than a great edifice, a huge classificational structure, providing accommodation for all the then known types of anomaly, and dwarfing all other competitive fabrics as well by its bulk as by its intricacy'.[80] The 'most serious fault' with this system, according to Ballantyne, is the notion that 'anomalous creatures form a world by themselves, a great kingdom or sub-kingdom like that of the plants or the animals'. This, he argued, is not justified 'for while species in Zoology are groups of living beings which transmit by generation a complex of characters . . . species in Teratology are simply individuals suffering from the same malformation'.

In spite of these reservations, Ballantyne did not discount the usefulness of the system, which he says can still be used 'without accepting the ideas of species, genera, and families which underlie' it, and by seeing them as 'larger and smaller divisions not related to each other in the intimate way suggested by the Saint-Hilaires'.[81]

A pair of conjoined twins that fitted the classic definition of a particular species set out by Saint-Hilaire was a little more knowable, albeit no less monstrous. Now placed securely within an accepted system, and along a scale based on degree of monstrosity, the double monster served to affirm the veracity of the system that could account for such a monstrosity. Confidence in medical knowledge and understanding of the condition allowed medical men to state confidently when a given specimen was rare for its type or common. For example, an American doctor wrote of his experience with conjoined male twins in 1861 that the case was of rare interest, in part 'on account of the infrequency of the cases of the kind reported'.[82]

The wide variety of monstrosities identified and classified, as evidenced by the accumulating number of cases of various types, may have contributed to the further medicalisation of the condition by reinforcing the notion that delivery of a monstrosity should not be left to an allegedly unskilled midwife or anyone else unfamiliar with the subject. Since the condition was not diagnosed before birth, this was, in a sense, an argument for the presence of trained medical men at all cases of childbirth.

Conclusion

For much of the nineteenth century, monstrosity and abnormality were conflated. Only gradually did notions of monstrosity come to be replaced by the binary notions of the 'normal' and the 'abnormal'. As the science of teratology became established and more cases of monstrosity were documented and disseminated, differences among monstrosities such as 'race' were de-emphasised (although not ignored), and similarities, based on seemingly more objective criteria, such as the anatomic location of conjoinment, were stressed. By the early to mid-twentieth century the medical gaze was on the abnormal aspects, and the perceived deficits ensuing from the abnormality became the centre of attention. In the nineteenth century, in contrast, the literature often remarked on what the individuals in question could do, in spite of their monstrous formation. The shift was from 'normal' within their own context, to 'abnormal' within a larger societal context in which difference was less acceptable. Advances in medicine and surgery reinforced the notions that 'abnormal' bodies were bodies in need of correction. The earlier nuanced understanding of monstrosity as existing in degrees did not translate well into the later notions of 'normal' and 'abnormal'.

68   *Sarah Mitchell*

After the deaths of Chang and Eng in 1874, the American doctor Robert Harris speculated about the never-attempted separation surgery on the two. He alluded to the fact that separation surgery itself would have rendered Chang and Eng abnormal – that, in fact, they were normal already. Their separation would have revealed that, individually, Chang and Eng possessed several physical defects, or abnormalities, which were somewhat masked by their 'monstrous' identities. For example, Harris speculated that, if separated, they would each have needed to learn to walk again and, 'compared with normal subjects', they 'would have presented a singular gait and figure'.[83] If they had ceased to be 'monstrous' they would have become merely abnormal, their individual physical deformities more noticeable and prominent.

The long-term consequences of the transformation from 'monstrous' to 'abnormal' had serious consequences for the medical and surgical treatment of conjoined twins and others with so-called 'abnormal' conditions. The desire for a 'normal' child as so defined by societal expectations has, in part, made children seen as 'abnormal' less desirable. The belief that a child who has a body dramatically different from the 'norm' will necessarily lead an unacceptable life, coupled with improved technological capability that promises to 'fix' these children, has contributed to decisions to attempt surgical correction.[84]

In the nineteenth century, though, before separation surgery became a viable option, the transformation of medical perceptions of double monsters from 'monstrous' to 'abnormal' reflected the perceptions medical men had of their own profession and aspirations. Monstrosity was something to learn from, to understand, to observe, to exhibit, and to dissect for the sake of scientific knowledge and, as a result, medical men themselves. The more they learned, however, the less medical men perceived what monstrosity had to teach. Even before there was a so-called technological fix for the condition, monstrosity was increasingly specialised into specific types, and pathologised. Abnormality became something to correct rather than to learn from. Ironically, the more that double monsters were 'normalised' in relation to other monstrosities, the more they became to be seen as 'abnormal' in relation to all other bodies.

Notes

1 See John Pearn, 'Bioethical Issues in Caring for Conjoined Twins and Their Parents', *Lancet*, 2001, 357, pp. 1968–71. In a recent case, a pair of conjoined twins born by Caesarean section at 32 weeks was contrasted to their 'normal singleton' sibling born at the same time. She Min Zeng, Jerome Yankowitz, and Jeffrey C. Murray, 'Conjoined Twins in a Monozygotic Triplet Pregnancy: Prenatal Diagnosis and X-inactivation', *Teratology*, 2002, 66, pp. 278–81.

2 In cases of identical twin births, this increases to one in every 200. Nancy L. Segal, *Entwined Lives: Twins and What They Tell Us about Human Behavior*, New York, Dutton, 1999, p. 297.

Conjoined twins 69

3 A few of these early surgical procedures on infants include the separation of Roger and Rodney Brodie, born joined at the skull and separated in Chicago in 1952; Carolyn Anne and Catherine Anne Mouton, separated in New Orleans in 1953; and Deborah Marie and Christine Mary Andrews, separated in New York in 1955. See, respectively, 'Day-Long Operation Parts Siamese Twins', *New York Times*, 18 December 1952, p. 1; 'Mouton Twins Well after Separation', *New York Times*, 19 September 1953, p. 17; and 'Twins Survive Surgery', *New York Times*, 23 April 1955, p. 22.

4 Denise Grady, 'Two Boys, Joined Skulls, One Goal: Two Lives', *New York Times*, 30 September 2003, p. 1.

5 See Mary Tiles, 'The Normal and Pathological: The Concept of a Scientific Medicine', *British Journal for the Philosophy of Science*, 1993, 44, pp. 729–42.

6 Ibid., pp. 733–4.

7 For examples of the medicalisation process, see Michael MacDonald, 'The Medicalization of Suicide in England: Laymen, Physicians, and Cultural Change, 1500–1870', in Charles E. Rosenberg and Janet Golden, eds, *Health and Medicine in American Society*, New Brunswick, NJ, Rutgers University Press, 1992, pp. 85–103; and Margaret Marsh and Wanda Ronner, *The Empty Cradle: Infertility in America from Colonial Times to the Present*, Baltimore, Johns Hopkins University Press, 1996.

8 John V. Pickstone, *Ways of Knowing: A New History of Science, Technology and Medicine*, Chicago, University of Chicago Press, 2000.

9 See Ian Hacking, *The Taming of Chance*, Cambridge, Cambridge University Press, 1990.

10 George Buckley Bolton, 'On the United Siamese Twins', *Philosophical Transactions of London*, 1830, p. 178.

11 See Gould's assessment of the nineteenth-century tendency to rank individuals and races into such a graded scale through 'objective' measures. Stephen Jay Gould, *The Mismeasure of Man*, New York, W. W. Norton, 1981, pp. 57, 62–104.

12 John C. Warren, 'Some Account of the Siamese Boys, Lately Brought to Boston', *Western Journal of the Medical and Physical Sciences*, 1830, pp. 286–8.

13 Bolton, 'On the United Siamese Twins', p. 178.

14 Robert P. Harris, 'Historical and Analogical Record of the Siamese Twins', *American Journal of the Medical Sciences*, 1874, 68, pp. 359–60.

15 Irving Wallace and Amy Wallace, *The Two: A Biography*, New York, Simon & Schuster, 1978, p. 47.

16 *The Times*, 25 November 1829, p. 2.

17 Anon., 'The Siamese Twins. Supplementary Report', *Lancet*, 1874, i, p. 493.

18 Bolton, 'On the United Siamese Twins', p. 179.

19 Quoted ibid., p. 178. For theories of acclimatisation, see Mark Harrison, *Climates and Constitutions: Health, Race, Environment and British Imperialism in India, 1600–1850*, Oxford, Oxford University Press, 1999.

20 For biographical details, see Irving Wallace and Amy Wallace, *The Two: A Biography*, New York, Simon & Schuster, 1978.

21 *The Times*, 23 November 1829, p. 3.

22 A noteworthy exception to this is the book by the historian John Kuo Wei Tchen, *New York Before Chinatown: Orientalism and the Shaping of American Culture, 1776–1882*, Baltimore, Johns Hopkins University Press, 1999.

23 Harrison, *Climates and Constitutions*.

24 *The Times*, 23 November 1829, p. 2.

25 Fannie Roper Feudge, 'The Siamese Twins in Their Own Land', *Lippincotts Magazine of Popular Literature and Science*, 1874, 13, p. 382.

26 Bransby Blake Cooper, 'Anatomical Description of the Foot of a Chinese

70 *Sarah Mitchell*

Female', *Philosophical Transactions of the Royal Society of London*, 1830, 119, pp. 255–60.

27 Leonard Cassuto, '"What an Object He Would Have Made of Me!" Tattooing and the Racial Freak in Melville's Typee', in Rosemarie Garland Thomson, ed., *Freakery: Cultural Spectacles of the Extraordinary Body*, New York, New York University Press, 1996.

28 James W. Hale, *An Historical Account of the Siamese Twin Brothers from Actual Observation*, London, W. Turner, 1830, p. 4.

29 Ibid.

30 John Crawfurd, *Journal of and Embassy from the Governor-General of India to the Courts of Siam and Cochin China; exhibiting a view of the actual state of those kingdoms*, London, Henry Colburn, 1828, pp. 313–14.

31 Ibid., p. 311.

32 Ibid., pp. 313–14.

33 Ibid., p. 341.

34 Ibid., p. 342.

35 Sander L. Gilman, *Disease and Representation: Images of Illness from Madness to AIDS*, Ithaca, NY, Cornell University Press, 1988, p. 141.

36 See, for example, J. L. Wooden, 'Pair of Twins a la Siamese', *Cincinnati Lancet and Observer*, 1860, 3, p. 669.

37 George M. Gould and Walter L. Pyle, *Medical Curiosities, Adapted from Curiosities of Medicine*, Philadelphia, W. B. Saunders, 1896; Wallace and Wallace, *The Two: A Biography*.

38 In 1876, geographer Frank Vincent, Jr, stated that Western knowledge of many 'Asiatic countries' was so limited that it 'might have been summed up in the words "Siamese Twins and Cochin-China chanticleers"'. Frank Vincent, Jr, 'Two Months in Burmah', *Journal of the American Geographical Society of New York*, 1876, 8, p. 162.

39 Douglas C. Baynton, 'Disability and the Justification of Inequality in American History', in Paul Longmore and Lauri Umansky, eds, *The New Disability History: American Perspectives*, New York, New York University Press, 2001, p. 36.

40 See Mark Jackson, 'Changing Depictions of Disease: Race, Representation and the History of Mongolism', in Waltraud Ernst and Bernard Harris, eds, *Race, Science and Medicine, 1700–1960*, London, Routledge, 1999, pp. 217–42.

41 Anon., 'Account of Another Case of United Twins in the East', *Edinburgh Journal of Science*, 1830, 3, p. 374.

42 Anon., 'The Case of Parasitic Fetus', *British Medical Journal*, 1888, 1, p. 436.

43 Ibid.

44 F. J. Shepherd, 'The Significance of Human Anomalies', *Popular Science Monthly*, 1884, 25, p. 722.

45 Pickstone has referred to the nineteenth century as the 'great age of "scientific" museums'. See Pickstone, *Ways of Knowing*, p. 73.

46 See Ruth Richardson, *Death, Dissection and the Destitute*, London, Penguin, 1988, and Michael Sappol, *A Traffic of Dead Bodies: Anatomy and Embodied Social Identity in Nineteenth-Century America*, Princeton, NJ, Princeton University Press, 2002.

47 See, for example, Kathryn Brammall, 'Monstrous Metamorphosis: Nature, Morality, and the Rhetoric of Monstrosity in Tudor England', *Sixteenth Century Journal*, 1966, 27, pp. 3–21; Javier Moscoco, 'Monsters as Evidence: The Uses of the Abnormal Body during the Early Eighteenth Century', *Journal of the History of Biology*, 1998, 31, pp. 355–82; Katharine Park and Lorraine Daston, 'Unnatural Conceptions: The Study of Monsters in Sixteenth and Seventeenth Century France and England', *Past and Present*, 1981, 92, pp. 20–54; Evelleen Richards, 'A Political Anatomy of Monsters, Hopeful and Otherwise: Teratogeny, Transcendentalism, and Evolutionary Theorizing', *Isis*, 1994, 85, pp. 377–411; and

Conjoined twins 71

D. B. Wilson, *Signs and Portents: Monstrous Births from the Middle Ages to the Enlightenment*, London, Routledge, 1993.

48 Richard Owen, quoted in Phillip Reid Sloan, ed., *The Hunterian Lectures in Comparative Anatomy, May–June 1837*, Chicago, University of Chicago Press, 1992, pp. 185–6.

49 H. V. N. Miller, 'Account of a Case of Double Monstrosity', *Southern Medical and Surgical Journal*, 1854, 10, pp. 79–84.

50 Ibid., p. 84.

51 Ibid.

52 John North, 'A Lecture on Monstrosities', *Lancet*, 1840, i, pp. 860–1.

53 Ibid.

54 Late examples from the medical literature include J. E. Benton, 'Monstrosity of Double Fetus', *Journal of the American Medical Association*, 1899, 33, p. 131; Milton E. Gregg, 'An Unusual case of Double Monster', *American Medical Journal*, 1903, 6, p. 390; Anon., 'Ischiopagus Double Monster', *British Medical Journal*, 1896, 1, p. 1394; and E. Smythe, 'A Double Bodied Monster', *British Medical Journal*, 1908, 2, p. 1680.

55 William B. Ball, 'A New Edition of the Siamese Twins', *Virginia Medical Journal*, 1858, 10, pp. 197–9; T. D. Mitchell, 'Newport Twins, Analogous to the Celebrated Siamese Twins', *Western Medical Gazette*, 1832, 1, p. 295.

56 This was not the first time the term 'abnormal' was used in a medical context, but is simply the first reference I have found thus far to the term being applied to a pair of conjoined twins.

57 J. W. Ballantyne, *Manual of Antenatal Pathology and Hygiene: The Embryo*, New York, Wm. Wood, 1904, p. 234.

58 Ibid.

59 The Anthropologist D. G. Brinton, for example, says that 'the fundamental question in anthropology is that of the causes which have led to the differences in the races of men'. He cites Dr Dareste's work on the artificial production of monsters, which suggests that 'monstrosities are not the result of pathological changes in the embryo, but are modifications of the processes of organic evolution, precisely analogous to those which bring about the differences which distinguish individuals and races in mankind'. D. G. Brinton, 'Current Notes on Anthropology', *Science*, 1892, 19, p. 202.

60 In nineteenth-century Britain, for example, 479 new medical journals were established. W. F. Bynum and Janice C. Wilson, 'Periodical Knowledge: Medical Journals and their Editors in Nineteenth-century Britain', in W. F. Bynum, Stephen Lock and Roy Porter, eds, *Medical Journals and Medical Knowledge: Historical Essays*, London, Routledge, 1992, p. 30.

61 See Judith Walzer Leavitt, *Brought to Bed: Childbearing in America, 1750–1950*, New York, Oxford University Press, 1986, and Irvine Loudon, 'Deaths in Childbed from the Eighteenth Century to 1935', *Medical History*, 1986, 30, pp. 1–41.

62 James M. Pendleton, 'Observations on Monstrosities', *Philadelphia Journal of the Medical and Physical Sciences*, 1826, 13, p. 259.

63 Ibid.

64 William F. Montgomery, 'Account of a Very Remarkable Case of Double Monster; with Some Observations on the Subject of Double Monstrosity', *Dublin Quarterly Journal of Medical Science*, 1853, 15, p. 258.

65 Joseph Eastman, 'Report of a Case of Double-Headed Monstrosity', *Journal of the American Medical Association*, 1884, 2, p. 89.

66 James Wands, 'A Case of "Siamese Twins', *British Medical Journal*, 1887, i, p. 1274.

67 Ibid.

72 Sarah Mitchell

68 R. W. O'Donovan, 'Case of Double Monster', *Dublin Quarterly Journal of Medical Science*, 1851, 12, p. 483.

69 Ruth Richardson, *Death, Dissection and the Destitute*, London, Penguin Books, 1988. William Burke and William Hare were tried in 1829 for the murder of 16 people whose bodies they sold to anatomist John Know in Edinburgh. For an American account of the subject, see Suzanne Shultz, *Body Snatching: The Robbing of Graves for the Education of Physicians in Early Nineteenth-Century America*, Jefferson, NC, McFarland, 1992. Also see Jonathan Sawday, *The Body Emblazoned: Dissection and the Human Body in Renaissance Culture*, London, Routledge, 1995.

70 They were occasionally also referred to as 'Siamese twins'. However, this term was not used as frequently by medical men as the term 'double monster' when they were involved in attempts to classify and categorise.

71 Harriet Ritvo, *The Platypus and the Mermaid and Other Figments of the Classifying Imagination*, Cambridge, MA, Harvard University Press, 1997.

72 For a concise summary of Saint-Hilaire's main arguments, see Anon., 'Review of "Histoire Generale et Particulière des Anomalies d'Organisation chez l'Homme et les Animaus, &c."', *Edinburgh Medical and Surgical Journal*, 1833, 39, pp. 166–78.

73 Francis H. Ramsbotham, *The Principles and Practice of Obstetric Medicine and Surgery*, London, John Churchill, 1841, p. 620.

74 Ibid., p. 494.

75 Vrolik, quoted in Montgomery, 'Account of a Very Remarkable Case', p. 259.

76 Joseph Jones, *Contribution to Teratology*, New Orleans, n. publ., 1888, p. 17. (Reprint from *Transactions of the Louisiana Medical Society*, 1888, 10, n.p.)

77 Ibid., p. 18.

78 Anon., 'Monsters and Teratology', *British Medical Journal*, 1891, ii, 440–1, p. 657.

79 Ballantyne, *Manual of Antenatal Pathology and Hygiene*, pp. 233–4.

80 Ibid., p. 229.

81 Ibid.

82 William H. Hawkins, 'A Case of Monstrosity', *New Orleans Medical and Surgical Journal*, 1861, 18, p. 5.

83 Harris, 'Historical and Analogical Record', p. 363. This was because the way they positioned themselves of necessity affected the development of their joints and muscles.

84 For an account of the historical and ethical considerations involved in separation surgery, see Alice Domurat Dreger, *One of Us: Conjoined Twins and the Future of Normal*, Cambridge, MA, Harvard University Press, 2004.

4   Eccentric lives
Character, characters and curiosities in Britain, *c.* 1760–1900

James Gregory

This chapter examines 'eccentric biography', a genre that placed abnormality on the national stage and in homes in Britain from the late eighteenth century. The genre's popularity is contextualised by considering a wider body of material, much of it commercially available, depicting remarkable or eccentric personalities and bodies. The ways these works conceived, categorised and commodified deviations are studied. Their expressed and latent uses in a specific cultural context are examined. Virtual display of the abnormal is not a-historical delight in bizarreness: how people are perceived as different 'has less to do with what they are physiologically than with who we are culturally'.[1]

The study is informed by approaches which suggest that the 'abnormal' are incorporated into society, not only because concerns, beliefs and roles render them, as Goffman termed them, 'normal deviants', but also because their presence is so culturally visible and desired.[2] The interpretation offered by Foucault, where the abnormal is increasingly the focus of normalising technologies that ultimately involve carceral institutions, fails to account for the *popularity* (as opposed to *ubiquity*) of the abnormal figure through biographies and related images of human curiosities and characters throughout this period.

The genre that is the focus of this chapter survives. Though eccentric biography was particularly popular in the early to mid-nineteenth century, collections like *Brewer's Eccentrics, Rogues and Villains* demonstrate modern interest in this subject.[3] But it will be clear that the genre's scope has altered during the past century, with the dropping of that 'singular physical conformation' which allowed dwarfs and giants to figure beside misers and others distinguished by their abnormal behaviour.

Eccentric biography: origins, history and readership

A fascination with physical and behavioural abnormality, which came to be expressed in eccentric biographies, dates from the earliest popular printing and drew on oral culture's interest in the strange, violent and dreadful.[4] Almost two centuries later, in the late seventeenth century, 'eccentricity'

74 James Gregory

entered the language (if not common discourse) as a description of personal attributes or qualities.[5] At the same time, the abnormal behaviours and physiologies that were to be comprehended in the concept of 'eccentricity' were documented in a collection that was one of the ancestors of eccentric biography. The Reverend Nathaniel Wanley's *Wonders of the Little World* (1678) studied 'what man hath been from the first ages of the world to these times: in respect of his body, senses, passions, affections, his virtues'.[6] This was partly stimulated by Francis Bacon's desire for a 'collection ... of the extraordinaries and wonders of human nature'.[7] As the reference to a 'collection' suggests, *Wunderkammern*, or cabinets of wonder, of the early modern period, may also be seen as ancestors of the eccentric biography in the sense of spaces arranged to display nature's extremes.[8] Even during the era identified by Foucault as the 'classical' episteme, the Royal Society's Repository provided a place for 'monstrous' or curious natural phenomena, and collections evoked a state of awe in relation to the second 'Book of Nature'.[9] Appropriately, some early-nineteenth-century works containing eccentric lives were entitled 'museums', for their miscellaneous natural and artificial wonders echoed such collections.[10] These publications invoked Francis Bacon's recommended project to suggest scientific and scholarly support for the enterprise.

Wanley's work included *terata*, which also appeared in some eccentric biographies.[11] More generally, interest in wonderful bodies, behaviour and talent was combined with an attention to 'character', with a moralistic gloss previously expressed in character books.[12] The anecdote book is another genre which, with its emphasis on the singular for diversion and instruction (and its apparent superficiality), had similarities to eccentric biography.[13]

In the eighteenth century, multifarious human curiosities appeared in scientific papers, broadsheets, commonplace books and popular collections of the wonderful.[14] The latter included the *Marvellous Chronicle and Wonderful Magazine* of 1764.[15] This reported natural wonders, Europe-wide superstitions, romances and elopements, the wagers of youths, pickpocketing, and accidents involving lightning, mad dogs, natal deformities and odd behaviour.[16] The eccentric biography emerged a few decades later as a development of the interest in abnormal bodies, behaviour, character and talent. Almost sixty works were dedicated to eccentric and remarkable characters in late eighteenth-century and early nineteenth-century Britain. They included serial literature, single- and multi-volume books, and compendia with an eccentric component in subtitles.[17]

One of the earliest was produced by the print-seller James Caulfield, who in 1788 commissioned engraved portraits for a project that was completed in 1795.[18] This presented individuals 'ushered into notice by circumstances of peculiar notoriety ... particularly such as have not been restrained by the laws of their country, or influenced by the common obligations of society', and was stimulated by the equivalent category in James Granger's *Biographical History of England* (on which more shortly).[19] Originally priced at 50s

Figure 4.1 'Chevalier Desseasau, Remarkable for his Vanity', from *The Book of Wonderful Characters: Memoirs and Anecdotes of Remarkable and Eccentric Persons in All Ages and Countries. Chiefly from the Text of Henry Wilson and James Caulfield* (London, Chatto & Windus, n.d.).

76 James Gregory

(about £140 in today's money), Caulfield's collection became sought-after, with copies selling for the high price of seven guineas (£7 7s); it was expanded and rearranged, chronologically, in 1813.

A *New Wonderful Magazine* appeared in 1793, its title a bid for readership by association with the earlier work.[20] It encompassed 'extraordinary productions, events, and occurrences, in providence, nature, and art' and 'such curious matters as come under the denominations of miraculous! queer! odd! strange! supernatural! whimsical! absurd! out of the way! and unaccountable!'. The work was justified by a curiosity about wonderful, but true, natural and artificial productions purportedly shared by all social ranks. There being no single compendium of such wonders, the collection drew on expensive or out-of-the-way sources, so it claimed, to 'present them to the Public, at an easy Rate'. It aimed to entertain and instruct through 'presentation of the human passions and general display of virtue, and hatred to vice'.[21] The readership was anticipated to include the serious and curious. The enterprise was also warranted by characterising modern England as producing 'enough of the WONDERFUL and the *ridiculous*, to furnish out more than a sixpenny monthly collection'; moreover, the absurdities of 'our blundering forefathers' could supply any deficiency.[22] As a rejoinder to those who might think a work of this nature contemptible, Bacon's proposal for a collection of 'ultimities ... or summities of humane nature' was used to imply high cultural support for this enterprise.[23]

The *New Wonderful Magazine* serialised *Gulliver's Travels*; printed whimsical notices of births, marriages and deaths; featured natural or human wonders from classical or antiquarian sources, some of them sent by readers; chronicled current wonderful events (such as the French National Convention); included poetry on freemasonry; anecdotes on female heroism; dialogues and sketches on husbands and wives, and effeminate man milliners; and a history of boxing. There was material on such categories as persons eating 'hardened substances' or those whose bodies had strange constitutions or properties. A correspondent declared, 'the oddities contained in your Wonderful Magazine, are often the topic of our conversation'.[24]

Memoirs and portraits 'of the most singular and remarkable persons of both Sexes, in every Walk of human Life' appeared monthly in William Granger's *New Wonderful Museum* from late 1802. Like a museum of curiosities, the title page jumbled natural and supernatural occurrences such as eclipses and 'strange Discoveries of long-concealed Murders' with biographies 'of many very eccentric Characters famous for Long Life, Courage, Extraordinary Strength, Avarice, astonishing Fortitude, as well as genuine Narratives of Giants, Dwarfs, Misers, Impostors, singular Vices and Virtues'.[25] Like the *New Wonderful Magazine*, it too paraded Bacon's authority. The work defined itself against compilations of the marvellous which evoked 'more Disgust than Satisfaction' through ridiculous narratives, and against meritorious works limited to 'remarkable Characters, human longevity, extraordinary occurrences, adventures &c'. Alleging the absence of any work of 'Respectability' uniting 'all the curiosities of nature and art', the *New Wonderful Museum*'s title page and preface stressed its veracity, a quality viewed as the chief recommendation for such works. Youth would not only be entertained but 'attain Knowledge of the World, all by Wonderful Providences related', and 'full Conviction of the Omnipotent Being!' The frontispiece depicted a feminine and classical Nature stimulating youthful admiration of the world's wonders. The work also appealed to the learned, curious, and lovers of nature and art by offering variety. The remarkable or eccentric of every walk of life who 'by their *deviations* from the *regular Path*, have created WONDER, or have rendered themselves REMARKABLE for *Courage, Strength, Avarice, Philanthropy*, or some *singular Vice* or *Virtue*' were included, since (citing Alexander Pope) 'the Proper Study of Mankind is Man'.[26] After this fanfare, the work featured individuals familiar from earlier productions and some novelties such as the miser Baron d'Aguilar, 'hitherto unnoticed in *any* publication', with information from a 'respectable' source.[27] Correspondents sent in poetry and information about new characters.[28]

Other early nineteenth-century publications included Wilson's four-volume collection of figures ranging from Jeanne d'Arc to obscure misers and long-lived black slaves.[29] The *Eccentric Magazine* was initiated by the bookseller and author Henry Lemoine, a contributor to the *New Wonderful Museum*.[30] An anonymous work of 1826 published in duodecimo format by Thomas Tegg contained 52 biographies and claimed to include 'almost every characteristic peculiarity that the modern world has seen'.[31] Tegg, wealthy through retailing cheap reprints, abridgements of popular works and remaindered stock, bought the copyright to Hone's *Everyday Book and Table Book*, which also featured eccentrics, and successfully serialised it.

Victorian eccentric biographies included the antiquarian Fairholt's *Eccentric and Remarkable Characters*; another *New Wonderful Magazine*; Russell's *Eccentric Personages*; and Timbs's *English Eccentrics and Eccentricities*.[32] Fairholt admitted that works like Caulfield's had familiarised the public with many of the characters (male, female, British and foreign) he presented. He was certain about the genre's popularity: the charm of 'counter-illustration' made it 'of interest to all'. As 'a mine of character' it also aided novelists. He incorporated new material: 'unconsidered trifles' from friends' collections of handbills, adverts and other 'evanescent' memoranda.[33] Also adding new material was Davidson's *New Wonderful Magazine*, which, unlike its similarly titled predecessors, largely ignored non-human wonders and instead presented queens, regicides, murders, *lusus naturae*, eccentrics and wonderful recent events such as Luddism and the Cato Street conspiracy.[34]

The next collection was that of John Timbs. Variously a druggist, printer, antiquarian, sub-editor of *The Illustrated London News*, and servant to the radical Sir Richard Phillips, Timbs wrote studies of metropolitan,

78 *James Gregory*

national and animal abnormalities and wonders. Admitting there were many eccentric biographies, he justified his own by selecting new examples. His categories were 'wealth and fashion', delusions, impostures, fanatic missions, hermits, fat people, giants, dwarfs, strong men, strong sights, sporting scenes, eccentric travellers, artists, theatrical people, men of letters and convivial eccentricities. There were lessons to be learned about thrift, humour, and the association between wit and madness, although eccentricity was often to be found in 'the minds of persons of good understanding'.[35] Eccentricity was a justifiable topic because 'man favours wonders'. Eccentricity was occasionally vicious, but his collection had few moral strays. Presenting his subjects as frequently grotesque or 'motley-minded', he argued that 'oddity of character' might coexist with 'goodness of heart' and that the strange fellow, defined by dictionaries as 'outlandish, odd, queer, and eccentric', had claims to attention that were ignored when the 'the fitness of things' was the principle.[36]

Since works were reprinted (for instance, Timbs's in 1874, 1875, 1877, 1898) or plundered for new collections, eccentric biographies were common.[37] Additionally, provincial versions were published throughout the period. One Newcastle publisher projected a compendium of the remarkable in 1819.[38] A late-Victorian pamphlet, *Human Wonders of the World*, was presented by a Sheffield stationer.[39] *Three Wonderful Yorkshire Characters* was another ephemeral version; its local emphasis was probably repeated elsewhere.[40] Cheaper collections appeared as chapbooks.[41] But no new collection was produced by London publishers in the late nineteenth century.

There was a transatlantic dimension, with British biographies enjoying a wider readership through reprinting.[42] An American imprint of William Russell's work, for instance, was reviewed as 'most popular and readable' and predicted to 'go through a very heavy edition'.[43] An American *Magazine of Wonders and Marvellous Chronicle* drew on English models but added native tales.[44] S. G. Goodrich's collection was part of a series that included books on benefactors, celebrated women, Native Americans, and signatories to the Declaration of Independence.[45] Such collections featured in the catalogues of British and American publishers or booksellers and appeared in private and public libraries.[46]

The 'eccentric' was not automatically appropriate for serious biographical dictionaries; Hole's work of 1866 was notable for *not* disdaining to include 'merely eccentric and odd characters'.[47] Yet lavishly illustrated and expensively bound copies of eccentric biographies appeared in aristocratic libraries. The *New Wonderful Magazine* of 1793 claimed to draw on material from 'the learned and the virtuosi', and appealed to these as readers. Caulfield's *Eccentric Magazine* was costly, with high-quality engravings. A copy of the *Magazine* belonged to George III's library, along with Wanley's *Wonders*.[48] The Victoria and Albert Museum's copy of Wilson's *Wonderful Characters* had been owned by an aristocratic clergyman.[49]

But the readership went well beyond the rich. The popularity of

THE BOOK
OF
WONDERFUL CHARACTERS

𝔐emoirs and 𝔄necdotes

OF

REMARKABLE AND ECCENTRIC PERSONS IN
ALL AGES AND COUNTRIES.

CHIEFLY FROM THE TEXT OF

HENRY WILSON AND JAMES CAULFIELD.

MATTHEW BUCHINGER,
The wonderful little man of Nuremburgh.

ILLUSTRATED WITH SIXTY-ONE FULL PAGE ENGRAVINGS.

𝔏ondon:
CHATTO AND WINDUS, PUBLISHERS.

Figure 4.2 Title page of *The Book of Wonderful Characters, Memoirs and Anecdotes of Remarkable and Eccentric Persons in All Ages and Countries. Chiefly from the Text of Henry Wilson and James Caulfield* (London, Chatto & Windus, n.d.).

80 *James Gregory*

this work is suggested by the readers who sent in anecdotes to the original *Wonderful Magazine*, including a Cheshire clergyman who 'conceived great hopes of entertainment'.[50] The *New Wonderful Magazine*, which also derived material from readers and advertisements,[51] was read 'by people of all classes and denominations throughout the kingdom, as well as in Ireland, Scotland, France and every country in Europe, and 'it's [*sic*] fame has reached already to many other polished nations in the world'.[52] It even printed an engraving of one reader, a lowly man of letters, with his eldest son portrayed reading the weekly paper to the family.[53] The doctors, clergymen and women who subscribed to the American *Magazine of Wonders* also demonstrate the genre's consumption by the educated and both genders.

One important market was the bourgeois family and its children. Presumably they accepted this literature as exemplars of character, moral instruction and entertainment, just as the reviewers seem to have done. An edition of Wilson published in 1842 advertised itself as 'worthy of a place in every library'.[54] Collections of human curiosities and natural or artificial wonders appeared throughout the century for home readership. Jane Austen's family subscribed to one; Edmund King's *Ten Thousand Wonderful Things* is a mid-Victorian example.[55]

Eccentric biographies were enjoyed by early-nineteenth-century children such as Robert Browning and Charles Darwin, who read Wanley's *Wonders*.[56] A reviewer of Fairholt's work described reading the *Wonderful Magazine* in school hours as 'such a notable pleasure a *few* years ago'.[57] Other references in memoirs and fiction document a humble and domestic status for such works. The biblical scholar John Kitto mastered reading through scripture and the *Wonderful Magazine*.[58] In a story in the American *Southern Literary Messenger* in 1851, an uncle's library comprised the *Wonderful Magazine*, *Universal History*, and a volume of farces and farming manuals.[59]

Popular culture's interest in the wonderful ensured a ready market for cheaper versions.[60] Henry Wilson's *Wonderful Characters* was available in cheap editions in the mid-Victorian period.[61] Mackenzie's collection of Glasgow eccentrics cost a shilling in the late-Victorian period.[62] They could be found in libraries and, as Boffin discovered in Dickens's *Our Mutual Friend*, at second-hand booksellers.[63]

Apart from a presence in *Our Mutual Friend*, references to this literature in nineteenth-century fiction are few. William Howitt in 1846 commented that one could, in England, write 'a dozen more volumes of the "Eccentric Mirror"' from one's own acquaintance.[64] In one of Thomas Hood's allusions to the genre, a character ironically lamented the absence of 'practical whims and oddities' such as 'bolting clasp-knives, riding on painted ponies', which had resulted in biographies in the *Wonderful Magazine* for 'sundry knaves, quacks, boobies'.[65]

Writers owned eccentric biographies: Thackeray, the poet Chauncey Townshend, the American Oliver Wendell Holmes; Dickens acquired his collection in researching *Our Mutual Friend*. One copy of J. C. Hotten's

Eccentric lives   81

edition of Wilson's *Wonderful Characters* belonged to Henry Tavener, who co-authored a biography of Dickens for Hotten.[66] An edition of Wilson was owned by the businessman, and patron of erotica, Henry Ashbee.[67]

Eccentricity portrayed

Prior to the development of the illustrated eccentric biography, portraits of remarkable and eccentric people had been published separately as prints, owing to a demand for representations of the extraordinary.[68] In the eccentric biography, where the subjects' abnormal appearance justified their presence, there was an interest, indeed requirement, for an accompanying image to prove or reinforce difference. A veridical basis in 'original portraits' was stressed. Caulfield emphasised the difficulty of obtaining authentic portraits of low-life characters: his engravings were 'of the greatest scarcity and value, and not a life or character is recorded, but is accompanied by a portrait of unquestioned authenticity'.[69]

While the popularity of portraiture (and biography) in Britain has often been asserted as characteristic, the popularity of images of abnormal characters has been neglected.[70] One further influence on the eccentric biography that has only been glanced at so far, was the influential typology of prints by James Granger (1769; continued by others), included as class 12, 'persons of both sexes, chiefly of the lower Order of the People, remarkable from only one Circumstance in their Lives; namely, such as lived to a great age, deformed persons, convicts &c' as part of his attempt to systematise national biography.[71] Their lowly origin became problematic for Granger, who was concerned about the potential for criticism of him for having 'given a place to mean engravings, and prints of obscure persons'. He feared that the work's range from monarchs to beggars was too extensive.[72]

Limitations of space preclude a more extensive examination in this chapter of the portrayal of eccentrics in a range of visual and three-dimensional media. Yet the ubiquity of representations of the abnormal can be indicated by reference to items ranging from inn signs depicting the vast bulk of a Daniel Lambert or Lucas the 'mad hermit of Hertfordshire', to full-size statues, and mugs, walking-stick tops and tobacco-stoppers presenting the likenesses of characters such as the blind fiddler William Purvis of Newcastle on a small scale.[73]

A proper study would need to consider the relationship of depictions of the physically and mentally abnormal to caricature, and explore the aesthetico-moral discussion of depictions of 'character' and deformity. It would also need to assess the influence of the popular genre of the 'Cries of London' on the provincial and local portrayal of odd, deformed and eccentric street characters. For it is clear that illustrated eccentric biographies drew on the genre of the 'Cries' and that professional or amateur artists across Britain were influenced by metropolitan models.[74] In the 1820s, watercolours recently attributed to the itinerant miniature painter and silhouettist John

82 *James Gregory*

Dempsey represented a British-wide version of the genre, with street vendors, beggars, town criers and maniacs.[75] Local versions included Sinclair's images from Thurso in the 1840s[76] and Edmund Holt's mid-Victorian portraits of Edinburgh street characters.[77] A thorough study would also need to chart the development and extent of new forms of representing the eccentric for a popular market, with late nineteenth-century postcards replacing the prints and woodcuts of earlier times.[78]

Although eccentric portraiture was considered low art, its popularity was not confined to the lowly. Print collecting, especially after Granger, might be costly. Some wealthy collectors are known through sale catalogues,[79] but others could be humble individuals, such as the Newcastle baker who collected curiosities.[80] Mark Noble, a continuer of Granger, might argue that it was fitting that 'worthy creatures' such as the 'Raree showman' Old Harry (*c.*1700) should be honoured with portraits, as they kept the populace in good humour.[81] But Bartholomew Fair and its textual or artistic analogues were attractions for all.

It should be clear from this survey of texts and portraiture that the eccentric was the focus of much commercial activity. An advertisement for the 6d monthly *Wonderful Magazine* made this commercialism explicit when it included acquiring 'The Ready Rhino' as a motive.[82] The variety of print media presenting eccentrics, ranging from almanacs and 'books of days' to tracts, national and local newspaper paragraphs and lavishly illustrated books such as Granger's *New Wonderful Museum*, simply reflected a wider commodification of abnormality.[83] The expectation of profit is demonstrated by the pricing of Granger's work, serialised in 1*s* numbers (*c.* £2.30 in today's money); subscribers had acquired two volumes of 24 numbers by 1805 (13*s* per volume by 1806; almost £30 in today's money). Wilson's *Wonderful Characters* sold in 3*s* monthly parts in 1822 (the equivalent of about £9 per month); the three volumes could be bought for £1 17*s* 6*d* (the equivalent in today's money of *c.* £110).[84] The potential profit explains why the *Eccentric Mirror*'s publisher challenged a rival's attempt to publish an 'improved' magazine in 1803.[85] If some collections were expensive, others emanated from hacks such as Thomas Prest and publishers of cheap sensationalist works like Thomas Tegg.[86] Profit was also envisaged by the artists, who expected the portrayal of well-known local figures to attract patronage.[87] In the era of the silhouette, for instance, a Newcastle newspaper observed of a well-known character: 'all the black profile men that ever visited the town used [to capture him] to a T'.[88]

Themes in eccentric material

The quotations from the frontispieces and the complete titles of the works consulted in this essay show that 'eccentric' kept company or was co-extensive with the following: 'curious', 'remarkable', 'singular', 'extraordinary', 'queer', 'odd', 'strange', 'whimsical', 'absurd', 'out of the way' and

Eccentric lives 83

'wonderful'. Does this 'eccentricity' equate with 'abnormality'? To ask that question is to raise more vexing questions: what is understood by the modern term 'abnormality'? Can a modern term (used by medical writers from the early nineteenth century) be applied to a concept, 'eccentricity', that antedates it?[89] Answered basically, since 'abnormality' has been defined simply (in a standard dictionary of psychology) as 'divergence from the normal', or (in a standard dictionary of the social sciences) as 'something that differs from what is generally considered normal', eccentricity *can* be equated with abnormality.[90] 'Eccentricity' and 'abnormality' are similarly expansive, for the latter, in its 'statistical' sense, embraces those superior as well as those inferior to a norm (to cite examples from the eccentric biography, those whose deviation from the average height takes the form of giantism and dwarfism; and those deviating from the average intellect either as idiot or genius). Just as the 'eccentric' comprehended the odd mind, so the term 'abnormal' has been applied to mental pathology, maladaptive behaviour and antisocial conduct.[91] The following examination of the functions of eccentric biographies (and related imagery) and their conceptualisation of eccentricity shows that this material offers a richness of themes related to the various senses of abnormality.

Abnormality is an inherently moralised concept, but in material concerned with the eccentric there was explicit moralisation and confirmation or reassertion of the social/moral order. Biographers commented on processes of *becoming* eccentric; through their categorisation of the abnormal they reveal how the concept of eccentricity reflected social and gender norms. The *Eccentric Mirror*'s title page summarised the fundamental categories – 'extraordinary qualifications, talents, and propensities, natural or acquired' – and then specified 'singular instances of longevity, conformation, bulk, stature, powers of mind and of body, wonderful exploits, adventures, habits, propensities, enterprising pursuits & & &'.

A central idea emerging from eccentric material is that *eccentricity is part of the normal*. Durkheim argued that a society of 'average individuals' without a profusion of individual anomalies was itself abnormal. Like Durkheim's understanding of crime, the logic of eccentric collections is that their subjects are always and *normally* there, rather than being 'a sort of parasite element, a strange unassimilable body, introduced into the midst of society'.[92] If compilers of eccentric biography identified eccentricity as a characteristic of 'men of extraordinary genius and talents', it was also observed that 'abundance of singularities' in ordinary people went unrecorded because of their unexceptional abilities.[93]

Cumulatively this material made abnormality familiar, even domesticated it. But how far was it seen as *necessary* to civilisation? This argument, about the *necessity of abnormality*, can be traced back, beyond Durkheim's discussion of normal and pathological, to John Stuart Mill, who defended 'experiments in living' and eccentricity as necessary for progress, and especially important when the 'merely average man' was becoming the predominant cultural force:

84 *James Gregory*

> In this age, the mere example of nonconformity, the mere refusal to bend the knee to custom, is itself a service. Precisely because the tyranny of opinion is such as to make eccentricity a reproach, it is desirable, in order to break through that tyranny, that people should be eccentric. Eccentricity has always abounded when and where strength of character has abounded.[94]

Most eccentric collections did not anticipate Mill's argument, but Timbs approached this viewpoint when describing hermits as 'firm abettors of freedom'.[95]

While eccentricity was partly understood to comprise those who were socially wayward, by presenting it as prevalent in all ranks, eccentric biographies *helped confirm a sense of common humanity*. Sailor eccentrics and musical coalmen were included with their social superiors.[96] Writers made a virtue of this. The *Eccentric Magazine* asked of London street-sellers, '[W]hy should they not find a nitch in history, as well as the gay, licentious noble?... Spurn not the humble efforts of the poor.'[97] The presence of beggars in Caulfield's *Eccentric Magazine* allowed the compiler to praise charity and deplore counterfeit beggars.[98] The social advance obtained by industry was stressed. Thus, an obscure character, John Baldock, was presented by Caulfield as an example for the young, and his work concluded with another life, that of Griffith Owen, exemplary for young readers.[99]

One of the key words used in eccentric literature and art in this period was 'character'. It was a word that had the potential to knit together the mental abnormalities (suggested in the *Mirror*'s title page by 'powers of mind' and 'propensities') which comprised one form of eccentricity, and the physical anomalies which contributed another major element. The discourse on 'character', in its sense of mental qualities and personality, valued independence and moral strength. To have a 'good character' was to mean being esteemed by peers and community. In another sense, however, 'character' meant the public reputation (and often label of 'eccentric') originating in odd personality. But 'characters' were also to be defined as those whose *physical* appearance both stimulated curiosity and suggested interior oddity. The literature of eccentricity was one manifestation of a keen interest in 'character' in British culture.[100]

Eccentric biographies included subjects who were physically disabled or physically abnormal; Langford neglects this important component in his examination of literary expressions of the eccentric cult. Those born lacking limbs figured frequently. Excessive or diminutive height, as in the cases of the giant Thomas Topham, Jeffery Hudson, the court dwarf of Charles I, and the little Count Boruwlaski (all the subject of portraits and engravings) commonly featured.[101] This category of 'unusual bodies' was also present as living curiosities in freak shows and similar places. Indeed, many of the lives presented in eccentric biographies *had* been exhibited long before the Victorian era, in which Erin O'Connor detects a 'new and improved individuality'

Eccentric lives 85

associated with emergent mass culture and industrialisation and expressed through 'deformito-mania'.[102] Wanley had viewed abnormalities of birth optimistically: there was 'oftentimes so much of ingenuity' in provident Nature's 'disorders' that, in comparison with her perfections, they could 'affect us with equal wonder'.[103] Fascination with deformity, and its commodification, was longstanding and Europe-wide.[104]

Eccentric biographies concerned themselves with those who were *innately* singular through being sports of nature, and those who *became* singular.[105] For if some were born into singular bodily states, there were others whose bodies were transformed into strange forms. Others had the misfortune to endure singular situations. Many acquired an eccentric reputation because they failed to observe conventional behaviour. When it came to certain forms of eccentric behaviour (as opposed to singular talents), acting strangely could be prompted in hitherto ordinary people by chance events. A few people, through their accidental isolation from normal society, made what was natural in mankind and what required education and civilisation into a matter of debate. The role of *nature* versus *nurture* was a central controversy in the treatment of feral children like 'Peter the Wild Boy', whose arrival in Britain had excited the curiosity of the Court, and savants such as James Burnett (Lord Monboddo) and Jonathan Swift.[106] Readers of Peter's biography were familiarised with Monboddo's view that man's natural state was gentle, 'at least until we become carnivorous and hunters or warriors'. But such cases were also felt to prove the importance of youthful instruction, social intercourse and civilisation. Given the variety of forms of eccentricity, the abnormal could be *both* a discrete state *and* a matter of degree. As Tegg's collection described it, using the metaphor of swerving from the beaten track (i.e. deviation), humankind could be classed as one comprehensive family, but there were 'a thousand ramifications and shades of character, which branch off from the main source'.[107]

Singular behaviour triggered reflections on the complexity of this 'character'. In the *Eccentric Mirror* the biography of the notorious Thomas Pitt, second Lord Camelford, a man whose assaults and general rakishness had been widely reported in the press, contrasted his rational scientific interests and virtues with dangerous eccentricities, extravagance and 'passions dangerous to peace and welfare of society'.[108] Misers occasioned expression of pieties about avarice, but also suggested contradictory traits: for some exhibited generosity to others. The multiplicity of character that Tegg identified allowed him to present his collection as a 'worthy' work of 'investigation', suitable for the 'reflective reader'.[109] For him, eccentricities were 'singular and subtler variations' contained within an unchanging 'character of mind' assigned from 'earliest time'.[110] Phrenological interpretations about the breaking of natural laws through the abuse of mental faculties might be referred to in later collections.[111] And remarkable mental talents like a great memory, or mathematical achievements by idiots savants, were discussed.[112]

86 James Gregory

When the abnormality being presented was behavioural, writers offered explanations that ranged from the impact of blighted romance,[113] inadequate guidance in youth,[114] or a generalised result of 'follies, failings or vices'.[115] Heredity was also accepted: thus, Russell observed, 'oddness or eccentricity of character, though differing in type and fashion, runs in the blood of the family'.[116] Frugality was recognised as having an element of heredity.[117] When the eccentricity took the form of a singular obsession, it could be related to insanity. Indeed, insane characters were a standard component of collections. A living madman of 'respectable parentage' who became a well-known street character through singular dress and walk appeared, for instance, in the *Eccentric Magazine*.[118]

Eccentricity partly entailed *transgression of the social order*. For example, artistic and intellectual talent in untutored plebeians was treated as eccentric, their fame and transgression of their normal station in life rendering them remarkable. Thomas Britton the 'musical small-coal man', a bibliophile, antiquarian and chemist in addition to being a connoisseur of ancient and modern music, featured in several biographies. Wilson observed that 'notwithstanding the meanness of his profession, a music concert was held at Britton's house, which was attended by the most distinguished professors, as well as by many persons of the highest rank and fashion'.[119] Less sympathetically, pretension to poetry in the lowborn was satirised in a portrait of one cobbler and radical 'Aesop of Eton' in Queen Anne's reign.[120] But this social deviation was rarely openly discussed in a way that suggested compilers were aware that eccentricity was a social construction. By apologising for including lives not 'perfectly coincident with the plan', on the grounds that it was hard to distinguish 'moderate eccentricity' from what was 'only an extension of the too arbitrary bounds prescribed by rigid regularity and decorum', Cundee's *Eccentric Biography* was unusually explicit about social definition.[121] More typical was Tegg's failure to expand on his observation, stimulated by the life of the 'white savage' Charles Martin of Jamaica, that in the present state of society 'the total and voluntary seclusion of an individual from the rest of his fellow creatures, may justly be considered as a very extraordinary circumstance'.[122] In a similar vein, Russell in 1864 felt that it hardly needed stating that eccentricity 'usually means one whose bent of mind prompts him or her to overleap or break through the conventional barriers which hedge in the different classes of society'.[123]

One of the most prominently featured social transgressions and instance of 'singular propensity' in eccentric biography was miserliness. This was stimulated by a general interest in misers, who were proverbial and represented in novels and plays.[124] Boffin's masquerade as miser in *Our Mutual Friend* involved the acquisition of an extensive library dealing with misers.[125] Other novels by Dickens show how well known miserly characters were.[126] The first number of Granger's *Wonderful Magazine* dealt with Daniel Dancer and moralised about the inability to derive happiness from wealth alone.[127] John Elwes was the most celebrated miser, a defence of him by

Caulfield in the *Eccentric Magazine* failing to rescue him from this category.[128] Nathaniel Bentley, or 'Dirty Dick', was the subject of cartoons, verse and memoirs.[129] One work, Merryweather's *Lives and Anecdotes of Misers*, was devoted solely, and in a markedly moralistic fashion, to the miser. The antonym of generosity, miserliness embodied the sin of avarice and misuse of talents, and an abnormal sociality similar to that of the hermit, another popular category.

Abnormality includes the *transgression of sexual morality*, and the *assumption of abnormal gender roles*. However, given the intended audience, sexual aberration rarely featured in eccentric biography. It was therefore unusual for Tegg's collection to mention the voracious carnal appetite of the debauchee Francis Charteris.[130] But there were reflections on gender, and gender transgressors in the form of transvestites. Wanley had defended including women in his collection: 'under the notion of Man both Sexes are comprehended'.[131] Later collections had proportionally more representations of men than women, although there were publications devoted to 'extraordinary deviation' (virtuous and vicious) from the generality of women.[132]

Masculine women who pursued academic, military, diplomatic and criminal careers were featured in general eccentric biographies. One was a highwaywoman.[133] Another was the book dealer Theodora Grahn; although her masculine occupation and apparel (her 'grotesque and striking appearance') and bibulousness explained her inclusion by Wilson, her 'excellent capacity' as linguist and mathematician was not considered odd.[134] Timidity and 'various circumstances' betrayed her sex. Her eccentricity was also indicated by her kissing John Wesley's coats: she was an enthusiast's enthusiast. Of the diplomat and spy the Chevalier d'Éon, a male transvestite whose sex was the subject of much public speculation until his death in 1810, Wilson observed, 'any woman with a good education and a sound understanding, might easily become as proficient in the arts of political intrigue'; but undercut this suggestion of intellectual equality by commenting that she exemplified the disappointment 'which sooner or later awaits those who step out of the path which nature designed them to pursue'.[135] And yet her 'services were certainly deserving of a permanent reward' – she had been a 'distinguished figure'.[136] Female soldiers who 'all pleaded the *tender* passion as an apology for assuming masculine pursuits and habits' appeared.[137] One, Mary Anne Talbot, was employed and published by the *Wonderful and Scientific Museum*'s publisher.[138] Her moral failings and her deficiency of 'firmness and rectitude of mind, which shield their possessors from error, as well as from crime' were criticised, rather than her transvestism.[139] Russell's biography of a '*very* eccentric American lady', the transcendentalist and feminist Margaret Fuller, revealed his prejudices in favour of a Christian femininity that was 'so delicate, so simple, so confiding, so affectionate', a 'true womanly heart and soul'.[140] Until Christianity, maternity and marriage had transformed her, Fuller merely possessed 'fluent, erratic cleverness'.[141]

88 *James Gregory*

The expressed functions of eccentric biographies, like contemporary displays of human and natural marvels, were entertainment and instruction. Even when the former was paramount, delight in wonders required justification, though compilers suggested that the mere fact of deviation made the eccentric 'an object of natural inquisition'.[142] The instructional aspect to narratives and depictions was maintained by asserting that they allowed that legitimate 'study of man' enjoined by Alexander Pope (quotations from Pope's *Essay on Man* became a cliché[143]); they showed the great variety and wonders of nature; and they provided inspirational or cautionary lessons in morality and vice. This material *moralised* the abnormal. Mere curiosity was deemed an insufficient justification, but it could be used to instil morality in an entertaining fashion.[144] Rather as character books extracted moral lessons through personifications of vices and virtues, so eccentric biographies offered warnings or encouragement. Judgements appeared in commentary on misers, spendthrifts, debauchees and other vicious types. As Wilson wrote, 'vice has its heroes as well as virtue'.[145] A celebrated mid-eighteenth-century case of falsely alleged abduction allowed observations on the folly of popular emotion.[146] A pickpocket turned colonial High Constable exemplified the counterbalancing of human evil and redemption.[147] Rather than being 'an object of admiration or as a model for the youthful mind to emulate', the soldier Mary Talbot was a 'beacon, to warn from danger'.[148] Caulfield's eccentrics were people whose talents might have brought them fame as statesmen or reputable entertainers. Crucial to moralistic claims was veracity. The *Biographical Curiosities* of 1797 argued that romances and novels, whatever their artistry, failed in their exemplary purpose, whereas 'the vicissitudes and incidents which biography present, press upon the mind with the weight of truth, and are applicable to the purpose of life'.[149]

It is significant that one publisher produced a version of the 'Newgate' genre of criminal biography as well as an eccentric biography.[150] The latter might include notorious murderers and highwaymen as a way of recycling material and as an expression of the open nature of the 'remarkable category'. The *Eccentric Magazine* justified including notorious 'thief-takers' because 'the historical genealogy of the lowest culprit, is of as much consequence to society, as that of the first minister of state, whose ambition has ruined his country'.[151] But since the Newgate genre was devoted to the criminally abnormal, eccentric biographies tended to limit their use. Whether categories of genre reflected attitudes about the eccentric as non-criminal or originated this separation is a moot point.

Even as they presented what would subsequently be described as the 'normal deviant', eccentric biographies could *comfort*. The category of 'eccentric' was extended to include providential acts experienced by the normally formed or normally behaved person, rendered remarkable because of luck or misfortune.[152] Wanley had documented the 'marvellous recompence [*sic*] of Nature in some Persons', including deaf and dumb people who could read well, blind musicians, and a women born with no limbs who used her tongue to spin.[153] Later works argued that absence of one sense was compensated for by hyper-development of others. Thus, the biography of one 'idiot' occasioned a reflection that 'however we may be deprived of some of the faculties, we have others given us'.[154] This comforting note incorporated readers: given the likelihood of impaired faculties through accident, overwork, insufficient nutrition and scientific ignorance, we should not undervalue the genre's message that if fate dealt hard blows, individuals could cope and be compensated.[155]

The *localisation* of abnormality is one of the themes explored by Sara Bergstresser in this book, and I have examined elsewhere the role of the local character in the north-east of England in the nineteenth century.[156] The texts considered here often made the same association of place with characters, and visual association was provided through recognisable backgrounds. 'As every nation has its favourite saint, so every village has its notability,' asserted one parochial version of the eccentric biography, which also pointed out, 'All large cities and towns have prominent features – in scenery, in public edifices, and in peculiar men.'[157] Eccentric characters were incorporated into the community and contributed to a local patriotism reflected in annals, guidebooks and newspapers. Visual material on abnormal characters was also organised by locality, as we have seen.

The compilers' inclusion of foreign and historically distant characters implied that humanity always had singularities and, paradoxically, common peculiarities. But eccentricity was also identified with notions of British characteristics and virtues.[158] Eccentric biographies were anecdotal rather than analytical, and made no attempt to examine cultural factors that might contribute to eccentricity; but another of their purposes was to assert that individuality was a national trait. Freedom to be different, and revelling in the variety that was the spice of life, enabled patriots to argue that Britain in the era of the French wars enjoyed true liberty. Wilson claimed it as a universally admitted truth that 'no country in the world produces so many humorists and eccentric characters' as Britain, through a constitutional and legal exceptionalism 'by which each individual is suffered to gratify every whim, fancy, and caprice, provided it be not prejudicial to his fellow-creatures'.[159] The unparalleled eccentricity originated in 'each feeling himself perfectly independent of all others', a belief encouraging an individual's peculiar propensities and caprices 'heedless of the censures or approbations of all the rest of the world'.[160]

Longevity, an enduring category of singularity in the eccentric biography, also stimulated patriotism, for, as a test of healthy climate, Britain was 'more highly favoured by nature in this particular, than almost any other region of the globe'.[161] There were few reflections otherwise on environmental factors. Caulfield said that London's Lewkener's Lane was notorious for the eccentricity of its characters and instanced the hangman Ketch, the grotesque 'Buckhorse', prostitutes, swindlers and others as proof that 'few places could boast of more originality of character'.[162] Caulfield also

90 James Gregory

presented London as a place of remarkable singularity for sound commercial reasons: street vendors relying on it for a livelihood.[163] This was making explicit that commercial motive which we have identified as an important element in the construction of abnormality.

Conclusions

Eccentric biographies partly acted as compendia of people renowned for reasons other than 'singularity', such as the Earl of Rochester, Hogarth and Jonathan Swift, and it is probable that a taste for biography, that interest in 'anecdote and personal history' which Noble thought a 'prevailing turn' in 1806, attracted readers.[164] Eccentric biographies flourished in the early to mid-nineteenth century, and it is tempting to associate a subsequent decline with the rise of rival cheap biographies of less marginal subjects, and to the commonplace use of eccentric material in popular journalism.[165]

The genre survives with other commodifications of abnormality, works such as Edith Sitwell's and Timpson's demonstrating the continued commerciality of the genre in the early and late twentieth century respectively.[166] But scope has narrowed. Eccentricity comprehended non-behavioural abnormality, with the category of singular physical conformation rendering the genre the literary equivalent of freak shows. Shifting attitudes towards physical disability and deformity mean that modern works of eccentric biography no longer possess the range of curiosities. The trend began with emerging polite and humane objections towards exhibition of deformity in the early nineteenth century, as seen in the partial attribution of Bartholomew Fair's demise to the opposition of all 'decent people'.[167] 'Eccentricity' is now more narrowly applied to behaviour. But if modern psychological and psychiatric knowledge has altered the explication of behavioural eccentricity, this has not filtered through to popular compilations, whose anecdotic level still precludes extensive analysis.[168]

Fundamentally, the notion of the 'eccentric' is normative, and publicising lives as 'abnormal' involves, explicitly or not, delineating the centric or normal. Eccentric biography instructed readers about diverse forms of otherness – forms whose 'marginal' status was underscored in the hierarchies of related collections such as Granger's. Some of this material was aimed at the home, and consumed as family reading and spectacle, or juvenile literature.[169] This can be envisaged as part of the technologies of normalisation. We need not consider this as the domestic parallel to the normalisation effected by the incarceration of abnormals, since imprisonment did not render them absent from society. Foucault emphasised the obsessive examination of abnormality *within* society; as part of the processes of normalisation, those classed as abnormal were presented to the population.

If our study of eccentric material shows that eccentrics were commonplace through their status as commodified objects of curiosity and titillation, this cultural prominence does not necessarily or automatically equate with

Eccentric lives 91

an acceptance understood as toleration. But interpreting narratives or images of deviation merely as resources for social control or moralism is simplistic. What if images of the abnormal continue to be relished or desired by society? What if abnormals remain cherished members of communities? It has been seen that eccentricity became one defining characteristic of English identity in this period: through text and portraiture, abnormality became incorporated, as it were, into the nation. It has also been suggested that eccentrics were rooted in localities as characters performing valued social or cultural roles. Robert Bogdan's interpretation of the freak shows, which were identical to the eccentric biographies in their display of the physically, mentally or behaviourally odd, offers an alternative approach to abnormality. Display, he argues, made abnormality 'valuable' and in that sense 'valued'. Therefore, characterisation of 'human variation' as 'stigmatized, rejected, and devalued' needs modification.[170] Bogdan identifies a 'sociology of acceptance ... by which demonstrable physical and mental differences became normalised, taken for granted'.[171]

The eccentric biography similarly suggested incorporation, rather than merely stigmatisation. It was a qualified inclusion, to be sure, as Goffman suggests in his discussion of the mascot or 'in-group deviant' whose indulgence by a community arguably allowed the social problems that led to the deviant's marginality (as in the case of the 'character' who was a beggar) to be treated less favourably.[172] But eccentric biography and associated art allowed sundry deviations to be valued not only as 'mere' objects of curiosity and moral lessons. They offered alternative behaviour and being to readers and their audience, or viewers.[173] There was the possibility of freedom through self-awareness and scrutiny.[174]

Notes

1 R. Bogdan, *Freak Show: Presenting Human Oddities for Amusement and Profit*, Chicago, University of Chicago Press, 1988, p. 10. See also S. L. Gilman, *Disease and Representation: Images of Illness from Madness to AIDS*, Ithaca, NY, Cornell University Press, 1988, p. 232.
2 E. Goffman, *Stigma: Notes on the Management of Spoiled Identity*, Englewood Cliffs, NJ, Prentice Hall, 1963, ch. 4.
3 W. Donaldson, *Brewer's Eccentrics, Rogues and Villains: An A–Z of Roguish Britons through the Ages*, London, Cassell, 2002.
4 B. Capp, *English Almanacs, 1500–1800: Astrology and the Popular Press*, Ithaca, NY, Cornell University Press, 1979, p. 222; D. Vincent, *Literacy and Popular Culture: England, 1750–1914*, Cambridge, Cambridge University Press, 1989, p. 205.
5 See *The Oxford English Dictionary*, 2nd edn, Oxford, Clarendon Press, 1989, hereafter *OED*, 'Eccentricity', 4b; and 'Eccentric', 6b.
6 N. Wanley, *The wonders of the little world, or, A general history of man in six books: wherein by many thousands of examples is shewed what man hath been from the first ages of the world to these times: in respect of his body, senses, passions, affections, his virtues and perfections, his vices and defects, his quality, vocation and profession; and many other particulars not reducible to any of the former heads*, London, T. Basset,

92 *James Gregory*

1678. On Wanley, see P. West, 'Wanley, Nathaniel (1632/3–1680)', in *Oxford Dictionary of National Biography*, Oxford, Oxford University Press, 2004, www.oxforddnb.com/view/article/28665 (accessed 19 October 2004). All subsequent references to the *Dictionary* use the abbreviation *ODNB*. Wanley's work was reprinted, serialised and abridged in 1704, 1788, 1790, 1791, 1796 and 1806. A similar collection was the Reverend William Turner's *A compleat history of the most remarkable providences, both of judgment and mercy, which have hapned in this present age...*, London, Dunton, 1697.

7 Wanley's Preface cites F. Bacon, *The Two Books of Francis Bacon: Of the Proficiency and Advancement of Learning, Divine and Humane* (1605), book 4, ch. 1, pp. 179–81.

8 E. Hooper-Greenhill, *Museums and the Shaping of Knowledge*, London, Routledge, 1992, p. 115; L. Daston, *Wonders and the Order of Nature, 1150–1750*, New York, Zone, 1998; B. M. Benedict, *Curiosity: A Cultural History of Early Modern Inquiry*, Chicago, University of Chicago Press, 2001.

9 Hooper-Greenhill, *Museums*, pp. 147–8 at p. 161.

10 Barbara M. Benedict rightly describes these as 'printed museums' or 'published curiosity museums', in Benedict, *Curiosity: A Cultural History of Early Modern Inquiry*, Chicago, University of Chicago Press, 2001.

11 K. Park and L. Daston, *Wonders and the Order of Nature, 1150–1750*, New York, Zone, 1998; J. Bondeson, *The Two-Headed Boy, and Other Medical Marvels*, Ithaca, NY, Cornell University Press, 2000; P. Youngqvist, *Monstrosities: Bodies and British Romanticism*, Minneapolis, University of Minnesota Press, 2003.

12 J. W. Smeed, *The Theophrastean 'Character': The History of a Literary Genre*, Oxford, Clarendon Press, 1985, chs 3, 6; *Household Words*, 1 May 1858, pp. 469–74.

13 See L. Gossman, 'Anecdote and History', *History and Theory*, May 2003, 42, pp. 143–68. For Gossman, anecdotes may be conventional in their views of history and human nature, or dissolvent 'by reporting "odd" occurrences' (p. 143). He associates this with the 'news in brief' of *faits divers* (including 'eccentricities') that French scholars have investigated, which reported 'a striking, disturbing, or perplexing event or behaviour' (p. 168).

14 S. West, 'The Darly Macaroni Prints and the Politics of the "Private Man"', *Eighteenth Century Life*, 2001, 25, pp. 170–82 at 175.

15 *The Marvellous Chronicle and Wonderful Magazine* (London), September 1764–January 1765.

16 *Marvellous Chronicle*, October 1764, p. 56: John Barker; and p. 88: Biggers, a glutton.

17 *Repository of Anecdote and Wit, containing smart sayings, singular adventures, eccentric biography, curious incidents, and a variety of other interesting Subjects*, 2 vols, London, n.d. [1784].

18 J. Caulfield, *Portraits, Memoirs and Characters of remarkable persons, from the reign of King Edward the Third to the Revolution*, 2 vols, London, Caulfield & Herbert, 1794; Caulfield and Harding, 1795. The 1813 edition was published in 3 vols by R. S. Kirby, London, 1813; Caulfield, *Portraits, Memoirs and Characters of remarkable persons, from the revolution in 1688 to the end of the reign of George II*, 4 vols, London, T. H. Whitely, 1819–20. On Caulfield, see T. Clayton, 'Caulfield, James (1764–1826)', in *ODNB*, www.oxforddnb.com/view/article/4910 (accessed 19 October 2004).

19 Caulfield, *Portraits, Memoirs and Characters*, 1819–20 edn, p. v.

20 *The New Wonderful Magazine and Marvellous Chronicle*, London, C. Johnson, 1793. The title varied, one variant being *The Wonderful Magazine*.

21 Ibid., 'Preface', p. 4.

Eccentric lives 93

22 Ibid.
23 Ibid. See F. Bacon, *Of the advancement and proficience of learning; or, The partitions of sciences. Nine books. Written in Latin by the most eminent, illustrious, and famous Lord Francis Bacon Baron of Verulam, Vicount St. Alban, Councellor of Estate, and Lord Chancellor of England. Interpreted by Gilbert Watts*, Oxford, Leon Lichfield, 1640, Lib. IV, pp. 179–80.
24 *New Wonderful Magazine*, 'T.L.', p. 163.
25 Title page, *The New Wonderful Museum and Extraordinary Magazine*, London, A. Hogg, 1804. Compiled with assistance from Caulfield and others, when completed this was a six-volume work.
26 From the first verse of 'Himself as an Individual', the second epistle (1732) of *Essay on Man*.
27 *New Wonderful Museum*, 1 November 1802, 1, p. 141.
28 Ibid., p. 214.
29 G. H. Wilson, *The Eccentric Mirror: Reflecting a faithful and interesting delineation of male and female character*, 4 vols, London, J. Cundee, 1806–7, 1813.
30 *The Eccentric Magazine; or, Lives and Portraits of Remarkable Characters* (G. Smeeton, 1814). See D. Goldthorpe, 'Lemoine, Henry (1756–1812)', *ODNB*, http://www.oxforddnb.com/view/article/16430. (accessed 19 October 2004)
31 *Eccentric Biography, or Lives of extraordinary characters, whether remarkable for their splendid talents, singular propensities, or wonderful adventures*, London, Thomas Tegg, 1826. See J. J. Barnes and P. P. Barnes, 'Reassessing the reputation of Thomas Tegg, London Publisher, 1776–1846', *Book History*, 2000, 3, pp. 45–60. The authors suggest he wrote this (p. 49); I have no evidence that Tegg did.
32 F. W. Fairholt, *Remarkable Characters: A Series of Biographical Memoirs of Persons Famous for Extraordinary Actions or Singularities*, London, Richard Bentley, 1849, 'vol. 1' (no other volume) W. Russell, *Eccentric Personages*, 2 vols, London, Maxwell, 1864; new edition 1868, Ward Lock – Russell published *Extraordinary Men* in 1851; J. Timbs, *English Eccentrics and Eccentricities*, 2 vols, London, Bentley, 1866.
33 On Fairholt, see J. Selborne, 'Fairholt, F. W. (bap. 1813, d. 1866)', in *ODNB*, www.oxforddnb.com/view/article/9098 (accessed 19 October 2004).
34 *The New Wonderful Magazine: consisting of a carefully selected collection of remarkable trials, biographies of wonderful or extraordinary characters, curious histories and adventures*, London, G. H. Davidson, 1849–50.
35 Timbs, *English Eccentrics*, vol. 1, Preface.
36 Ibid., pp. iii–iv. On Timbs, see J. R. MacDonald, 'Timbs, John (1801–1875)', rev. Nilanjana Banerji, in *ODNB*, www.oxforddnb.com/view/article/27460 (accessed 19 October 2004).
37 For instance, H. Wilson and J. Caulfield, *Book of Wonderful Characters*, London, J. C. Hotten, 1870.
38 Robinson Library, the University of Newcastle, RB Folio 92 8 BEL, G-O: William Hall.
39 G. Slater, *Human Wonders of the World. Containing a short account of the mental and physical deformities of the most remarkable characters who have lived*, Snighill, Sheffield, G. Slater, n.d.
40 W. Grainge, *Three Wonderful Yorkshire Characters*, Pateley Bridge, UK, Thomas Thorpe, 1864.
41 *Anecdotes of remarkable characters: Mary Squires, the Gipsy and others*, London, Bysch, c.1861?, London, Guildhall Library.
42 *Eccentric Biography or Sketches of Remarkable Characters Ancient and Modern*, Boston, Nathaniel Balch, Jr, 1825; E. Walker, *The Wonders of the World*, New York, Walker, 1850. In 1852 Putnam's *Book Buyers' Manual* listed Kirby's *Wonderful Museum* at $7.50.

94 *James Gregory*

43 *Debow's Review, Agricultural, Commercial, Industrial Progress and Resources*, Nashville, New Orleans and New York, April 1866, p. 447.

44 D. Fraser, *The American Magazine of Wonders and Marvellous Chronicle*, New York, Southwick & Pelsue, 1809.

45 S. G. Goodrich, *Curiosities of Human Nature*, part of 'Parley's Cabinet Library' of 20 volumes, 1844–5, was reprinted as *Lives of the Eccentrics*.

46 See the catalogue of the World Publishing House, no. 139, Eighth Street, New York, 1875, or the catalogue of J. & J. L. Gihon, no. 98, Chestnut Street, Philadelphia (advertisements reproduced on the 'Making of America' database, University of Michigan). For British advertisements, see *Notes and Queries*, e.g. 28 June 1862, Messrs Puttick & Simpson. See catalogue of the *Mercantile Library of Boston*, 1854; *Bibliotheca Dramatica. Catalogue of the theatrical and miscellaneous library of W. E. Burton*, 8 October 1860; J. Sabin, *A Catalogue of the books, autographs, engravings and miscellaneous . . .1864*. Reproduced on the 'Making of America' database, University of Michigan.

47 *Notes and Queries*, 8 February 1868, p. 138.

48 British Library, shelfmark 132.c.8.

49 National Art Library, Victoria and Albert Museum, donated by the poet Chauncey Hare Townshend in 1868.

50 *Wonderful Magazine*, October 1764, p. 67.

51 British Library, C.116.i.4, item 180, Prospectus, January 1793; and *New Wonderful Magazine*, 1793, no. 2, p. 50.

52 *New Wonderful Magazine*, 1793, p. 139.

53 Ibid., p. 338.

54 H. Wilson, *Wonderful Characters*, London, Walker, 1842, preface; the printer was W. Braithwaite, Stokesley.

55 See R. W. Chapman, ed., *Jane Austen's Letters to her Sister Cassandra and Others*, 2 vols, Oxford, Clarendon Press, 1932, vol. 1, p. 51: letter of 15 June 1808, concerning a Jefferson, probably William Jefferson, author of *Entertaining Literary Curiosities, consisting of Wonders of Nature and Art, remarkable characters; fragments, etc.*, 1808. E. F. King, *Ten Thousand Wonderful Things. Comprising the marvellous and rare, odd, curious, quaint, eccentric and extraordinary in all ages and nations, in art, nature, and science*, London, Ward Lock, 1859, priced at 3s 6d. This was republished.

56 C. A. Gross, 'The 2000 Thomas Hunt Morgan Medal: Evelyn M. Witkin', *Genetics*, February 2001, 157, p. 460.

57 *Athenaeum*, 10 February 1849, p. 141.

58 J. Kitto, *The Lost Senses – Deafness* (1845) reviewed in the *Athenaeum*, 1846.

59 'The Seldens of Sherwood', *Southern Literary Messenger*, July 1851, 17, 6, p. 358.

60 D. Vincent, *Literacy and Popular Culture*, p. 62.

61 Milner & Sowerby of Halifax, in a catalogue appended to a cheap edition of *Artemus Ward*, listed their edition in their 'cheap list' in 1866.

62 P. Mackenzie, *Curious and Remarkable Glasgow Characters*, Glasgow, T. D. Morison, Popular Shilling Books Series, 1891.

63 See *Notes and Queries*, e.g. 28 June 1862, Messrs Puttick & Simpson.

64 W. Howitt, 'English Scenes and Characters', *Shilling Journal*, 1846, 3, January–June, p. 38.

65 T. Hood, *The Choice Works of Thomas Hood*, 4 vols, New York, Kiggins & Kellogg, 1854, vol. 1, p. 40. His father was a partner in a publishing firm which published one *Eccentric Biography*, London, Vernor & Hood, 1801. For the second allusion see Hood, *Choice Works*, 1854, vol. 2, p. 138.

66 J. H. Stonehouse, ed., *Reprints of the Catalogues of the Libraries of Charles Dickens and W. M. Thackeray*, London, Fountain Press, 1935; author's own copy of J. C. Hotten edition of *The Book of Wonderful Characters. Memoirs and Anecdotes of*

Eccentric lives 95

Remarkable and Eccentric Persons in All Ages and Countries. Chiefly from the Text of Henry Wilson and James Caulfield, London, Chatto & Windus, n.d.; O. W. Holmes, *Over the Teacups*, London, Riverside Edition, Sampson Low, Marston, Searle & Rivington, 1891, p. 17.

67 British Library copy of Wilson, *Wonderful Characters*, London, Walker, 1842, shelfmark 10600.bb.28.

68 See S. O'Connell, *The Popular Print in England, 1550–1850*, London, Trustees of the British Museum, 1999.

69 Caulfield, *Portraits, Memoirs and Characters*, 1819–20 edn, p. ix.

70 On biography as *the* English form, and British fascination with individual likeness, see P. Langford, *Englishness Identified: Manners and Character, 1650–1850*, Oxford, Oxford University Press, 2000, p. 294.

71 J. Granger, *A Biographical History of England*, first published in 2 vols, London, T. Davies, 1769; 5th edn, 6 vols, London, W. Baynes, 1824; Henry Bromley, *A Catalogue of Engraved British Portraits, From Egbert the Great to the Present Time. Consisting of the Effigies of Persons in Every Walk of Human Life; as well those whose Services to their Country are Recorded in the Annals of the English History, as others whose Eccentricity of Character Rendered them Conspicuous in their Day...*, T. Payne and W. Otridge & Son, 1793; M. Noble, *A Biographical History of England*, London, W. Richardson, 1806. For a recent study of Granger, and these engraved portraits of the eccentric, see M. Pointon, *Hanging the Head: Portraiture and Social Formation in Eighteenth-Century England*, New Haven, CT, Yale University Press, 1993, ch. 3, 'Significant and Insignificant Lives'. For a biography, see L. Peltz, 'Granger, James (bap. 1723, d. 1776)' in *ODNB*, www.oxforddnb.com/view/article/11240 (accessed 19 October 2004).

72 Granger, *Biographical History*, 2nd edn, vol. 4, p. 356.

73 Stick of John Gale of London; tobacco-stopper of Dickinson of Scarborough; a $\frac{1}{2}$d trade token dated 1795, representing the 'Mayor of Garratt': catalogue of Falmouth stamp and coin shop, Falmouth, MA; Blind Willie represented on two mugs in the Tyne and Wear Museums collection; Blind Willie and Count Boruwlaski, by the sculptor David Dunbar: other North-Eastern eccentrics were depicted in wood. Staffordshire figures of the black musician Billy Waters (featuring in Pierce Egan's *Life in London*, and elsewhere depicted by the artist Thomas Lord Busby), and Black Sal *c*.1825, were reproduced in pottery. On commemorative ceramic representations of Lucas, and the oddly behaved James Hirst of Rawcliffe (died 1828), see J. Timpson, *English Eccentrics*, Norwich, Jarrold, 1994 [1991], p. 22, p. 79.

74 See S. Shesgreen, *The Criers and Hawkers of London: Engravings and Drawings by Marcellus Laroon*, Stanford, CA, Stanford University Press, 1990, and S. Shesgreen, *Images of the Outcast: The Urban Poor in the Cries of London*, Brunswick, NJ, Rutgers University Press, 2002. Important examples include J. T. Smith, *Vagabondiana, or, anecdotes of Mendicant Wanderers through the streets of London*, London, 1817; T. L. Busby, *Cries of London*, 1823; J. T. Smith (ed. J. B. Nichols), *The Cries of London: Exhibiting Several of the Itinerant Traders of Antient and Modern Times Copied from rare engravings or drawn from life*, London, J. B. Nichols, 1839.

75 D. Hansen, 'Dead Poet's Society', a description of the folio at the Tasmanian Museum and Art Gallery, at www.utas.edu.au/docs/siglo/mag/s12/hansen.html (accessed 31 October 2003).

76 J. Sinclair, *Scenes and Stories from the North of Scotland*, Edinburgh, James Thin, and London, Simpkin, Marshall, 1890.

77 On Holt, see Edinburgh City Libraries collections (8951 p; X28507 b plate 11 and plate 45), located through the Scottish Cultural Resources Access Network (Scran.ac.uk) database.

96 *James Gregory*

78 See Robert Jack's studies of 'Jethart Worthies', Scottish Borders Council Museum Service reference JA/P/92; Magnus Jackson's photographs of characters such as the pipeclay seller 'Blue Caum Kate'; and the newsagent and bookseller William Smith's photographs of local characters from c.1860, Perth and Kinross Council Archive and Perth Museum and Art Gallery, MJ 3567, Tain and District Museum Trust, TANDM:74.1. All this material was viewed via the Scran.ac.uk database.

79 For instance, *A catalogue of the genuine and extraordinary collection of British portraits and historic prints . . . collected with the true classic taste of the fine arts at a most liberal expense by the late Sir James Winter Lake, Baronet*, National Art Library, Victoria and Albert Museum, shelfmark Lugt: 7385.

80 *Catalogue of a choice collection of oil paintings, prints, books, eastern china, silver plate etc . . . the property of the late Mr Benjamin Thompson*, Gateshead, W. Stephenson, 1829, Newcastle Local Studies collection, L018.2, 0946.

81 Noble, *Biographical History*, vol. 1, p. 384; see vol. 2, p. 395 about a 'poor maniac' holding a print of Harry.

82 British Library, C.116.i.4, Prospectus for *The Wonderful Magazine*, January 1793. 'Ready Rhino' is [thieving?] slang for ready money. Brewer's *Dictionary of Phrase and Fable*: 'Some, as I know, / Have parted with their ready rhino', *The Seaman's Adieu* (1670).

83 W. Hone, *The Every-Day Book: or the guide to the year: relating the popular amusements, sports, ceremonies, manners, customs, events incident to the three hundred and sixty-five days, in past and present days. . .*, London, Tegg, 1825–6; R. Chambers, *The Book of Days: A Miscellany of Popular Antiquities in Connection with the Calendar, including Anecdote, Biography and History, Curiosities of Literature and Oddities of Human Life and Character*, 2 vols, London and Edinburgh, W. and R. Chambers, 1866. On tracts, see *Thomas Rodd's Booksellers Catalogue of Tracts and Pamphlets* (reprinted, Bloomfield Books and Publishers, 1975), Catalogue of Tracts, Part V, 1821.

84 My estimations are derived from John J. McCusker, 'Comparing the Purchasing Power of Money in Great Britain from 1264 to 2002', Economic History Services, 2003, URL: www.eh.net/hmit/ppowerbp/.

85 J. A. Morgan, *The Law of Literature*, New York, J. Cockcroft, 1875, vol. 2, p. 692.

86 *The Magazine of Curiosity and Wonder. . . Containing the Lives of the Most wonderful and eccentric individuals*, London, Drake, 1835, an illustrated penny magazine produced by Prest, a hack writer whose works included *Varney the Vampire* and *Sweeney Todd*. See L. James and H. R. Smith, 'Prest, Thomas Peckett (1809/10–1859)', *ODNB*, www.oxforddnb.com/view/article/41042 (accessed 19 October 2004).

87 H. P. Parker, 'Artist's Narrative', Newcastle City Library, L920 P239, pp. 26–7.

88 *Newcastle Weekly Chronicle*, 22 March 1873, p. 5.

89 According to the *OED*, 2nd edition, 1989, 'abnormality' is to be defined as 'The quality or state of being abnormal; irregularity of constitution' and 2. 'an instance or embodiment of such irregularity; and abnormal or unusual feature or act'. 'Abnormal' is defined as 'deviating from the ordinary rule or type; contrary to rule or system; irregular, unusual, aberrant'. Of the word 'abnormal', the *OED* notes, 'Few words show such a series of pseudo-etymological perversions'.

90 For definitions and admissions of major difficulties with the various meanings of the term for social scientists, psychologists and psychiatrists, see J. T. Zadrozny, *Dictionary of Social Science*, Washington, DC, Public Affairs Press, 1959, p. 1; J. Gould and W. L. Kolb, eds, *A Dictionary of the Social Sciences*, UNESCO, London, Tavistock Publications, 1964, p. 1; and D. A. Statt, *Concise Dictionary of Psychology*, London, Routledge, 1990, p. 1.

Eccentric lives 97

91 The three main definitions of psychological abnormality – statistical, social definition and medical definition – are summarised by D. R. Hemsley, 'Abnormal Psychology', in A. Kupar and J. Kupar, eds, *The Social Science Encyclopaedia*, London, Routledge & Kegan Paul, 1985, p. 1.

92 E. Durkheim, 'The Normal and the Pathological', in *The Rules of Sociological Method*, 8th edn, transl. S. A. Solvay and J. H. Mueller, ed. G. E. G. Catlin, Glencoe, IL, Free Press, 1950, pp. 65–73; 'Crime et santé sociale', *Revue Philosophique*, 1895, 39, extracted in A. Giddens, ed., *Emile Durkheim: Selected Writings*, Cambridge, Cambridge University Press, 1972, pp. 105–7.

93 Tegg, *Eccentric Biography*, p. 246.

94 J. S. Mill, *On Liberty*, London, 1859, ch. 3: 'Of Individuality, as one of the elements of well-being', Oxford University Press, World Classic edition, 1991, pp. 82–3 at p. 76.

95 Timbs, *English Eccentrics*, vol. 1, p. 158.

96 Caulfield, *Portraits, Memoirs, Characters*, 1819–20 edn, vol. 1, p. 79, Thomas Britton the coalman. Langford, *Englishness Identified*, pp. 286–7, also notes that eccentricity was not confined to the upper classes.

97 *Eccentric Magazine*, vol. 1, p. 280.

98 *Eccentric Magazine*, vol. 2, p. 294.

99 Ibid., pp. 111–12, p. 304.

100 Langford, *Englishness Identified*; S. Collini, 'The Idea of "Character" in Victorian Political Thought', *Transactions of the Royal Historical Society*, 5th series, 1985, 35, pp. 29–50.

101 For biographies of these, see R. Malcolm Smuts, 'Hudson, Jeffery (1619–1682)', *ODNB*, www.oxforddnb.com/view/article/14033 (accessed 19 October 2004); W. W. Wroth, 'Topham, Thomas (1710–1749)', rev. A. N. Harvey, *ODNB*, www.oxforddnb.com/view/article/27554 (accessed 19 October 2004); and M. Johnson, 'Boruwlaski, Joseph, styled Count Boruwlaski (1739–1837)', *ODNB*, www.oxforddnb.com/view/article/2925 (accessed 19 October 2004).

102 E. O'Connor, *Raw Material: Producing Pathology in Victorian Culture*, Durham, NC, Duke University Press, 2000, ch. 4. For further examination of Victorian interest in freaks, see R. Altick, *The Shows of London*, ch. 19: 'Freaks in the Age of Improvement'.

103 Wanley, Book 1, ch. 5, p. 5.

104 See D. Cressy, *Travesties and Transgressions in Stuart and Tudor England*, Oxford, Oxford University Press, 2000, and S. Pender, 'In the Bodyshop: Human Exhibition in Early Modern England', in H. Deutsch and F. Nussbaum, eds, *'Defects': Engendering the Modern Body*, Ann Arbor, Michigan University Press, pp. 95–126.

105 See *OED*, 2nd edn, for the etymology of 'singularity' in the sense of 'departing or deviating from what is customary, usual, or normal; peculiarity, eccentricity, oddity, strangeness', with the earliest example being from Steren in 1768.

106 See T. Seccombe, 'Peter the Wild Boy (*c*.1712–1785)', rev. D. Turner, *ODNB*, www.oxforddnb.com/view/article/22017 (accessed 19 October 2004).

107 Tegg, *Eccentric Biography*, Preface.

108 *Eccentric Mirror*, 4, p. 1. See Miles D. Barton, 'Pitt, Thomas, second Baron Camelford (1775–1804)', *ODNB*, www.oxforddnb.com/view/article/22335 (accessed 19 October 2004).

109 Tegg, *Eccentric Biography*, p. iv.

110 Tegg, *Eccentric Biography*, p. iv.

111 F. S. Merryweather, *Lives and Anecdotes of Misers; or the Passion of Avarice Displayed: in the parsimonious habits, unaccountable lives and remarkable deaths of the most notorious misers of all ages, with a few words on frugality and saving*, London, Simpkin, Marshall, 1850, pp. 28, 159, 175.

98   *James Gregory*

112 J. Timbs, *English Eccentrics and Eccentricities*, London, Chatto & Windus, 1875, pp. 29–30; 'Corner' Memory in Timbs, *Romance of London*, vol. 3, p. 261.
113 Wilson, *Eccentric Mirror*, 3, 30, p. 20.
114 Wilson, *Eccentric Mirror*, 4, 32, p. 28.
115 Wilson, *Eccentric Mirror*, 4, 34, p. 27.
116 Russell, *Eccentric Personages*, vol. 1, p. 308; see reference to the Stanhopes' hereditary craze', p. 106.
117 See Merryweather, *Lives and Anecdotes of Misers*, pp. 166–7.
118 'Valobra', in *Eccentric Magazine*, 2.
119 *The Book of Wonderful Characters*, London, Chatto & Windus, n.d., p. 291. See Douglas A. Reid, 'Britton, Thomas (1644–1714)', *ODNB*, www.oxforddnb.com/view/article/3459 (accessed 19 October 2004).
120 Noble, *Biographical History*, vol. 2, p. 397.
121 'Advertisement', *Eccentric Biography*.
122 Tegg, *Eccentric Biography*, p. 168.
123 Russell, *Eccentric Personages*, vol. 1, p. 70.
124 E. Cobham Brewer, *The Dictionary of Phrase and Fable*, 1894, lists misers.
125 C. Dickens, *Our Mutual Friend* (serialised 1864–5), ch. 5: 'Down among the Misers'. See also the titles referred to in ch. 6.
126 *Bleak House* (serialised 1852–3) [John Elwes, Daniel Dancer]; *Little Dorrit* (serialised 1855–7), 'The Clarionet-Player's Dwelling' [Dirty Dick].
127 On Dancer, see A. Vian, 'Dancer, Daniel (1716–1794)', rev. D. Turner, *ODNB*, www.oxforddnb.com/view/article/7100 (accessed 19 October 2004).
128 *Eccentric Magazine*, vol. 2, pp. 5–23. See the biography, *Gentleman's Magazine*, September 1791; E. Topham, *The Life of the Late John Elwes*, London, J. Ridgway, 1790); and A. Gordon, 'Elwes, John (1714–1789)', rev. A. McConnell, *ODNB*, www.oxforddnb.com/view/article/8776 (accessed 19 October 2004).
129 See P. Carter, 'Bentley, Nathaniel (1735?–1809)', *ODNB*, www.oxforddnb.com/view/article/2168 (accessed 19 October 2004).
130 Tegg, *Eccentric Biography*. Charteris had been a notorious character. See P. Life, 'Charteris, Francis (*c.*1665–1732)', *ODNB*, www.oxforddnb.com/view/article/5175 (accessed 19 October 2004).
131 Wanley, *Wonders of the little world*, preface.
132 For example, *Eccentric Biography; or memoirs of remarkable female characters, ancient and modern. Including actresses, adventurers, authoresses, fortune-tellers, gipsies, dwarfs, swindlers, vagrants. And others who have distinguished themselves by their chastity, dissipation, intrepidity, learning, abstinence, credulity &c &c. Alphabetically arranged. Forming a Pleasing Mirror of Reflection to the Female Mind*, London, J. Cundee, 1803, p. iv. A. Booth, 'Illustrious Company: Victoria Among Other Women in Anglo-American Role Model Anthologies', in M. Homans and A. Munich, eds, *Remaking Queen Victoria*, Cambridge, Cambridge University Press, 1997, pp. 59–78, has suggestive comments on anthologies of women.
133 A. B. Dawson, 'Mistric Hic and Haec: Representations of Moll Frith', *Studies in English Literature, 1500–1900*, Spring 1993, 32, pp. 385–404.
134 Wilson, *Eccentric Mirror*, vol. 3, no. 30, p. 27.
135 Ibid., vol. 3, no. 34, p. 1. See J. M. J. Rogister, 'D'Éon de Beaumont, Charles Geneviève Louis Auguste André Timothée, Chevalier D'Éon in the French nobility (1728–1810)', *ODNB*, www.oxforddnb.com/view/article/7523 (accessed 19 October 2004).
136 Wilson, *Eccentric Mirror*, vol. 3, 34, p. 14.
137 Caulfield, *Portraits, Memoirs, Characters*, 1819–20 edn, vol. 4, p. 112.
138 Wilson, *Eccentric Mirror*, vol. 4, no. 37. See Julie Wheelwright, 'Talbot, Mary Anne [John Taylor] (1778–1808)', *ODNB* www.oxforddnb.com/view/article/26935 (accessed 19 October 2004).

Eccentric lives 99

139 Wilson, *Eccentric Mirror*, vol. 4, 37, p. 22.
140 Ibid., vol. 1, pp. 144–64.
141 Ibid., vol. 1, p. 144.
142 Tegg, *Eccentric Biography*, p. iii.
143 A. Pope, *Essay on Man*, Epistle II: 'Of the Nature and State of Man, With Respect to Himself as an Individual', Stanza 1: 'Know then thyself, presume not God to scan, / The proper study of mankind is Man.'
144 Merryweather, *Lives and Anecdotes of Misers*, p. 3.
145 Wilson, *Eccentric Mirror*, 4, 36, p. 15.
146 Timbs, *English Eccentrics and Eccentricities*, p. 21.
147 Wilson, *Eccentric Mirror*, 4, 39, p. 31.
148 Ibid., 4, 37, p. 22.
149 Advertisement, *Biographical Curiosities; or Various Pictures of Human Nature Containing Original and Authentick Memoirs of Daniel Dancer Esq., the Extraordinary Miser &c &c*, London, Ridgway, 1797.
150 Hogg published the *Malefactor's Register*.
151 *Eccentric Magazine*, 1, p. 217.
152 For instance, see the biographies of the following victims of misfortune in Tegg, *Eccentric Biography*: Elizabeth Woodcock (who was buried in snow for eight days), John Orme (an innocent man who narrowly escaped punishment), John Holwell (who furnished an eyewitness account to the 'Black Hole of Calcutta').
153 Wanley, Book 1, ch. 10, pp. 14–16.
154 *Eccentric Magazine*, 2, p. 2.
155 See L. J. Davis, 'Dr Johnson, Amelia, and the Discourse of Disability in the Eighteenth Century', in Deutsch and Nussbaum, eds, *'Defects'*, for a discussion of the prevalence of impairment, pp. 56–7.
156 J. R. T. E. Gregory, 'Local Characters: Eccentricity and the North East in the Nineteenth Century', *Northern History* 2005, XLII, 163–86.
157 J. B. Robinson, *Derbyshire Gatherings a fund of delight for the antiquary, the historian, the topographer, the biographer*, London, J.R. Smith, 1866, p. 89.
158 Langford, *Englishness Identified*, pp. 301–10.
159 Wilson, *Eccentric Mirror*, 1, 4, p. 22.
160 Ibid., 3, 30, p. 1.
161 Ibid., 3, 28, p. 1.
162 *Eccentric Magazine*, 1, p. 269.
163 Ibid., 2, p. 129.
164 Noble, *Biographical History*, p. vi.
165 J. R. T. E. Gregory, 'Sensational Characters: Eccentric Biography c.1837–1900', paper read at the British Association of Victorian Studies, Fifth Annual Conference, Keele University, 4 September 2004.
166 E. Sitwell, *The English Eccentrics*, London, Faber & Faber, 1933.
167 Chambers, *Book of Days*, vol. 2, p. 267. The varied critique of exhibition is mapped in Pender, 'In the Bodyshop', pp. 104–13.
168 The only study of eccentricity providing a sustained scientific or psychological approach is D. J. Weeks and J. James, *Eccentrics: A Study of Sanity and Strangeness*, London, Weidenfeld & Nicolson, 1995, the first 'clinical' examination, by a clinical neuropsychologist and a journalist. See also D. J. Weeks, *Eccentrics: The Scientific Investigation*, Stirling, UK, Stirling University Press, 1988.
169 See R. G. Thomson, 'Introduction', in R. G. Thomson, ed., *Freakery: Cultural Spectacles of the Extraordinary Body*, New York, New York University Press, 1996, p. 7, on photographs and drawings circulating 'an iterable, fixed, collectible visual image of staged freakishness' that penetrated the Victorian parlour and family album.

100 *James Gregory*

170 Bogdan, *Freak Show*, p. 268.
171 Ibid.
172 Goffman, *Stigma*, pp. 141–5.
173 See Benedict, *Curiosity*, pp. 151–2 on vicarious transgression through printed depictions of transgressive bodies and themes.
174 As suggested in K. Magill, 'Surveillance-Free-Subjects', in M. Lloyd and A. Thacker, eds, *The Impact of Michel Foucault on the Social Sciences and Humanities*, Basingstoke, UK, Macmillan, 1997, pp. 54–77 at p. 67.

5 Constructing the common type

Physiognomic norms and the notion of 'civic usefulness', from Lavater to Galton

Lucy Hartley

> We learn to perceive the world through those cultural artefacts which preserve a society's stereotypes of its environment. . . . It is not merely flora and fauna, sunset and seascape which are seen through the prism of culture. We also see man in his infinite variety through the filters of stereotypical perspective.
>
> (Sander Gilman[1])

What do we understand by the term 'normal'? This relatively modern word has come to assume immense cultural significance as a marker of various different kinds of standards, a plumb line, if you like, by which we might measure consensus and commonality, both those things agreed upon and those things held in common. 'Normal', meaning 'constituting, conforming to, not deviating or differing from, the common type or standard', is a product of the nineteenth century, first cited in this form in the *Oxford English Dictionary* in 1821 and in common usage from 1840, but subsequently qualified by two other definitions of 'norm' as the 'standard, model, pattern, type' (*c.*1851) and 'normal' as 'a normal variety of anything; that which, or a person who, is healthy and is not impaired in any way' (1894).[2] The linguistic range of the term 'normal' indicated by these definitions points to a shift from an abstract conception of 'normal' as 'the common type' to its physical manifestation as 'healthy', 'not impaired'. Why, then, does the normative understanding of the first half of the nineteenth century, characterised as standard or pattern, seem to take on a rather different, indeed sharper, focus through its translation into an index of health in the second half of the century?

It is clear there is a political dimension to changing understandings of what constitutes or conforms to the normal. In an important essay entitled 'The Normal and the Pathological', Emile Durkheim argued that the normal contains, rather than opposes, its negatives, usually thought of in terms of the 'abnormal'. He claimed the 'abnormal', figured as the criminal, is not outside but integral to the function of the 'normal' and as such is necessary to the consensus-building activity of any democratic society.

102   *Lucy Hartley*

Crime is 'normal', according to Durkheim, because it pushes against the grain of the collectivity, of the rules and regulations of common life, and marks out the ground for consensus; it 'consists of an act that offends certain very strong collective sentiments' and therefore provides a referent for the proper functioning of law and morality.[3] The following illustration neatly encapsulates this thesis:

> Imagine a society of saints, a perfect cloister of exemplary individuals. Crimes, properly so called, will there be unknown; but faults which appear venial to the layman will create there the same scandal that the ordinary offence does in ordinary consciousness. If, then, this society has the power to judge and punish, it will define these acts as criminal and will treat them as such. For the same reason, the perfect and upright man judges his smallest failings with a severity that the majority reserve for acts more truly in the nature of an offence. Formerly acts of violence against persons were more frequent than they are today, because respect for individual dignity was less strong. As this has increased, these crimes have become more rare; and also, many acts violating this sentiment have been introduced into the penal law which were not included there in primitive times.[4]

Rather than presenting a model of society that alienates the criminal outside its bounds, then, Durkheim offers a model of assimilation that seeks to contain criminals in its midst because their actions constitute the plumb line that helps to maintain the balance in society, a balance forged on consensus and commonality (and to some large extent control). In effect, his suggestion that the 'abnormal' produces the conditions for the 'normal' is predicated on a principle of restitution in that he perceives crime as an extraordinary event, which involves changes to the social body that are healthy and normal and yet usually temporary in nature.

This chapter takes Durkheim's conception of the 'normal' as an inclusive term of assimilation and uses it to rethink the linguistic range and value attributed to normality in two distinct but related examples. The definitions from the *Oxford English Dictionary*, outlined earlier, suggest a translation from abstract to physical conceptions of what constitutes or conforms to the 'normal'; this is a double movement, for while the shift from common type to model and then variety maps the historical dimensions of the term 'normal', it constitutes also a cultural theory of reference with significant ramifications, then as now. I want, therefore, to consider some possible explanations for these shifts of understanding by examining, in particular, the idea of a 'common type'. A language of norms was central to descriptions of character in the nineteenth century, involving the construction of a typology that relied upon a correspondence between external appearance and internal character; and so I shall look at two key proponents of this kind of cultural stereotyping, namely Johann Caspar Lavater, who revived the phys-

Physiognomic norms   103

iognomic tradition, and Frances Galton, who extended it into the new science of eugenics.[5]

Physiognomists have long recognised an individual's face as an index of character that can be interpreted in relation to a common or general type. It is this notion of a type that eugenicists sought to identify and promote, for physiognomy and eugenics shared an ideological belief that the apparently circumstantial appearance of things, primarily glimpsed via the face, could reveal typical and emblematic traits that enabled the definition of normal types. Physical (health and beauty), sexual (desirability) and social (natural and regular) characteristics were necessary to this approach, which attempted to show how 'virtue beautifies, vice deforms'.[6]

Underpinning these discussions of character was a belief that what can be seen visibly on the body is meaningful, a register of signs to be interpreted for private and public purposes. But there is an important distinction to be made between the interpretation of types, based on facial profiles, and the prediction of behaviour or conduct, formulated from psychological or social profiles; the physiognomical is not the same as the pathological. A physiognomical reaction to an individual works on the assumption that there are certain essential types of character, denoted by particular facial features, while a pathological response attempts to outline the range of possible actions that will be determined by certain emotional, mental or physical symptoms. In an interesting (and timely) critique of the use of physical appearance to serve political ends, Sander Gilman isolates and identifies a dominant trend in the constitution of normality. Health and beauty together with the erotic and the good tend to be aligned with the 'normal', he contends, whereas the 'abnormal' is usually associated with illness and ugliness as well as the repulsive and the evil. He explains:

These idealized body types are paralleled by ideal 'moral' types, by 'good citizens'. The beautiful is the good citizen; the healthy citizen is the good citizen. And citizenship in this context is a reflex of the body. The good citizen cannot be ugly and therefore cannot be infected by, or infect, members of society with dangerous illnesses, illnesses that would be marked on their physiognomies.[7]

This may sound like a eugenic dream of citizenship, with its own theory of reference that classifies 'members of society' as morally good because they are beautiful and healthy or, alternatively, amorally bad because ugly and sick. But, as Gilman reminds us, the elevation of a normative typology predicated on vitality and virtue has had a marked, and overwhelmingly negative, impact on what it means to participate in and contribute to society. A comparison of Lavater's writings on physiognomy with Galton's ideas about eugenics will bring this into sharp relief.

104   *Lucy Hartley*

I

Physiognomy has a long history that stretches, roughly speaking, from Aristotle to Lavater.[8] Its popularity has varied in different historical moments, but the renaissance of the physiognomical tradition in the nineteenth century is an important phenomenon that must be accounted for in respect of not only the large sales of Lavater's increasingly famous volumes but also the changing notions of belief.[9] It is well known that the nineteenth century was a period in which man's place in nature was the subject of intense and often heated debate, specifically among the scientific community.[10] New ideas about the development of life on earth, and new explanations of its natural phenomena, offered compelling models of the history, structure and function of the organic world – for example, derived from the geology of Charles Lyell, the comparative anatomy of Georges Cuvier, the physiology of W. B. Carpenter and Alexander Bain, and the evolutionary theory of Charles Darwin and Alfred Russel Wallace – and demonstrated that it was no longer necessary to place humankind at the centre of explanations of change and transformation.[11] But this was also a period which inherited and went on to explain physiognomical teachings that seemed to affirm the purpose and design of a natural order of things, somewhat against the grain of these new ideas about humankind's origins, development, and transformation.

Originally published in German as *Physiognomische Fragmente* (1775–8), Lavater's work was translated into English by Henry Hunter in a luxury five-volume edition entitled *Essays on Physiognomy: Designed to Promote the Knowledge and Love of Mankind* (1789), and then a three-volume version (with the same title) translated by Thomas Holcroft (1789–93), followed within ten years by a much cheaper one-volume edition that enabled the popular dissemination of physiognomic teachings in the first half of the nineteenth century.[12] Thus, I want to claim that the definitions of 'normal' cited by the *Oxford English Dictionary* signal the parameters of a debate that emerged from the attempt to construct a 'common type' articulated in Lavater's work (and later extended in Galton's). *Essays on Physiognomy* started with a discussion of the truth of physiognomy, which included criticisms and testimonies of its teachings, and then explored the strengths and weaknesses, as well as the ease and difficulties, of physiognomical observation. A compendious collection of observations and aphorisms and an eclectic array of illustrations, silhouettes, and descriptions of individual character were contained within the covers of this work, which together presented a normative understanding of human character and conduct.[13] Defined as the 'science or knowledge of the correspondence between the external and internal man, the visible superficies and the invisible contents', physiognomy was a hermeneutic endeavour that relied on essentialism and determinism to make its points.[14] Expression was seen as a crucial form of mediation between a natural and a supernatural order because it was probably the most explicit of the physical states in the world, and so emotional expression, principally via the face, could be used to comprehend the actions of a higher mind. As Roger Smith has argued, such theories of man and mind produced by the natural philosophies of the seventeenth and eighteenth centuries tended to persist in using ideas of purpose, power and action to express the active part of physical events.[15] Physiognomy, therefore, represented a form of imagining something hidden from external appearances that, once revealed, made them more purposeful, more substantial and therefore more characterful.

At the heart of Lavater's teachings was a description of the 'threefold life' contained in the natural world, namely animal, moral and intellectual.[16] The first, 'animal' (or 'physiological') type corresponded to the belly and included the organs of reproduction; the second, 'moral' type linked to the breast, with the heart as its natural centre; and the third, 'intellectual' type referred to the head and had the eye as its locus. Lavater went on to claim that the face was exemplary of these three types, for its external features presented a crystallised version of an individual's internal character: thus, the mouth to the chin constituted the 'animal' type; the nose and cheeks represented the 'moral' type; and the forehead to the eyebrows exemplified the 'intellectual' type. Clearly, the idea was that these classifications marked out a hierarchy of description whereby the 'animal' type was linked to the function and structure of the digestive system and so provided the lowest order of description; the 'moral' type was correlated to the motions of the heart and acted as the middle order of description; and the 'intellectual' type connoted the head and therefore represented the highest order of description. Balance is the key here, because the language of norms articulated by Lavater sets up standards for animal, moral and intellectual types that related directly to social rank and function. The suggestion was that all three types contributed to the construction of a 'normal' understanding of character, finely weighted to incorporate complementary rather than competing aspects; but the discussion of high and low types also seems to involve an implicit warning that excess of any one type, and perhaps especially the animal kind, was likely to present a hermeneutic difficulty to the untrained eye of the ordinary observer.

All human beings, Lavater claimed, have the capacity to make judgements about other individuals in relation to their physical appearance. That is to say, the feeling that produced the 'physiognomical sensation' was universal; however, the thinking that legitimates it was peculiar to the physiognomist. The physiognomist was privileged in this respect, and therefore a specialist as distinct from the ordinary observer, as he could isolate the traits and identify the characteristics of emotional expression by using rational principles over emotional ones. The following passage, from a section on the 'rarity of the spirit of physiognomical observations', seeks to underline the distinction between the physiognomic practitioner as specialist and the ordinary observer as amateur:

106　*Lucy Hartley*

> Nothing can appear more easy than to observe, yet nothing is more uncommon. By observe I mean to consider a subject in all its various parts: first to consider each part separately, and, afterwards, to examine its analogy with contiguous or other possible objects; to conceive and retain the various properties which delineate, define, and constitute the essence of the thing under consideration; to have clear ideas of these properties, individually and collectively, as contributing to form a whole, so as not to confound them with other properties, or things, however great the resemblance.[17]

So the physiognomist was, according to Lavater, equipped with the special talent of seeing the general in the particular and the universal in the general; and further evidence of this talent was provided in the form of an illustrated comparison of types of faces (Figure 5.1). Sixteen heads are presented to the reader in profile, and there seem to be some quite obvious similarities between the male heads (numbered 1–12) and the female heads (13–16). Nonetheless, Lavater divides the profiles into three different categories and points out that close attention to these profiles will show up a number of dissimilarities between them: '1 to 6. – Have, to the unpractised, much resemblance, yet some of them have differences too vast to be imagined on a first view. The hasty observer will find some dissimilar, and the accurate all.' Consequently, we are told, the range of types develops from the 'understanding, but irresolution' of 1 through the 'goodness tinged with weakness' of 3 to the 'inanimate thoughtlessness' of 6, whereas 'imbecility is the character common to Fig. 7 to 12'.[18] In effect, the first six figures represent characters of the higher moral and intellectual types whose appearances are defined by their forehead, eyes and mouth; and the next six figures exemplify the lower animal types in that the negative qualities of their features outweigh the positive ones. We are, then, presented with the characteristics of normal types on the one hand, and abnormal characters on the other. But the four female figures at the bottom of the page, from 13 to 16, are perhaps the most interesting because, as Lavater explained, these figures represent ideal Grecian types and demonstrate the need for minute discriminations in physiognomical observation: for instance, 'the forehead of 14 will be found to possess a small superior degree of delicacy over that of 13; the forehead of 15 much inferior to 14, and the forehead of 16 still inferior to 15'.[19] The point that Lavater labours in this illustration is simply that physiognomists were equipped with special talents, not easily acquired, and so only they would have the ability to discern the degree of facial difference between these four sisters.

Evidentially, discrimination (or seeing difference) was the mechanism for physiognomy, as it enabled differences between individual appearances to be gathered up into generalisations about those appearances; and, in this way, a social calculus could be constructed according to types and their deviations. Lavater claimed that physiognomy was a generalised system of knowledge

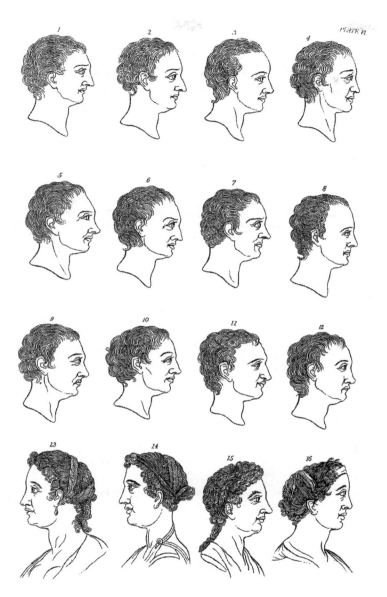

Figure 5.1 Illustration from Johann Caspar Lavater, 'On the Harmony between Moral and Corporeal Beauty', *Essays on Physiognomy: Designed to Promote the Knowledge and Love of Mankind. Written in the German Language by John Caspar Lavater: and Translated into English by Thomas Holcroft. To which are added one hundred physiognomical rules, a posthumous work by Mr. Lavater: and 'Memoirs of the Life of the Author'*, compiled principally from *'The Life of Lavater'*, by G. Gessner, 5th edn (London, William Tegg, 1848, Plate VI, p. 61). Author's copy.

108   *Lucy Hartley*

with an empiricist methodology derived from particular experiences. Physical appearance was, for him, the root of our social relations in that we make quite profound judgements of how an individual looks and therefore who they are without considering the reasons for doing so (and arguably as much now as then). The practice of physiognomy offered a means of defining and explaining the scope of these instinctive responses, stressing the fact that we make such judgements about character by means of physical characteristics and, more importantly, showing how to translate these judgements into a language of norms focused on common types. As a result, it is easy to see how the popularity of physiognomy became linked to the affirmation of social rank and class, 'from the most finished courtier to the lowest of the vulgar'.[20]

A chapter from Charles Dickens's *Sketches by Boz* (1836) on the subject of 'Our Next-Door Neighbour' provides a good satirical example of this connection between appearance, character and rank. Substituting 'the physiognomy of street-door knockers' for the study of the face, Dickens explained that

> whenever we visit a man for the first time, we contemplate the features of his knocker with the greatest curiosity, for we well know, that between the man and his knocker, there will inevitably be a greater or less degree of resemblance and sympathy.[21]

Four examples of door knockers are given: first, 'a large, round one, with the jolly face of a convivial lion smiling blandly at you' denoting hospitable people and a welcome invitation into the house; second, 'a heavy ferocious-looking fellow, with a countenance expressive of savage stupidity' indicating the selfishness and brutality of its inhabitants and often exemplified by 'a small attorney or bill-broker'; third, 'a little pert Egyptian knocker, with a long thin face, a pinched up nose, and a very sharp chin' representing the smugness of 'little spare, priggish men, who are perfectly satisfied with their own opinions, and consider themselves of paramount importance'; and finally, 'a new kind of knocker, without any face at all, composed of a wreath depending from a hand or small truncheon' pointing to the coldness and formality of people 'who always ask you why you *don't* come, and never say *do*'.[22]

Here, Dickens offers a damning indictment of the notion of neighbourliness whereby difference – what is unique rather than what is held in common – assumes importance as the characteristic feature of social life. As a result, the geniality of the first house-owner is emphasised in contrast to the varieties of aggression or aloofness, as well as racial stereotyping, exhibited by the three others. Not surprisingly, this caricature turns physiognomy on its head, so to speak, deeming differences between appearances to be the ground for social alienation and a notable absence of commonality. Lavater, on the other hand, sought to establish the similarities that can be gleaned from differences:

Physiognomic norms 109

[T]his physiognomical sensation is ever combined with a lively perception of what is beautiful, and what is deformed; of what is perfect and what imperfect. . . . How does my heart glow at the supposition that so high a sense of the sublime and beautiful, so deep an abhorrence of the base and deformed, shall be excited; that all the charms of virtue shall actuate the man who examines physiognomically; and that he who, at present, has a sense of those charms, shall, then, so powerfully, so delightfully, so variously, so incessantly, be impelled to a still higher improvement of his nature![23]

Beauty and deformity, perfection and imperfection, sublime and beautiful compared to base and deformed – these are the terms of Lavater's language of norms. We may see differently as individuals, but, he suggested, the establishment of a normative understanding of character (derived from types and their deviations) would allow for the translation of individual distinctiveness into a range of common types. In this way, the achievement, if that does not express it too strongly, of Lavater's teachings was to define the different types of physiognomic profiles and classify them in a representative framework that reduced complex (individual) features to simple (normal) types in the name of improving man's nature.

II

That the physiognomical tradition of the first two-thirds of the nineteenth century found a natural relation in the eugenics movement of the last third has been well documented.[24] The conventions of physiognomy, with the emphasis on natural types and unnatural deviations, clearly inform and inflect the development of Francis Galton's theory of eugenics.[25] For instance, a paper presented by Galton to the Sociological Society in 1904 explained that 'eugenics is the science which deals with all influences that improve the inborn qualities of a race; also with those that develop them to the utmost advantage'.[26] But while the essentialism that underpinned the practice of physiognomy is evident in the reference to 'inborn qualities', it is neatly referenced to the identification of 'influences', which might help to foster improvement, development and, ultimately, advantage in a race. This rather nebulous notion of 'influences' seems to be key to understanding how the term 'normal' becomes index-linked to health and impairment – because, as in physiognomy, the relation of external form to internal substance is paramount in constructing normative types but, unlike in physiognomy, the identification of types is explicitly directed towards advancement through the social range (rather than simply affirmation of it). It follows, then, that Galton's intellectual project aimed to improve the good and admirable qualities of an individual in terms not of morals but of civic usefulness:

110   *Lucy Hartley*

[S]ociety would be very dull if each man resembled the highly estimable Marcus Aurelius or Adam Bede. The aim of Eugenics is to represent each class or sect by its best specimens; that done, leave them to work out their common civilizations.[27]

The lesson is clear: 'best specimens' need to be encouraged to flourish by natural or artificial methods in order to enable the construction of 'common civilizations'.

Yet for all the similarities between Galton's eugenic ideas and the physiognomic tradition, there were also distinct differences. In the first place, Galton advocated the importance of intellectual progress espoused, in particular, by Herbert Spencer; and in the second, he applied the Darwinian principle of natural selection to explain social groupings as the product of fitness.[28] Spencer proposed a law of mental progress (or intelligence) in *Principles of Psychology* (1855) as follows:

It is a dominant characteristic of Intelligence, viewed in its successive stages of evolution, that its processes, which, as originally performed, were not accompanied with a consciousness of the manner in which they were performed, or of their adaptation to the ends achieved, become eventually both conscious and systematic. . . . Thus children reason, but do not know it. Youths know empirically what reason is, and when they are reasoning. Cultivated adults reason intentionally, with a view to certain results. The more advanced of such presently inquire after what manner they reason. And finally, a few reach a state in which they consciously conform their reasonings to those logical principles which analysis discloses.[29]

The development from childhood to youth to adulthood is marked in terms of increasing consciousness of the reasoning process, from having the ability to reason to the awareness of actually reasoning. Compare this to the opening page of Galton's *Hereditary Genius* (1869), which laid out the conditions for an investigation of the laws of inheritance:

I shall show that social agencies of an ordinary character, whose influences are little suspected, are at this moment working towards the degradation of human nature, and that others are working towards its improvement. I conclude that each generation has enormous power over the natural gifts of those that follow, and maintain that it is a duty we owe to humanity to investigate the range of that power, and to exercise it in a way that, without being unwise towards ourselves, shall be the most advantageous to future inhabitants of the earth.[30]

The rhetoric of this statement is hugely important, as Galton identifies hidden and powerful forces 'of an ordinary character' at work in society,

Physiognomic norms 111

capable of degrading or improving human nature, and so he appeals to a sense of moral obligation to emphasise that which is beneficial to 'future inhabitants of the earth' over that which is detrimental. The similarity of sentiment between Galton and Lavater is clearly evident, yet a difference in approach is also discernible, for Galton sets out not only to define the 'degraded' as compared to the 'advantageous', but also to regulate the activity of the former in order to encourage that of the latter.

Of course, contemporary debates about the progress of the intellect (and the moral sense) were hugely contentious, mainly, but not exclusively, because of the impact of Darwin's theory of evolution by means of natural selection.[31] The Darwinian thesis depended on the selective process; that is to say, change in social groups (or species) as a result of natural selection occurred through the evolution of instinctive responses intended to preserve the welfare of the community – those best able to express their moral impulses and perform behaviour appropriate for the benefit of the group were the most likely to survive. The moral feeling that prompted altruistic acts, and also caused pain when obligations were ignored, was responsible for the formation of social groups among animals, Darwin contended, as it enabled mutual cooperation and functional activity within the group, so allowing it to evolve at a level above that of egoistic individuals. Therefore, a description of human nature for Darwin necessarily involved consideration of the moral sense, which he claimed was a strain of social instinct. Indeed, he considered mental ability to be more or less equivalent within specific social groups, like the one formed by his contemporaries at Cambridge, and hard work and sustained effort caused only minor intellectual differences.

Axiomatic to the eugenic approach to human nature, and especially character, was a strongly utilitarian agenda that deemed it a matter of civic responsibility to separate the 'unfit' from the 'fit', as the 'unfit' (or 'degraded') upset the balance and proportion of society and so ought to be removed from its operations. It was well known that farmers and gardeners could create permanent breeds of animals and plants that were strong in particular characteristics. Galton believed that human stock might be improved in the same way if the strength of a specific quality of character, such as 'health, energy, ability, manliness and courteous disposition' as well as 'special aptitudes ... artistic faculties ... fearlessness of inquiry ... religious absorption', could be preserved, and possibly even improved, via selective reproduction.[32] His aim was to establish a system of social selection founded on a normative understanding of human nature derived from the basic rules of breeding, which would improve the races of man by presenting a practical way of measuring the usefulness of a nation's citizens.[33] It is noticeable that Galton's lecture on eugenics calls for 'the useful classes in the community to contribute more than their proportion to the next generation'; and he goes on to explain the need for a 'historical inquiry into the rates with which the various classes of society (classified according to civic

112 Lucy Hartley

usefulness) have contributed to the population at various times, in ancient and modern nations'.[34]

Central to the Galtonian project of improvement was a study of heredity, started in the 1860s and pursued throughout his career, which investigated the transmission of mental ability in human beings. Galton's first published essay, 'Hereditary Talent and Character' (1865), was intended to show the heritability of intellect: a pronounced mental talent would, he said, be evident in the various generations of a family, because an aptitude for science, mathematics, law, literature and painting was the result of the biological transmission of specific aspects of mind and character.[35] Galton examined a number of sources to substantiate his nascent theory, including the biographical dictionaries of distinguished people, the roll of past presidents of the British Association, lists of lord chancellors, and also lists of senior classics professors at Cambridge, and he discovered that the men noted seemed frequently to have quite close relatives who also had a pronounced intellectual ability. The implication was clear: '[W]hen a parent has achieved great eminence, his son will be placed in a more favourable position for advancement, than if he had been the son of an ordinary person.'[36] This distinction between ordinary and exceptional kinds bears a close resemblance to Lavater's comparison of the moral (intellectual) with the ideal Grecian types, but there is, of course, a third term missing from these classificatory schemes, for the binary division of 'this' type from 'that' one requires a negative 'other' to underline its force. Thus, Lavater distinguished between the abnormal, the normal and the ideal, while Galton configured these terms as the degraded, the ordinary and the exceptional. These three classificatory types provided the foundations of Galton's eugenic teachings, and the role of intelligence was especially important in measuring the degree of human development.

The fullest exposition of this theory can be found in *Inquiries into Human Faculty and Its Development* (1883), which investigated the 'varied hereditary faculties of different men, and . . . the great differences in different families and races' in order to uncover the 'practicability of supplanting inefficient human stock by better strains . . . thus exerting ourselves to further the ends of evolution more rapidly and with less distress than if events were left to their own course'.[37] Using a division of moral and intellectual faculties from physical ones that recalls Lavater's 'threefold life', Galton commenced his study with an analysis of the physical – features, bodily qualities and energy – followed by the moral and the intellectual – mental imagery, number forms, nurture and nature, associations. Yet, unlike Lavater, Galton showed no interest in claiming 'physiognomical sensation' as the special talent of an enlightened observer. He argued that the weakness of existing modes of facial analysis (and discrimination) meant that although the many differences in facial features enable us to recognise familiar faces amid a crowd of strangers, these differences are so numerous and small that they seem to elude measurement:

Physiognomic norms 113

[I]t is impossible ... to discover by ordinary statistical methods the true physiognomy of a race. The usual way is to select individuals who are judged to be representatives of the prevalent type, and to photograph them; but this method is not trustworthy, because the judgement itself is fallacious. It is swayed by exceptional and grotesque features more than by ordinary ones, and the portraits supposed to be typical are likely to be caricatures.[38]

Galton's objection to the construction of a common physiognomic type was connected to the process of selection of individuals judged to be representative of a specific characteristic. A subjective process of this kind could never escape the partiality and prejudice of the person judging, and so Galton sought a method of representation that was objective and impartial, replacing individual judgement with a composite machine that constructed similar and different types.

Setting aside momentary and accidental expressions as having little social value, Galton concentrated instead on the identification of different facial types (rather than individual features), for

the moral and intellectual wealth of a nation largely consists in the multifarious variety of the gifts of the men who compose it, and it would be the very reverse of improvement to make all its members assimilate to a common type.[39]

The frontispiece to *Inquiries into Human Faculty* (Figure 5.2) is presented as an illustration of how composite portraiture might solve 'the difficulty of procuring truly representative faces'.[40] The composite method appeared to offer an alternative approach to the construction of norms, both more robust than the often idiosyncratic observations evident in Lavater's teachings and, at the same time, less straightforward to interpret. Composite portraiture worked, quite literally, by collecting full-face photographic portraits, reduced to the same size, and securing them on separate pages of a blank book before photographing each page of the book in rapid succession without moving either the camera or the sensitised plate. The specimens presented by Galton were divided into eight different composite types – of Alexander the Great, two sisters, six members of one family, 23 Royal Engineers, 15 cases of tubercular disease, 12 cases of criminal types, and 56 consumptive and 150 non-consumptive cases – and grouped according to three main categories: 'Personal and family', 'Health, disease, criminality' and 'Consumption and other maladies'. The composite images were designed to emphasise the points that can be found in common from a range of different facial features, and, he explained, 'there are so many traits in common in all faces that the composite picture when made from many components is far from being a blur; it has altogether the look of an ideal composition.[41]

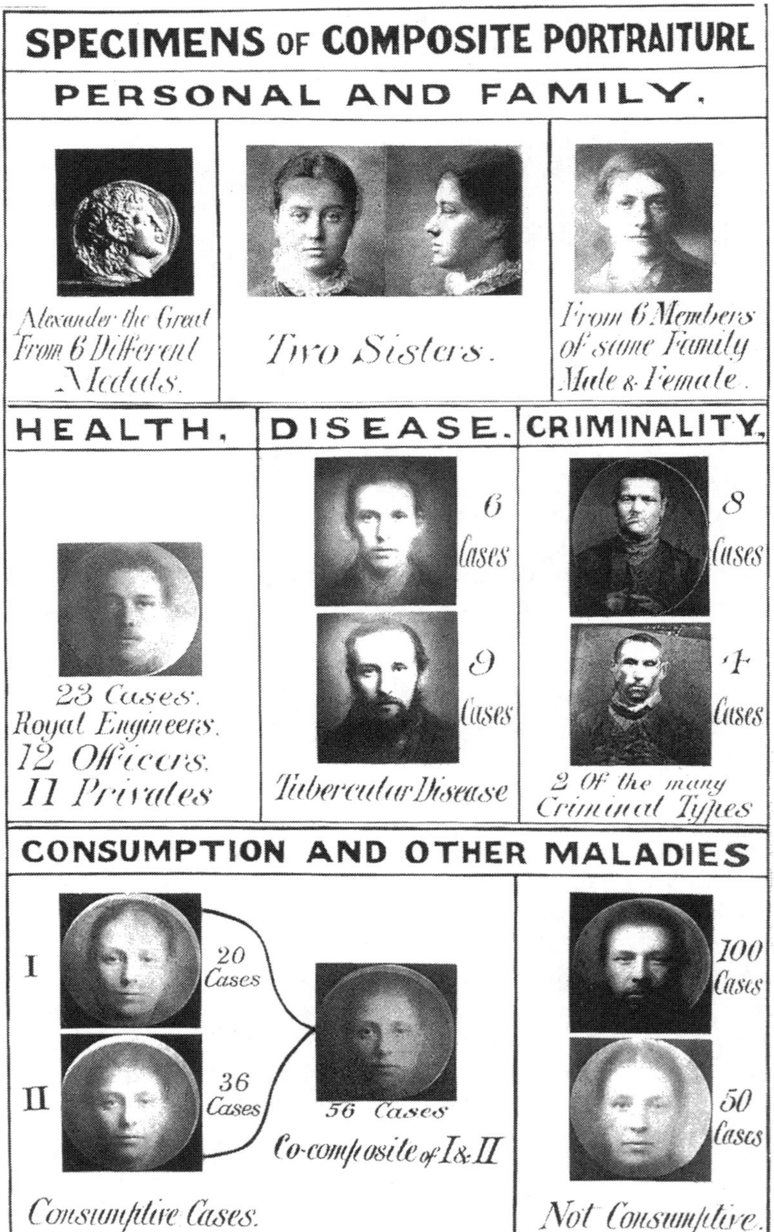

SPECIMENS OF COMPOSITE PORTRAITURE

PERSONAL AND FAMILY.

Alexander the Great From 6 Different Medals.

Two Sisters.

From 6 Members of same Family Male & Female.

HEALTH. DISEASE. CRIMINALITY,

23 Cases. Royal Engineers. 12 Officers. 11 Privates

6 Cases

9 Cases

Tubercular Disease

8 Cases

4 Cases

2 Of the many Criminal Types

CONSUMPTION AND OTHER MALADIES

I *20 Cases*

II *36 Cases*

56 Cases Co-composite of I & II

Consumptive Cases.

100 Cases

50 Cases

Not Consumptive.

Figure 5.2 Frontispiece from Francis Galton, *Inquiries into Human Faculty and its Development* (London, Macmillan, 1883), Wellcome Library, London.

Galton believed that the coherence of a race depended on the construction of a common type, crafted from the resemblances in the facial characteristics of a specific group of individuals. Where they were once a race characterised by 'high cheek-bones, long upper lips, thin eyebrows, and lank dark hair', the English are now, Galton claimed, 'a fair and reddish race' who contrast in physical stature and appearance with previous generations; thus, the 'types best adapted to prevail now' would not be the best adapted to prevail in previous periods of English history.[42] In an ideological system where the imperative was improvement towards the ideal – the healthiest stocks, the most suitable races and the best strains of blood – the aim was to select out as many examples of inferior variations as possible so as to allow the superior forms to flourish. Take the middle row of composites, representing 'Health, disease, and criminality': it contains examples of high physical types, diseased types, and 'coarse and low' criminal types. The composite of the Royal Engineers exemplifies health (not impairment), and so, Galton says, 'this face and the qualities it connotes probably gives a clue to the direction in which the stock of the English race might be improved'.[43] In other words, those who 'conform most nearly to the central type' should be encouraged to reproduce as a means towards the improvement of the human race, whereas 'those who deviate widely from it' should be restrained from reproductive activity.[44] This is a deceptively simple picture of human development; the use of composites to establish a normative typology provided 'pictorial statistics', which were intended to give us 'generic pictures of man ... the pictorial equivalents of those elaborate statistical tables out of which averages are deduced'.[45] Yet as Alan Sekula has persuasively argued, this sort of photographic portraiture is 'a double system: a system of representation capable of functioning both *honorifically* and *repressively*'.[46] Thus, degraded types are always held out as the measure against which the exceptional ones are calibrated, with the former designated as disagreeable and the latter desirable. Sekula concludes that the use of photography, specifically, to construct a normative typology can be seen 'to establish and delimit the terrain of the *other*, to define both the *generalized look* – the typology – and the *contingent instance* of deviance and social pathology'.[47]

III

In a series of lectures delivered at the Collège de France in 1974–5, and recently translated into English with the title of *Abnormal* (2003), Michel Foucault explores the scope and significance of the emergence of the abnormal individual in the nineteenth century.[48] Focusing on legal and penal institutions – as is now familiar to us from his other work on these subjects, especially *Discipline and Punish* (1977)[49] – Foucault examines

the emergence of the power of normalization, the way in which it has been formed, the way in which it has established itself without ever

116 *Lucy Hartley*

resting on a single institution but by establishing interactions between different institutions, and the way in which it has extended its sovereignty in our society.[50]

In the second lecture he identifies the two main models used to control individuals in the Western world: on the one hand, the 'exclusion of lepers' and, on the other, the 'inclusion of plague victims'.[51] These models are significant, Foucault suggests, because they illustrate two very different social responses to matters of public health (with opposing spatial organisations). It is noteworthy, according to Foucault, that the reaction to leprosy was a negative one, so boundaries were set premised on the importance of exclusion and alienation and rejection, whereas the reaction to the plague was more positive, thus inspections were established based on the need for observation and knowledge and power. Keeping the undesirable victims of leprosy out of the town reveals a principle of hygienic purification at work that divides the population into pure as opposed to impure. But, Foucault explains,

> With the plague there is no longer a sort of grand ritual of purification, as with leprosy, but rather an attempt to maximize the health, life, longevity, and strength of individuals. Essentially, it is a question of producing a healthy population rather than of purifying those living in the community, as in the case of leprosy. Finally, you can see that there is no irrevocable labelling of one part of the population but rather constant examination of a field of irregularity within which each individual is constantly assessed in order to determine whether he conforms to the rule, to the defined norm of health.[52]

Foucault then goes on to identify the three different figures or types of the 'abnormal' in the nineteenth century – that is, the 'human monster', the 'individual to be corrected' and the 'masturbator' – and their treatment at the hands of the medical and legal professions. However, he contends throughout the lectures that it is the inclusive model of the plague, with assimilation as a means of exercising control, that marks the beginning of a new, and distinctively modern, discourse of power: '[W]e pass from a technology of power that drives out, excludes, banishes, marginalizes, and represses, to a fundamentally positive power that fashions, observes, knows, and multiplies itself on the basis of its own effects'.[53]

There are clear connections between Foucault's conception of the plague as 'fundamentally positive' and Durkheim's notion of the criminal as 'normal'.[54] Both writers propose assimilatory systems where the 'abnormal', whether conceived as criminal or plague victim, functions as an integral part of the establishment and understanding of the 'normal'. The 'abnormal' is, in effect, that which calibrates the 'normal', establishing the conditions upon which a standard or pattern can be constructed. So, unlike Sekula, who posits the

Physiognomic norms   117

'normal' in opposition to the 'other' as 'generalized look' and 'contingent instance', therefore constructing a system based on alienation and exclusion, for Durkheim and Foucault the 'abnormal' is figured as complementary to the 'normal'. Something of the same impulse to construct types along normative lines has been evident in our historical examples. We have seen that an understanding of character and its typology was important to descriptions of human nature throughout the nineteenth century, in the form of both physiognomic profiles of 'higher' and 'lower' types, and eugenic composites of 'advantageous' and 'degraded' types. In effect, Lavater attempted to isolate the range of physiognomic profiles or common types in everyday life, while Galton worked to identify those individual types who did (and those who did not) make a contribution to civic society. Perhaps as importantly, though, the eugenic notion of 'civic usefulness', underscored by the physiognomic approach to character, speaks directly to what has come to be conceived as one of the most pressing issues of the twenty-first century concerning liberty and security: that is to say, how can 'abnormal' types be identified so that their activity can be controlled while 'normal' types can enjoy freedom?

Physiognomy, in the form proposed by Lavater, may not have provided a solution to this question, but its teachings relied on three related assumptions that would subsequently inform the eugenic solution. Physiognomic teachings suggested, first, that there are essential categories for understanding human nature, and especially character; second, that the appearances of individuals can be divided into the 'virtuous' (or 'normal') types and the 'vicious' (or 'abnormal') ones; and third, that a distinction ought to be drawn between privileged subjects who look and innocent objects who are looked at. At best, then, physiognomy proffered an explanation of human nature in terms of the common type, which worked by translating particular observations into general theories of character. At worst, it could be dismissed as a naive practice of interpretation, more akin to fortune-telling than to science, and cast as a poor resemblance of its family relations, phrenology and mesmerism. Galton's writings on the conformity of 'ideal average' types appear to affirm the place of these physiognomic assumptions in their descriptions of human nature and character. Yet his application of the theory of hereditary transmission to physiognomic teachings actually allowed him to transform an abstract view of character as type into a physical conception of character as useful and therefore potentially, at least, to be controlled and perhaps even corrected. Throughout *Inquiries into Human Faculty*, he investigated the anthropometrical differences of race, offering psychometric experiments that can be used to record the operations of mind, and suggesting the causes that hinder the 'unlimited improvement of highly-bred animals'.[55] Man has a moral obligation to maintain the natural order of things via improvement, he insisted, so 'furthering the course of evolution. He may use his intelligence to discover and expedite the changes that are necessary to adapt circumstance to race and race to circumstance, and his kindly sympathy will urge him to effect them mercifully'.[56] The most important

118   *Lucy Hartley*

aspect of the improvement of healthy types was its potential to enforce a substantial change in social attitudes and policy, Galton argued.[57]

What, then, can we learn from these historical examples and the cultural currency of debates about character and regulation? Constructions of the common type, such as the physiognomic and eugenic teachings of the nineteenth century presented, not only assumed, consensus but also concealed control. The kind of knowledge disseminated by these discriminatory practices was predicated on a language of norms that established a social calculus of high–low and advantageous–degraded character types. Yet these types were not constructed according to a model of opposition but rather to one of complement, where the 'abnormal' is part and parcel of the proper functioning of a 'normal' existence, included within the practices of everyday life. From 'common type or standard' to 'healthy, not impaired', the social consequences of the translation of 'normal' into a physical characteristic are now all too evident; for we live in a world that seems to be preoccupied with physical appearance, and that seems also to be increasingly concerned to classify individuals according to stereotypical understandings of what is or, more usually, what is not seen as 'normal' appearance or actions or conduct. To point out only the most obvious recent example, the Al-Qaeda terrorist attacks on New York on 11 September 2001 seem to have produced political responses of a particularly obnoxious kind from the United States government, though not by any means exclusively, and in the process, momentum has been given to the kind of social agenda that promotes the importance of classification via appearance as a means of attributing political value to, and so legitimating the public regulation of, certain (national and/or racial and/or religious) types. This profiling is, of course, based on the notion that all human beings can be described according to one of two typological categories, either 'normal' types, who usually do not commit crime, or 'abnormal' characters, who usually do. But, as we should all recognise, the health of a nation does not depend on a naive appreciation of character and conduct as types but rests, instead, on an understanding of the complex forces (physical and intellectual, moral and cultural, racial and national) that cannot simply be intuited from appearances.

A small section of this essay first appeared in *Physiognomy and the Meaning of Expression in Nineteenth-Century Culture*, Cambridge, Cambridge University Press, 2001. I am grateful to Cambridge University Press for permission to reprint.

Notes

1   Sander Gilman, *Seeing the Insane*, Lincoln, University of Nebraska Press, 1982, p. i.
2   *The Compact Oxford English Dictionary*, 2nd edn, Oxford, Clarendon Press, 1991.
3   Emile Durkheim, 'The Normal and the Pathological', *Social Deviance: Readings in Theory and Research*, ed. Henry N. Pontell, Englewood Cliffs, NJ, Prentice

Hall, 1993, p. 45. The fullest exposition of these ideas can be found in Durkheim's *The Rules of Sociological Method*, 1895, trans. S. A. Solovay and J. H. Mueller, Chicago, University of Chicago Press, 1938. See also Robert Alun Jones, *Emile Durkheim: An Introduction to Four Major Works*, Beverly Hills, CA, Sage, 1986, for a summary of Durkheim's intellectual project.

4 Durkheim, 'The Normal and the Pathological', p. 46.

5 My earlier work has traced the significance of the physiognomical tradition for the rise of new physiological doctrines about the expression of emotion; see *Physiognomy and the Meaning of Expression in Nineteenth-Century Culture*, Cambridge, Cambridge University Press, 2001.

6 Johann Caspar Lavater, 'On the Harmony between Moral and Corporeal Beauty', *Essays on Physiognomy: Designed to Promote the Knowledge and Love of Mankind. Written in the German Language by John Caspar Lavater, and Translated into English by Thomas Holcroft. To which are added one hundred physiognomical rules, a posthumous work by Mr. Lavater: and 'Memoirs of the Life of the Author', compiled principally from 'The Life of Lavater'*, by G. Gessner, 5th edn, London, William Tegg, 1848, p. 100. References throughout this essay will be to this edition.

7 Sander Gilman, *Health and Illness: Images of Difference*, London, Reaktion Books, 1995, p. 66.

8 The contours of the early history of physiognomy are outlined by Elizabeth C. Evans in 'Physiognomics in the Ancient World', *Transactions of the American Philosophical Society*, 1969, 59, pp. 5–97.

9 See Charles C. Gillispie, *Genesis and Geology: A Study in the Relations of Scientific Thought, Natural Theology, and Social Opinion in Great Britain, 1790–1850*, Cambridge, MA, Harvard University Press, 1951; and more recently Adrian Desmond, *The Politics of Evolution: Morphology, Medicine and Reform in Radical London*, Chicago, University of Chicago Press, 1989; L. S. Jacyna, 'The Physiology of Mind, the Unity of Nature, and the Moral Order in Victorian Thought', *British Journal of the History of Science*, 1981, 14, pp. 109–32; and 'Immanence or Transcendence: Theories of Life and Organization in Britain', *Isis*, 1983, 74, pp. 311–29.

10 Susan F. Cannon, *Science in Culture: The Early Victorian Period*, New York, Dawson and Science History Publications, 1978; David Knight, *The Age of Science: The Scientific World-View in the Nineteenth Century*, Oxford, Blackwell, 1996; and James Moore, ed., *History, Humanity and Evolution: Essays for John C. Greene*, Cambridge, Cambridge University Press, 1989.

11 There is a huge literature on these debates, but those with most relevance to this study include John W. Burrow, *Evolution and Society: A Study in Victorian Social Theory*, Cambridge, Cambridge University Press, 1966; William Coleman, *Biology in the Nineteenth Century: Problems of Form, Function, and Transformation*, New York, John Wiley, 1972; and Robert M. Young, *Darwin's Metaphor: Nature's Place in Victorian Culture*, Cambridge, Cambridge University Press, 1985.

12 The 'Address' to the fifth edition of Lavater's work explained that the production of yet another edition was justified by the need for a volume that combined 'uniformity, economy and portability . . . rendering it at once a book of utility, amusement, and instruction, suited to the man of intellect, study, and taste'. For details of the publication history of Lavater's famous work, see John C. Graham, 'Lavater's *Physiognomy* in England', *Journal of the History of Ideas*, 22, 1961, pp. 561–72.

13 There is an extensive literature on Lavater's famous work, most but not all of which concentrates on the application of physiognomic ideas to literary and artistic subject matter in the nineteenth century. See, for instance, Mary Cowling, *The Artist as Anthropologist: The Representation of Type and Character in Victorian Art*, Cambridge, Cambridge University Press, 1989; John Graham,

120   *Lucy Hartley*

Lavater's *'Essays on Physiognomy'*: *A Study in the History of Ideas*, Bern, Peter Lang, 1979; Christopher Rivers, *Face Value: Physiognomical Thought and the Legible Body in Marivaux, Lavater, Balzac, Gautier, and Zola*, Madison, University of Wisconsin Press, 1994; Ellis Shookman, ed., *The Faces of Physiognomy: Interdisciplinary Approaches to Johann Caspar Lavater*, Columbia, NY, Camden House, 1993; and Graeme Tytler, *Physiognomy in the European Novel: Faces and Fortunes*, Princeton, NJ, Princeton University Press, 1982.

14 Lavater, *Essays on Physiognomy*, p. 11.

15 See Roger Smith, 'The Background of Physiological Psychology in Natural Philosophy', *History of Science*, 1973, xi, pp. 75–123, as well as the dissertation from which this article is drawn, 'Physiological Psychology and the Philosophy of Nature in Mid-Nineteenth Century Britain', PhD Dissertation, University of Cambridge, 1970. Also invaluable is his edition of the *Fontana History of the Human Sciences*, London, HarperCollins, 1997.

16 Smith, *Fontana History*, p. 7.

17 Lavater, 'Of the Rarity of the Spirit of Physiognomical Observation', *Essays on Physiognomy*, pp. 57–8.

18 Ibid., p. 61.

19 Ibid., p. 62.

20 Lavater, 'Of the Universality of Physiognomical Sensation', *Essays on Physiognomy*, p. 32.

21 Charles Dickens, *Sketches by Boz: Illustrations of Every-Day Life and Every-Day People*, London, Chapman and Hall, 1836, p. 58.

22 Ibid., p. 59.

23 Lavater, 'Of the Advantages of Physiognomy', *Essays on Physiognomy*, p. 43.

24 Studies of Galton tend to concentrate on his eugenicist ideas at the expense of his debt to the physiognomic tradition, but see, in particular, Daniel J. Kevles, *In the Name of Eugenics: Genetics and the Uses of Human Heredity*, Harmondsworth, UK, Penguin, 1986; Karl Pearson, *The Life, Letters, and Labours of Francis Galton*, 2 vols, Cambridge, Cambridge University Press, 1924; Daniel Pick, *Faces of Degeneration: A European Disorder, c.1848–c.1918*, Cambridge, Cambridge University Press, 1989; and Ruth Schwartz, *Sir Francis Galton and the Study of Heredity in the Nineteenth Century*, New York, Garland, 1984.

25 In a lengthy note Galton explained that the term 'eugenics' was helpful in expressing 'the science of improving stock, which is by no means confined to questions of judicious mating, but which, especially in the case of man, takes cognisance of all influences that tend in however remote a degree to give to the more suitable races or strains of blood a better chance of prevailing over the less suitable than they otherwise would have had'. *Inquiries into Human Faculty and Its Development*, London, Macmillan, 1883, p. 25.

26 Francis Galton, 'Eugenics: Its Definition, Scope and Aims', *American Journal of Sociology*, 1904, 10, 1, pp. 1–25, p. 1.

27 Ibid., p. 2.

28 Galton published widely throughout his life on a number of topics related to inheritance; in addition to the above, see 'Hereditary Talent and Character', *Macmillan's Magazine*, 1865, 12, pp. 157–66, 318–27; 'Hereditary Improvement', *Fraser's Magazine*, 1873, 7, pp. 116–30; *English Men of Science: Their Nature and Nurture*, London, Macmillan, 1874; *Natural Inheritance*, London, Macmillan, 1889; *Memories of My Life*, 3rd edn, London, Methuen, 1909; *Essays in Eugenics*, London, Eugenics Education Society, 1909.

29 For a more detailed account of Spencer's work, see John C. Greene, 'Biology and Social Theory in the Nineteenth Century: Auguste Comte and Herbert Spencer', in M. Claggett, ed., *Critical Problems in the History of Science*, Madison, University of Wisconsin Press, 1959, pp. 419–46, and Robert M. Young, *Mind, Brain, and*

Physiognomic norms 121

Adaptation in the Nineteenth Century, Oxford, Oxford University Press, 1971, chap. 5.

30 Francis Galton, *Hereditary Genius: An Inquiry into its Laws and Consequences*, London, Macmillan, 1869, p. 1.

31 See note 8 above, and also Peter J. Bowler, *Theories of Human Evolution: A Century of Debate, 1844–1944*, Baltimore, Johns Hopkins University Press, 1986, and Robert J. Richards, *Darwin and the Emergence of Evolutionary Theories of Mind and Behavior*, Chicago, University of Chicago Press, 1987.

32 Galton, *Hereditary Genius*, p. 38.

33 See John R. Durant, 'The Meaning of Evolution: Post-Darwinian Debates on the Significance for Man of the Theory of Evolution, 1858–1908', PhD dissertation, University of Cambridge, 1977; and Lyndsay Andrew Farrall, 'The Origins and Growth of the English Eugenics Movement, 1865–1925', PhD dissertation, University of Indiana, 1970.

34 'Eugenics: Its Definition, Scope and Aims', p. 39.

35 Galton opposed the transcendentalist explanation of talent, which Charles Lyell, for example, had suggested occurred as the result of a sudden and dramatic leap in the progress of mind: 'the birth of an individual of transcendent genius, of parents who have never displayed any intellectual capacity above the average standard' was therefore comparable to the shift from 'unprogressive intelligence of the inferior animals' to the 'improvable reason manifested by Man'; see *The Geological Evidences of the Antiquity of Man*, London, John Murray, 1863, pp. 504–5.

36 Galton, 'Hereditary Talent and Character', p. 161.

37 Galton, *Inquiries into Human Faculty*, p. 2.

38 Ibid., pp. 5–6.

39 Ibid., p. 3.

40 Ibid., p. 8.

41 Ibid., p. 10.

42 Ibid., pp. 6–8.

43 Ibid., p. 14.

44 Ibid., pp. 14–15.

45 Galton, 'Generic Images', *Nineteenth Century*, 1879, 6, pp. 162–3. See also the companion pieces: 'On Generic Images: with autotype illustrations', *Proceedings of the Royal Institution*, 1879, 9, pp. 159–65; and 'Analytical Photography', *Nature*, 1890, 18, pp. 381–7.

46 Alan Sekula, 'The Body and the Archive', *October*, 1986, 39, p. 6.

47 Ibid., p. 7.

48 Michel Foucault, *Abnormal: Lectures at the Collège de France, 1974–1975*, ed. Valerie Marchetti and Antonella Salomoni, and trans. Graham Burchell, London, Verso, 2003.

49 Michel Foucault, *Discipline and Punish: The Birth of the Prison*, 1975, trans. Alan Sheridan, London, Penguin, 1977.

50 Foucault, *Abnormal*, p. 26.

51 Ibid., p. 44.

52 Ibid., pp. 46–7.

53 Ibid., p. 48.

54 A similar connection can also be made between the work of Foucault and Georges Canguilhem; see Christiane Sinding, 'The Power of Norms: Georges Canguilhem, Michel Foucault, and the History of Medicine', Frank Huisman and John Harley Warner, eds, *Locating Medical History: The Stories and Their Meanings*, Baltimore, Johns Hopkins University Press, 2004, pp. 262–84.

55 Galton, *Inquiries into Human Faculty*, p. 306.

56 Ibid., pp. 334–5.

57 Ibid., p. 337.

6 Norms and violations
Ugliness and abnormality in caricatures of Monsieur Mayeux

Nicola Cotton

A typical response to the question 'what is ugliness?' might be: 'the opposite of beauty'. I want to reject this binary notion from the outset. As Mark Cousins has argued, ugliness cannot be opposed to beauty in this way, because it does not exist in the register of aesthetics as theorised by Kant, where aesthetic judgements are judgements made exclusively about beauty.[1] The judgement 'This is beautiful', according to Cousins, does not have an opposite: 'The failure to form a judgement of beauty is just that; it is not an assertion of ugliness.'[2] This is because beauty and ugliness call forth different philosophical subjects: a judgement of beauty requires a subject who is entirely disinterested – that is, an impartial viewer whose pronouncements regarding the beautiful are true for everyone. The subject in relation to the ugly, by contrast, can never be disinterested because he or she is always forced to turn away from the ugly object physically or psychologically – or both. If ugliness cannot be explored in terms of traditional aesthetics on the grounds that it precludes a disinterested universal subject, which other areas of thought might prove helpful?

Following the anthropological arguments put forward by William James and Mary Douglas concerning dirt, Cousins defines the ugly as 'matter out of place'.[3] The ugly object is 'an object which is experienced both as being there and as something that should not be there'.[4] In other words, the subject perceives the object as being in 'the wrong place'. Viewed in this way, ugliness is a judgement that arises from a negative relation between the subject and the object. Crucially, however, that relation can only become apparent in the context of a particular situation. In this respect, the ugly object functions as an analogue of dirt: in itself, dirt is just meaningless 'stuff', but when that stuff intrudes on a space where it is not supposed to be – a fly in one's soup, for example – the subject responds to it as to a form of pollution because, as Mary Douglas argues, it threatens 'to confuse or contradict cherished classifications'.[5] There can be no dirt without a system for it to contravene. The fly would not pose a problem if the soup were to be served in a context where insects in food are considered normal. This brings me to my second reason for not exploring ugliness as the opposite of beauty. There is a much more interesting – and more appropriate – discussion to be

Ugliness and abnormality   123

had about the relation between the subject and the ugly object in the context of systems of rules that determine ideas about normality. In the discussion that follows, I propose to explore ugliness as a form of *ab*normality in relation to an aspect of visual culture that can itself be viewed as an art of abnormality: caricature.

Caricature and violations of the norm

Rudolf Arnheim argues that the particular significance of caricature is that it is 'a spectacular demonstration of expression by deviation', which can be likened to a 'pathological' symptom of how art in general makes its points.[6] The psychology of deviation is such, according to Arnheim, that 'just as a tilted rectangle is seen as a deviation from an upright one, each feature of the human body owes its expression to the deviation from norms that are inherent in perception'.[7] Not all morphological deviations result in caricatures, however. Arnheim describes how simple variations of the standard Cartesian coordinates in the work of the naturalist and mathematician D'Arcy Thompson (1860–1948) result in a study of different species where the choice of norm is arbitrary and no one species – to 'the unprejudiced eye', at least – can be seen as a caricature of the other.[8] He contrasts this with the work of the painter and printmaker Albrecht Dürer (1471–1528), who 'considers also irregular deformations of the network, which result in the ugliness of caricature'.[9] Thompson is interested in 'the rules of variation', Arnheim asserts, while Dürer studies 'violations of the norm'.[10]

The choice of language is significant here. Whereas the notion of variation, in theory at least, is neutral and harmless in relation to the norm, the violation associated with the ugliness of caricature implies a willed infringement or attack. The relationship between the ugly and the norm thus appears tense and antagonistic. Arnheim's distinction between variation and violation of the norm is useful because it points to a distinction which in practice is not always easy to make: in human terms, ideas about race (variations) can easily become confused with judgements about ugliness (violations). This confusion raises the key question of where the line between what is considered normal (a simple variation) and what is considered abnormal (a violation) might be drawn.

According to François Ewald, the separation between the normal and the abnormal occurs 'at the point in the relationship between a living entity and its environment where equilibrium is completely disrupted, and the distance between environmental requirements and individual performance becomes too great'.[11]

From the point of view of ugliness, this argument can perhaps best be developed with reference to Erving Goffman's analysis of stigma. For Goffman, 'ugliness ... is a stigma that is focused in social situations'.[12] As with other kinds of stigma, it relates to elements of 'undesired differentness' that are seen by so-called normals to depart negatively from the stereotypical

124 *Nicola Cotton*

cultural category to which it is felt a given person should belong in a given situation.[13] When it comes to judgements about 'physical comeliness', norms take the form of ideals that impose standards against which almost everyone falls short at some stage in their lives.[14] As an example of how the multiplicity of norms disqualifies many people, Goffman cites the only 'complete unblushing male in America' as being 'a young, married, white, urban, northern, heterosexual Protestant father of college education, fully employed, of good complexion, weight and height and a recent record in sports'.[15] Failure on the part of any male to conform to these standards will result, if only momentarily, in a feeling of inferiority. Goffman's list, of course, refers to norms that are culturally and historically specific – those operative in twentieth-century America – but the same principle holds true for other contexts, since what is at issue is the general process of normalisation and the position of an individual at a given time in relation to it.

In France the process of normalisation becomes apparent, according to Michel Foucault, in the eighteenth century when its effects begin to multiply in the fields of education, medicine and industrial production. Following the philosopher Georges Canguilhem (1904–95), Foucault defines the norm as a polemical concept with a capacity to make demands on people and to coerce them into behaving in certain ways. As such, far from being a natural law, it carries within it a pretension to power. The 'modern' notion of abnormality – a broadly post-revolutionary phenomenon, in Foucault's lectures on the subject – derives from the traditional normalising powers of medical knowledge and judicial authority.[16] As a hybridised instance of 'medico-legal expertise', it both gives rise to and seeks to control a new category of person: the individual who is abnormal, rather than the criminal (who is subject to the power of the judicial system) or the sick person (whose health is monitored by the medical establishment).[17] A fundamental characteristic of this new technique of power is that it operates from within. Instead of excluding abnormality (as would have been the case historically for the leper), the technique of normalisation incorporates it according to the 'plague' model:

> It is not a question of exclusion, but one of quarantine. It is not a question of driving out, but on the contrary of establishing, fixing, granting a space, assigning places, defining presences – presences, moreover, that are subject to strict control.[18]

The principle of normalisation, then, is to contain abnormality in order to control it.[19]

Foucault proposes a grand model for human abnormality: the figure of the monster. Contained within this overarching figure are a number of sub-categories of monstrosity, most notably in the present context that of King Louis XVI, from whom, Foucault argues, all human monsters are descended.[20] The essence of the monster is that it combines categories in

Ugliness and abnormality 125

such a way that it does not conform to 'the law'. From the Middle Ages to the eighteenth century the monster was something that transgressed the law of nature – a mixture of the human and the animal, for example. The modern monster, however, disturbs civil, canonical and religious law as well. It is defined more by aberrant behaviour than by irregular appearance. At the end of the eighteenth century, Foucault argues, the figure of 'natural irregularity' is overtaken by that of the moral monster, personified by the tyrannical, incestuous monarch, and memorably represented in the work of Sade.

In visual terms, if we recall Arnheim's definition of caricature, the modern monster is not so much a deviation from as a violation of the norm. Indeed, Foucault's argument, despite its juridical basis, explicitly makes a connection with caricature by drawing attention to the way in which, in the West, the point of origin of power – the king – is effectively 'disqualified' by his physical manifestation. Instead of standing as a figure of dignity and majesty, the monarch appears infamous, ridiculous and grotesque. Foucault's understanding of the term 'grotesque' is quite specific: he uses it to designate the situation in which an individual is invested with the effects of power while possessing none of the intrinsic qualities to suggest he should wield it. As such, the grotesque monarch is seen as 'ubuesque', a term borrowed from Alfred Jarry's scandalous tyrant, King Ubu.[21] The Larousse definition of 'ubuesque', reprinted in *Les Anormaux*, is given as follows: 'Refers to that which recalls the character of Ubu by its grotesque, absurd or caricatural nature.'[22] On this basis, I would suggest, Foucault's monsters appear inherently caricatural, and since caricature is an art of ugliness, they can also be seen as ugly.

The drive to normalise in nineteenth-century Paris

Having established a convergence of discourses of abnormality, monstrosity, ugliness and caricature, I want now to consider them in relation to a specific cultural context: Paris during the first half of the nineteenth century. This was a period of rapid change in the French capital when immigration from the provinces and from abroad almost doubled the population from about half a million to over one million.[23] As a result of this influx, the middle classes who had presided over the heart of the city at the beginning of the century found themselves having to share it with a host of newcomers. In the midst of this demographic upheaval there was a growing preoccupation, obsession even, with recognising and distinguishing social types as a means of fixing identity. Pierre Bourdieu's assertion in *Outline of a Theory of Practice* that in transitional situations seemingly negligible details of social behaviour such as dress, bearing and physical and verbal manners take on particular significance is relevant here, despite its twentieth-century frame of reference.[24] So too is his contention in *Distinction* that 'social identity defines and affirms itself through difference'.[25]

126   *Nicola Cotton*

In nineteenth-century Paris, different elements of middle-class society felt compelled to affirm their adherence to a particular social group, identified by its distinctive habits and mannerisms, by attempting to assert their difference from other, equally distinctive social groups. This tendency to consolidate identity through difference reveals the presence of the norm, which, as François Ewald states, 'is most effective in its affirmation of differences, discrepancies, and disparities'.[26] It would seem that middle-class Parisian culture was engaged in the self-conscious creation of social norms, even though the practice of normalisation was not theorised as such for another hundred years.[27]

Tangible evidence of the drive to normalise during the nineteenth century is to be found in the array of hugely successful publications that aimed to classify people according to type. French editions of Lavater's famous essay on physiognomy, for example, quickly became important reference works for observers of city life, both amateur and professional.[28] Lavater's pseudo-scientific theory that inner moral character could be reliably inferred from external features appealed greatly to anxious Parisians who, in the fluid social space they now inhabited, wanted to know where they stood in relation to their fellow citizens. Balzac too made use of physiognomic principles to create many of the characters in *La Comédie humaine* and to describe the social types in the *Physiologies*: illustrated, semi-comic texts developed by Balzac in the 1830s, which set out to classify humans using the methodology of contemporary zoology. A passage from the self-parodying *Physiologie des physiologies* makes this approach clear:

> Thanks to these little books, filled with science and wit, man will be better classified, better divided, better subdivided than his fellow animals. Each person will know his origin, his species, his family, his kind. Every man will have his allotted space within humanity.[29]

The emphasis in these short texts on identifying social types in a humorous way reveals the serious underlying need within contemporary middle-class society to normalise.[30]

In *Distinction* Bourdieu demonstrates that the social class most acutely aware of the need to hold itself and express itself correctly (i.e. of social norms) in French culture in the 1970s was the petit bourgeoisie. This analysis applies equally to French culture in the nineteenth century, despite the obvious changes in material circumstances. It is no accident, according to Bourdieu, that this group is designated by the adjective *'petit'* (small):

> Small concerns, small needs, the petit-bourgeois is a bourgeois who lives in a small way. Even his bodily hexis, through which his entire objective relationship to the social world is expressed, is that of a man who has to make himself small in order to pass through the narrow gateway to the bourgeoisie.[31]

Ugliness and abnormality   127

Bourdieu characterises the petit bourgeois as strict, sober, discreet, severe in manner of dress and manner of speech, and lacking in stature, breadth and largesse. There is nothing natural about the petit bourgeoisie as Bourdieu describes it, to the extent that it relentlessly models itself on a hyper-correct – and hence, I would argue, distorted or caricatural – set of norms established by the dominant social class. In the nineteenth century, efforts to incorporate the values of that class in an exaggerated way offered rich pickings for the caricaturists.[32] Henry Monnier's *Physiologie du bourgeois* (1832), for example, portrays a bourgeois family in which the wife, obsessed with appearances, insists that her husband wear shirt collars so highly starched that his head resembles a bouquet of flowers. The fussiness of her own toilette shows clear signs that she, too, is trying too hard. Her tendency to overcompensate for that which she is not makes her a caricature of that to which she aspires, namely the status of the *femme comme il faut* – the well-bred woman who succeeds in every respect in appearing 'very proper'.

But who acts as the judge of 'properness'? The impersonality of the phrase *'comme il faut'* is telling. It speaks of a set of rules, or norms, which has no single point of origin, yet is recognised by all those who are, or aspire to be, respectable bourgeois citizens. According to Ewald,

> [i]n a normative order, there is no room for the sovereign. No one can pretend to be the subject that establishes the norm; norms are created by the collectivity without being willed by anyone in particular. The norm is the group's observation of itself: no one has the power to declare it or establish it.[33]

A good illustration of the normalising power of the collectivity and the superfluous nature of the monarch is to be found in France during the reign of Louis-Philippe (1830–48). As a constitutional monarch brought to the throne following the republican July Revolution, Louis-Philippe made a point of dispensing with many of the trappings of office and of dressing down and behaving like one of the citizens he was supposed to represent. *Le roi bourgeois*, as he was known, made every effort to appear 'normal' and so enacted, in a literal way, the relative absence of sovereign power and the corresponding force of norms willed collectively by the dominant social class, namely the bourgeoisie.

One unintended result of Louis-Philippe's efforts to integrate himself with bourgeois society was that the aspects of middle-class existence he set out to imitate were thrown into stark relief. In other words, he succeeded in making certain norms visible because of his inability – as a king – to embody them effortlessly.[34] In this respect, his position relative to bourgeois norms was no different from that of the family in Monnier's *Physiologie*. If we recall Ewald's argument that the separation of the normal from the abnormal occurs at the point when the distance between environmental requirements (in this case bourgeois social norms) and individual performance (that

128   *Nicola Cotton*

of the king and of the bourgeois family) becomes too great, it would seem that, in practice, this distance can be minimal. In the social situation in 1830s and 1840s Paris, which required participants to look and behave in a manner *comme il faut*, even small 'inadequacies' proved highly visible, and almost no one satisfied the criteria in every respect. Indeed, the bourgeois who could claim to be consistently 'proper' was rather like Goffman's unblushing American male – a rare and fleeting entity.

Such widespread failure to realise social norms provided the caricaturists – most famously those working with Charles Philipon at the Maison Aubert – with an endless source of material.[35] However, as the contemporary author, historian and essayist known as Champfleury observed in his *Histoire de la caricature moderne* (1865), 'it is annoying for man to see himself reflected constantly in a mirror that shows nothing but his moral deformities'.[36] This explains in part why fictional caricatures were so successful: they enabled the caricaturists to pursue their attack on the shortcomings of middle-class culture while the public could laugh at images of greed, hypocrisy, vanity and credulity safe in the knowledge that they did not appear to refer to them.[37]

The case of Monsieur Mayeux

One of the most enduring of these caricatures was the infamous Monsieur Mayeux, who featured in the pages of the popular satirical newspapers.[38] It is widely acknowledged that Mayeux was the creation of Charles-Joseph Traviès (1804–59), although Traviès never made such a claim – understandably so, given the objectionable and fiercely critical nature of the character. What distinguished Mayeux from other well-known contemporary caricatural figures, notably Robert Macaire and Monsieur Prudhomme, was the fact that, in his many and varied guises, he served as the embodiment of petit-bourgeois physical and moral imperfections and as such was consistently judged to be ugly.

Alfred de Musset describes how, in addition to having a hunched back, 'this deformed and hideous individual is made up of all the aberrations of nature: the lustful eye of the toad, the long hands of the monkey, the spindly legs of the cretin, all the ignoble vices, all the moral and physical monstrosities'.[39] Such a characterisation is clearly influenced by Romanticism, with its taste for excess, but also by contemporary science and its emphasis on comparative anatomy.[40] The human–animal connection was frequently evident in caricatures of Mayeux, as in Figure 6.2, where he is portrayed as the star of a sideshow attraction. In the foreground, a group of bourgeois look on towards Mayeux, who is dressed as Pierrot and engaged in an angry altercation with a monkey. The similarity of the facial expressions of man and monkey implies an unmistakable physical link, which is intended to be read physiognomically as a sign of similar levels of intelligence. Meanwhile, in the background the sideshow owner points to a poster

Ugliness and abnormality 129

Figure 6.1 'M. Mayeux. Dessiné d'après nature par Hippolyte Robillard' (Mr Mayeux, a life drawing by Hippolyte Robillard') (19 February 1831). Bibliothèque nationale de France, Paris, Cabinet des Estampes, Tf. 52. Robillard was a portrait painter who exhibited in the Paris salons during the 1830s and early 1840s. As Elizabeth Menon observes, the phrase 'dessiné d'après nature' suggests that Mayeux actually sat for the artist; and grotesque forms which appealed to Romantic tastes, and were often found in nature, were also described as being 'after nature'. See Menon, *The Complete Mayeux*, p. 64.

advertising 'Le véritable Mayeux vivant' (the genuine living Mayeux), with Mayeux pictured as a monkey alongside a camel and a hunched, long-billed bird.

Mayeux's complex character was aimed at a sophisticated audience familiar not only with contemporary scientific (or pseudo-scientific) discourse, but also with numerous political and social references. Conceived as a savage

Figure 6.2 'Le célèbre Mayeux, il n'est point empaillé, il est vivant... vous le verrez liant ses cordons de souliers sans es baisser, entrez-vous voir, venez voir, montez voir, vous allez voir...' ('The famous Mayeux: not stuffed, but alive. You will see him tie his shoelaces without bending down. Go in and see, come and see, come up and see, you will see...') (unsigned, 11 June 1831). From *Histoire complette* [*sic*] *de M. Mayeux* no. 54. Bibliothèque nationale de France, Paris, Cabinet des Estampes, Tf. 53.

Ugliness and abnormality 131

indictment of the former revolutionary turned power-hungry petit-bourgeois, his foul-mouthed, lewd behaviour was intended to shock and offend (Figure 6.3).

At the same time, however, he could not be taken too seriously, partly because he was fictional and partly because of the comic tradition to which he belonged: that of Pulcinella, *Punch*, Maccus and Priapus, referred to by Champfleury as 'this deformed, facetious and cynical generation'.[41] Mayeux's obvious physical difference was also a convenient device that disguised the fact that his (often reprehensible) behaviour did not differ from that of many of his 'normal' peers. The dynamics of Mayeux's situation are illustrated in an image by Traviès showing Mayeux in military attire with a *grisette*

Figure 6.3 "Oui Madame Mayeux, j'ai obtenu les suffrages de mes concitoyens, je suis nommé ... ça m'était dû nom de D——!' ('Yes Mrs Mayeux, I received the votes of my fellow citizens, I have been elected ... I bloody deserved it too!') (unsigned, 11 June 1831). From *Histoire complette* [*sic*] *de M. Mayeux* no. 57. Bibliothèque nationale de France, Paris, Cabinet des Estampes, Tf. 53.

(a nineteenth-century term for an attractive working girl) pulling gently on his arm (Figure 6.4). In the background a disgruntled bourgeois man turns to look at the unlikely couple. His expression and puffed-up manly stance betray a sense of outrage that the young woman might prefer to entertain someone like Mayeux rather than someone like himself. The gaze of the bourgeois from the back of the picture is intended to mirror the gaze of a

Figure 6.4 'Out of the question, my dear. I'm on duty now ... Later perhaps...' (Charles-Joseph Traviès, 1831). Bibliothèque nationale de France, Paris.

Ugliness and abnormality   133

possible male bourgeois viewer looking in: both, it is implied, must resent the way in which Mayeux occupies the position for which they consider themselves more eminently suited. But the fact is that such resentment reflects negatively not on Mayeux (who in any case rejects the *grisette*'s advances and so assumes, temporarily at least, the moral high ground), but on the bourgeois onlooker. In this instance the figure of the ugly, abnormal 'outsider' exposes bourgeois respectability – presumed normality – as a pretence.

Writing in the periodical *Le Livre des cent-et-un* in 1831, the social critic Anaïs Bazin placed Mayeux in the tradition of all the hunchbacks to have mocked humanity since Aesop and Thersites. The malformed outsider, he argued, was in fact

> the best judge of the events of our era, the person who seemed to have personified our anger, our enthusiasm, our credulity, the typical man of 1830 and 1831, the mask behind which we could recognise ourselves just as we are without distress because we charged his account, or should I say loaded his back, with all our follies and all our blunders.[42]

In other words, Mayeux performed a specific function as a scapegoat, drawing derisive laughter on to his physical abnormality and so obscuring his moral position as an accurate representative of that society – an insider perceived wrongly as an outsider. In Figure 6.5, for example, Mayeux is seen seated at a table in the dining room of his favoured procuress with two arrogant-looking young bourgeois seated at another table close by. Hunched over more than ever to express a sense of humiliation, Mayeux exclaims: 'Bloody hell, I think those sly young rascals are making fun of me and drawing a caricature of me!' The point is, however, that all three are seated in the same place waiting to entertain the same female company, and Mayeux has no more reason to feel ashamed than the other clients. In passing judgement on Mayeux for his physical appearance, the bourgeois youths unwittingly confirm their own hypocrisy.

Historically, the figure of the scapegoat harks back to the ritual of the *pharmakos* – an ancient ceremony in which the scapegoat, who was explicitly the ugliest man of all, was called upon to fulfil the role of expiation for the sins of the city. At times of crisis, he (and it seems the *pharmakos* was always a man) was cast out, beaten and burned to death in order that the city might be purified. The ritual expulsion of the 'personification of evil' developed into an annual event re-enacted on the sixth day of the festival of Thargelia.[43] In his *Ambiguïté et renversement. Sur la structure énigmatique d'Oedipe-Roi* (1970) J. P. Vernant considers the scapegoat ritual of Thargelia in terms of its 'symmetrical inverse' – the 'institution' of ostracism.[44] Vernant's description of the threat posed to the city from above by Oedipus and from below by the *pharmacos* [*sic*] bears a striking resemblance to Foucault's theory of abnormality in so far as it relates to the dual figure of the

Figure 6.5 'Je crois que ces mâtins-là se f——— de moi et me tirent en caricature, nom de D———!' ('Bloody hell, I think those sly young rascals are making fun of me and drawing a caricature of me!') (unsigned, 30 April 1831). From *Histoire Complette* [sic] *de M. Mayeux* no. 46. Bibliothèque nationale de France, Paris, Cabinet des Estampes, Tf. 53.

outlaw, which comprises the king, who breaks the social pact from above, and the criminal, who breaks it from below.[45] The passage from Vernant reads as follows:

> With the ostracised person, the City expels the person from within who is too elevated and who embodies the harm which might befall it from above. With the scapegoat, it expels its vilest elements and the person who embodies the harm which might come from below. Through this double and complementary rejection, the City sets its own limits in relation to a notion of what is up here and what is down there. It takes the proper measure of the human in opposition to the divine and the heroic on one side and to the bestial and the monstrous on the other.[46]

What emerges from Vernant's text is a clear sense that the institution of ostracism is strongly normative and that it originates from an implied

Ugliness and abnormality 135

middle ground. In relation to French culture in the context of the 1789 Revolution, Foucault locates that middle ground specifically with the bourgeoisie, invoking two monstrous outlaws — the despotic king and the people in revolt — who inhabit the field of anomaly 'according to bourgeois thought and bourgeois politics'.[47] Perceptions of abnormality on which ideas of monstrosity in France are based are determined by the middle classes.

It is significant that after the Revolution, Foucault's two great outlaws give way to a notion of the abnormal person as 'un monstre quotidien, un monstre banalisé' (an everyday monster, a banal monster).[48] With this in mind, Foucault's monstrous monarch and people in revolt (or Vernant's ostracised king and scapegoat) might be recast under the July monarchy as Louis-Philippe and Mayeux respectively. The bourgeois king and the former revolutionary could then represent banal monsters in relation to the 'law' of bourgeois normality. An image of Louis-Philippe with Mayeux as his tailor published in the satirical journal *La Caricature* would appear to support this idea (Figure 6.6). While measuring the length of the king's back, Mayeux observes, 'Vous n'êtes pas grand, mon cher!' The word '*grand*' conveys a double meaning: a literal assessment by the tailor of the king's physique, 'You are not tall, my dear fellow'; and a political judgement, 'You are not a

Figure 6.6 'Vous n'êtes pas grand, mon cher!' (unsigned, *La Caricature*, 26 July 1832). Bibliothèque nationale de France, Paris, Cabinet des Estampes, Tf. 70a.

136   *Nicola Cotton*

great man'. In other words, Mayeux is invoking two sets of norms: first and most obviously the notion of the average body,[49] and second the discourse of republicanism – the latter providing a clear example of Foucault's claim that the norm carries within it a pretension to power. Louis-Philippe lacked stature from the point of view of disillusioned republicans, who condemned him for his failure to deliver on the republican agenda he had proclaimed on his accession. The caricature expresses their disappointment, but also seeks to lay claim to power by reasserting a sense of republican idealism. As for Mayeux, his critique of the king establishes his political credibility despite his diminutive, crooked stature.

Beyond Mayeux: ugliness and modernity

Viewed from a wider perspective, the function of caricatures of Mayeux was to show what was wrong not just with the king, but with middle-class Parisian society under the July Monarchy more generally. Through his failure to realise existing norms physically, morally and politically, Mayeux made those norms visible and, as an insider perceived wrongly as an outsider, presented the bourgeois public with images of its own imperfections in a palatable, entertaining way. In doing so, he made an important contribution to the growing sense of modernity in French culture and the role of ugliness within it. Already, in 1827, Hugo had argued in his famous *Préface de Cromwell* for a modern artistic muse who would recognise that 'creation is not all humanly beautiful, that the ugly exists alongside the beautiful, the deformed alongside the graceful, the grotesque behind the sublime, the wicked with the good, the darkness with the light'.[50]

By the middle of the century the notion of modernity and a desire to capture the essence of the present had become a major preoccupation for Baudelaire. Writing in praise of the work of Constantin Guys (specifically a series of etchings of fashions from the Revolution to the Consulate) as 'the painter of modern life', Baudelaire argued that 'these etchings can be translated as beautiful or as ugly; as ugly they become caricatures; as beautiful, ancient statues'.[51] The modernity of the etchings for Baudelaire lay in the way a sense of eternal beauty could be perceived through the transitory 'ugliness' of outdated fashions and in Guys's unique ability to extricate poetry from history. Baudelaire's own poetry took this modern aesthetic a stage further by combining ideas of ugliness and beauty in the paradoxical and undecidable figure of the beautiful monster, or the monstrous beauty. Significantly, the words '*laid*' (ugly) and '*laideur*' (ugliness) themselves were never used in his poems – quite possibly because they seemed too banal, too trivial and too vulgar. Baudelaire chose to evoke instead the exquisite attractions of '*le mal*' (sorrow, pain, harm, evil), of misfortune, of the bizarre, the enigmatic, the grotesque and the horrible.[52] In the poem 'Petites vieilles', for example (dedicated to Victor Hugo), the little old women of the title are described not as ugly, but as 'dislocated monsters . . . broken, hunchbacked, twisted monsters'.[53] The absence of the word does nothing to lessen the presence of the idea, however. In fact, if anything, this calculated omission strengthens the underlying sense of ugliness.

In Baudelaire's critical writing, meanwhile, references to the ugly appear undisguised: in an 1846 article for *Corsaire-Satan*, for instance, he wrote that 'pleasure in the face of ugliness comes from a mysterious feeling which is the thirst for the unknown and the taste for the horrible'.[54] This thirst for the unknown and taste for the horrible developed as a means of reinvigorating the traditional discourse of aesthetics, which, as the nineteenth century progressed, seemed increasingly jaded and inappropriate to the new culture of mass production and consumption.

The connection made by Baudelaire between the nature of modern life and a profound sense of the ugly was to prove inspirational to the Anglo-American modernist writers of the twentieth century who belonged to what Ezra Pound termed 'the cult of ugliness'.[55] In his essay 'The Serious Artist' (1913), Pound defended the 'delineation of ugliness' in the following terms:

> As there are in medicine the art of diagnosis and the art of cure, so in the arts, so in the particular arts of poetry and of literature, there is the art of diagnosis and there is the art of cure. They call one the cult of ugliness and the other the cult of beauty.
>
> The cult of beauty is the hygiene, it is sun, air and the sea and the rain and the lake bathing. The cult of ugliness, Villon, Baudelaire, Corbière, Beardsley are diagnosis. Flaubert is diagnosis. Satire, if we are to ride this metaphor to staggers, satire is surgery, insertions and amputations.[56]

If we ride the metaphor a little further still, Pound's view of satire might extend beyond poetry and literature to the art of caricature. The insertions and amputations could then refer to the morphological exaggerations of the caricaturist's pen and to images of the hunchbacked M. Mayeux in particular. Although Mayeux was not part of a self-conscious 'cult of ugliness', he played a significant role in the development of a sense of what was wrong with modern culture – specifically, the shortcomings of the Parisian petit bourgeoisie. Images of Mayeux thus constituted an 'art of diagnosis' that enabled the nineteenth-century French public to see, indirectly, what ailed it. There was, of course, an element of frustrated idealism in this, but there was also a sense that the sordid, negative aspects of modern life could be indulged in by the artist and enjoyed by members of the public even as they were being criticised. Such delight in the repulsive both anticipates Baudelaire's aesthetics and looks forward to the modernist discourse of the ugly. Thus, as we have moved away at the beginning of this discussion from the field of traditional aesthetics towards a socio-politics of abnormality viewed in terms of caricature, it would seem that a return to an aesthetics of a different, non-Kantian order – one in which the ugly is granted a privileged position as a powerful source of creativity – is possible. Indeed, one might

138   *Nicola Cotton*

speculate, finally, that an appreciation of ugliness as prefigured by caricatures of Mayeux offers vital insight into the Baudelairean sense of modernity and the nature of the modernist literature that it inspired.

Notes

1 Cousins presented this argument in an inspirational lecture series, 'The Ugly', at the Architectural Association in London during the academic year 1994–5. Cousins's strong psychoanalytic reading of 'The Ugly' is published in the *AA Files*: Part 1, vol. 28 (Autumn 1994), pp. 61–4; Part 2, vol. 29 (Summer 1995), pp. 3–6; Part 3, vol. 30 (Autumn 1995), pp. 65–8.
2 Cousins, *AA files* no. 28, p. 62.
3 William James, Lecture VI, 'The Sick Soul', in *The Varieties of Religious Experience* [1902]. Mary Douglas, *Purity and Danger: An Analysis of the Concept of Pollution and Taboo* [1966], London, Routledge, 2002, p. 44. Cousins, *AA Files* no. 28 p. 63.
4 Cousins, *AA Files* no. 28, p 63.
5 Douglas, *Purity and Danger*, p. 45. The sense of challenging cherished classifications has been memorably represented by the artist Mark Hutchinson. His installation *Leak* (a small army of lifelike rats emerging from a notional hole in the gallery wall to invade the pristine white space above, below and around other artworks) was first shown as part of 'Nausea: Encounters with Ugliness' – an exhibition of contemporary art curated by Mark Hutchinson and Nicola Cotton at the Djanogly Art Gallery in Nottingham in April 2002.
6 R. Arnheim, 'The Rationale of Deformation', *Art Journal*, Winter 1983, pp. 319–24 at p. 321.
7 Ibid.
8 Thompson's most famous work, *On Growth and Form* (1917), seeks to understand plants and animals in terms of mathematics.
9 Arnheim, 'The Rationale of Deviation', p. 321. Dürer's *Four Books on Human Proportions* (1528) stress geometry and measurement as the key to understanding Italian Renaissance art in contrast to the emphasis on observation of real life seen in the fifteenth century in his native Germany.
10 Ibid.
11 François Ewald, 'Norms, Discipline and the Law', translated and adapted by Marjorie Beale, *Representations*, Spring 1990, 30, pp. 138–61 at p. 157. With the exception of this essay, all translations are my own.
12 Erving Goffman, *Stigma: Notes on the Management of spoiled Identity* [1963], London, Penguin, 1990, p. 67.
13 Ibid., p. 15.
14 Ibid., p. 153.
15 Ibid.
16 See M. Foucault, *Les Anormaux: Cours au Collège de France, 1974–1975*, Paris, Gallimard/Le Seuil, 1999, p. 38. (Published in English as *Abnormal: Lectures at the Collège de France, 1974–1975*, ed. Arnold Davidson, trans. Graham Burchell, London, Picador, 2004.)
17 Foucault, of course, has a specific reason for wanting to explore the nature of a third, medico-legal hybridised source of power, namely to understand the history of normalisation as it applies to sexuality.
18 'Il ne s'agit pas d'une exclusion, il s'agit d'une quarantaine. Il ne s'agit pas de chasser, il s'agit au contraire d'établir, de fixer, de donner son lieu, d'assigner des places, de définir des présences, et des présences quadrillés.' Foucault, *Les Anormaux*, p. 43.

Ugliness and abnormality 139

19 Foucault's argument refers to Canguilhem's *Le Normal et le pathologique*, 2nd edn, Paris, Presses univesitaires de France, 1972, pp. 169–222.

20 Up until the beginning of the twentieth century, the monster is one of three distinct discourses of abnormality – the other two being the 'incorrigible' and the onanist. The discourse of the monster is the most important until the end of the twentieth century, when, according to Foucault, that of the onanist comes to the fore.

21 The repulsive, cowardly Ubu was created by Alfred Jarry (1873–1907) as the principal character of his infamous satirical play *Ubu Roi* (1896).

22 'Se dit de ce qui, par son caractère grotesque, absurde ou caricaturale, rappelle le personnage d'Ubu.' Foucault, *Les Anormaux*, p. 26.

23 See James Cuno, 'Violence, satire et types sociaux dans les arts graphiques durant la monarchie de Juillet', in Maria Tersa Caracciolo and Ségolène Le Men, eds, *L'Illustration. Essai d'iconographie. Actes du Séminaire CNRS (GDR 712) Paris 1993–1994*, Paris, Klincksieck, 1999, p. 291. The exact figures cited by Cuno for the increase in population are from 546,846 in 1801 to 1,053,261 in 1851.

24 P. Bourdieu, *Esquisse d'une théorie de la pratique, précédé de trois études d'ethnologie kabyle*, Geneva, Droz, 1972, p. 197.

25 '. . . l'identité sociale se définit et s'affirme dans la différence'. P. Bourdieu, *La Distinction: critique social du jugement*, Paris, Minuit, p. 191.

26 Ewald, 'Norms, Discipline and the Law', p. 154.

27 According to Ewald, the term 'normalisation' dates from the late 1920s. Once identified, however, the concept appeared to apply in retrospect to social development throughout history. See Ewald, 'Norms, Discipline and the Law', p. 148.

28 His study was first published in Germany in 1775–8 and translated into French as *Essai sur la physiognomonie destiné à faire connaître l'homme et à le faire aimer* between 1781 and 1803. Moreau de la Sarthe's highly successful illustrated edition, *L'Art de connaître des hommes par la physionomie*, appeared in 1806–9.

29 'Grâce à ces petits livres, pétris de science et d'esprit, l'homme sera mieux classé, mieux divisé, mieux subdivisé que les animaux ses confrères. Chacun connaîtra: Son origine; Son espèce; Sa famille; Son genre; Chaque homme aura sa case dans l'humanité.' Anon., Paris, Desloges, 1841, pp. 19–20.

30 It is significant that at the height of their popularity during the 1830s to 1850s, half a million copies of the *Physiologies* were sold in Paris to a population of less than one million, of whom half were illiterate. Figures quoted are taken from Judith Wechsler's *A Human Comedy: Physiognomy and Caricature in Nineteenth-Century Paris*, London, Thames & Hudson, 1982, p. 34. For a fuller introduction to the *Physiologies*, see Wechsler, pp. 31–6.

31 'Petits soucis, petits besoins, le petit bourgeois est un bourgeois qui vit petitement. Son hexis corporelle même, où s'exprime toute sa relation objective au monde social, est d'un homme qui doit se faire petit pour passer par la porte étroite qui donne accès à la bourgeoisie'. Bourdieu, *La Distinction*, p. 390.

32 In France in the 1830s, the formation of a non-aristocratic dominant social class was a relatively new (post-1789) phenomenon. Although stratifications soon became apparent within that class, the terms 'petit bourgeois' and 'grand bourgeois' as such did not yet exist.

33 Ewald, 'Norms, Discipline and the Law', p. 155.

34 For a detailed discussion of satirical representations of Louis-Philippe, see Nicola Cotton, 'The Pun, the Pear and the Pursuit of Power in Paris: Caricatures of Louis-Philippe (1830–1835)', *Nottingham French Studies*, 2003, 42, 2, pp. 12–25.

35 These included Honoré Daumier, Henry Monnier and Charles-Joseph Traviès.

36 '[l]'homme s'irrite de trouver sans cesse sa figure réfléchie par un miroir où n'apparaissent que ses difformités morales'. *Histoire de la caricature moderne* [1865],

140 Nicola Cotton

2nd edn, Paris, Dentu, 1871, p. xii. Champfleury's real name was Jules François Félix Husson (1821–89).

37 The other important reason for their success being the fact that, after the 1835 censorship law came into force, images which did not mock real people were less likely to be banned.

38 Mayeux also featured on the stage, inspired characters in literature (e.g. La Mayeux in Eugène Sue's *Le Juif Errant*) and was even fashioned into small figurines. For a comprehensive illustrated account of Mayeux, see Elizabeth K. Menon, *The Complete Mayeux: Use and Abuse of a French Icon*, Berne, Peter Lang, 1998.

39 '. . . ce type difforme et hideux est composé de toutes les aberrations de la nature. L'oeil lubrique du crapaud, les longues mains du singe, les jambes frêles du crétin, tous les vices ignobles, toutes les monstruosités morales et physiques.' 'Revue Fantastique', *Le Temps*, 7 March 1831, p. 2. Quoted in Menon, *The Complete Mayeux*, p. 93, f/n 33.

40 The foremost exponent of comparative anatomy at the time was the zoologist Georges Cuvier (1769–1832). Among other studies, Cuvier co-published with Geoffroy Saint-Hilaire *Histoire naturelle des orangs-outangs* (1795).

41 'cette génération difforme, facétieuse et cynique'. Champfleury, *Histoire de la caricature moderne*, p. 195.

42 '. . . celui qui a le meilleur jugé les événements de notre époque, qui semblait avoir personnifié en lui nos colères, nos enthousiasmes, nos crédulités, le type de 1830 et de 1831, le masque dans lequel, tous tant que nous sommes, nous pouvions sans chagrin nous reconnaître, parce que nous placions sur son compte, je dirais mieux sur son dos, toutes nos folies, toutes nos bévues. A. Bazin, 'Nécrologie', *Paris ou Le Livre des cent-et-un*, 1831, 3, pp. 361–2. Quoted in Champfleury, *Histoire de la Caricature moderne*, 1871, p. 203.

43 See Jacques Derrida, *La Dissemination*, Paris, Seuil, 1979 [1972], p. 152.

44 'Ambiguity and inversion: on the enigmatic structure of King Oedipus'.

45 See Foucault, *Les Anormaux*, pp. 86–97.

46 'Dans la personne de l'ostracisé, la Cité expulse qui en elle est trop élevé et incarne le mal qui peut lui venir par le haut. Dans celle du *pharmacos*, elle expulse ce qu'elle comporte de plus vil et qui incarne le mal qui commence par le bas. Par ce double et complémentaire rejet, elle se délimite elle-même par rapport à un au-delà et un en deçà. Elle prend la mesure propre de l'humain en opposition d'un côté au divin et à l'héroïque, de l'autre au bestial et au monstrueux.' Quoted in Derrida, *La Dissemination*, footnote p. 150.

47 'selon la pensée bourgeoise et la politique bourgeoise'. Foucault, *Les Anormaux*, p. 97.

48 Foucault, *Les Anormaux*, p 53.

49 Further evidence of a conscious drive to normalise in French culture in the 1830s and 1840s is to be found in Alphonse Quetelet's theory of the average man. Such a man does not, in fact, exist; rather, he is a projection of the mean that would occupy the middle of a given distribution. In terms of average height, Quetelet makes an important point: the extreme limits of the distribution, such as giants and dwarfs – and, we might add, hunchbacks – are rare but not anomalous, because they form the necessary outer limits of the total sample. For an introduction to Quetelet's theory, see Ewald, 'Norms, Discipline and the Law', pp. 143–6.

50 '. . . tout dans la création n'est pas humainement *beau*, que le laid y existe à côté du beau, le difforme près du gracieux, le grotesque au revers du sublime, le mal avec le bien, l'ombre avec la lumière'. Victor Hugo, *Préface de Cromwell* [1827], ed. Maurice Souriau, Geneva, Slatkine, 1973, p. 191.

51 '[c]es gravures peuvent être traduites en beau et en laid; en laid elles deviennent

des caricatures; en beau, des statues antiques'. Charles Baudelaire, 'Le Peintre de la vie moderne' (1863), in *Curiosités esthétiques. L'Art romantique et autres œuvres critiques* [1868], ed. Henri Lemaitre, Paris, Garnier, 1962, p. 455.

52 For a more detailed analysis of Baudelaire's aesthetic, see Lydie Krestovsky, *Le Problème spirituel de la beauté et de la laideur*, Paris, Presses Universitaires de France, 1948, pp. 126–36.

53 'monstres disloqués . . . Monstres brisés, bossus, tordus'.

54 'la jouissance devant la Laideur provient d'un sentiment mystérieux qui est la soif de l'inconnu et le Goût de l'Horrible'. Quoted in Krestovsky, *Le Problème spirituel*, p. 133.

55 A comprehensive study of Anglo-American, modernist ugliness in relation to the work of Pound, Eliot, Hulme and Lewis can be found in Lesley Higgins, *The Modernist Cult of Ugliness: Aesthetic and Gender Politics*, Basingstoke, UK, Palgrave Macmillan, 2002.

56 Quoted ibid., p. 122.

7 Made to measure?

Tailoring and the 'normal' body in nineteenth-century France

Alison Matthews David

During the late eighteenth and nineteenth centuries, scientists, administrators, artists and doctors abstracted and depersonalised the human body using a new tool: statistics. As Ian Hacking argues in *The Taming of Chance*, the nineteenth century established the hegemony of statistical measurement as a mode of scientific and social investigation.[1] I am interested in the profound effects this growing determinism had on conceptions of the male body. The Renaissance artist Leonardo da Vinci revived classical canons of bodily proportions based on abstract geometry in his drawing of Vitruvian Man. By contrast, early statisticians such as Adolphe Quetelet mathematically quantified the height, weight and chest measurements of flesh-and-blood populations and used his measurements to calculate bodily means or norms. In effect, he defined the concept of the 'average man'. All individual variations could literally be measured against this normative but abstract body. The quirks of the asymmetrical human being – who had uneven shoulders, a curved spine or a large stomach – became abnormal deviations rather than personal traits. Many contemporary social commentators read these infinite variations as visible markers of the degenerative effects of urban modernity.[2] The depressing 'realities' of these pathological symptoms came into increasing conflict with classical, medical and fashionable models of the ideal body. The contrast between the ideal and the average man was debated in the realms of art, medicine and the military, domains that often overlapped in nineteenth-century discourse.[3] This chapter focuses on the practice of tailoring – a process of production and consumption in which the problem of dressing actual, not ideal, bodies was a constant and compelling concern.

Because of his close contact with the body and the clothing that had to cover it, few male artisans were more interested in minute variations in physical conformation than the tailor.[4] His professional pride rested on his ability to study fashionable silhouettes, conceal asymmetries, flatter deformities and help his customer correspond to the norm in vogue. The study of the nineteenth-century tailoring trade allows me to consider the body from both a post-structuralist and an experiential perspective. Corporeal norms were imposed externally in the form of fashion plates representing the body beautiful and paper patterns designed for an 'average' male body. These norms later found expression in garments made in standardised sizes. At the same time, this standardisation was experienced, often negatively, by many men who felt that they had become impersonal numbers rather than unique customers. The tensions between democratic yet normative principles of sartorial uniformity and more personal needs for individual identity informed the heated debates over tailoring in the nineteenth century.

During the early nineteenth century, tailoring was at the forefront of technological and anthropometric innovation. A mathematically precise fit was central to the marketing of tailoring as an 'exact' science. The intensely competitive commercial environment and race for patents led to the idea of proportionate, geometrically scaled sizes, a principle which a new breed of clothing entrepreneurs appropriated for mass-producing garments. Thus, a profession that now epitomises hand-crafted tradition was in fact instrumental in the industrialisation of clothing production.

The average man

During the 1830s Adolphe Quetelet, founder of the science of statistics, was the first to extrapolate average heights, weights and life expectancies for the general civilian population from records the military had long collected for its own purposes. He was the inventor of the concept of the *homme moyen* (average man), whose height, weight, strength and life expectancy fall exactly within the statistical mean. For him, this average man was the new ideal, a physical manifestation of the new political regime of the *Juste Milieu*, translatable as 'happy medium' or 'golden mean', and of the democratisation of society after the fall of the *Ancien Régime*. He writes:

> This determination of the average man is not merely a matter of speculative curiosity; it may be of the most important service to the science of man and the social system. . . . The average man, indeed, is in a nation what the centre of gravity is in a body.[5]

Statistical ideologies shifted concepts of the unique and individual body to a quantifiable and comparable unit, a stabilising force in the national body.

Though Quetelet used data obtained from records of military conscripts, the average man was a civilian, and statistical averages would soon be applied to regular citizens, especially in medical and orthopaedic discourse. For example, in 1864 the medical practitioner R. Hubert published a printed table, 'Proportions ordinaires du corps humain'.[6] These tables gave proportions at birth and maturity for both men and women in three sizes, 'elongated, ordinary and short'.[7] In addition to height, the tables gave measurements for three sizes, from the circumference of the waist to the distance from the chin to the mouth or the ground to the hips.

In the field of tailoring, the physical results of this impersonal, metrical approach to the human body were wide-ranging. A disgruntled novelist and

144 *Alison Matthews David*

playwright commenting on the products of the clothing industry at the 1867 World's Fair in Paris complained that now everyone was forced to wear the three sizes invented by the military:

> The sculptural age of Staub and Kleber is no more – it died with the well-fitted suit and the frock coat. They have been replaced by the paletot-sack on every man's shoulders. There are no more measurements, there are sizes. Just like the old National Guard, chasseurs, voltigeurs and grenadiers. Metres and centimetres. One is no longer a client, one is a size eighty! A hundred vestimentary factories are leading us towards the absolute and indifferent uniform.[8]

He laments that the era of artisanal tailoring exemplified by the work of the celebrated early nineteenth-century master tailors Staub and Kleber is long past. In the second half of the century, civilian men are dressed in small (*voltigeurs* or light infantry), medium (*chasseurs* or light cavalry) and large (*grenadier* guards, the tallest men in the army). He also complains that measurements have become sizes, and that he is no longer a tailor's personal client, but a ready-made garment manufacturer's size 80.

Luchet's writing in the second half of the century reflects the changing class status of ready-made clothing. In the early 1800s it was the province of the labouring classes and army, but by the 1850s the petits bourgeois and middle classes began to supplement their wardrobes with ready-made garments.[9] In the following sections I return to the *Ancien Régime* to examine the history of the tailoring trade in France and explore how the transformation from client to size 80 came about.

Making men: the bespoke tailor's art

From a linguistic standpoint the English word 'bespoke' denotes a garment that has been 'spoken for' – in other words, ordered by a specific individual. By contrast, the Latinate French word *confection*, used to describe ready-made garments, implies the notion of completely made objects, produced without a specific client in mind. In France, *confection* was to make its first appearance only after the Revolution. During the *Ancien Régime* the tailor's trade was strictly hierarchical and catered to individual clients. An eighteenth-century manual illustrates the model interior of a tailor's workshop[10] (Figure 7.1). The image, from de Garsault's *L'Art du tailleur* (1769), depicts the activities of a bustling atelier. The division of labour is clear. At the top of the hierarchy the well-dressed master-tailor takes the measure of his client's torso. He uses a paper band in which he cuts little V-shaped notches showing each dimension needed to construct a suit.

Each client had a personal band upon which his measures were stored. The dimensions of the clothing were based on the client's own dimensions, hence the clothing fitted the body whatever its size or shape. Though there were

Tailoring and the 'normal' body 145

Figure 7.1 The interior of an eighteenth-century tailor's workshop. From François de Garsault, *L'Art du tailleur* (1769).

desirable or fashionable silhouettes that changed from decade to decade, there was no absolute norm, no standard size. At the time, precise measurements by unit in *aunes*, *pouces* and *lignes* were reserved for bolts of cloth, not human bodies.[11] The unique strip of paper or cloth gave the tailor the personal dimensions of the chest, arm and inseam of Monsieur X or the Comte de Y, not a list of abstract numbers. De Garsault's text notes that measuring the body was the tailor's first task and it describes the method he used:

> [I]t is executed with inch-wide strips of paper sewn end to end to the required length, which is called a measure. You take this measure from the side you have determined to be the top by a notch cut into that end, and bring it successively to the parts whose dimensions you must know either in width or in height. You mark each dimension on the measure by one or two little snips of the scissors. The tailor must then recognise all of these cuts and notches; with a bit of practice he will be able to do this easily. During the time he takes the measures, the tailor must also observe that which he cannot mark on the paper; that is, the structure of the body, for example high or sloping shoulders, the curve and bearing of the stomach, the flat or raised chest, etc., so as to cut in consequence.

146   *Alison Matthews David*

> With regard to faults in conformation, his art is to remedy them by paddings of canvas, wool or cotton. For the most considerable faults, you cut a stiffened casing in proportion to them, you open it in two and line it with the horse-hair [*crin*] used in mattresses.[12]

Though de Garsault describes a system, it is a flexible and qualitative one. The tape measure he recommends is not graduated, and the tailor acknowledges the importance of direct physical contact and visual observation in the pursuit of his art. As for 'flaws' in conformation, he takes these in his stride. He gives a simple way in which to remedy them, one that does not suggest typologies for these flaws or deviations from a given norm, as would be the case in the nineteenth century, when this discourse became medicalised.

The nineteenth-century tailor's art

At the end of the eighteenth century, artistic ideals celebrated in neoclassical painting and sculpture were incorporated into men's tailoring. Tailors began to use woollen broadcloth for formal dress instead of the felts, velvets, velours and silks of the *Ancien Régime*. Whereas the sumptuous textiles and dazzling patterns of elite eighteenth-century dress attracted the eye to the surface of clothing rather than its construction, woollen cloths and simple unified colours shifted the focus of attention towards a garment's cut and the way in which it defined the body within it. The high quality of woollen broadcloth allowed tailors to 'sculpt' it with hot irons and mould it to the bodies of their clients.

Anne Hollander argues that this approach to the dressed body made men into modern versions of ancient heroes. The new 'heroes in wool' were both elegant and sexually attractive in their sculptural garments.[13] At the dawn of the nineteenth century the well-tailored man was a modern Apollo Belvedere. During the first decades of the nineteenth century a new system of quantifying the human body came into competition with traditional artistic canons, began to inform them and eventually supplanted them. This system, which was prized for its scientific exactitude, consisted of measuring the actual human body for statistical data. The army was the seedbed for this classifying activity, which was later dubbed anthropometry and eventually used in racial comparisons. Those who had 'scientifically' measured the Venus de Medici's bust and the Apollo Belvedere's legs turned their calculations to live bodies.

The French Revolution produced an important change in concepts of the body and the clothing it wore. This shift was the invention and spread of the metric system. All measurements were originally anthropometrical, since man used his own body as a yardstick: feet, *pouces* (thumbs), etc.[14] The traditional unit for measuring lengths of cloth was also bodily, and it was called the *aune*, or ell in English (short for elbow, the length of the forearm). This system was used exclusively for cloth and did not correspond to the methods

Tailoring and the 'normal' body 147

then in use for measuring other lengths or widths. In addition, the length of an ell varied according to region.

As one writer observed, 'As for the ell, in such wide use for the purchase of cloth, a popular saying had made it a symbol of fraud. In the north of France alone there were eighteen different kinds.'[15] The Revolution sought to rationalise these systems and replace traditional feudal rights, which included setting measurements, weights and calibrations.[16] With the support of scientists and reformers such as Lavoisier and de Condorcet, the provisional meter was established as early as 1793 but was not definitively fixed until 1799. Military tailors were using the metric system at least as early as 1800. Civilian tailors took their metrological principles to heart and began to invent systems that measured and abstracted the male body. These systems contributed to the process that transformed men from personal clients into numerical sizes.

Bespoke tailors made real progress during the first decades of the nineteenth century. Long before modern techniques of mass production were in operation, tailors were inventing systems that quantified the male body and improved the fit of clothes.[17] In order to achieve a perfect fit, the tailor adopted a new tool: the flexible tape measure. Invented around 1800, this graduated instrument became central to his professional practice.[18] In the tailor's eyes, and under his hands, men were measured and the suit became the measure of a man.

In 1816 the tailor Christian Beck received a government patent for his *costumomètre* and *longimètre*. These geometrical measuring systems were approved by the Institut Royal de France in 1818. In 1819 Beck published *Note explicative sur le costumomètre et le longimètre*, measuring tools designed to give a much more precise fit than a simple tape measure.[19] The text explains his scientific tailoring system, a scaled, proportional method that uses either the meter or the *pied du roi* as a basic measure.[20] In a sales prospectus, he writes that the principal difficulty in producing a suit is translating the two-dimensional surface of the cloth to the three-dimensional surface of the body. Referring to himself in the third person, Beck frames this procedure as an advanced exercise in mathematics:

> The greatest difficulty is to elaborate the exterior shape of the body, for the fabric that is originally a planar surface has to clothe the body, which is a surface with a double curvature. . . . The system of Mr Christian Beck has developed the exterior shape of the body in a rectangular parallelogram in which the height of the individual forms one of the sides; the other measurement is calculated according to the width of the person and is subject to variations. . . . In this parallelogram, Mr Christian Beck has fixed all of the principal points, such as the collar, waist, armholes, etc. By means of perpendicular lines between them, and which form the X and Y axes of the traced curve, Mr Christian Beck finds the exact contour of the suit or whatever sort of garment he wishes to cut.[21]

148   *Alison Matthews David*

By comparison with the qualitative approach of de Garsault's eighteenth-century tailor, this mathematical language turns tailoring into a geometric exercise: the human body becomes a conjunction of parallelograms, double curvatures and points on a graph. The garment he constructs for this fictive person is equally abstracted, and cloth is conceived of as a planar surface upon which he performs similarly geometrical operations.

Despite these elaborate calculations, Beck's *costumomètre* and his *longimètre* were designed to produce not a customised suit as de Garsault had done, but a garment in a set scale of sizes. In theory, the *costumomètre* enabled the tailor to make garments in 33 different proportionate sizes. The tailor claimed that this number was more than sufficient to cater to the clients he encountered in his daily practice. However, he also encountered clients who did not fit the norm, men who were either too long for their width or too wide for their height, geometrically speaking.[22] In these cases, the tailor had the *longimètre* at his disposal. In his small book on tailoring, which doubles as an advertisement, Beck then offers to sell the authorisation for the use of his patented instruments to a certain number of privileged tailors. The use of different instruments for 'normal' clients and those who did not correspond to the norm points to a problem that would become increasingly important in the nineteenth century.

Tailors marketed a multitude of instruments designed to measure the male body with a hitherto unimaginable precision. In 1834 the tailor F. A. Barde, an author of theoretical treatises on tayloring, even marketed an *anthropomètre* ('man-meter'), recalling the emerging science of anthropometry. His tripartite tool consisted of a 'shoulder-metre' a 'back-meter', and a 'body-meter'.[23] One of the most striking images of such an instrument is George Delas's *somatomètre*, derived from the Greek *somatos* (body-meter) (Figure 7.2). Using the same pseudo-scientific vocabulary as Beck, Delas's elaborate sales prospectus from 1839 proclaims that the tailor has a patent for the invention and perfection of his 'regulating mechanism'. The image reproduces the original patent drawing itself as an unfurled scroll with the inventor's name in the top centre, wreathed in laurels. Two young dandies stand on either side of the patent like heraldic figures and illustrate the use of Delas's contraption, which resembles nothing so much as a torture device. These men's faces, hairstyles and conformations are models of the ideal male body of the period. The machine itself seems to consist of adjustable bands of cloth or thin metal marked with sliding centimetres. The man on our left seems to have been poured into a black body suit (with coat-tail dangling behind him) and then fitted with the *somatomètre*, which encases him like a metallic skeleton. This cage encircles him from neck to toes, measuring everything from the length of his forearm to the circumference of his thigh. He is the man of fashion quantified.

His counterpart on the right, a younger man with stylishly long hair, seems to be undergoing the same process of measurement, though we see him from the back. He gestures towards the drawing of the machine worn

Tailoring and the 'normal' body   149

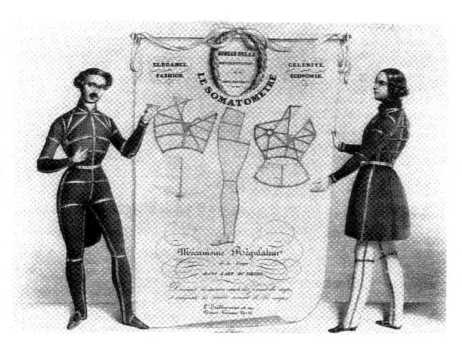

Figure 7.2 Illustration from George Delas, *Le Somatomètre* (1839). Bibliothèque nationale de France. Paris, Cabinet des Estampes.

by his companion. There is a leg in the centre of the patent, with several bands for measuring and constructing trousers. Both men wear this leg-apparatus. In 1839, the same year as Delas's prospectus, the tailor Couanon, editor of the *Journal des marchands-tailleurs*, describes the invention of M. Gilet (Mr Waistcoat), a fictitious tailor whose system resembles that of Delas. Couanon's tongue-in-cheek approbation of this system celebrates its ability to trap clients who do not pay:

> Two little pieces of iron that project from 6 to 8 centimetres are placed on the steel circle that occupies the bottom half of the body, that is to say the waistline, in which you adjust the large metric band of steel, which, from this point, falls perpendicularly the length of the leg, and is fixed on a sort of shackle that fits over the whole foot ... once all of this paraphernalia is well adjusted, the client is well bound and well muzzled, and the fear that he will escape you should entirely disappear when you use such a method.[24]

These contraptions certainly placed the tailor in an unaccustomed position of power over his client. Geometric cutting systems maintained their vogue throughout the century, but their complexity ensured that many

150   *Alison Matthews David*

tailors simply used them as pseudo-scientific jargon to sell their garments, cutting systems or private courses. Entrepreneurs of ready-made clothing, known as *confectionneurs*, were quick to capitalise on the bespoke tailors' innovative procedures for making clothing in scaled sizes. Ironically, these systems paved the way for the large-scale production of civilian clothing. As Christopher Breward writes,

> The introduction of the tape measure and an interest in standardized measuring and cutting techniques from the 1820s which eased the move into mass-production, simply offered the promise of democratization to a tailoring industry already enamored with the potential of platonic notions of the 'model' body.[25]

I would nuance this statement to argue that in fact tailors were torn between the desire for perfection and the actuality of the daily round of body types that filed through their shops.

Tissue paper patterns provide us with another material trace of this increasingly normative approach to the male body. The ghostly reminders of the sleeves, backs and collars, which tailors carefully cut out and assembled to produce suits in more durable materials, are still wedged into tailoring journals of the 1830s and 40s.[26] In a more technological register, these patterns, which are often constructed on a decimal one-tenth scale, are physical evidence of the ways in which the nineteenth century produced a template for the 'normal' or 'average' male body. Some social scientists have examined these concepts in the writings of early nineteenth-century statisticians such as Adolphe Quetelet. However, the current literature on fashion and body image tends to focus on the ways in which fashion images encourage women to desire unrealistic, unattainable and unhealthy body shapes.[27] Though scholarship has only recently begun to study male body image, men were negatively affected by fashionable ideals as well. In fact, my research suggests that this process occurred in tailoring during the early nineteenth century. As one tailor's manual observed in 1841, journals had begun to send out patterns for clothing, and many men wished their bodies to follow these templates as closely as possible:

> Now journals give a description and send patterns ... it's a great advantage ... but can the patterns they send dress everyone? I don't think so, because not all men are fashioned alike. Some are pleasantly formed, others are not, yet they all want to be well built, or at least to appear to be so. They want to have arched backs, slender waists. They have seen a sculptural man [*homme moulé*] and they want to be like him.[28]

This association of a readily available, mass-produced template for men's fashions in the form of a paper pattern with a customer's more personal desire to resemble a stylish man summarises the tension between ideal and actual bodies.

The technology of beauty: art, orthopaedics and the male body

In his 1858 essay 'De la mode', Théophile Gautier wrote that antique physical perfection was but a memory in contemporary urban society:

> Without the admirable remains of ancient statuary, the tradition of the human form would be entirely lost.... What kinship exists between these abstract figures and the dressed spectators who gaze at them? Is it possible to believe that they spring from the same race? Not in the least.... Beauty and strength are no longer typical traits in the man of our time.[29]

Certainly, the Frenchman of the Second Empire did not always measure up to the Greek statues on display at the Louvre. If one scrutinised the differences between the spectator and the spectated, the physical inadequacy of modern bourgeois man was glaringly obvious. Since the reality of urban bodies that were under- or overnourished and underused, confined to the office or the bank, was not always pretty, this intense scrutiny led to insecurities, mockery, and theories of degeneration. While Apollo hardly seemed to need clothing, the office clerk was a despicable specimen of humanity; his average height, weight and strength did not recommend him to the sculptor.

Yet most tailors were reluctant to abandon the Apollonian model of the male body. Many used it as the stock model to construct their patterns. In bespoke tailoring of the July Monarchy (1830–48) the ideal male conformation was called a straight or upright posture, or *tenue d'Apollon*, the most common classical ideal of masculine beauty in both the eighteenth and the nineteenth centuries.[30] The inaugural issue of the tailor's journal *Le Dandy* (1838) describes the body of the man who will fit tailors' patterns perfectly: 'For men's suits, our general proportions are based on an upright, well-formed model, exact in his proportions, having the height of five feet three inches. The Apollo Belvedere represents this man as Buffon has described him.'[31]

The most typical deviations from this norm were a posture that slumped forward or curved back, but other common problems were sloping, raised and unequal shoulders. Yet even in the face of endless variations in posture and body shape, the tailor had abstract ideals, whether these corresponded to canons of ancient statuary or the heights of fashion. Fashionable ideals also competed with classical ideals, and, unlike the eternally beautiful artist's canon, fashion's favourite was subject to temporal fluctuations. The fashionable man's silhouette and physique, like the fashionable woman's, changed from year to year and decade to decade. During the 1840s, style demanded that tailored clothing hug the forms of the body, and it helped if this body was already close to perfect:

152   Alison Matthews David

> For imagine, if you can, in the actual state of things, in 1841, an undressed man! What would become of him, the unlucky one?... Yet all the same, I ask you, what is the great ambition of today's clothing, if not to reproduce, to delineate the nude, to accentuate the body's exact shape; and you apprehend by his body he who, better than all of you and for less money, succeeds at attaining the *beau réel*, at attaining your ideal![32]

There were varied responses to the shift in emphasis from the *beau idéal* to the *beau réel*. While some considered it a triumph of modern ugliness over classical beauty, others celebrated the new mode of thinking. The egalitarian Quetelet attacked classicism in art, arguing that modern artists should leave the heroic male nude body aside and study the average man:

> The ancients have represented the physical and moral man with infinite art, such as he then was; and the greater number of the moderns, struck with the perfection of their works, have thought they had nothing to do but servilely to imitate them; they have not understood that the type has been changed; and that, when imitating them for the perfection of art, they had another nature to study. Hence the universal cry, 'Who shall deliver us from the Greeks and the Romans?'[33]

For Quetelet, the modern 'type' or norm was not one based on classical canons of beauty derived from abstract geometric principles but one calculated from statistical means based on systematically measuring actual adult male and female bodies. It was clear that the modern type did not have the physical perfection of the ancient, yet Quetelet's cry was not echoed by most nineteenth-century critics. For most, the *réel* was anything but *beau*.

A new branch of the medical profession both reinforced the idea that modern man was ugly and tried to correct the flaws culture had imposed on nature. During the mid-eighteenth century, medicine had begun to study irregularities in posture, particularly in children. This science was called orthopaedics, or the art of making the body 'right', from the Greek *orthos*, right, straight, and *pais*, child.[34] Orthopaedists studied the infinite variations and deformities of the body and attempted to straighten those that were extremely malformed. Children were the first focus of their attention, since their growing bones were easier to manipulate. Soon the general population began to frequent their establishments. Systems developed during the early nineteenth century used gymnastic exercises and mechanisms such as steel corsets and restraining beds for straightening crooked spines. Many of the instruments they used recall 'regulating mechanisms' like Delas's cage-*somatomètre*.

Many treatment centres were aimed at the well off who wished to rid themselves or their children of their unsightly physiques. At the time, deformities were thought to be hereditary. In fact, nutritional problems such as rickets and childhood diseases like polio were responsible for crippling many children. Ironically, contemporary observers noticed that rickets (*rachitisme*) seems to be more common among rich young girls, who were never exposed to the sun, than in working-class girls, who developed their muscles and went outdoors.[35]

Tailors profited from this vogue for orthopaedics as well. A vaudeville play from 1826 entitled *Orthopaedics, or the Tailor for Hunchbacks* satirises the charlatanism and profiteering nature of many of these new 'orthopaedists' springing up in Paris.[36] The tailor Monsieur Dubélair ('Of the beautiful appearance') invents and markets 'dissembling apparatuses' used to right the wrongs of nature.[37] He soon attracts a large clientele of hunchbacks, including one Monsieur Malplaquet (or *mal-plaqué*, badly built), who is a building contractor. He wishes his spine to be as straight as his buildings, and Dubélair promises to make the twisted man as beautiful as an Apollo. He calls on his assistant for help in applying his instruments:

'– Give me the epigastric cinch, (to Malplaquet) we will clothe you in antique forms.'
'...Release him a tiny bit (writing the numbers named below in chalk on Malplaquet's suit). [L]et us apply the movable chest with a diaphragmatic valve so as not to hinder the movements of the thorax, no. 1, second series. Stand up straight!'[38]

Covered in chalk numbers, cinched in a rigid corset and ordered to stand up straight, the hunchback hopes he will be transformed into an attractive man of fashion. Despite the claims of Dubélair's advertising, Malplaquet's wishes are not realised, and the trussed and numbered bundle becomes a source of ridicule for the audience.[39] Though this interpretation of quantifications of the male body is humorous, it does attest to a larger public interest in issues of measurement and ideals of beauty.

Victor Hugo's popular *Hunchback of Notre-Dame*, published in 1830, attests to the extent of contemporary public fascination for deformed bodies. Hugo's description of the severely twisted and malformed Quasimodo corresponds with many medical typologies of the period. In fact, the author's use of extremely technical terminology strikes the modern reader as anachronistic in the context of a medievalising novel. However, less extreme versions of Hugo's character were being spotted everywhere by careful observers. For example, Honoré Daumier satirises the ugly and misshapen bodies of denuded urban men in his series of caricatures entitled 'The Bathers' produced during the 1840s and 50s.[40] A caricature from 1842 entitled *Le Conseil de révision* (Figure 7.3) shows the army's selection process. The caption reads, 'It's a glorious spectacle to see the noble French youth, full of ardour, force and elegance, dispute the honour of serving the country under the flags of Mars!'[41] The god of war might be less thrilled to see the reality of the glorious spectacle. A doctor raises the chin of a stunted, skeletal

LE CONSEIL DE REVISION

Figure 7.3 Honoré Daumier, 'The Military Review Board' (*Le Charivari*, 1842).

youth, naked from the waist up, in order to make him tall enough to be conscripted into the army. Behind him cluster a group of similarly imperfect male specimens. One turns his back to us so that we may see his curved spine, uneven, bony elbows and tilted hips. He is so deformed as to be a candidate for an illustration in an orthopaedic manual. In 1855 an orthopaedic doctor observed that deformities were the general rule, whereas a normal conformation was a rare exception:

> The examples of curvature of the upper body are numerous ... would one not say (if one knows how to look) about the appearance of these bodies, short and massive, of these hunched backs, of these compressed chests, of these irregularly protruding shoulders, of these stiff and halting gaits, that spinal curvature is the universal rule, and the normal upper body is the exception.[42]

One tailor was instrumental in devising, producing and marketing systems based on concepts of the 'normal' and 'deformed' body. Alexis Lavigne was born in the Pas-de-Calais in northern France in 1818. He

Tailoring and the 'normal' body 155

settled in Paris, where he worked as a master tailor, instructor and inventor. As both an entrepreneur and a labour activist, he agitated for the rights of the working classes and fought against the long hours and low wages of fellow tailors.[43] At the same time, this demagogue was a skilful self-promoter who invented and patented numerous products, then marketed and mass-produced them. In 1841, at the age of 23, he published the first of many editions of his cutting manual and founded the professional school that is now called the École Supérieure des Arts et Techniques de la Mode (ESMOD), an institution that currently has branches from Japan to Brazil. In 1847 he patented a flexible metric tape measure that still bears his name. In 1849 Lavigne expanded his business and presented busts for tailors at the tenth Industrial Exhibition in Paris, the predecessor of the World's Fairs.[44] He advertised these busts as tools 'for the use of tailors in fitting and perfecting the cut of suits'.[45] His prospectus looks like an advertisement for an orthopaedic establishment. In 1846 Alexis Lavigne published a large lithographic plate comparing 'the diverse structures and several types of garments' (Figure 7.4). The diverse structures are the conformations of a wide range of male body types. This large-scale print illustrates these men and the garments designed for them, and publicises the tailor-entrepreneur's cutting manual, first published in 1841, his metric tape measure, granted a

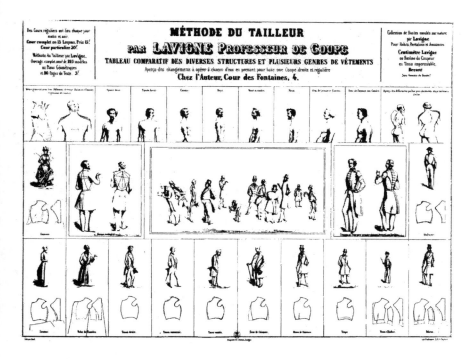

Figure 7.4 Illustration from Alexis Lavigne, *Méthode du tailleur* (Tailoring Method) (1846). Bibliothèque nationale de France. Paris, Cabinet des Estampes.

156   *Alison Matthews David*

government patent in 1847, as well as his collection of individually cast busts for suits, trousers and riding habits.[46]

The top row is divided into orderly boxes that organise men into a quasi-scientific taxonomy of physical conformations. Each box contains the undressed torso of a man with a description. There are men with high or low shoulders, slight hunches or arched backs, and to the far right the two most extreme examples are meant to give the future tailor 'a look at the deformities that may present themselves and which are infinitely variable'. To preserve modesty, these naked men are cropped at the waist. However, they are objects of intense scrutiny. The frontal and profile views recall the iconography of contemporary criminal line-ups. They also evoke the typological analysis of bodies central to anthropometric, orthopaedic and ethnographic studies.

Closer to the centre, Lavigne displays his ordinary rules for taking measurements to the left, while to the right he illustrates yet another of his inventions, a canvas bodice (*corsage*) for taking measures. This contraption appears to be an adjustable vest shut with straps and buttons that measures the dimensions of the torso. However, as we have seen, for example, with Delas's *somatomètre*, Lavigne's invention was not unique or particularly novel.

In the centre of Lavigne's advertisement a group of men of all sizes and shapes mill about. At the bottom of the print, Lavigne shows us how to clothe the conformations of the men we saw naked in the top row. He illustrates the idea of the tailor as agent of civilised masculinity typical of the period: with a cut of the tailor's shears, these men progress from being naked 'savages' to becoming well-dressed gentlemen. Underneath the three-dimensional figure we see a model of how the cut of a jacket should be altered according to the conformation of a given individual. In Lavigne's system, as in most geometrical cutting methods, there is a standard model, called the *tenue droite* (upright posture), which requires no alteration.[47] Every other garment is a variation on this one standardised pattern, even the horsewoman's riding habit. Lavigne's diagrams illustrate how a variation in the three-dimensional shape of a human body transfers on to paper – into an abstract, two-dimensional pattern ready to cut from the cloth. Lavigne's system recalls the geometrical principles of Beck, yet Lavigne illustrates each of these variations in conformation. Many of the changes required to adapt a flat pattern to fit different body shapes are intuitive. For example, Lavigne instructs the tailor to add fabric at the stomach and the back for a man with a large girth, whereas he removes fabric by darting the bottom of the pattern for a thin-waisted man. However, some variations are more subtle. For example, a suit for a man with a slight hunch must be altered everywhere. Just over a decade after Lavigne's prospectus appeared, changes in clothing styles that favoured looser cuts rendered his exacting methods for fitting clothing almost obsolete.

One branch of his business is still very much alive in contemporary fashion production and retailing: the eerie body double called a mannequin.

Like bespoke tailoring, the early mannequin or tailor's dummy was made to measure. In a text written later in his career, Lavigne scripted his own origin myth concerning his revolutionary product, his 'mannequins cast upon the live model and after the live model'. He frames his 'invention' of the mannequins as a quasi-medicalised 'study of bodily malformations':

> One day, one of my students came to request my help in dressing a new client who was very rich, very hard to please, and who had a deformity that defied description. . . . I accepted this opportunity with pleasure, for it allowed me to embark on a study of bodily malformations. In such cases one is almost always obliged to have several fitting sessions without being certain of success. As it proves impossible to have the client at one's entire disposition, I pondered the difficulties we often encounter in our trade, and remembered that I had sometimes used a non-penetrating liquid that waterproofs fabrics and that by adding another substance I could make fabrics as stiff as felt and even as cardboard.
>
> These casts are made swiftly and without inconvenience for the person who is posing and they do not stain a man's shirt or trousers or a woman's chemise, corset or petticoat. After successfully experimenting with casting the bust of my client, I have since taken advantage of opportunities to take casts of all irregular body types by the same method. For normal types I use a much simpler procedure to make busts after nature without using casts. By uniting all of these materials I have been able to establish a large factory for manufacturing busts, whose products have been awarded medals at different exhibitions since 1849 and are now making their way around the globe.[48]

The nineteenth century saw a renaissance in the ancient art of casting bodies after nature. These direct casts were used for artistic, scientific and medical purposes.[49] In the 1840s, when Lavigne was 'inventing' his busts cast after nature, casting techniques were increasingly in use in scientific domains such as palaeontology and ethnography, and the pseudo-science of phrenology.[50] Though modelling in wax was fairly common, plaster casting was the technique used most frequently to reproduce the human body or body parts in three dimensions.

Tailoring styles emphasised the shapes of the male body during the first half of the century and were often described as '*moulant*' (form-fitting, from '*moule*', meaning cast). It was logical for Lavigne to invent or copy techniques designed to reproduce the contours of the natural body as closely as possible. Men who would benefit from such a customised procedure appear in the centre of his prospectuses for his method and are repeated in his mannequin sales prospectus from the 1849 Industrial Exhibition. In the second image, men stroll through the Bois de Boulogne like so many animals on display in a zoo. There are short hunchbacked men, tall fat men, men with one shoulder higher than the other, men with bow legs, and a few relatively 'normal' specimens. How to clothe these varied bodies was the constant concern of the tailor in an age of increasing mass production. In the minds of tailors like Lavigne, modern man was an endless set of deviations from a norm, and they seemed to relish the challenge of dressing him in flattering clothing. However, in comparison with the perfectly formed and impeccably dressed silhouettes appearing in contemporary magazines like *Le Dandy*, *Le Fashionable* and *Le Narcisse*, Lavigne's advertisement is a tailor's journal gone mad.

While Lavigne's prospectus for the Industrial Exhibition markets made-to-measure busts for a limited and elite clientele, his original bespoke casting experiment for a deformed client and pseudo-scientific interest in bodily variations heralded the production of mass-produced busts in standardised sizes. Though he was not the first to invent the tailor's dummy, he was the first to mass-produce it. This industrialised version of the tailor's dummy embodied a statistical mean, an average, and its invention is contemporary with the rise in demand for ready-made clothing for a more modest clientele. Garments in standardised sizes could clothe dummies made according to the same mathematical calculations.[51] However, anatomical accuracy was not his only criterion for making mannequins. According to his advertisements, Lavigne calculated the shape of the industrial mannequins he began to produce during the Second Empire both mathematically and according to proportions taken from ancient statuary, a combination of the scientific and the beautiful typical of the nineteenth century.[52] During the July Monarchy another phenomenon embodied the tension between mathematical and aesthetic ideals.

Patented regulating mechanisms, geometrically scaled paper patterns and tailor's mannequins embody the way in which tailoring abstracted and quantified the nineteenth-century male body. These models of the body contrasted the 'normal', if rare, upright Apollonian body with the multitude of variant body shapes and sizes found in the modern urban bourgeois population. In a sartorial landscape increasingly dominated by an emphasis on perfect cut and fit, these variations were no longer catered to in the sensitive, qualitative and tactile manner typical of eighteenth-century tailoring. Tailors increasingly saw these bodily variations as 'deviations', 'deformations' and even abnormalities that required scientific and medical technologies for cutting and fitting cloth to the body. With tailors such as Beck, Delas and Lavigne drawing on geometric and orthopaedic discourses for inspiration, it is no wonder that many modern men felt that their 'degenerate' bodies were subject to unwelcome scrutiny. Unlike his gentlemanly ancestors, the nineteenth-century bourgeois was measured against mathematical templates and medical norms and was almost always found wanting.

Conclusion

While many felt uncomfortable at first with new methods of precise bodily measurement and the standardisation of their clothing, innovations in tailoring did democratise dress for the majority of men. While the early bespoke tailors applied their theories of norms and deviations only to a limited circle of clients, they were used on a far greater scale and for entirely different purposes by the new science of anthropometry. During the second half of the nineteenth century, criminologists, anthropologists and eugenicists such as Alphonse Bertillon and Francis Galton developed more complex mathematical and representational strategies to measure human bodies. They turned these systems to more nefarious ends, cataloguing criminal types, ethnic characteristics and physical degeneracies. These 'scientific', normalising views of the body enabled them to create taxonomies of other races and classify them as inferior to white European males. In the twenty-first century, when the manufacturing, marketing and consumption of clothing is an important part of the global economy, it is worth remembering that our standardised system of small, medium and large sizes originated in ideologies of man as a statistically quantifiable concept, a body made to measure.

Notes

1 Ian Hacking, *The Taming of Chance*, Cambridge, Cambridge University Press, 1990. See especially the chapter on Quetelet, 'Regimental Chests', pp. 105–14.

2 Christopher Breward, 'Manliness, Modernity and the Shaping of Male Clothing', in Joanne Entwistle and Elizabeth Wilson, eds, *Body Dressing*, Oxford, Berg, 2001, p. 175.

3 See for example, Dr Jean-Galbert, *Anatomie du gladiateur combatant, applicable aux beaux-arts*, Paris, [self published],1812; Étienne Bardin, *Texte du règlement sur l'uniforme de l'Armée de Terre*, Paris, Musée de l'Armée, 1818; Paul Topinard, *Le Canon des proportions de l'homme européen*, Paris, Masson, 1889; Paul Richer, *L'Anatomie dans l'art: proportions du corps humain, canons artistiques et canons scientifiques*, Paris, Administration des Deux Revues, 1893.

4 Traditionally, tailors worked in wool while female dressmakers worked in silks, cottons and velvets. Because of the strength required to manipulate the heavy shears and irons used to cut and shape woollen cloth, they were almost always men and they closely guarded their trade against the rare incursions of the 'tailoress'.

5 Adolphe Quetelet, *A Treatise on Man and the Development of His Faculties*, Gainesville, FL, Scholars' Facsimiles and Reprints, 1969 [1842], p. 96.

6 R. Hubert, *Proportions ordinaires du corps humain*, Paris, A. Appert, 1864.

7 It gives, as the large, medium and small measurements for men, 2 metres, 1.75 metres and 1.5 metres, and 1.90, 1.662 and 1.425 metres for women.

8 The author's pseudonym was the 'Baron de Pourcelt', a name that highlights his class allegiances with aristocratic ideals of bespoke tailoring. 'Le temps sculptural des Staub et des Kleber n'est plus; il est mort avec le frac et la redingote ajustée. Le paletot-sac à toutes épaules l'a supprimé. Il n'y a plus de mesures maintenant, il y a des tailles. Comme dans l'ancienne garde nationale, chasseurs, voltigeurs et grenadiers. Mètres et centimètres. On n'est plus un *client*, on est un *quatre-vingts*. Une centaine d'usines vétissantes nous conduisent à l'uniforme

160 *Alison Matthews David*

indifferent et absolu.' Auguste Luchet, *L'Art Industriel à l'exposition universelle de 1867*, Paris, Librairie Internationale, 1868, p. 379.

9 Philippe Perrot, *Fashioning the Bourgeoisie*, Princeton, NJ, Princeton University Press, 1994, p. 54

10 François de Garsault, *L'Art du tailleur*, Paris, Académie Royale des Sciences, Descriptions des Arts et Métiers, 1769.

11 Army recruitment was the only context in which men's height was measured.

12 '[E]lle s'exécute avec des bandes de papier larges d'un pouce et cousues de bout à bout jusqu'à la longueur suffisante, ce qui s'appelle une mesure. On porte successivement cette mesure depuis le bout qu'on a déterminé être celui d'en haut par une hoche qu'on a faite à son extremité, aux endroits dont on doit connoître les dimensions soit en longueur, soit en largeur; on marque chacune sur la mesure par un ou deux petits coups de cizeau. Le tailleur doit reconnoître par la suite toutes ces hoches et entailles; un peu d'habitude y parvient aisément. Dans les tems que le tailleur prend la mesure, il doit encore observer ce qu'il ne peut marquer sur le papier; c'est la structure du corps, comme les épaules hautes ou avalées, la rondeur et la tournure du ventre, la poitrine plate ou élevée, & c. afin de tailler en conséquence . . .

A l'égard des défauts de la conformation, son art est de les pallier par des garnitures, soit de toile, de laine, de coton, & c. pour les plus considérables, on taille au prorata une houette gommée, on l'ouvre en deux, & on la garnit de crin à matelas.' François de Garsault, *L'Art du tailleur*, Paris, Académie des arts et sciences, 1994 [1769], p. 14.

13 Anne Hollander, *Sex and Suits*, New York, Kodansha, 1995, p. 89.

14 Yannick Marec, 'Autour des résistances au système métrique', in Bernard Garnier and Jean-Claude Hocquet, eds, *La Naissance du système métrique*, Caen, Diffusions du Lys, 1989, pp. 135–44.

15 'Quant à l'aune, en si grand usage pour l'achat des tissus, un dicton populaire en avait fait un symbole de fraude. Rien que dans le nord on en comptait dix-huit sortes.' J. Tarnier, *L'Adoption universelle du système métrique à l'occasion de l'exposition universelle*, Paris, Belin, 1867, p. 8. In the new decimal system the litre replaced the pint, the gram replaced the pound, the metre the *aune* or ell, the *are* the *toise* for measuring land, the franc replaced various monetary systems then in use, and the *stère* became the acceptable measure for quantities of wood.

16 Traditional systems had been used to profit those in power, who bent them to serve their needs and often to cheat the less fortunate. Garnier and Hocquet, *La Naissance*, p. 16.

17 Before 1840 many of them worked interchangeably with metric and imperial measures.

18 Naomi Tarrant, *The Development of Costume*, London, Routledge, 1994, p. 12. He sported it as an accessory, hanging it around his neck like a scarf when it was not in use. Many bespoke tailors still follow this practice. In an increasingly competitive market the nineteenth-century master-tailor aspired to be more than a simple artisan, for he tried to combine the talents of sculptor and engineer, artist and mathematician.

19 Beck advertises his address as 35, rue de Richelieu, the street that was the centre of custom tailoring activity in Paris, much like Savile Row in London.

20 The use of the *pied du roi* may be a concession to the monarchy whose favour he curried, but it was perfectly legal to use either system of measurement, and a system that used both was more marketable.

21 'La grande difficulté est de développer la forme extérieure du corps, car l'étoffe qui est dans l'origine une surface plane, doit revêtir le corps qui est une surface à double courbure. . . . Le système de M. Ch. Beck a développé la forme extérieur du corps dans un parallelogramme rectangle duquel la hauteur de l'individu

forme un de ses côtés; l'autre dimension est calculée d'après la grosseur de l'individu et peut subir des variations..... Dans ce parallèllogramme, M. Ch. Beck a fixé tous les points principaux, tels que l'encolure, la taille, les emmanchures, etc.; et au moyen de lignes perpendiculaires entre elles, et qui forment comme les abscisses et les ordonnés de la courbe développée, M. Ch. Beck trouve le countour exact de l'habit ou du vêtement quelconque qu'il veut couper.' Christian Beck, *Notice explicative sure le costumomètre et le longimètre*, Paris, [no publisher], 1819, pp. 1–12.

22 Ibid., pp. 17–19.

23 Farid Chenoune, *Des modes et des hommes*, Paris, Gallimard, 1993, p. 44.

24 'Sur le cercle d'acier qui occupe la partie inférieure du corps, c'est-à-dire la ceinture, sont placés deux petits morceaux de fer qui saillissent de 6 à 8 centimetres, dans lesquels s'adapte la grande bande d'acier métrique qui, de ce point, va, en tombant perpendiculairement le long de la jambe, se fixer sur un espèce d'entrave qui emboîte tout le pied ... une fois tout cet attirail bien ajusté, la pratique est bien liée et bien garrottée, et la crainte qu'elle ne vous échappe doit entièrement disparaître devant un semblable procédé.' *Journal des marchands-tailleurs*, September 1839, pp. 258–9.

25 Breward, 'Manliness', p. 166.

26 For example, the tailor's journal *Le Capricieux* of 25 May 1838 advertises: 'patrons, en grandeur naturelle, aux prix de 1 fr. 25, ceux d'habits, 1 fr. 50, ceux pour pantalons, et 75c. ceux pour gilets.' *Le Capricieux*, p. 32. It also sells the plates that accompany the patterns separately for ten sous. At the end of the bound journal, the life-sized patterns are folded neatly into the binding and can still be unfolded. Other journals have the cut-out pieces inserted unbound.

27 Marianne Thesander, *The Feminine Ideal*, London, Reaktion, 1997.

28 '...mais les patrons qu'on envoie peuvent-ils habiller tout le monde? Je ne le crois pas, car tous les hommes ne sont pas faits de la meme manière; ils sont plus ou moins bien conformés, et cependant tous veulent être bien faits, ou du moins le paraître. On veut etre cambré, avoir la taille fine. On a vu un homme moulé, on veut être comme lui. Ici donc est la difficulté de l'état, celle de corriger, d'atténuer autant que possible les défauts de la conformation. D. Desaulnée, *Description d'une nouvelle coupe géometrique pour l'habillement de l'homme*, Versailles, Montalant-Bougleux, 1841, p. 7.

29 'Sans les admirables restes de la statuaire antique, la tradition de la forme humaine serait entièrement perdue.... Quel rapport existe-t-il entre ces figures abstraites et les spectateurs habillés qui les regardent? Les croirait-on de la même race? En aucune manière.... La beauté et la force ne sont plus les caractères typiques de l'homme à notre époque'. Théophile Gautier, *De la mode*, Paris, Poulet-Malassis, 1858, pp. 6–13.

30 For example, under 'Tenue droite, dite d'Apollon' one tailor writes, 'On nomme tenue droite et proportionnée toute conformation d'homme qui offre dans son ensemble un accord parfait de régularité; cette perfection ne peut s'appliquer qu'à une faible partie du genre humain. Avec un homme de cette structure, on n'eprouve aucune difficulté dans l'éxécution; avec un peut de pratique et de goût ... on est sûr de toujours réussir avec ce modèle.' [n.n.] Ruelle, *Guide du Tailleur*, Paris, [no publisher], 1845, p. 10.

31 'Nos proportions générales sont prises, pour les costumes d'hommes, sur un modèle droit, formé, exact dans ses proportions, ayant la taille de cinq pieds trois pouces. L'Apollon du Belvedere réprésente cet homme tel que Buffon l'a décrit.' *Le Dandy*, January 1838, 1, p. 2.

32 'Car, figurez-vous, si vous pouvez, dans l'état actuel des choses, en 41, un homme non vêtu! que deviendrait-il, l'infortuné?... Et pourtant, quelle est, je vous prie, la grande prétention des vêtements actuels, sinon de reproduire, de

162   *Alison Matthews David*

dessiner le nu, d'accuser les formes exactes; et vous appréhendez au corps celui qui, mieux que vous tous et à moins de frais, arrive au beau réel, à votre idéal!' D. Desaulnée, *Description d'une nouvelle coupe géométrique pour l'habillement de l'homme*, Versailles, Montalant-Bougleux, 1841, pp. 13–14.

33 Quetelet, *Treatise on Man*, p. 97.

34 Leonard Peltier, *Orthopedics: A History and Iconography*, San Francisco, Norman, 1993.

35 One orthopaedist states, 'Les difformités de la taille sont beaucoup plus communes chez la femme que chez l'homme.' L. Bienaimé, *Courte notice sur l'orthopédie*, Paris, [self-published], 1839, p. 57.

36 For example, a Mr Milli, who is accused of being a charlatan, set up shop on the quai de Billy near the Champs-Élysées in 1823. His clinic, which even provided its wealthy clients with a chapel, had a certain vogue. See Anon. [A Doctor from the Paris Faculty of Medicine], *La Vérité sur les progrès récens de l'orthopédie ou l'art de corriger les difformités du corps humain*, Paris, de Feugeray, 1826, p. 9.

37 His newspaper advertisement reads, 'Monsieur Dubélair, patented merchant-tailor, inventor of the mannequin-man, known for the felicitous conception of his suits, which unite the daring of their cut with the polish of their collars, has discovered, after considerable studies, that the man badly built in all his parts, cannot be good on the whole.... [He] has the honour of announcing to the public, that with his dissembling apparatuses, he has found the secret of righting the wrongs of nature. Hunchbacks who wish to honour him with their confidence, will find him at his academy, rue Villedot, etc.'
The action takes place in Paris, and the location of his 'academy' on the rue Villedot may be a reference to the rue Villedo situated right next to the rue Richelieu. 'Avis aux gens mal faits: monsieur Dubélair, marchand tailleur breveté, inventeur de l'homme mannequin, et connu par l'heureuse conception de ses habits, qui joignent à la hardiesse de la coupe, le fini du collet, ayant découvert après de mûres études, que l'homme mal fait dans toutes ses parties, ne pouvait être bien dans son ensemble.... A l'honneur de prévenir le public, qu'au moyen d'appareils dissimulatoires, il a trouvé le secret de redresser les torts de la nature. Les bossus qui voudront bien l'honorer de leur confiance, le trouveront à son academie, rue Villedot, etc.' Edmond Rochefort and Georges Duval, *Le Tailleur des bossus, ou l'Orthopédie, contrefaçon en 1 acte et en vaudeville*, Paris, Barba, 1826, p. 14.

38 'Donne-moi la sangle épigastrique, (à Malplaquet) nous allons vous revêtir de formes antiques.'
'...Lâchez monsieur d'une ligne (écrivant avec de la craie sur l'habit de Malplaquet, les chiffres nommés plus bas). [A]ppliquons ici une poitrine mobile à soupape diaphragmatique pour ne pas gêner les mouvements du thorax, no. 1, deuxième serie. Tenez-vous droit.' Ibid., pp. 23–4.

39 In the same year as the vaudeville, a doctor proclaimed that despite all of the advertisements there were no miracle cures for certain deformities: 'In seeing this sort of orthopaedic frenzy, in reading the pompous announcements of the daily newspapers, does one not believe that the race of hunchbacks and rickety men will disappear from French soil? But, alas, it is all for naught!' Anon., *La Vérité*, p. 9.

40 He also satirised pretensions to classical beauty in his series mocking ancient myths of the same period.

41 'C'est un glorieux spectacle que de voir cette noble jeunesse française, pleine d'ardeur, de force et d'élégance se disputer l'honneur de servir la patrie sous les drapeaux de Mars!', published in *Le Charivari*, 21 August 1842.

42 'Les exemples de déviation de la taille sont nombreux ... ne dirait-on pas (si l'on sait regarder), à l'aspect de ces tailles, courtes et massives, de ces dos bombés, de

Tailoring and the 'normal' body   163

ces poitrines déprimées, de ces épaules irrégulièrement saillantes, de ces démarches raides et saccadées, que la taille déviée est la règle universelle, et que la taille normale est l'exception.' A. Tavernier, *Simple avis sur quelques préjugés et abus en orthopédie*, Paris, Labbé, 1855, p. 18.

43 During the revolution of 1848 he wrote a pamphlet entitled *Organisation du travail*, entreating the new Republican government to employ tailors during the off season and to pay proper wages for work made cheap by the new *confectionneurs*, producers of ready-made clothing. For more information on the rise of ready-made clothing, see Philippe Perrot, 'Traditional Trades and the Rise of Ready-Made Clothing', in Philippe Perrot, *Fashioning the Bourgeoisie*, Princeton, NJ, Princeton University Press, 1994, and François Faraut, *Histoire de la belle jardinière*, Paris, Belin, 1987.

44 For an overview of the bibliography of these fairs, see Jacqueline Viaux, 'Les Expositions des produits de l'industrie, 1798–1849', in Abraham Horodisch, ed., *De Arte et Libris: Festschrift Erasmus 1934–1984*, Amsterdam, Erasmus Antiquariaat en Boekhandel, 1984.

45 During the first half of the nineteenth century, tailors vied with each other in their patenting of inventions and their publication of new geometric cutting methods. They produced instruments like Beck's *costumomètre* (1819), Sylvestre's *corsage mécanique* (1829) and Delas's *somatomètre* (body-meter) (1839). Farid Chenoune, *Des Modes et des Hommes*, Paris, Flammarion, 1993.

46 French tailors and workers in the clothing industry still use Lavigne tape measures today.

47 The other main variations on the *tenue droite* were the *tenue cambrée* (arched-back posture) and the *tenue voûtée* (hunched-back posture).

48 'Un jour, un de mes élèves vient me prier de lui venir en aide pour habiller un nouveau client très riche, très difficile et d'une difformité impossible à décrire. Satisfaire ce client qui recevait et qui était reçu dans les meilleurs salons c'était doubler sa clientèle; j'acceptai avec plaisir cette occasion qui me permettait de faire une étude sur les conformations exceptionnelles où presque toujours on est obligé d'essayer plusieurs fois sans être certain de réussir à son gré. Comme il est impossible d'avoir son client ou sa cliente à son entière disposition et en songeant aux difficultés que l'on rencontre souvent dans notre métier, je me suis rappelé que j'avais quelques fois fait usage d'un liquide non pénétrant qui imperméabilise les étoffes et qu'en ajoutant un autre produit on pouvait donner aux tissus la fermeté du feutre et même du carton.

Ce modelage se fait vivement et sans inconvénient pour la personne qui pose et ne tache ni la chemise, ni le pantalon chez l'homme, ni la chemise, ni le corset, ni le jupon chez la femme. Après avoir expérimenté avec succès le moulage du buste de mon client, j'ai depuis lors profité des occasions qui se sont présentés pour mouler par le même procédé toutes conformations qui ne sont pas régulières. Dans les cas ordinaires j'emploie des moyens beaucoup plus simples pour faire les bustes sur nature sans avoir recours au modelage. Tous ces matériaux réunis m'ont permis de fonder une grande fabrique des bustes dont les produits depuis 1849 ont été médaillés au différentes Expositions et font aujourd'hui le tour du monde.' Alexis Lavigne, *Origine des mannequins modernes moulés sur nature et d'après nature*, Archives Esmod, Paris, n.d.

49 Musée d'Orsay, *A fleur de peau: le moulage sur nature au XIXe siècle*, Paris, RMN, 2001.

50 Édouard Papet, 'Le Moulage sur nature au service de la science', ibid., pp. 88–108.

51 Of course the mathematics were not exact, and even now clothing sizes vary over time and from brand to brand, so that a size ten dress in the 1950s is not a size ten now, nor is a size ten by Donna Karan necessarily proportioned the same as a size ten by Vivienne Westwood.

52 Sales prospectus for patented 'Bustes Lavigne', *c.*1868. As Lavigne's two-tier commercial practice demonstrates, the standardised bust aimed at the mass market and the made-to-measure bust cast individually for an elite few coexisted in the nineteenth century. By 1900 the commercial directory for Paris lists only three of ten mannequin manufacturers who offer made-to-measure busts to their clients.

8 'A masculine mythology suppressing and distorting all the facts'

British women contesting the concept of the male-as-norm, 1870–1930

Lesley A. Hall

The male norm, and constructing the female as abnormal

There is a very long tradition of men regarding the male body and male bodily functions as the norm, and the female body and its functions as therefore abnormal or deviant. Exactly how this abnormality of the female has been conceptualised has differed over time. While Laqueur's *Making Sex* posits a rather too sharp and definite historical shift around 1800 from perceptions of the female as lesser, defective male to a new construction of the female as opposite and different (the 'other', in fact),[1] both these approaches operated from an assumption that the standard of measurement was the male and that female difference required explanation and analysis.

Though 'woman' might sometimes have been included under the heading 'man', this could never be taken an absolute given, and the boundary kept shifting: as the pioneering feminist Charlotte Carmichael Stopes noted in 1907, in English law '"man" always includes "woman" when there is a penalty to be incurred but never includes "woman" when there is a privilege to be conferred'.[2] The presumption that female difference formed a deviation from the standard model produced a vast literature – as Virginia Woolf in *A Room of One's Own* asked in 1928: 'Have you any notion how many books are written about women in the course of one year? . . . Are you aware that you are, perhaps, the most discussed animal in the universe?'[3] This gender imbalance, testifying to the idea of the female as abnormal variant to be closely examined, is by no means superseded. There has been a vast amount of feminist scholarship on the extent to which the 'default setting' for humanity has been taken to be male over a wide range of fields and the extent to which social arrangements have been made on this understanding.

The persistence of such assumptions has been demonstrated in an elegant paper by Susan Lawrence and Kae Bendixen on representations of male and female anatomy in standard US textbooks of anatomy over the period 1890–1989. Lawrence and Bendixen point out that there is a disproportionate use of male figures for illustrations, far more than either female figures,

166   *Lesley A. Hall*

or diagrams lacking any specific gender attributes, and that even when a structure is not specified as male or female, it frequently includes male, rather than female, characteristics: for example, the posterior abdominal wall is shown with testicular arteries and veins. They suggest that this 'creates an anatomical ideal in the form of the male body'. Meanwhile, the text in these works persistently 'demarcate[s] the female as a "different" human type compared to the standard (male) human'. Male anatomy is presented as the norm which students must master before proceeding to the female variant. 'The' anatomy is that of the male, while the female is marked as distinctive. Comparisons frequently feature terms such as ' "smaller", "feebler", "weaker", or "less developed" ', and female structures 'presented as those that "fail" to develop'. Overall, in order to learn female anatomy, male anatomy must be learned first, a process that can lead to 'useless comparisons, careless inaccuracies and errors'. The authors conclude: 'This process reveals how far Western culture is from creating a non-gendered human anatomy, one from which both male and female emerge as equally significant and intriguing variations.'[4]

The extent to which hegemonic models of anatomy omitted the specific features of over 50 per cent of the population was further evidenced by the work of Helen O'Connell, an Australian urological surgeon, in 1998. In the article 'Anatomical Relationship between Urethra and Clitoris', she revealed that '[a] series of detailed dissections suggest that current anatomical descriptions of female human urethral and genital anatomy are inaccurate', and that the densely nerved clitoral structure extended far beyond its externally visible glans.[5] This clearly has significant implications in the context of surgical operations in the female urogenital area.

Only in 1993, following revelations in that year casting serious doubts on the findings of drug trials and population studies, did the United States mandate the inclusion of women in clinical trials.[6] Researchers had frequently applied evidence from a single-sex (usually male) study without ensuring that this generalisation was in fact valid.[7] It has recently been suggested that although approximately 52 per cent of subjects in large-scale trials are women, this represents less progress than would seem apparent, as it includes women-only studies for female-specific disorders such as breast cancer, while tests for other medications may unhelpfully lump together male and female subjects' results. While these figures apply to the United States, the situation in the United Kingdom is not much better.[8]

If this applies to scientific medical textbooks and otherwise carefully designed clinical trials, how much more so have unexamined assumptions about the male as norm inflected beliefs about sexuality. Pioneer sexologist Havelock Ellis suggested, in his essay 'The Sexual Impulse', that it was unnecessary to deal extensively with the nature of the male sexual impulse, because, 'since the constitution of society has largely been in the hands of men, the nature of the sexual impulse in men has largely been expressed in the written and unwritten codes of social law'.[9]

Women contesting the male-as-norm 167

This chapter considers attempts by British women from the late nineteenth to the mid-twentieth century, writing in a range of genres including polemic essays, advice to parents, marriage manuals and social observations, to critique the hegemonic assumptions about the relative nature and importance of male and female sexuality. Two aspects of the subject on which women made significant interventions are discussed. First, the attack on the social institutions constituted upon the belief that male sexual drives necessitated the existence of prostitution and the concomitant double standard of morality – whereby men's sexual needs had, at least tacitly, to be catered for, but any sexual peccadillo on a woman's part made her a complete outcast from society. Second, attempts by women to construct a model of female sexual desire, proceeding from the belief both that women were naturally neither frigid nor wantonly sexually promiscuous, and that their desire was neither a mere response to, nor a reflection of, that of men, with the concomitant re-visioning of sexual interactions so that they would be pleasurable and satisfying to women.

'[S]ome radical defect in . . . training for men'

Ellis's comment on the institutionalisation of the male sexual impulse was echoing arguments advanced by late nineteenth-century feminists embattled against the injustices to their sex encoded in British laws, in particular the Contagious Diseases Acts of the 1860s. These Acts were intended to safeguard the health of the armed forces, an issue of pressing concern following the debacle of the Crimean War and the subsequent government investigations into the health of the army and navy. One of the major threats to military health was venereal disease, running at a shockingly high rate among the ranks. The measure taken to deal with this particular threat was to create certain 'designated districts' around port and garrison towns, within which any woman suspected of being a prostitute could be compulsorily examined for venereal disease and, if found to be infected, incarcerated until cured. While this seemed to many an appropriate public health approach, these Acts aroused great hostility on grounds of religion and morality, as well as by their implicit violation of understood civil liberties (prostitution as such was not a crime, yet these women were, in effect, being incarcerated). They also aroused huge indignation among women already active in campaigns to improve women's civil and legal status.[10]

British women had already been contesting in various ways the pervasive societal assumptions that the male was to be taken as the norm and femaleness as the exception. The Contagious Diseases Acts, by this overt proclamation of the tacit double standard of morality, catalysed both campaigning and theorising by women. Josephine Butler, the charismatic leader of the Ladies' National Association for the Repeal of the Contagious Diseases Act, analysed the situation as follows:

168 *Lesley A. Hall*

> Our open defiance of governments, and of that false public opinion which made it possible for governments to enact such a law, has done what years – even centuries – of more silent and private work had never done, and could never do. It compelled the enemy to show himself, and to declare his nature and principles. It forced men once more to call things by their right names. The upholders of this law were obliged only to declare as their belief, and as the basis of this legislation, the doctrine of the *necessity of vice* for man, and of the impossibility of self-restraint; and then was called forth the public denial of that doctrine. For the first time in the world's history *women* came to the front in the controversy. The whole cruelty of the law falling on their own sex for the fancied preservation of the health of men, woke up the womanhood of this land.[11]

Butler emphasised the pervasiveness of the assumptions which formed the basis of the Acts: 'Even those men who are personally pure and blameless become persuaded by the force of familiarity with male profligacy around them, that this sin in *man* is venial and excusable.'[12] This view of the preconceptions about male sexuality in society was elaborated by a number of other women who were Butler's contemporaries, along with strategies for altering the situation. In endeavouring to establish a new and different norm for sexual behaviour in society, women were not positing something entirely new. They were looking at the standards demanded of women, which were based in a morality founded in Christian religious teaching that in theory applied to both sexes, and suggesting that these should become the societal norm.

A major assumption they made was that the sexual urge was more plastic and educable than patriarchal double-standard morality alleged. Elizabeth Blackwell, the pioneer woman doctor, advanced the argument that,

> under the effect of training to a moral life and the action of public opinion, a great body of women in our own country constantly lead a virtuous life, frequently in spite of physical instincts as strong as those of men, and always in spite of mental instincts still more powerful.[13]

At least for rhetorical purposes in making this argument, Blackwell claimed that women were not the sexless angels of Victorian ideology, but beings capable both of experiencing passion and, through training and the expectations laid upon them, able to restrain it.

Formulating the issue as being about the outcome of a learning process rather than the inevitable manifestation of innate attributes of male nature was a productive means of suggesting ways in which the norm might be altered. In her exhortations to parents to provide moral guidance on the problems of sex to their children, Blackwell presented the situation of the young man as follows:

Women contesting the male-as-norm   169

If at an early age, thought and feeling have been set in the right direction, and aids to virtue and to health, surround the young man, then this period of time, before his twenty-fifth year, will lead him into a strong and vigorous manhood. But where the mind is corrupted, the imagination heated, and no strong love of virtue planted in the soul, the individual loses the power of self-control, and becomes the victim of physical sensation and suggestion. When this condition of mental and physical deterioration has been produced, it is no longer possible for him to resist surrounding temptations.[14]

She painted a cautionary picture:

> Opportunity tempts his wavering innocence, thoughtless or vicious companions undertake to 'form' him, laugh at his scruples, sneer at his conscience, excite him with allurements. Or a deadly counsel meets him, meets him from those he is bound to respect. The most powerful morbid stimulant that exists – a stimulant to every drop of his seething young blood – is advised, viz.: the resort to prostitutes.[15]

Similar views on the possibility of changing the situation, and the pervasiveness of the views she contested, were adumbrated by the influential social purity writer Jane Ellice Hopkins:

> There must be some radical defect in that training for men to take the attitude they do. I do not mean bad, dissipated men, but men who in all other relations of life would be designated fairly good men. Once let such a man be persuaded – however wrongly – that his health, or his prospect of having some day a family of his own, will suffer from delayed marriage and he considers the question settled. He will sacrifice his health to over-smoking, to excess in athletics, to over-eating or champagne drinking, to late hours and overwork; but to sacrifice health or future happiness to save a woman from degradation, bah! it never so much as enters his mind.[16]

Hopkins suggested that besides inculcating a generally higher moral standard in the growing youth, it was appropriate to give medical warnings concerning the danger of indulgence:

> [Y]oung men require a plain, emphatic warning as to the physical dangers of licentiousness and of the possibility of contracting a taint which medical science is now pronouncing to be ineradicable and which they will transmit in some form or other to their children after them. We want a strong cord made up of every strand we can lay hold of, and one of these strands is doubtless self preservation.[17]

170   *Lesley A. Hall*

Making changes in the socialisation of boys, so that they would eschew vicious ways and not indulge in sexual immorality, was one strategy advanced by women critiquing the existing male norm and resisting assumptions that it was an unalterable law of nature.

The growing concern over the public health threat posed by venereal diseases by the end of the nineteenth century, made yet more acute by the revelation of the Wasserman test of the hitherto unsuspected prevalence of asymptomatic syphilis in the population, provided further stimulus and opportunity for women to attack the social institutions that facilitated the spread of these incurable diseases. Michael Worboys has plausibly argued that as a result not only of the rise of bacteriological science in the late nineteenth century, but also of the feminist arguments about the pernicious societal effects of male promiscuity, gonorrhoea was, by the beginning of the twentieth century, re-gendered as a disease spread by men. Formerly it had been assumed to be conveyed to men from women, probably by some toxic natural secretion of the vagina. But by the 1900s it was a disease contracted by immoral men and conveyed to their innocent wives, causing hidden disease and sterility.[18]

Frances Swiney, in *The Awakening of Womanhood* (first published 1905, into its third edition by 1908), wrote of the 'far-reaching effects of immorality in the case of the man, and in the present sex-biased inequality of the moral law'. A man 'unrestrained by legal restrictions, unhampered by medical supervision, may at any time, and under any circumstance and condition of disease, contract marriage with a healthy innocent woman', thus producing 'offspring tainted from birth with the worst of human scourges'. While women who chose 'a life of shame', she conceded, 'should bear the full measure of its guilt and degradation', it was 'still more necessary . . . to make the way of the male transgressor hard . . . so too should the man be branded: and not, as at present, be courted, feted, forgiven'.[19] Her conclusion was, similar to that of her predecessors, that

> throughout the whole code affecting sexual relations . . . male vice is safeguarded in every possible manner. . . . It is indeed a matter of surprise, not that men are immoral, but they are not more so, for man-made legislation has made the path of vice easy, and carefully excluded such restrictions and penalties as would be inconvenient and compromising to the male offender.[20]

In her essay 'The State Regulation of Vice', Swiney – aided by the recent developments in medical science around the understanding of venereal diseases, and appealing also to the eugenic concerns prevalent at the time – turned on their head the arguments from nature so often used to justify male licence:

> Nature is fundamentally moral. . . . Nature makes no provision for sex-obsession, except through the righteousness of immutable law governing cause and effect, diseasing, weakening, and ultimately extirpating

Women contesting the male-as-norm 171

those who transgress in the way of life.... If the human male is in so low a grade of physical and ethical development as to be incapable of the self-restraint and self-regulation of the lower species, he will look in vain to Nature for sanction to exploit the most highly evolved of organisms – the woman of the race. He can only fall back upon a man-made law, recognising a double standard of morality, providing means for prostitution, and authorising a commercial system built on vested interests of greed and lust under the aegis of Church and State.[21]

Louisa Martindale, writing with the authority of her medical qualification as well as feminist passion in *Under the Surface* (1908), analysed the socially-constructed factors, rather than innate viciousness, that accounted for women falling into prostitution: 'seduced . . . ashamed to return to her home she finds herself alone without credentials or testimonials and unable to find employment. It is then that she is forced to go on the streets.' Martindale reasoned that it was so easy for women to be seduced as a result of their socialisation rather than any libidinous urges:

[F]rom her earliest days, she has been imbued with the belief in the superior knowledge of the other sex. She has been taught to be obedient and to be affectionate and charming, and above all to be unselfish. She has been taught to regard her future husband as master, and one she must obey. Surely if she falls into the hands of a scoundrel, there is very little chance that she may successfully resist him.

She cited in support of this contention, 'the hundreds of cases I have come in contact with in my profession', which had struck her forcibly

with the helplessness of the young girl, the physical paralysis that creeps over her; her utter ignorance of the result of her acquiescence, and her faith in the man she believes is in love with her. She has been trained from her earliest years in the very qualities which make her an easy prey to the professional seducer or procurer.[22]

The best-known polemic against the double moral standard, the existence of prostitution and the outcome of widespread venereal disease was *The Great Scourge*, published by the militant suffragette Christabel Pankhurst in 1913. As can be seen, she was far from the first to make these connections or to reveal the underlying assumptions, and her arguments in fact drew on points with which her readers would already have been familiar:

We shall hear the usual balderdash about 'human nature and 'injury to man's health'. Human nature is a very wide term, and it covers a multitude of sins and vices which are not on that account any the more to be tolerated. . . .

172 *Lesley A. Hall*

> Why is human nature to have full scope only in the one direction of sexual vice? The answer to that question is that men have got all the power in the State, and therefore make not only the laws of the State, but also its morality.[23]

She also made the connection between diseases conveyed to women within marriage by their husbands, and their consequent ailing, rather than this being simply attributable to inherent female fragility: 'Women are not naturally invalids, as they have been taught to believe. They are invalids because they are the victims of the sexual diseases known as syphilis and gonorrhoea.'[24]

Such arguments were not only associated with the most militant wing of the suffrage movement. Martindale, for example, was a constitutional suffragist, as was A. Maude Royden, who in 1917 (after the publication of the report of the Royal Commission on Venereal Diseases, which made relatively humane and equitable recommendations for dealing with them, but during increased wartime agitation lamented about the 'harpies' allegedly infecting the troops) wrote bitterly in *Women and the Sovereign State*:

> The extremity of the exploitation is even more naked than before, since it is said that the prostitute is necessary for men's health, and it is now known that she herself, in the exercise of her trade, very frequently becomes diseased. Syphilis and gonorrhoea are the industrial diseases of prostitution, but they do not fall within the Employers' Liability Act. On the contrary, it is continually urged that when one of her employers has infected a prostitute, she should be punished for it. It is not suggested that she herself should be protected in the exercise of what is held to be a necessary and known to be a highly dangerous trade. She plies it in the interests of men's health; for this purpose alone is she allowed to exist. How, then, can any penalty be too harsh when she gives to her patron not health but a disease? Should we not, indeed, regard it as an extraordinary exercise of Christian charity – or perhaps a maudlin sentimentality – that she is not at once taken out and shot? What does it matter that she herself was infected by a man? He has a right to infect her, if his health or ease required it. She has no right except the right to be exploited.[25]

These views on the iniquity of a male-defined system of sexual morality were shared by a somewhat younger generation of feminist writers (to be discussed in more detail later) associated with 'sex reform' and a more liberal attitude towards the positive potential of sexuality. The extreme sex radical and advocate for free love, Stella Browne, wrote of the pernicious division of women into 'two arbitrary classes, corresponding to no psychological or ethical individual differences: (a) The prospective or actual private sex property of one man. (b) The public sex property of all and sundry.'[26] She was

Women contesting the male-as-norm   173

scathing about existing 'sexual institutions founded on the needs and preferences of a primitive type of man'.[27] Josephine Butler was one of her great heroines.[28]

The tradition of critique of the existing patriarchally inflected sexual institutions of society thus did not vanish during the interwar period, although there was a widespread perception that commercial prostitution was undergoing decline, as a result of the rise of consensual 'promiscuous' relationships between the sexes, and it therefore became less of an overriding cause for concern. Furthermore, a new system for tackling the problem of venereal disease was implemented as a result of the recommendations of the Royal Commission on Venereal Diseases in 1916, and this was strongly influenced by preceding feminist debates. The commissioners included the feminist social purity campaigner Dame Mary Scharlieb, and the commission heard evidence from many women activists and propagandists. Thus, at least in principle, there was no invidious division of sufferers into the innocent and the guilty, or discrimination by gender.[29]

'[A]n enormously wider range of variation; and much greater diffusion'

From at least the later nineteenth century, women were arguing that their sex was not divided into passionless angels in the house on the one hand and lustful fallen women on the other. At first the claims tended to be adduced for the rhetorical purpose of pointing out that women, unlike men, were expected to, and in the great majority of cases did, control their sexual desires: reference has already been made to Elizabeth Blackwell's comments on this subject. She additionally remarked that '[n]o solution of the difficult problem of sexual relationships is possible, until the complete parallelism (not identity) of the sexual nature in the two sexes is recognised.'[30] Jane Clapperton, a free-thinker and a supporter of the Malthusian League, which advocated the use of birth control, similarly indicated that women were not passionless creatures, but that it was in girls' nature 'to throw out tender tentacles of human feeling'. However, social pressures meant that

> girls are never able to be free and natural ... with the other sex, they must be formal, cold, unnatural, or run the risk of being taken for husband-hunters, and condemned as wanting in the very quality they eminently possess – delicate womanliness.[31]

Her fellow Malthusian and freethinker Annie Besant, in *The Law of Population* (1889), her pamphlet advocating contraception, made a case for sexual activity as both healthful and pleasurable:

> Celibacy is not natural to men or to women: all bodily needs require their legitimate satisfaction, and celibacy is a disregard of natural law.

174   *Lesley A. Hall*

The asceticism which despises the body is a contempt of nature, and a revolt against her.[32]

But there were also, initially somewhat coded, allusions to women's adverse experiences of sex within marriage. Besant herself, in *Marriage, as It Was, as It Is, and As It Should Be: A Plea for Reform* (1882), advanced forthright arguments about the state of affairs as it was legally and socially constituted by the doctrine of 'conjugal rights':

A married woman loses control over her own body; it belongs to her owner, not to herself; no force, no violence, on the husband's part in conjugal relations is regarded as possible by the law; she may be suffering, ill, it matters not; force or constraint is recognised by the law as rape, in all cases save that of marriage . . . no rape can be committed by a husband on a wife; the consent given in marriage is held to cover the life, and if – as sometimes occurs – a miscarriage or premature confinement be brought on by the husband's selfish passions, no offence is committed in the eye of the law, for the wife is the husband's property, and by marriage she has lost the right of control over her own body. The English marriage law sweeps away all the tenderness, all the grace, all the generosity of love, and transforms conjugal affection into a hard and brutal legal right.[33]

Ellice Hopkins presented a similar picture (though she condemned Besant's agenda of free love and birth control) of women physically debilitated and emotionally repelled by thoughtless and selfish male demands:

Whilst the sight is so familiar of wives with health broken down and life made a burden, possibly even premature death incurred, by their being given no rest from the sacred duties of motherhood, to say nothing of the health of the hapless child born under such circumstances, can we wonder that the modern woman often shows a marked distaste to marriage and looks upon it as something low and sensual? Or can we wonder that married men, with so sensual an idea of so holy a state should, alas! so largely minister to the existence of an outcast class of women? [34]

Although there was an obvious contrast being made by several of these writers between male lustfulness and female self-control, the beginnings of a construction of sexual desire as good in itself, when not corrupted by exploitative and inequitable male assumptions and practices, can be discerned. This featured not only in the works of self-declared radical freethinkers and Malthusians such as Besant and Clapperton but also in works of those such as Blackwell and Hopkins who were arguing from a basis of Christian morality. Blackwell indeed went so far as to claim:

The physical pleasure which attends the caresses of love is a rich endowment of humanity, granted by a beneficent Creative Power. There is nothing necessarily evil in physical pleasure. Though inferior in rank to mental pleasure, it is a legitimate part of our nature. . . . The sexual act itself, rightly understood in its compound character, so far from being a necessarily evil thing, is really a divinely created and altogether righteous fulfilment of the conditions of present life.[35]

But while she saw sexual desire and pleasure as, in the right circumstances, benign, she also expressed some doubts as to the extent to which women might be experiencing these benefits within marriage:

A delicate wife will often confide to her medical adviser . . . that at the very time when marriage love seems to unite them most closely, when her husband's welcome kisses and caresses seem to bring them into profound union, comes an act which mentally separates them, and which may be either indifferent or repugnant to her. . . . It is the profound attraction of one nature to the other which marks passion; and delight in kiss and caress – the love-touch – is physical sexual expression as much as the special act of the male.[36]

However, desire and the possible pleasures of sex tended to be regarded with some suspicion by feminists fighting for civic recognition. Periodicals published by the various suffrage societies did touch on sexual matters, but largely in the context of oppression. For example, the relatively light sentences imposed for crimes of violence and sexual abuse against women and girls were contrasted with the heavy penalties imposed for crimes against property. The underlying notions of female sexuality largely presupposed the prime importance of chaste monogamous marriage, and women's maternal role, both of which were threatened by male vice and hypocrisy.[37]

A significant moment in changing the terms of the argument was the publication of the radical feminist journal *The Freewoman* from late 1911 to the end of 1912. It was unaligned with any of the suffrage societies and cast a critical eye on what its founding editor, Dora Marsden, considered an undue emphasis on gaining the vote. *The Freewoman* took up a position of revolt against what it perceived as the puritanism, even prudery, pervading the suffrage movement. The heated debates in its columns about such issues as whether women had sexual desires, and, if not, whether this made them superior to men, have been extensively analysed.[38] Discussing the overall significance of *The Freewoman* some 15 years after its founding, Rebecca West, who had been a contributor, even though she was forbidden to bring the journal into her mother's house, claimed that 'the greatest service' it performed was 'through its unblushingness' and because

176 *Lesley A. Hall*

it smashed the romantic pretence that women had as a birthright the gift of perfect adaptation: that they were in a bland state of desireless contentment which, when they were beautiful, reminded the onlooker of goddesses, and when they were plain were apt to remind him of cabbage.

Instead, it revealed that 'women were vexed human beings who suffered intensely from male-adaptation to life, and that they were tortured and dangerous if they were not allowed to adapt themselves to life.'[39]

The feminist, socialist and sex-radical Stella Browne, a significant contributor to the Freewoman debates, summed up the still prevalent assumptions about female sexuality in her 1915 paper 'The Sexual Variety and Variability of Women, and its Bearing upon Social Reconstruction' (published 1917) as follows:

The belief that the majority of women, those not belonging to the prostitute class, feel neither curiosity, nor desire on these matters, while they are maidens. And that when their sexual life has begun, its physical side is quite subordinate, and merely a *response* to their husbands.

Browne went on to disruptively redefine the female sexual impulse as follows:

The sexual emotion in women is not, taking it broadly, weaker than in men. But it has an enormously wider range of variation; and much greater diffusion, both in desire and pleasure, all through women's organisms. . . . The variability of the sexual emotion in women is absolutely basic and primary. It can never be expressed or satisfied by either patriarchal marriage or prostitution.

She further claimed that

this variety and variability . . . would militate against any real promiscuity, if women were all economically secure and free to follow their own instincts, and to control their maternal function by the knowledge of contraceptives (a most important part of women's real emancipation). Most people are apt to under-rate the real strength of desire, and at the same time, to exaggerate its indiscriminate facility.[40]

Stella Browne represented a radical vanguard, being active in the Malthusian League and the British Society for the Study of Sex Psychology, as well as an early member of the British Communist Party and an advocate for and practitioner of free love. She was the first woman to speak up for the legalisation of abortion at a time when even birth control was mentioned in hushed undertones. However, the ideas being voiced in the progressive circles of

Women contesting the male-as-norm 177

which Browne was part were adapted for and disseminated to a much wider audience by Marie Stopes.

Stopes was a distinguished woman scientist who had turned to the investigation of sexual matters as a result of her disastrous first marriage, which ended in annulment.[41] 'Knowledge gained at such a cost', she later stated, 'should be placed at the service of humanity'.[42] She did this in *Married Love: A New Contribution to the Solution of Sex Difficulties* (1918). Her name is predominantly associated with birth control, but in *Married Love* the use of contraception was implied rather than explicitly described, the central theme being the necessity of female sexual pleasure within marriage. Central to Stopes's message was her vision of female desire as very far from being merely a reflection of or response to that of the male.

In Chapter 3 of *Married Love* she vigorously dissented from the common masculine notion that women were simply 'contrary'. Stopes – an ardent feminist who had been a suffragette – argued that 'it has suited the general structure of society much better for men to shrug their shoulders and smile at women as irrational and capricious creatures, to be courted when it suited them, not studied'. In fact, she claimed that women experienced a periodic recurrence of natural desire at approximately fortnightly intervals. However:

> Woman, so long coerced by economic dependence, and the need for protection while she bore her children, has had to mould herself to the shape desired by man wherever possible, and she has stifled her natural feelings and her own deep thoughts as they welled up.

The demand that wives should be sexually available on male terms had thus been detrimental to their own responses and potential for sexual pleasure.

Stopes depicted 'woman's nature [as] set to rhythms over which man has no more control than he has over the tides of the sea' (metaphorically identifying female desire with powerful natural forces: no frail wilting and fading flowers here). Apart from its most obvious manifestations in menstruation and pregnancy, 'the subtler ebb and flow of woman's sex [had] escaped man's observations or his care', and thus the husband found 'only caprice in his bride's coldness when she yields her sacrificial body while her sex-tide is at the ebb'. Another side to the problem was even less recognised: the woman whose husband did not recognise 'the delicate signs of her ardour' when her 'love-tide is at the highest'. The initiate of 'love's mysteries' would realise by 'a hundred subtle signs' when 'the tide is up', but many husbands were blind, unresponsive and behaved in such a fashion as to inhibit their wives' responsiveness.[43]

Male desire, by contrast, was in 'our anaemic artificial days . . . a surface need, quickly satisfied, colourless, and lacking beauty'.[44] Husbands claimed wives 'when [they] would naturally enjoy union and when it is to some degree repugnant', and this 'tended to flatten out the billowing curves of . . . natural desire'.[45] Female desire was represented by Stopes as much richer and

178 Lesley A. Hall

more complex than men's: 'wonderful tides, scented and enriched . . . urging her to transports and self-expressions'.[46]

This concept of female sexuality as equally powerful, or even more powerful than that of the male, but different in kind, not simply the same, became a recurrent motif in a range of writings by women on sexuality throughout the 1920s and 1930s in Britain. A popular preacher and writer on religious matters, the Reverend Dr Maude Royden, for example, wrote in *Sex and Commonsense*, a work which went into several editions following its first publication in 1921:

> I did not say that men and women suffered in the same way. I said they suffered equally . . . passion comes to a man with greater violence, and is more likely to leave him in peace at other times. And in the case of a woman . . . very often the strain on her is much less dramatic, much less violent, and more persistent. . . . That kind of strain is easily denied by the very people who are enduring it. It is so customary, so much a part of their life, that they are unconscious of it.[47]

This new vision of female desire also led to the critique of male sexual practice as too often failing to provide requisite mutual satisfaction. As Stella Browne commented,

> The diffused sexuality of women, again, is the enemy of very abrupt transformations and transitions: no social order which took this fact adequately into consideration, could tolerate the present forms of marriage, with the outrage on decency and freedom alike involved in the ideas of 'conjugal rights'.
>
> No woman has been given her full share of the beauty and the joy of life, who has not been very gradually and skilfully initiated into the sexual relation.[48]

Maude Royden, writing from a specifically Christian viewpoint for a religious audience, declared:

> I wish men could . . . understand that to enforce physical union when a woman's psychical and emotional nature does not desire it, is definitely and physically cruel. Woman is not a passive instrument, and to treat her as such is to injure her.
>
> Perhaps I may be forgiven for labouring this point because, in fact, misunderstanding here is so disastrous. Marriage, after all, is a relation into which the question of physical union enters, and if there is no equality of desire, marriage will be much less than it might be.[49]

Leonora Eyles, in *The Woman in the Little House*, based on her observations of the lives of working-class women, deplored the insistence of husbands upon their 'conjugal rights'. As a result, for the women she was describing, marital sex had

> grown, through their husbands' selfishness and carelessness, to be unendurably distressing to nerve and body and mind alike. . . . Men must be taught that what amounts to forcing their wives' imitation love is not going to make for comfortable homes, married harmony, and even lasting physical pleasure.[50]

Similar comments and insights could be multiplied in a range of works produced by women during the interwar years.[51] There was a continuing tradition of resistance to the assumption that existing male patterns of sexual behaviour were simply something to which women had to adapt themselves to or uncomplainingly endure.

Conclusion

Unfortunately, it does appear that these attempts to overturn perspectives on the sexual institutions in British society based on the assumption that particular types of male behaviour formed the standard became increasingly occluded and dismissed following the Second World War. Although in 1951 legislation finally restored some of the civil liberties that had continued to be denied to the 'common prostitute', the concerns about visible street prostitution addressed by the Wolfenden Committee in 1954–6 resulted in the Street Offences Act of 1959, which effectively removed these again. Prostitution was largely considered in the light of a problem of public order and cleaning up the streets, and the prostitutes themselves seen in terms of deviancy and pathology: socio-economic explanations no longer seemed valid in an era of economic prosperity and the welfare state, while issues of demand and the customer were not addressed. During the 1950s and 60s many marriage guidance manuals, instead of asserting women's right to sexual pleasure, exhorted them to be compliant and agreeable partners for their husbands, even if they were not themselves in the mood.[52]

In more recent decades there have been initiatives aimed at the male customers of prostitutes, in particular 'kerb-crawlers'. However, the approach is largely based in a perception of these men being a public nuisance in the same way as overtly soliciting prostitutes, rather than in any broader consideration of the factors leading to the demand for prostitution. The 1999 Swedish law prohibiting the purchasing, rather than the sale, of sex is a still-rare attempt to address 'the demand, the men who assume the right to purchase persons for prostitution purposes'.[53]

Recent discussions about a 'female Viagra' point up the extent to which ideas of female sexuality are still modelled on the assumption that the male model can simply be extended to women, or that women need to be fixed to conform to male specifications. However valuable and appropriate medical

180   Lesley A. Hall

interventions may be in certain specific cases, it seems improbable that 43 per cent of US females, as claimed, suffer from a pharmacologically treatable 'female sexual dysfunction' disorder. The sex therapist Leonore Tiefer, author of *Sex Is Not a Natural Act* (1994), commented: 'If almost half the population has the disorder, is it more likely that they all suffer from some physical defect, or that there is a social or cultural problem that needs to be addressed?' A survey of 2,600 American women reported that they saw their sexual problems as more to do with lifestyle issues such as being too tired and too busy, rather than as physical difficulties that just needed a 'quick fix'. However, the emphasis of the medical approach, strongly encouraged by aggressive marketing strategies by drug manufacturers, seems to be on providing a 'magic bullet' to make women match up to what is considered the masculine norm of sexual functioning, even to the extent of dosing them with testosterone.[54] Dr John Bancroft of the Kinsey Institute is reported as pointing out that, far from being a malfunction, 'an inhibition of sexual desire is in many situations a healthy and functional response for women faced with stress, tiredness or threatening patterns of behaviour from their partners'. The issue is complicated by the fact that, while male sexual function and dysfunction can be simply (if possibly misleadingly) assessed by erection capacity, 'female sexual responses have proved much more difficult to quantify' and remain relatively under-researched.[55]

It can therefore be seen that the male body and its sexual responses are still presumed to constitute the norm, something for which society has to cater and to which women are required to adapt themselves. While this is being contested by contemporary feminists, the earlier analyses by late nineteenth- and twentieth-century feminists remain relevant to current debates.

Notes

1 T. Laqueur, *Making Sex: Body and Gender from the Greeks to Freud*, Cambridge, MA, Harvard University Press, 1990.
2 C. Stopes, *The Sphere of Man in Relation to That of Woman in the Constitution*, London, T. Fisher Unwin, 1907.
3 V. Woolf, *A Room of One's Own*, Harmondsworth, UK, Penguin, 1970 [1928], p. 28.
4 S. Lawrence and K. Bendixen, 'His and Hers: Male and Female Anatomy in Textbooks for US Medical Students, 1890–1989', *Social Science and Medicine*, 1992, 37, pp. 925–34.
5 Reported in S. Williamson, 'The Truth about Women', *New Scientist*, 1998, 2145, p. 34. The extent of the hidden structure of the clitoris was already known among sex researchers. See J. Bancroft, *Human Sexuality and Its Problems*, 2nd edn, London, Churchill Livingstone, 1989, pp. 39–40. But clearly this information had not made any impact on more general anatomical and surgical knowledge.
6 'His Pain, Her Pain', *New Scientist*, 19 January 2002, 2326, p. 32.
7 '"Gender Offenders" skew results in many studies', *New Scientist*, 1993, 1861, p. 8.
8 'His Pain, Her Pain'.

9 H. Ellis, *Studies in the Psychology of Sex*, vol. 3: *Analysis of the Sexual Impulse, Love and Pain, The Sexual Impulse in Women*, London, privately printed for the Society of Psychological Research, 1904, p. 217.

10 There is an extensive historiography on the Acts and the campaigns against them. P. McHugh, *Prostitution and Victorian Social Reform*, London, Croom Helm, 1980, and J. Walkowitz, *Prostitution and Victorian Society: Women, Class and the State*, Cambridge, Cambridge University Press, 1980, remain the best introductions.

11 J. Butler, *Social Purity*, London, Morgan & Scott, 1879, pp. 30–1.

12 Ibid., pp. 10–11.

13 E. Blackwell, *Counsel to Parents on the Moral Education of Their Children*, London, Hirst Smyth & Son, 1882, p. 75.

14 Ibid., pp. 36–7.

15 Ibid., p. 37.

16 E. Hopkins, *The Power of Womanhood or Mothers and Sons: A Book for Parents, and Those in Loco Parentis*, London, Wells Gardner, 1899, pp. 59–60.

17 Ibid., p. 147.

18 M. Worboys, 'Unsexing Gonorrhoea: Bacteriologists, Gynaecologists, and Suffragists in Britain, 1860–1920', *Social History of Medicine*, 2004, 17, pp. 41–59.

19 F. Swiney, *The Awakening of Women or Woman's Part in Evolution*, London, William Reeves, 1905, 3rd edition 1908, pp. 127–8.

20 Ibid., p. 219.

21 F. Swiney, 'State Regulation of Vice', in *The Sons of Belial and Other Essays on the Social Evil*, London, C. W. Daniel for the League of Isis, *c.*1912, pp. 38–42.

22 L. Martindale, *Under the Surface*, Brighton, The Southern Publishing Company, 1908, pp. 70–1.

23 C. Pankhurst, *The Great Scourge and How to End It*, London, E. Pankhurst, 1913, p. 6.

24 Ibid., p. 65.

25 M. Royden, *Women and the Sovereign State: The State and Prostitution*, London, Headley Bros., 1917, pp. 54–5.

26 S. Browne, *Sexual Variety and Variability among Women, and Its Bearing upon Social Reconstruction*, London, British Society for the Study of Sex Psychology, 1917, p. 2.

27 S. Browne, 'Women and Birth-Control', in E. Paul and C. Paul, eds, *Population and Birth-Control: A Symposium*, New York, Critic and Guide Company, 1917, pp. 247–57.

28 S. Browne, 'Current Notes', *The New Generation*, May 1928, 7, p. 53.

29 L. Hall, 'Venereal diseases in Britain from the Contagious Diseases Acts to the National Health Service', in R. Davidson and L. Hall, eds, *Sex, Sin and Suffering: Venereal Disease and European Society since 1870*, London, Routledge, 2001, pp. 120–36.

30 Blackwell, *Counsel to Parents*, p. 75.

31 J. Clapperton, *Scientific Meliorism and the Evolution of Happiness*, London, Kegan, Paul, Trench, 1885, pp. 150–1.

32 A. Besant, *The Law of Population: Its Consequences, and Its Bearing upon Human Conduct and Morals*, London, Freethought Publishing Company, 1889, p. 28.

33 A. Besant, *Marriage, as It Was, as It Is, and as It Should Be: A Plea for Reform*, London, Freethought Publishing Company, 1882, pp. 13–14.

34 Hopkins, *The Power of Womanhood*, p. 143.

35 E. Blackwell, *The Human Element in Sex, being a Medical Inquiry into the Relation of Sexual Physiology to Christian Morality*, London, J. & A. Churchill, 1894, p. 14.

36 Ibid., p. 50.

37 L. Garner, *Stepping Stones to Women's Liberty: Feminist Ideas in the Women's Suffrage Movement*, London, Heinemann, 1984, pp. 21–2, 38–40.

182   *Lesley A. Hall*

38 There are significant discussions on *The Freewoman* in L. Bland, *Banishing the Beast: English Feminism and Sexual Morality, 1885–1914*, London, Penguin, 1995; L. Garner, *A Brave and Beautiful Spirit: Dora Marsden, 1882–1960*, Aldershot, UK, Avebury, 1990 (Marsden was the originator and founding editor of *The Freewoman*); L. Hall, 'The Next Generation: Stella Browne, the New Woman as Freewoman', in A. Richardson and C. Willis, eds, *The New Woman in Fiction and in Fact: Fin-de-Siècle Feminisms*, Basingstoke, UK, Palgrave, 2001, pp. 224–38; M. Jackson, *The Real Facts of Life: Feminism and the Politics of Sexuality, c.1850–1940*, London: Taylor and Francis, 1994; and S. Jeffreys, *The Spinster and Her Enemies: Feminism and Sexuality, 1880–1930*, London, Pandora, 1985.

39 R. West, 'The Freewoman', first published in *Time and Tide*, 16 July 1926, reprinted in D. Spender, ed., *Time and Tide Wait for No Man*, London, Pandora, 1984, p. 66.

40 Browne, *Sexual Variety and Variability*, pp. 4–6.

41 There are several biographies of Stopes: for a short overview of her writings on marriage in the light of her own experiences, see L. Hall, 'Uniting Science and Sensibility: Marie Stopes and the Narratives of Marriage in the 1920s', in A. Ingram and D. Patai, eds, *Rediscovering Forgotten Radicals: British Women Writers, 1889–1939*, Chapel Hill, NC, University of North Carolina Press, 1993, pp. 118–36.

42 M. Stopes, *Married Love: A New Contribution to the Solution of Sex Difficulties*, London, A. C. Fifield, 1918, p. xiii.

43 Ibid., pp. 20–1.

44 Ibid., pp. 19–20.

45 Ibid., p. 28.

46 Ibid., p. 20.

47 M. Royden, *Sex and Common-Sense*, London, Hurst & Blackett, 1921, 8th edn, *c.*1922, pp. 117–18.

48 Browne, *Sexual Variety and Variability*, p. 8.

49 Royden, *Sex and Common Sense*, p. 181.

50 L. Eyles, *The Woman in the Little House*, London, Grant Richards, 1922, pp. 147–8.

51 For examples, see L. Hall, *Outspoken Women: British Women Writing about Sex, 1870–1969*, London, Routledge, 2005, sections 3 and 4.

52 Ibid., Section 5.

53 G. Ekberg, 'The Swedish Law That Prohibits the Purchase of Sexual Services: Best Practices for Prevention of Prostitution and Trafficking in Human Beings', *Violence against Women*, 2004, 10, pp. 1187–218.

54 D. Martindale, 'What Women Want', *New Scientist*, 17 March 2001, 2282, p. 28.

55 R. Moynihan, 'The Making of a Disease: Female Sexual Dysfunction', *British Medical Journal*, 2003, 326, pp. 45–7.

9 Interpreting abnormal psychology in the late nineteenth century

William James's spiritual crisis

Francis Neary

> I went one evening into a dressing-room in the twilight to procure some article that was there; when suddenly there fell upon me without warning, just as if it came out of the darkness, a horrible fear of my own existence. Simultaneously there arose in my mind the image of an epileptic patient whom I had seen in the asylum, a black-haired youth with greenish skin, entirely idiotic, who used to sit all day on one of the benches, or rather shelves against the wall, with his knees drawn up against his chin. *That shape am I*, I felt, potentially. I became a mass of quivering fear. After this the universe was changed for me altogether. I awoke morning after morning with a horrible dread at the pit of my stomach, and with a sense of the insecurity of life that I never knew before, and that I have never felt since.[1]

This often-quoted passage from *The Varieties of Religious Experience* turned out to be William James reflecting thirty years later upon his own spiritual crisis in the late 1860s and early 1870s. James was both an important founding father of American psychology and the first American philosopher to have wide appeal in Europe. In the original text of the *Varieties* he described the episode in the guise of a memoir given to him by an anonymous Frenchman, but afterwards he admitted that the experience was his own, on multiple occasions.[2]

The *Varieties* started life as the 1900–1 series of Gifford Lectures delivered in Edinburgh, and the resulting monograph sought to bring religion within the realm of normal science. He argued against medical and scientific materialists who either ignored spiritual experiences or associated them with pathological malfunctions of the physical body. James's empirical approach to religion sought to give religious experiences power as guides for life, guides validated through science and not faith. This project led him through early work on 'multiple personalities'[3] by the French doctors Pierre Janet and Alfred Binet to the investigations of the Society for Psychical Research, and especially the work by F. W. H. Myers on the subliminal self. By the turn of the twentieth century James saw religious experience to be the result of collective subliminal consciousness finding its way into our individual supraliminal consciousnesses. This was the only way that the phenomena

184   Francis Neary

that he had investigated throughout the 1880s and 1890s, such as automatic writing, possession and hypnotism, could be explained. Like so many psychical investigators in the late nineteenth century, James felt that science needed to be expanded to be able to explain a host of abnormal psychological phenomena that were real but remained outside the boundaries of scientific thought. He sought to normalise the abnormality of exceptional mental states and bring them within the bounds of scientific explanation:

> Science, so far as science denies such exceptional occurrences, lies prostrate in the dust for me; and the most urgent intellectual need which I feel at present is that science be built up again in a form in which such things may have a positive place.[4]

Taylor and Wozniac show how James attempted 'to transcend the shortcomings of the analytic, associational empiricism of the "new" scientific psychology'.[5] Their case is that James's thought was not a reworking of German idealism or British empiricism, but should be seen as more uniquely American in the tradition of Swedenborgian transcendentalism and Emerson's psychology of personality. There is continuity in the transition from James's seminal work *The Principles of Psychology* to his later philosophy in the work that he did on abnormal psychology and psychology of religion in the 1890s. In abandoning positivism and reductionism of the natural sciences he began to look beyond waking consciousness towards the margin that surrounds our thoughts. This can be seen in the *Principles* as another centre of gravity, which did not explain intuitions in terms of habits and reflexes.[6] Hence, continuity is forged by giving the *Principles* two centres of gravity, one drawn from the natural sciences, the other drawn from abnormal psychology. James's thought after the early 1890s is discontinuous with only one of these: the 'scientific' centre. Furthermore, James's interest in abnormal psychology can be traced back to his spiritual crisis in the late 1860s, and projected forward on to the seeking of something beyond our normative ways of carving up the world in his later philosophy.

In this chapter I take a single period in James's life (his 'spiritual crisis') and compare and contrast the different interpretations of it by philosophers, literary theorists, historians of science and biographers. My aims are both to look at how James's abnormal psychology has been reconstructed by twentieth-century scholars and to discuss how James's own experience of abnormality led him to write about psychology in his own period. Ian Hacking describes how Comte's depressive period allowed him to reflect on Broussais's idea of the pathological as a deviation from the normal bodily state. His illness was 'just variation from his normal state produced by irritation and inflammation of tissues'.[7] Normality relieved Comte of responsibility for his illness and he later translated the concept into the sphere of social illness and added a progressive dimension. For Comte, the normal state became not the ordinary, healthy state of Broussais but the idealist,

William James's spiritual crisis   185

purified state that we are striving to. Comte creates a tension between normal as the average, correct state of being and normal as only average and something to be improved upon. This tension is felt most markedly in the late nineteenth century in the work of Emile Durkheim and Francis Galton.[8] James drew upon both approaches to the normal and used his illness to reflect upon the normal and abnormal, as Comte had done. However, unlike Comte, James embraced spirituality and looked to explaining abnormal states of consciousness to normalise his illness. As a result, he came to believe that progress of humankind could not be achieved by striving for an ideal type based on current scientific principles. He shared with Galton the idea that abnormal was an interesting indication of genius that we should strive to explain by scientific principles. Progress for James was made only when abnormal phenomena were explained by a new, more inclusive science.

Philosophical interpretations

I shall now discuss a number of different interpretations of James's spiritual crisis, which slowly built up to a peak in the early 1870s. This episode has received much attention from biographers and scholars of James because it has been seen as a turning point in his development as a self. Each interpretation differs from the others in its attribution of causes of the crisis itself and of James's eventual recovery. The interpretations emphasise certain sources as crucial to the understanding of James's motivations behind the crisis and reconstruct the sequence of events into a coherent narrative around these. However, as will become clear, the sources emphasised are different, and sometimes radically different, in each case. The sheer number and diversity of these interpretations lend themselves well to a comparative study, not in order to establish which interpretation is correct, but to comment on the interests of the historians at play, and the relationship between historian and actor, in highlighting some sources rather than others in their accounts. This will allow us to think about how an abnormal psychology has been interpreted in the late nineteenth century and how James's experience of it directed his later thought.

I start with the first major biographer and personal friend of James, Ralph Barton Perry, who states: 'The spiritual crisis was the ebbing of the will to live, for lack of philosophy to live by – a paralysis of action occasioned by a sense of moral impotence.'[9] For Perry, the crisis was purely philosophical in nature, and his interest is in the 'specific quality of the philosophy which his soul-sickness required'.[10] The interpretation hinges around two diary entries. The first is from 1 February 1870, when James attempts to acknowledge the supremacy of morality in the face of the existence of evil:

> Today I about touched bottom, and perceive plainly that I must face the choice with open eyes: shall I *frankly* throw the moral business overboard, as one unsuited to my innate aptitudes, or shall I follow it, and it

186 *Francis Neary*

alone, making everything else merely stuff for it? I will give the latter alternative a fair trial. Who knows but the moral interest may become developed. . . . Hitherto I have tried to fire myself with the moral interest, as an aid to accomplishing certain utilitarian ends.[11]

The second is from three months later, 30 April, which Perry sees as a revolutionary insight in James's thought. On reading Renouvier, James adopted the moralist alternative with the vigour of will which springs from the belief in freedom of the will:

I think that yesterday was a crisis in my life. I finished the first part of Renouvier's second *Essais* and see no reason why his definition of free will – 'the sustaining of a thought *because I choose to* when I might have other thoughts' – need be the definition of an illusion. At any rate, I will assume for the present – until next year – that it is no illusion. My first act of free will shall be to believe in free will.[12]

Perry makes the point that for James, philosophy was never 'a detached and dispassionate inquiry into truth'; it was never a mere theory, but 'a set of beliefs which reconciled him to life and which he proclaimed as one preaching a way of salvation'.[13] However, Perry does not go on to show how James's philosophy was intimately tied to his personal life at any given time. Perry provides a rationalistic reconstruction in the sense that philosophical pondering helped him to struggle with problems in his life, rather than seeing James's life experience and philosophy as so intimately tied that they have a reciprocal relationship of mutually generating each other. Perry seeks to separate James's life from his philosophy, seeing the latter as primary in his account. Consequently, he does not see the reading of Renouvier as a conversion experience that enabled him to deal with his depression once and for all. He sees the recovery as a slow process, and points to other events which contributed to James's recovery in the winter of 1872–3: the beginning of a correspondence with Renouvier and his appointment as lecturer in comparative anatomy and physiology at Harvard College. The former 'curing factor' is supported by his first letter to Renouvier (2 November 1872), in which he states:

I must not lose this opportunity of telling you of the admiration and gratitude which have been excited in me by the reading of your *Essais*. . . . Thanks to you I possess for the first time an intelligible and reasonable conception of freedom.[14]

What are we to make of Perry's interpretation? He was a student and later friend and designated biographer of James who won the Pulitzer Prize for his work *The Thought and Character of William James*. In many aspects his lengthy, comprehensive interpretation has only been questioned by those

William James's spiritual crisis 187

who have looked beyond the easily accessible published works towards the archives. Eugene Taylor has noted that he even exercised editorial power over the William James collection by not wanting to include medical and psychological sources (e.g. his medical school notebook from 1867–8) because they were not philosophical.[15] He also suggests that Perry was 'ultimately a Western philosopher in the American academic tradition' and he 'tended to gloss over James's activities in psychical research, his psychology of the subconscious, the Asian influences, and the impact of the New England Mind-Cure Movement on James's thinking as a *psychologist*'.[16] It is clear from the last two chapters of Perry's biography that Perry saw James as a sick soul without an adequate philosophy to live by, and it is this assumption that if he only had had the right philosophy he would have been happy which puts Perry's interpretation squarely in a rationalistic camp. Perry's James is a benign and morbid figure whose philosophy was never finished, an endless quest, but it was the *philosophy* that was most important to him. Perry's interpretation of James's breakdown is a philosophical crisis that could only be cured by new ideas.

Bruce Kuklick follows Perry in seeing James's crisis as for the most part philosophical. He points to the environment of the Cambridge Metaphysical Club, of which James was a member, and especially the tightly argued nihilist position of Chauncey Wright in providing a catalyst for the crisis.[17] Kuklick augments his position that the philosophical climate James found himself in is crucial to understanding the circumstances of his crisis with an auxiliary hypothesis. This is that James 'was a pampered child of the upper classes' who 'had never had to work and had received from his father – the crucial figure of his youth – no practical help whatever on what to do with himself'.[18] With much the same references as Perry, Kuklick then asserts that Renouvier lifted James out of his 'psychological doldrums'. Perry and Kuklick seek to explain James's abnormal psychology as a crisis in ideas, for which James takes full responsibility. James becomes normal again by reading philosophy and exercising his will – factors that are within his conscious control.

Psychoanalytical interpretations

Let us now consider two psychoanalytic interpretations of the breakdown, where the sources of abnormality shift to the level of the subconscious. Cushing Strout's 'William James and the Twice-Born Sick Soul' dwells on James's search for a vocation in the 1860s and James's relationship with his father to explain the period of neurasthenia. He appropriates the psychoanalytical approach to history of Erik Erikson to frame James's problems. In particular, the notion that 'born leaders seem to fear only more consciously what in some form everybody fears in the depths of his inner life; and they convincingly claim to have an answer'[19] is projected on to James as the conscious fear that 'scientific determinism ... would leave no meaningful space

188   *Francis Neary*

for the human will'.[20] If you add the quest for moralism, this seems very much in line with Perry's interpretation, until Strout goes on to contend that the fear described was closely connected with his fears as a member of the James family.

Strout proposes 'to analyse that linkage in narrative form, trying to do justice to the relevant claims of psychoanalysis, history and philosophy'.[21] Much is made of the paralysing recollection of an image of a greenish, withdrawn epileptic idiot whom James had seen in an asylum. James had confessed in a letter to his friend Tom Ward that he potentially saw himself as this terrifying figure.[22] Strout points to the similarity of description with that found in William Acton's *The Functions and Disorders of the Reproductive Organs*.[23] Acton used the description to indicate what might happen to those who do not 'wilfully break the habit of introspection in order to ward off the temptation of masturbation, luridly imagined as a threat to sanity'.[24] The fact that James was unsuccessfully courting in the 1860s and that he did not marry until 1878, at the age of 36, suggests that sexual frustration may have plagued him. However, Strout feels that James's respect for his father as a metaphysician and James's feeling of being trapped in a medical career (which seemed his only option after his disillusionment with natural history) that his father did not wholly approve of is most important in the interpretation of the hideous figure in the recollection. Strout's James is fleeing from science until 1899, when he is finally freed from laboratory work and can devote himself fully to the philosophical questions that interested him years earlier. Philosophy was not for him in the early 1870s because 'he was not yet prepared to make that much of a bid for autonomy' from his father.[25]

The crux of Strout's interpretation of the crisis is that William had followed his father's wish for a scientific career knowing that his father ultimately believed that science was inferior to metaphysics and religion. He had felt in the late 1860s that he had become fatally committed to what he was not believing in.[26] The cure came with a growing sense of independence from his father, which was precipitated through his job at Harvard and marriage in the 1870s, and culminated in James Sr's death, when he wrote to Henry Jr that he was 'a different man', amazed that a 'change of weather could effect such a revolution'.[27] James was also progressively able to devote more and more time to metaphysical issues as the century drew to a close, and to pursue further a project that his father would have approved of: defending the moral and spiritual domains against the enemy of scientific determinism. Through his focus on the father–son relationship Strout gives an interpretation of James's crisis that differs radically from the 'philosophical' account of Perry. The coherence of narrative depends upon interplay between psychoanalytic theory drawn from Erikson's work and the personal letters of James to family and friends.

A practising clinical psychologist, James William Anderson, provides a more recent psychoanalytic interpretation.[28] His interpretation does not focus on specific conflicts and defensive strategies but follows the wave of psychoanalytic theorists in the 1960s and 70s who focused on the entire self as the primary unit for analysis. Like Strout, he prioritises James's search for a vocation as central to his illness, but he sees this confusion over choice of career as a symptom of James not having a fully consolidated self.

For Anderson, James did not lack morals or ideas, but for psychological reasons he was unable to draw upon them. He cites Kohut's psychoanalytic work to see James as unable to forge a link between his inner motives and his actions: 'Such a person often feels impoverished because his self is thin, and the split-off parts of himself do not fuel his personality.'[29] The thesis of a weak state of self, interacting with his philosophical concerns about materialism drawn from his scientific education and the superstition he saw in his father's work, is further supported by his inability to sustain intimate friendships in the period. The argument for the weakness of James's self is further bolstered by what Anderson describes as a fragmentation experience. The very same image of the epileptic which Strout interpreted as a result of the fear of being trapped in a medical career is here seen through the psychoanalytic theories of Winnicott and Kohut[30] as James's self giving way:

> As a result of his 'horror' of the patient and his realisation of 'my own merely momentary discrepancy from him', James explained, 'it was as if something hitherto solid within my breast gave way entirely, and I became a mass of quivering fear'. His image of something giving way within his breast is a particularly graphic metaphor for a self-fragmentation experience.[31]

Another passage from James's personal notes in the summer of 1869 is mobilised by both the Strout and Anderson articles to different effect. The direct quotation of the note reads: 'Three qualities to determine. (1) how much pain I'll stand; (2) how much other's pain I'll inflict (by existing); (3) how much other's pain I'll "accept", without ceasing to take pleasure in their existence.'[32] Strout makes use of the quotation to show that pain was at the 'centre of things' for James after he had passed his medical exams. To continue to follow this path would be a kind of suicide, because he 'could not find himself in medicine nor the acting self in the medical materialist's picture of the world'.[33]

Anderson, on the other hand, uses the quotation in his thesis to show that James was concerned about the isolation from intimate relationships his illness had brought upon him. He sees the passage in terms of James's reflections on two basic approaches to life: self-sufficiency and sympathy with others. The first approach denies the possibility of true intimacy but the second gives pain. In considering the perils of closeness, the quotation provides James's conditions for choosing it. Anderson feels that the passage ought to be interpreted in terms of James's thinking about the pain he was inflicting on others with his sickness. Both interpretations clearly allude to the fact that James was considering what reasons would justify suicide, but

190 *Francis Neary*

they make them coherent with their general thesis in different ways. Anderson takes a holistic view of James's entire self not being fully consolidated, and sees his inability to forge intimate relationships as a symptom of this. The quotation represents a reflective moment of James's thinking about his relations with others. In contrast, Strout highlights a specific conflict in James's career path and sees the quotation as one of the many expressions of this. This disparity in the interpretations of one passage shows scholars at work fitting the evidence in with their respective theories of the self.

Interestingly, for Anderson there is no direct cure for James's condition: the problems persist throughout his life but his sense of self becomes gradually stronger and much more able to deal with them. His interest in psychopathology and abnormal states continued and was to be a major concern in the 1890s, but by the publication of *The Varieties of Religious Experience* in 1901 he was content with his morbid-mindedness. This was because he felt that evil facts existed and could not be glossed over, and he felt that the sick soul gave truer values and opened up one's eyes to the deepest levels of truth. In short, the melancholia did not go away but his discontentment with it did, because the insight he felt it produced made it all worthwhile.

Strout and Anderson see James's abnormality in terms of narratives and conceptual resources that were unavailable to him. The boundary between the normal and the abnormal is hidden from James and can only be correctly assessed in terms of psychoanalytic theories by professional practitioners. The claim is that James had neither the resources nor the perspective to diagnose his own condition. Further to this, James's normalisation was not brought about by the conscious act of his will, as in Perry's account; it was through changes in his circumstances that were mostly beyond his control.

Traditional historical interpretations

How have more traditional historians tackled James's crisis? I now consider three historical approaches. Mark Schwehn provides a middle ground between all the positions discussed so far. He takes on board Perry's conviction that James' work, and especially *Principles of Psychology*, must be understood in terms of James's readings, professional associations and education. However, unlike Perry he does not see cultural strains or psychological struggles as one and the same, and contends that neither can give a full explanation on their own. Schwehn agrees with Strout and Anderson that the pertinent biographical contexts in which to read James's depression are conflicts with his father and vocational indecision. However, he does not seek to give a psychological account of James's intellectual development, like the two authors discussed previously. Instead, James's work is the primary unit for interpretation, rather than his state of mind. We see in Schwehn a moderate who wants to steer a middle course between

William James's spiritual crisis   191

psychobiography and intellectual history. He wants to say that James's work is a product of his intellectual and professional contexts, but its rhetoric must be interpreted in terms of biographical and cultural contexts. The only position he decisively disagrees with is that of James's son, Henry, who argues that James's depression was a result of genuine physical afflictions, which were the actual causes rather than the symptoms of his illness.[34]

In the style of a true intellectual historian, Schwehn wants to play down the importance of James's depressive period (which he sees as lasting from 1867 to 1873) and play up the importance of the later period of 1876–82. This is because the 36 articles James published before 1876 were merely occasional pieces, but after that date he published major articles prolifically, which later became his greatest work – *Principles*. This change is explained by the biographical event of meeting, and courting for two years, his future wife, Alice Howe Gibbens. Thus, Schwehn emphasises James's unsettled vocational path from art to comparative anatomy to medicine with some dabbling in physiology in Germany as important in explaining the crisis. James's scientific studies had given him a grim, mechanistic view of the world as 'morally and aesthetically reprehensible', but 'he could find no intellectual escape from it, least of all in his father's theology'.[35] Then the stock Perry line is partially followed: that his saviour Renouvier came along on 30 April 1870 and reactivated his will, and by 1873 he was in such a comparatively healthy state of mind he was able to take up the post at Harvard.

The conversion experience line certainly suits the intellectual historian, but the twist in Schwehn's tale is that he uses this well-trodden line to play down the significance of the healing potion of Renouvier and the job at Harvard: 'By James's own reckoning, his relationship with Alice, not the discovery of Renouvier nor his decision to believe in free will nor even his choice of vocation, had made him a healthy man.'[36] The letters between James and his wife were only released to scholars in 1980, and Schwehn was keen to make use of the novel resource when his article was published in 1982. He charts the tragic struggle of their courtship and what James would later refer to as 'the strenuous moral life'. For Schwehn, James's contact with Alice's spiritual piety was the major curing factor. It was this intimate relationship that provided a partial corrective and an escape from the compelling arguments of scientific materialists, and enabled him to make peace with his father.[37]

Schwehn adds little to the interpretation of the cause of James's crisis, but provides an intriguing hypothesis of James's marriage as the main curing factor. He sticks very closely to James's writings to explain his passage from morbid, abnormal to healthy, normal state. He paints a much more detailed and meticulous picture of the transition than Perry, but, like Perry, and unlike Strout and Anderson, he sees James as grappling with his own abnormality and bringing himself to normality through his thinking about philosophy, and through personal relationships.

192 *Francis Neary*

Taylor is in broad agreement, seeing that James being 'tossed back and forth between the materialistic determinism of science and the free will of philosophy ... was perhaps symbolic of the struggle between his own choices and the will of his father'.[38] However, he is much more cautious about giving such weight to James's marriage as a cure. Perhaps with a more sober attitude towards the new archival resource of the marriage letters, he contends that Renouvier's essays and Wordsworth's poems put him on the road to recovery, and the job at Harvard and subsequent marriage 'solidified his health and gave his energies definite direction'.

Most interesting about Taylor's account is the context in which he sets James in the late 1860s and early 1870s. Taylor, as lecturer in psychiatry and clinical associate in psychology turned historian, is keen to portray James as a pioneer and a distant lost prophet for the future of psychology. As a committed disciple, his James is busy reviewing A. A. Liebeault's work on magnetic sleep in 1867 before anyone had heard of him.[39] He is looking beyond orthodox medicine to therapeutic alternatives to cure his condition: mineral baths, later a stream of mental healers and, finally, injections of animal extracts. His relationship with his wife is not portrayed in high philosophical terms, as by Schwehn, but she was the woman who fuelled his interest in psychic health, cooked, cleaned and played the piano for him, tended the children, 'travelled with him and protected his time from the innumerable cranks who flocked to his door'.[40] She gave the best possible practical environment for his recovery, and most of his ailments 'disappeared after he settled into a family atmosphere of his own'.[41] Before meeting her in the early 1870s James had become deeply interested in insanity and its possible cause, reviewing many contemporary texts in the area.[42] This interest, coupled with his obsession with the mind-cure movement and alternative medicine, seems to provide the evidence for another interpretation of his crisis. The knowledge gained from his medical training and his explorations beyond orthodox medicine fuelled his neurasthenic condition. Although Taylor concedes that the symptoms are hypochondriacal, he sees the causal chain in the opposite direction: the state of depression promotes these new interests. Taylor is keen to promote James's abnormal state as having the positive effect of taking his thought into new realms – his abnormal state inspires his work rather than hampering it.

Robert J. Richard's claims about James's breakdown are much bolder. He begins by alluding to the many breakdowns of nineteenth-century notables (e.g. John Stuart Mill, Herbert Spencer, Francis Galton and Charles Darwin), stating almost without irony: 'To be an intellectual in the mid-nineteenth century required that one suffer a severe spiritual crisis or mental breakdown.'[43] The comment is telling, in that the figures he includes in his list of melancholic geniuses map out the intellectual territory in which Richards intends to frame his analysis. The respective crises may have little in common in their details but we will meet these figures again in his interpretation. He quickly moves to what reads as an apology for considering

William James's spiritual crisis 193

James's emotional life. It is not something historians of science should be doing, at least in 1982:

> Little effort has gone to assessing the impact of private crises on the philosophical and especially the scientific ideas of these men, and generally little return would be paid to the historian who tried. After all, these philosophers and scientists did not produce imaginative works fired in passion.[44]

The argument tells us much about the temptation to stick to the published works and keep scientists' personal lives out of historical accounts, and Richards is resisting in holding up James as a special case. James is different because he made 'subjective preference . . . reason to accept or reject a scientific hypothesis. . . . We are authorised, then, to recover his subjective state in an effort to explain his adoption and use of certain scientific ideas'.[45]

For Richards, James's crisis had three major components: 'professional, interpersonal and psychometaphysical'.[46] The first two components are treated relatively rapidly. Again we see the job at Harvard easing James's despair over his professional prospects, after he felt that 'his education had left him unprepared for serious scientific work and that he had wasted his years in desultory study'.[47] Next we see material from James's diary from Germany in 1868 regarding Kate Havens, interpreted as a repeated inability to act on his desires for women. This is given a biopsychological twist by reading the experiences in terms of James's later work on cognition. He later felt that its function was to produce action, and wrote: 'Cognition, in short, is incomplete until discharged in act.'[48]

However, this mature scientific pronouncement of 1882 is a far cry from the diary jottings, expressing that he should not dwell on thoughts he could not act upon in 1868, that Richards links it with. Richards is very eager to push James's experiences of his crisis into a coherent theory. James's cognition about women was finally discharged into action with his marriage, and Richards follows the Schwehn line of the therapeutic effects of this. By far the most space is devoted to the third, psycho-metaphysical dimension of the crisis. Richards maintains that James was a Spencerian in the 1860s and believed in determinism, and that his 'palsied will . . . could all be understood and justified if mind were a puppet to nature's laws'.[49] Richards analyses Renouvier's second essay, *Traité de psychologie rationnelle*, in considerable detail and comes to the conclusion that

> the remedy of Renouvier, taken alone, was not potent enough for a lasting cure. The French Kantian demonstrated that the determinist position was not more logically persuasive than the libertarian; yet he failed to counter the full strength of Victorian science which seemed to support determinism. James required objective evidence to compound with his subjective preference for freedom. This he found, oddly

194　*Francis Neary*

> enough, in the ideas of one usually credited with introducing a pervasive mechanism in biology – Charles Darwin.[50]

Thus Richards provides a lengthy, Darwinocentric account of how James cured himself through the appropriation of Darwinian ideas. James pitted Darwin against Spencer in forging an argument for the independence of mind from the brain machinery: '[I]f conscious mind is an evolved trait . . . then it could have been naturally selected only if it added some utility to the material of the brain.'[51] This utility for James was the conscious selection of interests from the environment, thus stabilising the machinery of the brain. Richards attempts to show that James forged this argument in the early 1870s and that it relieved his condition by providing him with an argument for the efficacy of human consciousness, within the confines of the natural sciences. Darwinism was the main instrument of his emotional therapy for Richards. However, he conflates James's emotional state with his philosophical arguments concerning subjectivity. He hardly discusses James's private emotional states beyond a few allusions to diary entries in the late 1860s; he sticks to the published philosophical works and professional lectures.

The narrative is only weakly anchored to his emotional state by the contention that philosophical arguments for the efficacy of consciousness enabled him to act freely and aided his recovery.[52] The argument appears to be a detailed and sophisticated philosophical analysis in the Perry vein, but replacing James's reading of Renouvier with that of Darwin as the prime mover in his recovery. For Richards, James's abnormal emotional state is a symptom of the philosophical turmoil in his thought and is resolved by developing new philosophical arguments.

Biographical interpretations

Let us now consider several broadly biographical approaches to James's crisis. Gay Wilson Allen wrote the first full-scale biography of James in 1967. The work makes much of his visit to Europe during 1867–8 in explaining the crisis. In particular, Allen highlights the time spent in Germany studying physiology and spending much time in solitary confinement reading German philosophy and literature. During this period he wrote frequently to his parents, his brother Henry, sister Alice and friends Tom Ward and Oliver Wendell Holmes about his failing health. This correspondence provides an insightful chronicle detailing what James's illness meant to him at various stages of his removal from the Bostonian context.

Allen emphasises James's shame at the fact that all his younger brothers were now supporting themselves and he was still reliant on the parental purse. But by far the most important factor for Allen in the crisis comes from James's ideas about relationships with women at the time.[53]

Fear of madness plagued James in his felt determinism, and there were ample examples of unsavoury traits in other members of his family to suggest that he was fated by heredity to suffer the crisis for the rest of his life. He saw himself as unfit for marriage and especially worried over passing his condition to potential offspring in any possible matrimonial match. According to Allen, facing up to this tragedy of fate was key in James's agenda, and he found fatal courage in two works he had purchased in Europe: the much-cited Renouvier's *Essais* and the more surprising *The Senses and the Intellect* by Alexander Bain. Both works highlighted action over speculation: Renouvier's act of belief in free will to attain the moral consequences that come with it; and Bain's idea of acquisition of ordered habits leading to wilful choice through passionate initiative.

By the end of spring 1870 James was no longer hanging around for the external world to determine all for him, but acting with his will and believing in his 'individual reality and creative power'.[54] Through belief in the power of his will James had conquered the temptation to commit suicide through seeing this as a possible act of will, and positing *life* as another possible act. Allen's close analysis of diary entries of the period is used to show the centrality of James's reflections on relationships with women in causing his crisis and throwing up the problems that led him to seek a particular philosophical solution. The conflict between longings and idealisation is shown to be central to his depressed emotional state by the linkage of despair and encounters with women in his diary entries and letters. The death of his favourite cousin, Minny Temple, shocked him into accepting life as tragedy and pushing back the darkness by accumulated acts of thought, leading him to a cocktail of European philosophy, which was conducive to this agenda.

Allen's position on the attribution of causes of the breakdown is very different from Perry's: for rather than the philosophical problems causing the crisis and personal discomfort, personal problems lead to the crisis and dictate the philosophical problems to be considered. This biographical approach can also be seen in stark contrast to the psychoanalytic approaches discussed earlier, as Allen posits no theoretical unconscious constructions to explain the crisis. Instead, he looks for an explanation purely at the level of James's conscious narrative, emphasising the more intimate and personal sources as more crucial in his explanation. In the vein of Taylor, the abnormal state is not caused by philosophy; philosophy comes from it. However, it was his existential philosophy rather than his work on abnormal states of consciousness that led to normalisation.

Feinstein's detailed account of James's depressive period throws up many contributing factors to the crisis. He paints a lucid picture of the paranoia that can be seen in James's correspondence from Germany and his drawings of staring eyes from this period. His frame of mind was secretive and he demanded discretion from all his correspondents. These demands were especially manifest in the letters to his friends in Cambridge, and he made them swear not to show their contents to his father.[55]

196 *Francis Neary*

For Feinstein, the irreconcilability of his wants and the perceived wants of his father were at the heart of James's spiritual crisis. James's existential reflections on the events of his life in the 1860s had been distilled in a radical choice of either suffering himself or making his father suffer. The question that reverberated in his mind in 1869 was: 'How could he follow his desires, which delighted in art and of late were drawn toward speculation on the borders of science and philosophy, and still give his father a scientist son?'[56]

Feinstein considerably elaborates on, and brings much more evidence to, Strout's thesis that vocational struggles with his father precipitated the crisis. For example, they were both seeking resolution of a prolonged vocational crisis, overwhelmed by panic and terrified by a vision of a seated figure. The comparison adds more weight to two of Feinstein's main narrative-linking themes running through his text: first, that the issue of autonomy was at the centre of the James family politics, and second, that history was inclined to repeat itself in the familial generations.

In a radical departure from the other interpretations, Feinstein sees James using Renouvier fused with Bain not as an emancipatory force but as 'one more justification for James's effort to restrain himself. Instead of freedom of the will, William needed to be freed from the will – his own and the testamentary shadow cast by William James of Albany'.[57] In balancing his tolerance of pain with his reluctance to cause pain, the focus of 'the moral business' was not evil in general but the specific evil of hurting his father. The breakdown of spring 1870 was just one expression of this stifling process that continued until at least 1872, long after James's reading of Renouvier.

There are plenty of diary entries after the much-used one regarding Renouvier of 30 April 1870 detailing James's continued melancholia. Feinstein sees the work of Bain and Maudsley, in the British associationist tradition, on forming ordered habits as providing the discipline James needed to separate himself enough from the excesses of his father's doctrine of self-expression, and perhaps cure his perceived madness.[58] Familial relationships are the key to explaining James's abnormality, as in Strout's account, but normalisation occurs through him engaging with and acting upon literature on habit.

Another 1980s biographer, Daniel Bjork, feels that the importance of James's spiritual crisis has been greatly overemphasised, to the extent of an impoverishment of the analysis of the later period of his life. He feels that the abundance of detailed diary entries from the period 1868–73 is partially to blame, but also attributes the fixation to 'the fashion of writing about Victorian neurosis and about the persistence of self-help mythology'.[59] He notes that scholars 'have worried about James's youthful anxieties to a point well beyond their actual importance in his experience', and in turn such an emphasis has led to a 'de-emphasising of the intrinsic importance of his ideas'. For Bjork, the health question was curiously crucial in encouraging his creative endeavour, and 'it never prevented James from being a strikingly original and productive scholar'. It is unsurprising, then, that the key to Bjork's treatment of the crisis is James's worry that he had nothing especially original and creative to say.

Instead of being forced into an unwanted scientific career and needing to find himself in philosophy, Bjork's James has a far greater sense of autonomy from his father and the rest of his family. To be sure, he perhaps 'oscillates around too many centers' in the 1860s, but this is not seen as a vocational crisis so much as a creative crisis – having too many centres to make his creative mark on any of them. His brothers had found their centres of oscillation, and Henry Jr was beginning to make his mark on his as a novelist; William simply needed to find his.

Bjork feels he had a genuine interest in the new physiology, but was 'too intellectually ambitious to simply follow a scientific career'.[60] He deplored the fact that nothing original had emerged in his own mind, and his despair was that he was not making original scientific discoveries. Furthermore, William's principal point of difference with his father was not a clash of the old, theological worldview with the 'modern', scientific one in which William had been trained. For Bjork, it was over William wanting to be an active, creative participant rather than an awed spectator. William was not on earth simply to prove the existence of God or deny material nature: '[C]hoosing between science and God, or nature and spirituality, would not clear his way, but would be a creative dead end.'[61]

Bjork's picture of James at the time of his crisis is much more positive than that of the other commentators discussed. Even in Germany, James is 'full of mental activity and vigour', reviewing scientific works for journals back home and beginning a project on art in the Dresden gallery. Bjork cites sections from his diary of 1868, unplundered by other scholars, regarding James's enthusiasm for a project on consciousness and object in art. The novel evidence serves to support two important strands of Bjork's thesis. The first is that James's 'ill health' did not stop him creating, and the extents of his depths of despair have been significantly overplayed. The second is that because the project is a juxtaposition of two fields of James's creative experience – art and psychology – vocational labels cannot be seen as explanatory in his case, and creative experience provides a more authentic focus.

The various combinations of Renouvier, Darwin, Bain and Maudsley in a curing tonic, concocted by each of the commentators mentioned above, are all played down in Bjork's account. For Bjork, 'the storms of personal crisis' kept blowing until James could make his own creative mark. Normality here is gained through creativity, and the extent of James's abnormality in the first place is played down.

A more recent biographer, Linda Simon, departs from the crisis and recovery narrative in her assessment of the significance of James's illness.[62] Rather than playing down the crisis altogether or identifying the cause as a

198   *Francis Neary*

sexual, career, identity, family or philosophical problem and citing a cure in the form of a change in appropriate sphere of James's life, Simon asserts that James simply never recovered. She sees his crisis in terms of late twentieth-century ideas about depression in that the condition stayed with him throughout his life and he was constantly relapsing when his attentions were not focused on a goal or challenge. Simon cites evidence of further prolonged depressive periods from his letters during his courtship with Alice Gibbens in the mid-1870s, in the early 1890s after completing *The Principles*, in the late 1890s after discovering his heart condition and again in the year before his death.

Simon's James was consistently and persistently ill, and no amount of changes in his personal, professional or philosophical outlook would cure his depressive character, because his depression was not something that could be cured; it was part of him and inspired and shaped his work. James's life toggled between normal and abnormal states, and his lifelong periods of abnormality inspired him to look deeply into the psychology of insanity, religion and abnormal states of consciousness.

Returning to James's description of the epileptic patient in *The Varieties of Religious Experience* where we started, Louis Menand maintains that this haunting passage and the Renouvier diary entry are 'experiences of different kinds of distress alleviated by quite different kinds of self therapy'.[63] The iconic status of both writings in almost every version of James's life is questioned. The facts that James's experience of the epileptic patient could be dated any time from 1861 to 1878 and that there are significant gaps in James's diary entries from the late 1860s and early 1870s (including 21 pages simply cut out between February and December 1869) make the evidence for linking the two episodes into a convenient breakdown and recovery narrative sketchy.

Menand follows Linda Simon's line of seeing the epileptic case as 'pre-cooked' to fit the genre of a medical case history in a book about religious experiences. He points to the coda to the piece (where the fictitious Frenchman clings to scripture texts to avoid insanity) not sounding much like William James and the cross-referencing to Bunyan's *Pilgrim's Progress* and James's father's account of his spiritual crisis as evidence. In general, the epileptic patient case as a description of the crisis and the diary entry of the response to reading Renouvier as a description of the recovery are seen as two pieces of evidence plucked from a fragmentary record that all too conveniently match themes in James's later philosophy of 'the will to believe' and 'pragmatism'. They are just too symmetrical with James's philosophy 'to act "as if" in the face of uncertainty – to believe that if we take a risk, the Universe will meet us halfway'.[64]

These two ingredients used by Perry to construct the official biography (and perhaps the very idea of a single spiritual crisis in the first place) by reading James's later philosophy back on to his earlier letters and diary entries have influenced Jamesian scholarship markedly. However, Menand plausibly argues that the iconic episodes were about different problems with different solutions. The story of the epileptic patient highlights the problem of 'fear of catastrophe', and the solution is 'religious consolation', whereas the Renouvier case is about 'intellectual paralysis', with the solution of 'belief in the efficacy of self assertion'.[65]

Menand's account further complicates the story in that, on the evidence available, it is difficult to assess the relationship between James's abnormal and normal states. He even provides a critique of accounts that have placed James as the patient in an asylum but concludes that, although it is plausible that James was a patient of McLean Hospital (given the number of cures that he tried for his condition), there is no hard evidence. James was a 'sick soul' constantly shifting from normal to abnormal states, but exactly when these changes occurred and how they affected him in local contexts has not been committed to the historical record.

Conclusion

The scant and ambiguous legacy of James in the form of notebooks, diaries and letters has led to a plethora of interpretations of his 'spiritual crisis', with each author playing up some sources and playing down others to construct a coherent narrative. If read chronologically, the literature on James's crisis also provides a history of the James archival material and indicates how, when a new batch of sources became available, a new interpretation of the crisis would soon follow. His iconic status as the quintessential American intellectual whose thought straddled both philosophy and the fledgling discipline of psychology and his seductive and personal writing style have led to a fascination with James's life and its twists and turns. Not only is his life rich and idiosyncratic enough to produce riveting prose but its reconstruction has also been an exercise in the definition of the intellectual in American culture and in building a distinctive American history of academia and American contributions to philosophical and psychological thought.

This survey of the thicket of interpretations of James's spiritual crisis has provided us with many approaches to interpreting and reconstructing an abnormal psychology in the late nineteenth century. The nexus of interlocking narratives with common themes and ideas provides a bewildering array of views on the causes and cures of abnormality and the relationship between the normal and the abnormal. James's abnormality is constituted in many different spheres, from the physical to the mental and the philosophical to the experiential. The different interpretations afford James with different levels of responsibility for his illness and the resulting cure. Temporally they range from defining James's period of abnormality as a specific moment to a lifelong condition.

The abnormal state is pitched in terms of philosophy, familial relations, friendship relations, James's general character, mental illness, consolida-

200 *Francis Neary*

tion of selfhood, James's perceived lack of creativity or as not so abnormal after all or in terms of combinations of these factors. The normalisation either never happens or is brought about by factors ranging from reading and reflecting on philosophy (Renouvier, Darwin or Bain), working out his own existential philosophy, marriage, embarking on an academic career to making his own creative mark. The interpretations as to the effect of the abnormal state also differ markedly and range from its being a crippling condition to a springboard for new ideas and areas of thought to explore.

The main transitions from abnormal to normal states are also covered in these accounts; be it crisis and recovery, transcendence, accommodation, conversion, negation and the constant switching between the two states. Each scholar reads their own particular interests into James's work and makes the most of the sources and concepts available to them. Although there is concordance between interpretations in some of the general themes, the disagreements and differences are too great to forge a coherent account.

But what would James have made of all this and how does his crisis relate to his own work on insanity and abnormality? James would have seen these discrepancies through his psychological idea of 'the stream of thought', where human beings with unique interests forge a coherent account of the world through streams of connected thoughts. An individual's picture of James's abnormality is built up by looking at the sources available with unique interests based on their stream of thought that has gone before. When another individual looks upon old and new sources with different unique interests a different, equally coherent narrative is created.

So James would have expected and actively encouraged different interpretations to fit with his own psychological ideas. However, the interpretations also express psychological ideas that James might have taken issue with. For instance, it is likely that he would have eschewed a psychoanalytic interpretation. He did review Breuer and Freud[66] in 1894, but as part of a trilogy of reviews which also included Janet's dissertation under Charcot[67] and L. E. Whipple's *Philosophy of Mental Healing.*[68] The critical notice appeared in the *Psychological Review* and was one of the first airings of Freud's work in the United States. However, James played down the significance of Freud and Breuer's work, and merely saw it as a comment on F. W. H. Myers's earlier work on the subliminal self, and an independent corroboration of Janet's views. He did not seem to see the difference between Janet and Freud over the automaticity of changes in principal consciousness from emotional venting in the hypnoid state. Janet did not articulate Freud's doctrine of abreaction.

James also thought that these studies showed that the methods of the American mental healers had been vindicated.[69] Unlike Freud, James was not drawn to the content of inner images in hysterical patients, and when he listened to Freud at the Clark conference in 1909 he could make nothing of the dream theories. He wrote to Flournoy that he felt Freud to be possessed by fixed ideas, and walking with him did little but bring on an attack of angina.[70] The main disagreement was over the impersonality of Freud's concept of the unconscious. James felt that 'an item experienced unconsciously must be conscious to a secondary or subconscious self', for what could be 'the point of calling something both unconscious and mental . . . if it is not impressed upon someone's consciousness at least a little bit?'.[71] It is the positing of impersonal motives beyond any consciousness that James could not stomach. This smacked of taking the personal context out of consciousness and would allow constructions of an individual self with resources that were never available to it.

James would have also rejected the numerous approaches that saw philosophy as an adequate response to his despair, because he thought the foundation of philosophy was that it starts and ends with the recognition of its own limitations

> Philosophy is a moralism: it is for people who feel strong enough to face the universe on its own terms, knowing that there is, in the end, nothing to back them up, nothing to guarantee that their vote will be counted.[72]

Whatever the real story behind the case of the epileptic patient, James was certainly using the case to rehearse or re-rehearse his idea that the boundary between the normal and abnormal person was paper-thin and that there was no sharp line between healthy and unhealthy minds. James clearly grappled with his own abnormality throughout his adult life, and, like so many late nineteenth-century thinkers, he struggled to square a religious upbringing with new scientific ideas. James saw religion as a branch of abnormal psychology and as real as any other mental state because it must have evolved for the purpose of helping us cope with our environment. In maintaining that consciousness played an active role in human destiny and that all conscious states were useful, he attempted to tame what was seen as abnormal, to bring it into the sphere of normal science. In doing so he also attempted to normalise his own soul-sickness. The specific details of James's crisis may remain speculative and be ultimately unrecoverable, but his bold attempt to collapse the barrier between the normal and abnormal was extremely ambitious and remained unfinished. Perhaps this is why his soul-sickness remains with him.

Notes

1 William James, *The Varieties of Religious Experience: A Study in Human Nature*, New York, Modern Library, 1994, p. 179.
2 For instance, see a letter to Frank Abauzit dated 1 June 1904: 'The document . . . is my own case – acute neurasthenic attack with phobia. I naturally disguised the provenance!' (quoted in Gerald E. Myers, *William James: His Life and Thought*, New Haven Yale, CT, University Press, 1986, p. 608). It is interesting

202 *Francis Neary*

to note that James uses the medical term 'neurasthenic', and the line that James was simply psychically ill suffering from a diagnosed medical condition is followed by his son in the first edited collection of his letters (Henry James, ed., *The Letters of William James*, 2 vols, London, Longman's, Green, 1920). Neurasthenia was a nervous condition brought about by the rigours of urban living and popularised by the New York doctor and advocate of electrotherapy G. M. Beard in the late 1860s (round about the time of James's crisis). For an excellent study of the condition's medical contexts and dissemination, see Marijke Gijswijt-Hofstra and Roy Porter, eds, *Cultures of Neurasthenia from Beard to the First World War*, Amsterdam, Rodopi, 2001.

3 The category of 'multiple personality' was forged in the last decades of the nineteenth century and it became a primary topic for James's 1896 Lowell Lectures on 'exceptional mental states'. It was developed further by his student Morton Prince (for example, see Morton Prince, *The Dissociation of a Personality*, London, Longman's, 1906).

4 William James, *The Will to Believe and Other Essays in Popular Philosophy*, London, Longman's, Green, 1899, p. 236.

5 Eugene Taylor and Robert Wozniak, *Pure Experience: The Response to William James*, Bristol, Thoemmes Press, 1996, p. xviii.

6 Ibid., pp. xxiii–xxiv. See E. Taylor, *William James on Consciousness beyond the Margin*, Princeton, NJ, Princeton University Press, 1996 for a more sustained argument for this view.

7 Ian Hacking, *The Taming of Chance*, Cambridge, Cambridge University Press, 1990, p. 168.

8 See E. Durkheim, 'The Normal and the Pathological', in M. Wolfgang, L. Savitz and N. Johnston, *The Sociology of Crime and Delinquency*, London, Wiley, 1970, pp. 11–14, and Francis Galton, *Hereditary Genius*, London, Macmillan, 1869.

9 R. B. Perry, *The Thought and Character of William James*, 2 vols, Boston, Little, Brown, 1935, vol. 1, p. 322.

10 Ibid., p. 323.

11 Ibid., p. 322.

12 Ibid., p. 323.

13 Ibid., pp. 323–4.

14 Ibid., pp. 661–2.

15 Taylor, *William James on Consciousness*, p. 15.

16 Ibid., p. 7. The influence that Perry has had over Jamesian scholarship, and his interest exclusively in the Western philosophical tradition, is further indicated by the fact that when Harvard was offered the several thousand volumes in the James Family Library in 1923, only 50 classics of Western Philosophy were chosen by Perry for the Treasure Room. The rest were either sold off or committed to the stacks, and those that Perry felt were particularly unimportant (such as F. C. S. Schiller's work) were sold first.

17 Bruce Kuklick, *The Rise of American Philosophy: Cambridge, Massachusetts, 1860–1930*, New Haven, CT, Yale University Press, 1977, p. 161.

18 Ibid., p. 160.

19 E. Erikson, *Young Man Luther: A Study in Psychoanalysis and History*, New York, Norton, 1958, pp. 14–15.

20 Cushing Strout, 'William James and the Twice-Born Sick Soul', *Daedalus*, 1968, 97, p. 1064.

21 Ibid.

22 Letter to Tom Ward, January, 1868, reprinted in Perry, *Thought and Character*, vol. 2, p. 675.

23 William Acton, *The Functions and Disorders of the Reproductive Organs in Youth, in Adult Age, and in Advanced Life*, London, John Churchill, 1857.

William James's spiritual crisis 203

24 Cushing Strout, 'William James', p. 1066.
25 Ibid., p. 1068.
26 Ibid., p. 1071.
27 Ibid., p. 1074.
28 James William Anderson, ' "The Worst Kind of Melancholy": William James in 1869', *Harvard Library Bulletin*, 1982, 30, p. 373.
29 Ibid., p.377.
30 D. W. Winnicott, 'Fear of Breakdown', *International Review of Psycho-Analysis*, 1974, 1, pp. 103–7; H. Kohut, *The Analysis of the Self*, New York, International Universities Press, 1971, pp. 8–11.
31 Anderson, ' "The Worst Kind of Melancholy" ', p. 382.
32 Personal note in William James Papers cited by Anderson, ' "The Worst Kind of Melancholy" ', p. 381; Strout, 'William James', p. 1067.
33 Strout, 'William James', p. 1068.
34 Henry James, *Letters of William James*, vol. 1, p. 84.
35 Mark Schwehn, 'Making the World: William James and the Life of the Mind', *Harvard Library Bulletin*, 1982, 30, p. 432.
36 Ibid., p. 439.
37 Ibid., p. 443. Presumably he had in mind agnostics and materialist members of the 'Scratch Eight' (an elite philosophical dining club of which James was an honorary member when he visited Britain), as he wrote about one of their meetings from England in the same letter.
38 E. Taylor, 'William James on Psychopathology: The 1896 Lowell Lectures on Exceptional Mental States', *Harvard Library Bulletin*, 1982, 30, p. 461.
39 'Du sommeil et des états analogues'. See *Nation*, 1868, 7, pp. 50–2.
40 Taylor, 'William James on Psychopathology', p. 462.
41 Ibid.
42 Between 1869 and 1878 James reviewed I. Ray's *Contributions to Mental Pathology*, H. Maudsley's *Responsibility in Mental Disease*, W. B. Carpenter's *Principles of Mental Physiology: A Winter's Borderlands of Insanity and Other Allied Papers* and R. L. Dugdale's *'The Jukes': A Study in Crime, Pauperism, Disease and Heredity*.
43 R. J. Richards, 'The Personal Equation in Science: William James's Psychological and Moral Uses of Darwinian Theory', *Harvard Library Bulletin*, 1982, 30, p. 387.
44 Ibid., p. 388.
45 Ibid.
46 Ibid., p. 392.
47 Ibid., p. 393.
48 Ibid., p. 422.
49 Ibid., p. 394.
50 Ibid., p. 398.
51 Ibid., p. 423.
52 To be fair, there may be a little more support for seeing James's emotional life through his published work in that in his very early published works there are some coded references to his relationship with Alice, incomprehensible to 'outside' readers. However, this evidence seems very peripheral and Richards does not cite it anyway.
53 G. W. Allen, *William James: A Biography*, New York, The Viking Press, 1969, p. 149.
54 Ibid., p. 169.
55 Howard M. Feinstein, *Becoming William James*, New York, Cornell, 1984, p. 208.
56 Ibid., p. 221.
57 Ibid.

204   *Francis Neary*

58 A. Bain, *The Senses and the Intellect*, London, Henry King, 1855; H. Maudsley, *Responsibility in Mental Disease*, London, Longman's, 1874.
59 Daniel W. Bjork, *William James: The Center of his Vision*, New York, Columbia, 1988, p. xvi.
60 Ibid., p. 78.
61 Ibid., p. 80.
62 Linda Simon, *Genuine Reality: A Life of William James*, New York, Harcourt, Brace, 1998.
63 Louis Menand, 'William James and the Case of the Epileptic Patient', *New York Review of Books*, 17 December 1988, p. 14.
64 Ibid., p. 13.
65 Ibid., p. 14.
66 'Über den psychischen Mechanismus hysterischer Phänomene'.
67 'État mental des hystériques'.
68 *Psychological Review*, 1894, 1, pp. 195–200.
69 See Taylor, *William James on Consciousness*, p. 52.
70 Ibid., p. 146.
71 G. E. Myers, *William James: His Life and Thought*, New Haven, CT, Yale University Press, 1986, p. 60.
72 Louis Menand, 'William James and the Case of the Epileptic Patient', *New York Review of Books*, 17 December 1988, p. 15.

10 Can kinship be designed and still be normal?

The curious case of child adoption

Ellen Herman

'Although there is no such thing as a perfect home, there is such a thing as a normal family,' declared Dorothy Hutchinson, a national authority on child placement at the Columbia School of Social Work in New York in 1943. 'Normality is something that is hard to define, yet easy to feel and see.'[1] The case of child adoption shows how central norms have been to defining families, deciding who legitimately belonged in them, and governing the practices that turned strangers into kin.[2] Between the 1910s and the 1960s in the United States, the evaluation of personal and interpersonal norms in children and adults increasingly shaped adoptive family-making, and the appearance of novel techniques that sought to define this hard-to-define quality reveals a great deal about the evolution of adoption over the course of the twentieth century.

The project of establishing, measuring and enforcing norms – which promised that kinship without blood might escape the stigma of difference by closely matching the look and feel of blood ties – helps to explain why shifting qualifications for family membership were simultaneously prized and virtually impossible to attain. In the regulated, scientific and therapeutic operation that modern adoption came to be, normalisation rivalled and eventually overtook charity, sentiment, commerce, impulse, accident and other traditional or haphazard family-making paradigms.[3] The triumph of normalisation was never monolithic, but it was a historically novel development, a hallmark of twentieth-century modernity.

By emphasising normality, Hutchinson intended to offer reassurance. 'Of all types of child-placing, adoption comes closest to normal.'[4] This was her way of stating the obvious. Permanent, legal adoption was preferable to temporary family placements or institutional residence, both of which denied children permanent, secure belonging. Arranged intelligently and supervised with care, adoption was a desirable option for parentless children. It was almost as safe, natural and real as biological kinship, but not quite. 'No one who is not willfully deluded would maintain that the experiences of adoption can take the place of the actual bearing and rearing of an own child,' wrote Jessie Taft in 1929.[5] Taft was a leading social work educator as well as one of the country's most articulate voices for adoption reform.

206 Ellen Herman

Taft's conviction that a purely social family-making process might simulate, but could never replicate, blood ties was as poignant as it was telling. Taft was the mother of two children, Everett and Martha, both adopted.

Normal and abnormal as moral standards for 'kinship by design'

The adoption case reveals a great deal about normalisation as a form of government uniquely suited to the administrative requirements of modern welfare states.[6] In 1934 Ruth Benedict suggested that 'the concept of the normal is properly a variant of the concept of the good'.[7] Benedict's 'normal' amounted to rules about what was (and was not) approved at particular times and in particular places. Her view was steeped in the culture concept, which grew out of the well-known efforts of anthropologist Franz Boas and his students (including Benedict and her colleague Margaret Mead) to introduce a pluralistic and relativistic conception of culture compatible with the interdependence and mobility of modern life. Their fieldwork among 'primitive peoples' in the Americas and the Pacific aimed to elucidate the meanings of given cultures for their participants and repudiated the project of ranging cultures on a hierarchy from superior to inferior, from civilisation to savagery.

The upshot of their collective efforts was that lofty moral universals and absolute values were downgraded to local variations on a wide spectrum of normality. Famous examples included Margaret Mead's portrayal of an easy, sexually free adolescence in *The Coming of Age in Samoa* (1928) and Benedict's own work for the Office of War Information during the Second World War, which strove to shape US policy towards Japan by attending to that country's distinctive norms. The heightened awareness of ethnocentrism instilled by the culture concept was very explicit in relation to racial and national identities, but the fact of multiple normalities transformed how virtually every form of social difference was perceived. People who stubbornly 'identify our local normalities with the inevitable necessities of existence,' Benedict warned, were 'handicapped in dealing with human society'.[8] For Benedict, the implications were straightforward. Fears of being different and pressures towards conformity were foolish. Diversity – not sameness – and toleration – not dogmatism – were imperative values in a culture – and a world – where norms varied significantly and changed rapidly.

More recently, Ian Hacking has pointed out that norms claim to be objective descriptions of statistical typicality while simultaneously functioning as cultural ideals.[9] They live under the sign of science, but they defy the commonplace distinction between facts and values. This has made norms an especially attractive form of power in spheres of human action characterised by indeterminacy and lack of consensus, as the historian Theodore Porter has shown in relation to such activities as different as census-taking and accounting.[10] Family-making is a case in point. Assessments of human

Child adoption   207

worth, mushy notions like clinical judgement, and worries about arbitrary decision-making are recipes for value conflicts, and such conflicts have been enduring features of modern adoption history. By substituting confidence in objective practices and scientific methods for the conviction that family-making is inevitably subjective, normalisation aspired to generate a consensus about what was good for children, rationalise court and agency procedures on their behalf, and promote a new, improved ideal of family formation – what I call *kinship by design*.

In the United States, special-purpose adoption laws began to appear in the middle of the nineteenth century. Legal historians usually consider the Massachusetts Adoption of Children Act of 1851 the first to display a uniquely modern preoccupation with child welfare, its language suggesting that the core purpose of adoption was to benefit children rather than meet adults' needs for heirs.[11] The United States was well ahead of other Western nations in this regard. For example, the first UK Act of Parliament to regulate adoption was the Adoption of Children Act 1926. And in significant parts of the non-Western world, adoption remained formally proscribed by law and secretive and exceptional in practice even at the end of the twentieth century.[12] In many different contexts the distance between adoptive ties and blood ties defined adoption as more than exceptional. It was abnormal.

Abnormality was synonymous with danger as well as deviation. The modern machinery of public investigation and regulation by agencies, courts and professionals was erected precisely to manage the multiple risks believed to be inherent in adopting children who were not one's 'own'. This machinery – a defining feature of kinship by design – was institutionalised during the early twentieth century in the United States. In 1917 Minnesota passed the first law mandating that children's adoptability and prospective parents' suitability be investigated before adoption decrees were granted.[13] In 1921 Ohio stipulated that adoption studies be conducted by duly accredited children's agencies.[14] By 1935 more than 20 states had translated similar standards into law.[15] At mid-century virtually all states in the country required individual and organisational child-placers to be licensed, and the vast majority required that adoptive families be studied in advance, supervised after placement, and kept on probation for a lengthy period (6–12 months) before adoptions were finalised.[16]

In spite of such changes, kinship by design never achieved a monopoly over adoption. The federalism that characterises the United States meant that states were entitled to pass and administer family laws as they saw fit, and this included allowing 'independent' or 'private' (i.e. non-agency) adoptions, which tended to skimp on the 'safeguards' professionals cherished. (Only two states ever banned non-agency adoptions altogether – Delaware in 1952 and Connecticut in 1957 – and because jurisdiction-shopping was easy, these were largely symbolic restrictions.) The country's legal patchwork frustrated standardisation. In their determined quest for children, Americans easily crossed state and, increasingly, national lines to circumvent any unwelcome regulations close to home. Still, most states incorporated the formal managerial requirements of kinship by design by mid-century. Most also made adoption records confidential and had finally taken steps to equalise the inheritance rights of natural and adopted children.[17]

Political and legal reforms illustrated that standardisation explicitly aimed to alleviate fears about bad children and bad outcomes by the 1930s and 1940s, but concerns also surfaced about the moral fitness of adults – birth parents as well as those adults who volunteered to become parents to other people's children. Several other institutional and cultural factors also served to normalise adoption. A move towards environmentalism (nurture over nature) in the human sciences, prompted by appreciation of the genocidal link between Nazism and biological determinism, and the relatively greater availability of public social welfare services, thanks to the New Deal of the 1930s, also countered the perception that adoption was extremely risky.

Together, these developments helped to popularise adoption. In contrast, formalising adoptive kinship had been exceedingly rare among ordinary Americans in 1900, according to one keen observer. Appearing in court was 'thoroughly formidable to families who have never in their lives had anything to do with "the law". They naturally shrink from it and from the possible publicity entailed'.[18] Anecdotal evidence suggests that adoptions increased steadily during the first several decades of the century, but after 1945, when the US Children's Bureau and the National Center for Social Statistics began collecting national data, the numbers climbed dramatically. Adoptions doubled in the decade following the Second World War and reached a century-long high point of 175,000 adoptions annually in 1970. Most were non-relative adoptions, and the vast majority of these were arranged by agency professionals.[19]

New forms of inspection and documentation turned modern adoption into a uniquely legible social institution. According to James Scott, 'legibility' has been the premier achievement of modern statecraft.[20] It turned exceedingly complex and varied private transactions into simplified exchanges subject to monitoring, quantification and other forms of public regulation. Accompanying this new level of legibility was a firm commitment to making adoption better by making it more scientific.[21] The adoption research industry, an entirely unique twentieth-century phenomenon, manifested the very same worry that galvanised state-making: that the distinction between adoption and 'real', blood-based kinship disadvantaged the former and made a powerful case for authoritative knowledge and supervision. Novel forms of empirical inquiry into adoption might generate such knowledge, and these flourished after the 1910s, taking four primary forms. *Field* studies and *outcome* studies were done primarily by social work researchers determined to document what they considered an appalling number of irregular adoptions, make the case for stiffer regulation, refine adoption standards, and improve matching practices by assessing the results of adoption many years after placement. *Nature–nurture* and *clinical* studies were conducted by developmentalists in psychology, psychiatry and what is now called behavioural genetics. Abnormality was their starting point, with nature–nurture inquiries using adoption as a counterpoint to nature, and clinical inquiries probing the relationship between adoption and psychopathology.[22]

Adoption research reinforced the conviction underlying adoption reform, that effective public regulation and knowledge production were mutually reinforcing enterprises, equally necessary to control adoption and other serious social problems such as crime, sexual immorality and economic dependence. This belief had animated the progressive politics of maternalist thinkers and activists before the First World War, was dramatically institutionalised in the form of the New Deal state, and was nowhere more obvious than in policy arenas linked to childhood and family life.[23] Developing refined techniques for assessment and prediction was considered by most researchers, policy-makers and helping professionals to be a prerequisite for enhancing social welfare. Virtually all adoption research aimed to normalise adoption, in the sense of reducing the hazards confronted by children and adults, making the adopting families more like other families, and improving its subjective experience and cultural reputation.

The adoption research industry was nothing if not benevolent. Yet each research genre inevitably reiterated and reinscribed the distinctiveness that was unavoidable in adoption, exposing the questions that defined modern adoption as a managerial problem in the first place. Could social operations successfully simulate natural operations? If identity and belonging were typically ascribed to birth and blood, and were not achieved by purely social means, what could compensate the members of adoptive families? *Could kinship be designed and still be normal?*

The zealous campaign to subject family-formation to new forms of legal, intellectual and scientific authority during the first part of the century initially answered these questions by publicising facts which proved that adoption, and all its participants, were abnormal. What were these facts? First, children unlucky enough to need new parents were frequently presumed to be mentally subnormal – 'defective' or 'feeble-minded' in the vocabulary of the time.[24] (*Sub*normality was a species of abnormality in which deviations fell consistently below norms.) Histories of antisocial or criminal behaviour in natal parents were also cited as ubiquitous among children in need of placement. To have 'vicious', 'shiftless', 'worthless', 'ignorant' or 'cruel' relatives was not merely unfortunate,[25] but a sign of bad inheritance and a barometer of future trouble. The close pairing of mental subnormality and social abnormality decreased children's chances of being judged adoptable. Progressive-era reformers may have celebrated the family as the 'the highest and finest product of civilization'[26] in theory, but in practice, families were destinations only for 'normal' children.

Second, adults who wanted to raise other people's children were also suspected of living on the wrong side of normality. Cases of criminals,

210   *Ellen Herman*

alcoholics, single men and women, and immoral characters of all kinds surfaced regularly during the period around the First World War. The fact that they were frequently able to adopt with ease appalled reformers even as it stiffened their resolve to prevent such horrors from recurring in the future. These adults violated the rapidly evolving norms of bourgeois parenthood. They often expected adoptees to do farm work or domestic chores, for example, just like indentured children, servants or even slaves. Adopting child workers, during this period of historical transition in the meaning of childhood, signalled exploitation. Mixing love and labour in families, a statistical norm for the vast majority of American families in the nineteenth century, violated a cultural norm consolidated during the early decades of the twentieth century, as a culture of consumption emerged along with a new and self-conscious middle class. Children had become emotional investments rather than economic assets. In a market context where everything had its price, children were supposed to be priceless rather than productive.[27]

Finally, reformers believed that many of the institutional mechanisms available for adoption early in the twentieth century – from orphanages and baby farms to commercial maternity homes and philanthropic baby bureaux – were grossly inadequate for ensuring that normality was probed in either children or adults. The earliest field studies of adoption in the United States – conducted in the late 1910s and 1920s – compiled piles of factual data revealing many irregularities and repeated norm violations. Ida Parker, a researcher with the Boston Council of Social Agencies, found that most Massachusetts adoptions between 1922 and 1925 involved physicians, hospitals and newspaper ads – not authorised social agencies. She also found mental deficiency and immorality everywhere she looked in the natal backgrounds of the 900 children she studied. Parker concluded: '[T]his is not the human stock which people contemplating adoption desire but many times ... it is what they secure. ... Normal families of good stock seldom give away their children.'[28] For reformers like Parker, market values, sentimentality, and naiveté were primary reasons why mental and moral norms were ignored and why adoption remained perilous.

Normalisation and therapeutic adoption

Anxieties about normality contributed directly to the reconceptualisation of adoption as a social problem requiring significant reform in law and practice. Adoption reformers included leaders in the new profession of social work, policy-makers affiliated with bureaucracies such as the US Children's Bureau, founded in 1912, and public and private child welfare organisations federated under the umbrella of the Child Welfare League of America after 1921. They formulated arguments about the correspondence between legal uniformity, agency professionalism and state responsibility to protect vulnerable children. Their promise was that 'standards' and 'safeguards'

Child adoption 211

(terms used interchangeably for decades) would make adoption safer and more natural, hence bringing it closer to normality.[29]

The premise of their normalising campaign was that adoption was abnormal and had to be approached therapeutically. Systematic concern with identifying and adjusting abnormalities, including (perhaps especially) those that consistently escaped the conscious notice of the parties to adoption themselves, was a defining characteristic of therapeutic technique and philosophy. Therapeutic adoption called for thorough personality studies, copious documentation, objective measurements, repeated investigations, and a dose of scrupulously non-judgemental 'interpretation' that heralded adoption's arrival as a full-fledged subject of casework and counselling.[30] The historical origins of therapeutic adoption can be traced to the child study and parent education movements, the tradition of maternalist reform, foundation-supported developmental science, and the spread of psychoanalysis in American culture.[31]

First and most forcefully articulated in the work of Jessie Taft in the late 1910s, therapeutic adoption was also advocated by other social work educators, including Charlotte Towle and Dorothy Hutchinson, as well as psychiatrists Viola Bernard and Florence Clothier.[32] These were elite women, born between 1882 and 1907. They were educated at the country's top colleges and professional schools, including Smith, Vassar, the New York School of Social Work, Johns Hopkins and Cornell.[33] All worked in child placement and adoption agencies and all (except Clothier) eventually ended up in academic positions. They taught at Columbia, the University of Chicago and the University of Pennsylvania. Of the five, only Clothier led a conventional married life. Taft and Towle shared their lives with other women, while Bernard's marriage quickly ended in a messy divorce. Taft adopted two children with her partner, Virginia Robinson, but Towle, Bernard and Hutchinson never raised children themselves.

These life patterns were not unusual among female reformers and intellectuals at the time, but they are notable, and curious, among women who boldly set out to define and enforce norms related to heterosexual marriage, childrearing and family life. Like so many other dimensions of therapeutic culture, therapeutic adoption exuded a feminine sensibility while imposing new restrictions on women's lives. Its theoretical foundations were laid during the first several decades of the century, but it reached the height of its popularity after 1945.

Advocates of therapeutic approaches presumed that without systematic help and oversight to counterbalance its many weaknesses and abnormalities, adoption was a disaster waiting to happen, and their constant invocation of norms suggested that these were moral as well as statistical indices of value. Unmarried birth mothers, for instance, were abnormal by definition because they had already flouted the widespread sanction against illegitimacy. Could unmarried birth mothers lead *normal* lives by keeping their babies or giving them up? And were their babies less likely to be *normal*

212 Ellen Herman

than those born to married parents? Whatever the marital status of birth parents, infants and children who needed new families were automatically suspected of having subnormal minds and bodies because their parents had taken the abnormal step of giving them away. Which children were mentally and physically *normal* enough to qualify for family rather than institutional placements? There were a host of other practical questions related to detecting normality in the less-than-normal parties to adoption. Did couples who wished to adopt have *normal* motivations? Would they provide home environments suitable for *normal* development? Could adoption be *normal* for fertile couples, or only for infertile ones? What configurations of religion, age, race, income and sex roles made a family *normal*?

Over time the answers changed, and the quest for personal and interpersonal norms in children, adults and families faltered on evidence that such supposedly essential qualities could also be so transitory. Early in the century, for instance, children with mental retardation or physical disabilities were rarely adopted, and it was considered sensible to adopt older children, who were known quantities, rather than riskier newborns or toddlers.[34] By 1950 the discourse of 'special needs' made adoption theoretically normal for every child, and older children had been redefined from desirable to 'hard to place'.[35] Most demand was for infants, and placing babies became more normal, statistically and ideologically, as a result.

Reformers clearly understood that norms had shifted dramatically, but they still believed that normalisation was the best way to address adoption's numerous hazards and authenticity problems. From the 1910s through to the 1960s, quests to make adoption normal converged on the goal of matching reproductive nature. Matching normalised adoption by hiding the most obvious fact about it: it was a different way to acquire children and make families.

Detecting norms and deviations in children

Two brief examples illustrate how the normalisation process worked in the new regulatory, scientific and therapeutic practices that redefined adoption as kinship by design from the 1910s onwards. The first has to do with detecting norms and deviations in children. The second has to do with detecting norms and deviations in adults.

Determining objectively whether children were adoptable was the first goal of normalisation in modern adoption. During the early part of the century, eugenic worries about the quality of available children drove efforts to distinguish between normal children, who were qualified for family membership, and feeble-minded and defective children, who were not. Stories of superficially adorable children who turned out to be tragically flawed, breaking the hearts of well-meaning adoptive parents, were common. One baby girl, 'in the "cute" stage of development which conceals her limitations . . . was just the kind of child who would smite the heart of questing adoptive parents,' noted Arnold Gesell. Gesell was a Yale psychologist whose standardisation of developmental norms, beginning at birth, during the 1920s and 1930s transformed him from a talented technologist into the most popular childrearing celebrity in the country during the era before Benjamin Spock.[36] Gesell predicted that this baby would probably never complete high school and that 'there may be genuine pangs of regret' in store for any parents foolish enough to adopt her.[37]

Reformers used such cases as object lessons to advertise the riskiness of adoption and the necessity of practices that offered safety through precise measurement and close supervision. The border between normal and abnormal in children was not a bright line readily apparent to casual observers, they warned, but a complex set of qualifications that required training to discern and even more training to predict. Reformers like Gesell called on the judicial system to require professional oversight of every placement in order to prevent the suffering associated with 'bungled adoption'.[38] 'Heartaches for the adult; injustice and personality-distortion for the child' were ever-present risks whether adoptions were arranged by well-intentioned amateurs or by profit-hungry entrepreneurs. These 'can be enormously reduced by intelligent social control,' Gesell stressed.[39] He also trusted that expert assessment 'will serve to reveal children of normal and superior endowment beneath the concealment of neglect, of poverty, or of poor repute'.[40] This accomplishment made normalisation synonymous with fairness to the individual as well as with safety. It allowed for both impartial inclusion and appropriate exclusion from families.

More worrisome to public authorities than children whose bad appearances obscured their essential normality, however, were children who seemed normal, but actually were not. In 1911, Henry Herbert Goddard, Director of the Vineland Training School, authority on feeble-mindedness and a pioneer in the field of special education, warned that this kind of adoption was a eugenic time bomb. 'It is neither right nor wise for us to let our humanity, our pity and sympathy for the poor, homeless, and neglected child, drive us to do injustice to and commit a crime against those yet unborn.'[41] Children of dubious pedigree who needed new parents deserved compassionate care in institutional settings where their reproductive sexuality might be contained and the quality of the gene pool preserved.[42]

One of the first adoption standards formulated by the Child Welfare League in 1938 was that 'the child have the intelligence and the physical and mental background to meet the reasonable expectations of the adopting parents'.[43] From the 1910s on, mental and developmental tests – from the Binet Scale to the Gesell Scale – were administered to assess children and decide whether or not they were appropriate candidates for adoption. The first professional child-placing manual, W. H. Slingerland's *Child-Placing in Families* (1919), called for professional psychologists to conduct 'a scientific study of mentality and personality' in every case of possible placement, along with a careful physical examination.[44] Such studies would serve two purposes. First, they would eliminate 'constitutionally defective' children

214   *Ellen Herman*

from consideration. Second, they would provide technical assistance to child-placers seeking to match like with like.

Mental matching was considered at least as important as matching skin or eye or hair colour during this period, and tests were utilised as a way to avoid the much-discussed errors of 'under-placement' and 'over-placement'. (The first gave bright children to dull parents; the second gave dull children to bright parents.) 'To put a low grade mental defective in a family home where a normal child was expected is a social crime, once to be condoned because of ignorance, but now inexcusable in a well-ordered and progressive child-placing agency,' Slingerland chided his colleagues.[45] Like the social managers who inspected the mentality of immigrants, soldiers and school-children, child-placers embraced mental and developmental norms as proxies for social status that could withstand the egalitarianism of American democracy. 'You must bear in mind that there are first-class, second-class, and third-class children,' Slingerland added, 'and there are first-class, second-class, and third-class homes.'[46]

Normalising inspection remained more of an aspiration than an accomplished fact in adoptions before the Second World War, but as early as 1915, testing for placement-related purposes was routinised at leading agencies such as the New England Home for Little Wanderers, which operated throughout New England.[47] Sophie van Senden Theis, a prominent early adoption professional who spent her career at the New York State Charities Aid Association, claimed in the late 1940s that mental and psychological testing was utilised by most agencies around the country.[48] An ambitious national survey conducted by the Child Welfare League at mid-century showed that 75 per cent of all public and private agencies in the United States utilised tests to determine eligibility for adoption, reduce risks, and match children with parents. By 1950, selective mental matching was considered slightly more important than matching by race or religion, even by Catholic and sectarian agencies.[49]

The spread of techniques such as mental and developmental testing exposed an ideology of family belonging in which physiological resemblance and intellectual similarity were considered the chief products of reproductive nature. The absence of biological connection in adoption, according to this theory, could be compensated for by increasing the chances that unrelated adults and children would look, feel and be alike. Equating parent–child sameness with familial normality represented, at best, a partial reading of nature, since heterosexual reproduction produced significant intergenerational variation as well as continuity. Advocates of normalisation nevertheless believed deeply that their techniques would safeguard adoption in a cultural context that classified kinship without blood as inferior, unnatural, second best – in short, as abnormal. It is a paradox of adoption history that the very social design operations that marked adoption as a voluntary means of family formation subject to enlightened design and control also defined it as a form of kinship prone to unusual hazards and mistakes.

Detecting norms and deviations in adults

Efforts to ascertain the suitability of potential parents were evident early in the century too. Child-placers inspected the cleanliness of homes, the religious practice of would-be parents, their drinking habits and their public reputation. All were proxies for moral character, and fairly simple to determine. But it was not until adoption became more popular and visible, in the 1930s and 1940s, that efforts to deliberately select normal parents became systematic and widespread. By mid-century, when the demand for healthy white infants had increased dramatically, professionals considered it dangerously naive to assume that adults interested in adopting actually were who they said they were and meant what they said. Like children earlier in the century who had been suspected of underlying deviations, adults needed to be objectively scrutinised so that elusive dangers might be detected before families were formed.

The home investigation (called the 'home study' by mid-century) evolved as a normalising approach to applicant fitness that was at once evaluative and therapeutic. It assessed adults' practical and psychological readiness to care for children. Age, duration of marriage, occupation, education, income and spending habits, religion, and experience with child care were all surveyed. Emotional health was considered among the most salient and difficult-to-determine qualifications, as important by mid-century as physical health.[50] Home studies probed capacity for parenthood by exploring marital adjustment and household division of labour, feelings about infertility, and motivations for adoption. Marriage itself hardly guaranteed normality, to be sure, and most state laws did not explicitly require adopters to be married, although most were. Any child born to unmarried adults was 'practically foredoomed ... to become one of the "neurotic personalities of our time"', one social worker declared in 1939, and that made it all the more important for adopters to be married.[51] By 1940, adoptions by single adults were on the wane. The quest to normalise adoption had narrowed the definition of an acceptable family and placed adoption off limits to many kinds of adults – especially single women and female couples – who had adopted earlier in the century.[52]

No issue was a more sensitive index of emotional normality in would-be parents than 'sterility', a term more common than 'infertility' before the 1960s. Infertility was a frequent motivation for adoption that professionals also considered a very sensitive indicator of marital adjustment and parental capacity. Inability to conceive had not always been a decisive prerequisite for adoption, but childless couples were probably always attracted to adoption. By mid-century, infertility loomed so large that most agencies refused even to consider applications from couples able to produce children on their own. In 1943, Louise Wise Services, a prominent New York agency, began rejecting couples who already had or could have children of their own, even when they expressed a preference for adoption, and began requesting confidential

216 Ellen Herman

medical reports from physicians to verify applicants' infertility and use as a diagnostic tool in the course of the adoption process.[53] By the early 1960s, infertility was so well established as a qualification that to apply for adoption was itself 'an overt admission of biological failure', according to one Mayo Clinic psychiatrist.[54]

Tying requirements for parenthood to adoption's status as a last resort posed an enormous obstacle to the normalisation of adoptive kinship and functioned as a double bind for adults wishing to adopt. Making infertility a prerequisite for adoption required that couples first work long and hard to correct their reproductive breakdown and have children of their 'own'. Home studies explored how long they had been trying to conceive, how many doctors they had seen and how much time they had devoted to treating their infertility. The more strenuously couples resisted their infertility, the more they appeared to want children, but the more strenuously they resisted their infertility, the further away they were from the 'resolution' of infertility that proved they were ready to adopt. This conflict was poignantly illustrated by couples who honestly admitted they preferred to have their 'own' children and wished to adopt because adoption might cure infertility and induce pregnancy.[55] Although they were merely expressing the dominant cultural preference for natural, and therefore normal, kinship, their reason for pursuing adoption was viewed sceptically, as evidence of neurosis and a sign of trouble.[56] Couples were expected to want their own children above all else, but they were also expected to want adopted children for their own sake.

Why infertility existed was as important as, if not more important than, whether it had been medically documented, especially during the golden age of psychoanalysis after the Second World War. According to the psychiatrist and adoption agency consultant Viola Bernard, who studied the psychosocial dynamics of reproduction at Columbia Medical School, childlessness might be 'organic' or 'psychogenic', and the difference made all the difference in assessments of parental capacity.[57] 'Organic' causes for infertility were medically explicable and figured infertility as a bodily state located in the reproductive physiology of husband, wife or both. Couples afflicted with infertility of this kind were childless against their will. Innocent victims of reproductively uncooperative bodies who negotiated their infertility with emotional maturity, many agencies agreed, 'offer the most hopeful prognosis for adoption and for adopted children'.[58] In contrast, the causes of 'psychogenic' infertility were located in the mind, and that made childlessness at once mysterious and suspicious. Couples without children, but without any authoritative reason for not having them, might overcome their infertility at any moment. Giving them a child might deprive another couple with absolutely no hope of ever having their own. Even couples who had experienced multiple miscarriages were sometimes denied children because their reproductive potential was theoretically intact.[59]

The most serious risk was that psychogenic infertility might represent hostility towards parenthood unknown to the applicants themselves, making them potential threats to vulnerable children. Would-be parents whose childlessness could not be medically explained might actually be terrified of pregnancy and childbirth, reproductively paralysed by neurosis, or convinced they would make inadequate parents. 'Psychogenic factors . . . may be far from evident to the casual observer,' noted a Louise Wise Services intake report for 1943 and 1943, but they betrayed dangers 'which we most desire to avoid for the adopted child'.[60] 'This is one of the most difficult things to get at,' social worker Helen Fradkin admitted, 'because the woman is not, certainly, going to come to the adoption agency and say, "I am afraid to have a child of my own, I'd rather adopt one."'[61] Like adoption itself, infertility deviated from the norm. By posing risks that were subtle if not unconscious, it presented thorny challenges for interpretation and adjustment.

During the period I have examined, protection from risk was the single most important justification for turning the home study into a full-fledged object of help, supervision, empirical inquiry, and a new apparatus of legal and social control. Kinship by design promised to increase the chances of making happy, stable families by determining whether applicants for adoptive parenthood were normal or not. But the normalising operations involved in probing adult motivations reinforced the authenticity problems that plagued adoption. Getting close to realness was the best that adoptive families could hope for, because realness was a quality that could not be achieved, no matter how great the effort, or perhaps especially with great effort. The kind of realness that resided in normality was ascribed to blood, and blood meant kinship that was automatic and taken for granted. If real family ties were positioned as fixed and insulated from social arrangement, adoption contrasted sharply. It was 'made up'. The acts of social planning and consent that marked adoption as exemplary therefore also marked it as inauthentic and deviant.

Conclusion

At the heart of adoption normalisation there was a paradox. Adoption was at once an ideal and a problem. It was the most desirable goal for many children in need of new parents, yet it was defined as a deviation rather than a variation. It was not normal because it was at once less real than 'the real thing' and more social than 'the real thing'. In addition to adoption's close relationship to illegitimacy, a source of great shame until at least the 1960s, the measure of realness in modern American kinship ideology was blood, as in 'blood is thicker than water'.[62] The equivalence between blood and belonging makes normalisation appear to be a primary strategy for managing the stigma of purely social kinship and allocating children and parents according to a changing cultural hierarchy of characteristics that were more and less desirable in each. Adoption was distinctive because it was excruciatingly deliberate. No one, after all, ended up in an adoptive family by

218 *Ellen Herman*

accident. Choice – typically lauded as an exemplary value in a liberal, individualistic culture like the United States – was precisely what made adoption appear weak and distant from the kind of permanent and unchosen kinship that nature made.

Normalising techniques were well-intentioned efforts to bring dignity and equality to adoption through social design. Their architects were dedicated advocates who wanted to move beyond protecting vulnerable dependants from harm and set out to enhance child and family welfare by designing families that were safe, natural and real – hence normal. They were confident that the powerful combination of a benevolent state, enlightened science and therapeutic insight would help them to achieve their goals.

They did not ultimately succeed, nor could they have done so. Purposeful cultural operations that made families necessarily deviated from natural operations that made families. Today, in the age of the human genome, nature, that ultimate norm, is not what it used to be, and neither is culture.[63] Advances in reproductive technology during the past few decades have exposed nature as more manipulable and therefore less powerful and constant than ever, yet its allure as a source of legitimation for family-making persists undiminished.[64] From the early twentieth century through to the 1960s, however, nature was a family-making ideal still held apart from and exalted over the human agency that made adoption possible as a kinship arrangement. Adoption never got all the way to normal, because its kin ties were achieved entirely through social action rather than ascribed to nature and then validated socially and legally after the fact. Adoption history consequently illustrates some of the impediments to normalising authority as well as its historical progress. Kinship could not be designed and, at the same time, be entirely normal.

Notes

1 Dorothy Hutchinson, *In Quest of Foster Parents: A Point of View on Homefinding*, New York, Columbia University Press, 1943, pp. 91, 52.

2 The term 'adoption' is used here to refer to adoption by non-relatives ('biological strangers'), because child welfare reformers, regulators and researchers have been almost exclusively interested in this type of adoption. Whereas adoption by blood relatives was presumed to be natural and easy, the difficulties associated with adoption by strangers justified public regulation, professional oversight and scientific inquiry. Most children adopted during the twentieth century in the United States were placed with non-relatives, but there have always been a substantial number of adoptions by natal relatives and stepparents, and this proportion has increased since 1970. See note 19 below for references to historical statistics on adoption's changing profile.

3 On child placement and adoption prior to the era of normalisation, see Bruce Bellingham, 'Waifs and Strays: Child Abandonment, Foster Care, and Families in Mid-Nineteenth-Century New York', in Peter Mandler, ed., *The Uses of Charity: The Poor on Relief in the Nineteenth-Century Metropolis*, Philadelphia, University of Pennsylvania Press, 1990, pp. 123–60; Sherri Broder, *Tramps, Unfit Mothers, and Neglected Children: Negotiating the Family in Nineteenth-Century*

Child adoption 219

Philadelphia, Philadelphia, University of Pennsylvania Press, 2002; Matthew A. Crenson, *Building the Invisible Orphanage: The Prehistory of the American Welfare System*, Cambridge, MA, Harvard University Press, 1998; and Stephen O'Connor, *Orphan Trains: The Story of Charles Loring Brace and the Children He Saved and Failed*, Boston, Houghton Mifflin, 2001.

4 Dorothy Hutchinson, 'Re-examination of Some Aspects of Case Work Practice in Adoption', *Child Welfare*, 1946, 25, p. 4.

5 Jessie Taft, 'Concerning Adopted Children', *Child Study*, 1929, 6, p. 87.

6 Peter Miller and Nikolas Rose, 'On Therapeutic Authority: Psychoanalytical Expertise Under Advanced Liberalism', *History of the Human Sciences*, 1994, 7, pp. 29–64.

7 Ruth Benedict, 'Anthropology and the Abnormal', in Margaret Mead, ed., *An Anthropologist at Work: Writings of Ruth Benedict*, Boston, Houghton Mifflin, 1959, p. 276. Originally published in the *Journal of General Psychology*, 1934, 10, pp. 59–82.

8 Ruth Benedict, 'The Individual and the Pattern of Culture', in *Patterns of Culture*, Boston and New York, Houghton Mifflin, 1934, p. 271.

9 Ian Hacking, *The Taming of Chance*, New York, Cambridge University Press, 1990, ch. 19. Other important perspectives include Georges Canguilhem, *The Normal and the Pathological*, trans. Carolyn R. Fawcett in collaboration with Robert S. Cohen, New York, Zone Books, 1989; Michel Foucault, *Abnormal: Lectures at the Collège de France, 1974–1975*, ed. Arnold I. Davidson, trans. Graham Burchell, New York, Picador, 2003; and Michel Foucault, *Discipline and Punish: The Birth of the Prison*, trans. Alan Sheridan, New York, Vintage Books, 1979.

10 Theodore M. Porter, *Trust in Numbers: The Pursuit of Objectivity in Science and Public Life*, Princeton, NJ, Princeton University Press, 1995.

11 For the text of the Massachusetts law, see The Adoption History Project, Online, darkwing.uoregon.edu/~adoption/archive/MassACA.htm. For more on the Massachusetts law and the early legal history of adoption, see Stephen B. Presser, 'The Historical Background of the American Law of Adoption', *Journal of Family Law*, 1971–2, 11, pp. 443–516, and Jamil S. Zainaldin, 'The Emergence of a Modern American Family Law: Child Custody, Adoption, and the Courts, 1796–1851', *Northwestern University Law Review*, 1979, 73, pp. 1038–89.

12 Jamila Bargach, *Orphans of Islam: Family, Abandonment, and Secret Adoption in Morocco*, Lanham, MD, Rowman and Littlefield, 2002.

13 In 1891 Michigan was the first state to call on judges to 'investigate' before entering final adoption decrees, but that law did not specify any investigatory methods or standards, nor did it authorise judges to have third parties conduct such investigations. In contrast, the 1917 Minnesota law directed the state 'to verify the allegations of the petition, to investigate the conditions and antecedents of the child for the purpose of ascertaining whether he is a proper subject for adoption, and to make appropriate inquiry to determine whether the proposed foster home is a suitable home for the child'. The inquiry was to be conducted by the state welfare department, a licensed children's agency, a court social worker, or another qualified investigator, with the results to be submitted to courts in a written form that included a specific recommendation. For more of the text of the Minnesota statute, see US Children's Bureau, *Adoption Laws in the United States: A Summary of the Development of Adoption Legislation and Significant Features of Adoption Statutes, with the Text of Selected Laws*, ed. Emelyn Foster Peck, Bureau Publication 148, Washington, DC, Government Printing Office, 1925, pp. 27–8.

14 US Children's Bureau, *Adoption Laws in the United States*, pp. 32–4.

15 Agnes K. Hanna, 'Some Problems of Adoption', *Child*, December 1936, p. 4.

See also Carl A. Heisterman, 'A Summary of Legislation on Adoption', *Social Service Review*, 1935, 9, pp. 270–5.

16 The *Social Work Year Book* (renamed the *Encyclopedia of Social Work* in 1965) was conceived as a comprehensive reference guide to the varied activities of social work professionals. Its entries on adoption, which begin in 1929, offer a useful introduction to the expansion of adoption regulation and illustrate how deeply professionals believed child welfare depended on the expanding jurisdiction of state authority. See also US Children's Bureau, *Essentials of Adoption Law and Procedure*, Bureau Publication 331, Washington, DC, Government Printing Office, 1949.

17 The 1917 Minnesota law was the first law in the United States to seal all records in adoption proceedings, except for 'parties in interest and their attorneys and representatives of the State board of control'. For more on the history of confidentiality and secrecy in adoption, see E. Wayne Carp, *Family Matters: Secrecy and Disclosure in the History of Adoption*, Cambridge, MA, Harvard University Press, 1998, and Elizabeth J. Samuels, 'The Idea of Adoption: An Inquiry into the History of Adult Adoptee Access to Birth Records', *Rutgers Law Review*, Winter 2001, pp. 367–436. A useful historical summary can be found in Joan H. Hollinger, 'Introduction to Adoption Law and Practice', in Joan H. Hollinger, ed., *Adoption Law and Practice*, New York, Matthew Bender, 1994.

18 Sophie van Senden Theis, *How Foster Children Turn Out*, Publication 165, New York State Charities Aid Association, 1924, p. 127.

19 The 1945–77 period was the only part of the twentieth century when a national reporting system existed, based on data voluntarily supplied by states and territories. Penelope L. Maza, 'Adoption Trends: 1944–1975', Child Welfare Research Notes no. 9, US Children's Bureau, August 1984, table 1, CWLA Papers (SW55.1), Box 65, Folder: 'Adoption – Research – Reprints of Articles'; Kathy S. Stolley, 'Statistics on Adoption in the United States', *The Future of Children*, Spring 1993, 1, pp. 26–42. In spite of increases in international and transracial adoptions since 1970, which have made adoption literally more visible than it was in the past, numbers of adoptions have declined significantly to around 125,000 annually in recent years. Of these, relative adoptions (by step-parents, for instance) have increased substantially. For more recent data, see the statistical profile compiled by the Evan B. Donaldson Adoption Institute, Online, www.adoptioninstitute.org/research/ressta.html; Anjani Chandra, Joyce Abma, Penelope Maza and Christine Backrach, 'Adoption, Adoption Seeking, and Relinquishment for Adoption in the United States', *Advance Data from Vital and Health Statistics of the Centers for Disease Control and Prevention/National Center for Health Statistics*, 11 May 1999, no. 306; and US Census Bureau, 'Census 2000 Special Reports, Adopted Children and Stepchildren: 2000', Washington DC, US Department of Commerce, Economics and Statistics Administration, August 2003.

20 James C. Scott, *Seeing Like a State: How Certain Schemes to Improve the Human Condition Have Failed*, New Haven, CT, Yale University Press, 1998.

21 Ellen Herman, 'Families Made by Science: Arnold Gesell and the Technologies of Modern Child Adoption', *Isis*, December 2001, 92, pp. 684–715.

22 One early field study, conducted by the Boston Council of Social Agencies, was reported in Ida R. Parker, *'Fit and Proper?': A Study of Legal Adoption in Massachusetts*, Boston, Church Home Society, 1927. The first large-scale outcome study was Theis, *How Foster Children Turn Out*. An early nature–nurture study can be found in Barbara Stoddard Burks, 'The Relative Influence of Nature and Nurture upon Mental Development: A Comparative Study of Foster Parent–Foster Child Resemblance and True Parent–True Child Resemblance', *27th Yearbook of the National Society for the Study of Education*, part 1, 1928,

pp. 219–316. Clinical studies began somewhat later. An early example can be found in David M. Levy, 'Primary Affect Hunger', *American Journal of Psychiatry*, November 1937, 94, 643–52.

23 Linda Gordon, *Pitied but Not Entitled: Single Mothers and the History of Welfare, 1890–1935*, New York, The Free Press, 1994; Molly Ladd-Taylor, *Mother-Work: Women, Child Welfare, and the State, 1890–1930*, Urbana, University of Illinois Press, 1994; Kriste Lindenmeyer, *'A Right to Childhood': The U.S. Children's Bureau and Child Welfare, 1912–46*, Urbana, University of Illinois Press, 1997; Sonia Michel, *Children's Interests, Mothers' Rights: The Shaping of America's Child Care Policy*, New Haven, CT, Yale University Press, 1999; Robyn Muncy, *Creating a Female Dominion in American Reform, 1890–1935*, New York, Oxford University Press, 1991; Theda Skocpol, *Protecting Soldiers and Mothers: The Political Origins of Social Policy in the United States*, Cambridge, MA, Harvard University Press, 1992.

24 'Mental retardation' or 'developmental disability' are the terms in use today.

25 Such terms were commonplace in the records of child-placing agencies. See Sophie van Senden Theis and Constance Goodrich, *The Child in the Foster Home, Part I: The Placement and Supervision of Children in Free Foster Homes: A Study Based on the Work of the Child-Placing Agency of the New York State Charities Aid Association*, New York, School of Social Work, 1921.

26 This often-quoted declaration about family life originated with the first White House Conference on Children in 1909. Its rhetorical success obscured the fact that the theory of institutional care was repudiated long before its practice ended. Not until the 1950s did the number of children living in temporary foster families exceed the number of children living in institutions, and it was not until the 1960s that the number of adoptive placements surpassed the number of institutional placements. See Bernadine Barr, 'Spare Children, 1900–1945: Inmates of Orphanages as Subjects of Research in Medicine and in the Social Sciences in America', PhD dissertation, Stanford, CA, Stanford University, 1992, fig. 2.2, p. 32.

27 Viviana A. Zelizer, *Pricing the Priceless Child: The Changing Social Value of Children*, New York, Basic Books, 1985. The classic work on the history of Western childhood is Philippe Ariès, *Centuries of Childhood*, trans. Robert Baldick, New York, Vintage Books, 1962.

28 Parker, *'Fit and Proper?'*, p. 26.

29 Ellen Herman, 'The Paradoxical Rationalization of Modern Adoption', *Journal of Social History*, Winter 2002, 36, pp. 339–85.

30 'Interpretation' had another, more specific and limited meaning. It also referred to the process of educating an uninformed public about the need for adoption standards and agency professionalism so as to decrease the numbers of risky, independent placements. For example, see Bernice F. Seltz, 'Interpreting Good Adoption Practice', *Child Welfare*, October 1950, pp. 16–17.

31 General sources include Mari Jo Buhle, *Feminism and Its Discontents: A Century of Struggle with Psychoanalysis*, Cambridge, MA, Harvard University Press, 1998; Hamilton Cravens, *Before Head Start: The Iowa Station and America's Children*, Chapel Hill, University of North Carolina Press, 1993; Estelle B. Freedman, *Maternal Justice: Miriam Van Waters and the Female Reform Tradition, 1887–1974*, Chicago, University of Chicago Press, 1996; Julia Grant, *Raising Baby by the Book: The Education of American Mothers*, New Haven, CT, Yale University Press, 1998; Nathan G. Hale Jr, *The Rise and Crisis of Psychoanalysis in America: Freud and the Americans, 1917–1985*, New York, Oxford University Press, 1995; Kathleen W. Jones, *Taming the Troublesome Child: American Families, Child Guidance, and the Limits of Psychiatric Authority*, Cambridge, MA, Harvard University Press, 1999.

222   *Ellen Herman*

32 For just a sample of their work, see Jessie Taft, 'The Need for Psychological Interpretation in the Placement of Dependent Children', *Child Welfare League of America Bulletin*, no. 6, April 1922, and 'Relation of Personality Study to Child Placing', paper presented at the National Conference of Social Work, 1919, pp. 63–7; Charlotte Towle, 'The Evaluation of Homes in Preparation for Child Placement', *Mental Hygiene*, July 1927, 11, pp. 460–81; Hutchinson, *In Quest of Foster Parents*; Viola W. Bernard, 'Psychiatric Consultation with Special Reference to Adoption Practice', *Casework Papers*, 1954, pp. 70–83; Florence Clothier, 'Some Aspects of the Problem of Adoption', *American Journal of Orthopsychiatry*, July 1939, 9, pp. 598–615.

33 Only Taft, the best known of the group, has been the subject of significant historical research, and biographical details have been pieced together from a number of obscure sources. A profile of Taft can be found on The Adoption History Project, Online, darkwing.uoregon.edu/~adoption/people/taft.htm.

34 Albert H. Stoneman, 'Adoption of Illegitimate Children: The Peril of Ignorance', *Child Welfare League of America Bulletin*, February, 1926, 5, p. 8.

35 Address by Marshall Field to the National Conference on Adoptions, 26 January 1955, pp. 1–2, 4, Child Welfare League of America Papers, Box 16, Folder 8, Social Welfare History Archives, University of Minnesota. See also Michael Schapiro, *A Study of Adoption Practice*, vol. 3: *Adoption of Children with Special Needs*, New York, Child Welfare League of America, 1956.

36 Ann Hulbert, *Raising America: Experts, Parents, and a Century of Advice about Children*, New York, Alfred A. Knopf, 2003, ch 6. A profile of Gesell can be found on The Adoption History Project, Online, darkwing.uoregon.edu/~adoption/people/gesell.htm.

37 Arnold Gesell, 'Psychoclinical Guidance in Child Adoption', in *Foster-Home Care for Dependent Children*, US Children's Bureau Publication 136, Washington, DC, Government Printing Office, 1926, pp. 200–1.

38 Arnold Gesell, 'Child Adoptions in Connecticut', p. 3, Arnold Gesell Papers, Box 45, Folder: 'Adoption', Library of Congress, Manuscript Division.

39 Arnold Gesell, draft manuscript, 'Is It Safe to Adopt an Infant?', n.d, p. 2, Arnold Gesell Papers, Box 45, Folder: 'Subject File: Adoption [Law]', Library of Congress, Manuscript Division.

40 Arnold Gesell, *The Guidance of Mental Growth in Infant and Child*, New York, Macmillan, 1930, p. 217.

41 Henry H. Goddard, 'Wanted: A Child to Adopt', *Survey*, 14 October 1911, 27, p. 1006.

42 Henry H. Goddard, 'The Basis for State Policy', *Survey*, 2 March 1912, 27, pp. 1852–6.

43 'Minimum Safeguards in Adoption', approved by the CWLA Board of Directors on November 3, 1938, Child Welfare League of America (SW55), Box 15, Folder 5, Social Welfare History Archives, University of Minnesota. These safeguards were published under the title 'A Program in Education', *Child Welfare League of America Bulletin*, November 1938, 17, p. 4.

44 W. H. Slingerland, *Child-Placing in Families: A Manual for Students and Social Workers*, New York, Russell Sage Foundation, 1919, p. 73.

45 Ibid., p. 69.

46 Ibid., p. 118.

47 At the New England Home for Little Wanderers, Rose Hardwick instituted a comprehensive mental testing programme in September 1915 and eventually wrote a dissertation about her experience as a mental tester working with hundreds of young children between June 1918 and October 1923. Rose S. Hardwick, 'The Stanford–Binet Intelligence Examination Re-interpreted with Special Reference to Qualitative Differences', PhD dissertation, Radcliffe College, 1924.

Child adoption   223

48 Frances Lockridge and Sophie van S. Theis, *Adopting a Child*, New York, Greenberg, 1947, ch. 6.

49 Schapiro, *A Study of Adoption Practice*, vol. 1: *Adoption Agencies and the Children They Serve*, pp. 54–8, table of 'matching factors' on p. 84.

50 Ibid., p. 75, table 6.

51 Mary S. Brisley, 'Parent–Child Relationships in Unmarried Parenthood', *Proceedings of the National Conference of Social Work*, New York, 1939, pp. 436, 437–8, 439.

52 For more on non-traditional adoptions early in the century, see Julie Berebitsky, *Like Our Very Own: Adoption and the Changing Culture of Motherhood, 1851–1950*, Lawrence, University Press of Kansas, 2000, ch. 4. For a narrative of a professional woman who adopted on her own in 1934, see 'I Just Adopted a Baby', *Ladies' Home Journal*, August 1937, 14–15, 96. For fictional representations of single adoptive mothers during this era, see Claudia Nelson, *Little Strangers: Portrayals of Adoption and Foster Care in America, 1850–1929*, Bloomington, Indiana University Press, 2003, pp. 124–32, and Claudia Nelson, 'Nontraditional Adoption in Progressive-Era Orphan Narratives', *Mosaic, a Journal for the Interdisciplinary Study of Literature*, June 2001, 34, pp. 181–97. For a general discussion of the narrowing of adoption standards and the quest for 'ideal' families, see Brian Paul Gill, 'The Jurisprudence of Good Parenting: The Selection of Adoptive Parents, 1894–1964', PhD dissertation, University of California, Berkeley, 1997. It is interesting that the increased emphasis on marriage among adopters corresponded to a shift in the demographic profile of birth parents. Statistical analyses suggest that before the Second World War, a majority of birth mothers were married women. By the mid-1960s, single women had taken their place. See E. Wayne Carp and Anna-Leon Guerrero, 'When in Doubt, Count: World War II as a Watershed in the History of Adoption', in E. Wayne Carp, ed., *Adoption in America: Historical Perspectives*, Ann Arbor, University of Michigan Press, 2002, pp. 181–217.

53 The only exception involved couples for whom reproduction meant risking serious hereditary illness, such as haemophilia and Tay-Sachs. See Minutes of Dr Bernard's Seminar, 8 April 1952, Viola W. Bernard Papers, Box 161, Folder 5, and Minutes of Dr Bernard's Seminar, 14 June 1954, Viola W. Bernard Papers, Box 161, Folder 6, Archives and Special Collections, Augustus C. Long Library, Columbia University.

54 Maurice J. Barry, 'Emotional Transactions in the Pre-adoptive Study', in Robert Tod, ed., *Social Work in Adoption: Collected Papers*, London, Longman, 1971, p. 52.

55 This belief was strongest at mid-century, when normalising approaches to adoption were at their height. It was based on the theory that the unconscious emotional currents causing infertility could be unblocked if couples adopted. Having a child would relax them and remove whatever stresses prevented pregnancy. There was a great deal of controversy about adoption as a cure for infertility in the medical literature. See Margaret Marsh and Wanda Ronner, *The Empty Cradle: Infertility in America from Colonial Times to the Present*, Baltimore, Johns Hopkins University Press, 1996, ch. 5.

56 Helen Fradkin, *The Adoption Home Study*, Trenton, NJ, Bureau of Children's Services, 1963, p. 11.

57 Viola W. Bernard, 'Application of Psychoanalytic Concepts to Adoption Agency Practice', in I. Evelyn Smith, ed., *Readings in Adoption*, New York, Philosophical Library, 1963, pp. 420–1; Free Synagogue Child Adoption Committee, Staff Meeting With Dr Bernard, 20 January 1943; Confidential Medical Report on Fertility Status of Prospective Adoptive Couple, n.d., but early 1940s; Viola Bernard Papers, Box 157, Folder 1. Other terms in vogue included 'psychosomatic' and 'functional'. Sometimes, 'sterility' was used to designate reproductive

224   *Ellen Herman*

failure with an obvious cause, while 'infertility' suggested that no such cause existed. See, for example, Richard Frank, 'What the Adoption Worker Should Know about Infertility', in Schapiro, *A Study of Adoption Practice*, vol. 2: *Selected Scientific Papers Presented at the National Conference on Adoption, January, 1955*, pp. 113–18.

58 Report to the Board of the Free Synagogue Child Adoption Committee of One Year's Intake Service to Prospective Adoptive Parents, 1 December 1942–1 December 1943, p. 4, Viola W. Bernard Papers, Box 157, Folder 1, Archives and Special Collections, Augustus C. Long Library, Columbia University.

59 Ernest Cady and Frances Cady, *How to Adopt a Child*, New York, Whiteside, and William Morrow, 1956, p. 41.

60 Report to the Board of the Free Synagogue Child Adoption Committee of One Year's Intake Service to Prospective Adoptive Parents, 1 December 1942–1 December 1943, p. 4, Viola W. Bernard Papers, Box 157, Folder 1, Archives and Special Collections, Augustus C. Long Library, Columbia University.

61 Fradkin, *The Adoption Home Study*, p. 49.

62 David M. Schneider, *American Kinship: A Cultural Account*, 2nd edn, Chicago, University of Chicago Press, 1980.

63 Marilyn Strathern, *After Nature: English Kinship in the Late Twentieth Century*, Cambridge, Cambridge University Press, 1992.

64 Richard Lewontin, *It Ain't Necessarily So: The Dream of the Human Genome and Other Illusions*, New York, New York Review of Books, 2000; Dorothy Roberts, *Killing the Black Body: Race, Reproduction, and the Meaning of Liberty*, New York, Pantheon Books, 1997; Arlene Skolnick, 'Solomon's Children: The New Biologism, Psychological Parenthood, Attachment Theory, and the Best Interests Standard', in Mary Ann Mason, Arlene Skolnick and Stephen D. Sugarman, eds, *All Our Families: New Policies for a New Century*, New York, Oxford University Press, 1998, pp. 236–55. The profound impact of the new reproductive technologies on adoption is poignantly illustrated in Jill Bialosky and Helen Schulman, eds, *Wanting a Child: Twenty-two Writers on Their Difficult but Mostly Successful Quests for Parenthood in a High-Tech Age*, New York, Farrar, Straus & Giroux, 1998.

11 Flexible norms?

From patients' values to physicians' standards

Christiane Sinding

The construction of medical norms is a complex process. It begins with the patient who reports her or his experience of disease to the doctor, and ends with the establishment of medical standards considered to be universal. According to sociologists, norms are general rules of action and behaviour belonging to specific social groups, whereas values express individuals' desires and choices. Although norms may reflect those values, they are not identical with them; this becomes apparent when individuals contest social norms.

One of the earliest theoreticians of medical norms, Georges Canguilhem, opposes *normality* (the result of statistical observation) to *normativity* (the capacity to invent new norms). Disease, stress, and changes in the living environment constitute particularly useful sites to investigate normativity. 'Being healthy means being not only normal in a given situation but also normative in this and other possible situations,' Canguilhem asserted. 'What characterises health is the possibility of transcending the norm.'[1] Disease reduces this capacity to innovate, and sick persons live in a reduced world, inventing for their lives new norms that vary from one patient to the next.

To Canguilhem the pathological is never entirely objective; it always retains an element of subjectivity. Before being an object of science, disease is above all an experience reported by the patient to her/his doctor. Diagnoses may be made on the basis of objective examinations; however, preceding these, individual patients would have drawn their doctor's attention to their symptoms and illness experiences. Even in the case of a patient's death, when the earlier clinical observations are compared with the autopsy report, resulting in new conclusions said to be 'objective', these still remain bound up with the patient's initial subjective descriptions. As Canguilhem put it, 'We think *that there is nothing in science that did not first appear in consciousness*, and . . . it is the patient's point of view that is basically correct.'[2]

In this sense Canguilhem can be considered as one of the first defenders of what was later to be called the 'patient's view'. This refers to patients' values and norms concerning life as well as the knowledge they acquire about their illnesses. From the 1980s, historians of medicine increasingly came to employ a perspective 'from below'.[3] They sought to replace earlier

226 *Christiane Sinding*

hagiographic stories of great doctors by patient-oriented accounts of illness or daily realities that urban or rural practitioners had to face.[4] Some of these historical studies focused on transformations in doctor–patient relations, while sociologists began to observe the patient–doctor encounter closely. Although Canguilhem insisted that vital norms had individual components as well as social ones, he did not analyse the subject in depth. His philosophical thesis overlooked the question of the professional norms of the medical profession. In a seminal article, the sociologist Nicholas Jewson asserted that a great shift occurred in the general pattern of relationships between patients and their doctors at the end of the eighteenth century. To him this shift led from 'bed-side medicine' to 'hospital medicine', and then to 'laboratory medicine'.[5] Ten years earlier, Foucault had published his *Birth of the Clinic*, a complex inquiry into conceptual, institutional and political configurations that made it possible to constitute anatomo-clinical medicine as a new experience of disease.[6] His hypothesis was that

> [f]or clinical experience to become possible as a form of knowledge, a reorganization of the hospital field, a new definition of the status of the patient in society, and the establishment of a certain relationship between public assistance and experience, between help and knowledge, became necessary; the patient had to be enveloped in a collective, homogeneous space.[7]

For Foucault, medical norms are produced by doctors – a social body belonging to an institution (the hospital). With anatomo-clinical medicine, he asserted, the patient experience became anonymous, collective, and controlled by the institution. A new type of hospital emerged as a place for administering care and training, where priority was given to the constitution of a system of knowledge based on individual cases. The patient was no longer the subject of her/his disease, but an example of the universal. By gathering together large numbers of patients in the same place it was possible to observe individuals continuously and comparatively. Physicians established medical standards that considered only those medical symptoms and anatomical lesions that were shared by the patients who appeared to have the same disease.[8] In this context the patient became an object subjected to a gaze which was normalised by a medical corps that considered itself competent and authoritative, confined within an institution that legitimised the relationship between watched and watcher. Thus his analysis, although more complex and complete than Jewson's, is consistent with it: for both authors, the patient's values became partly neglected with the birth of hospital medicine.

In the mid-1950s, medical sociologists began to study more closely the system of norms and values governing the relationship between patients and their doctors. For Talcott Parsons, this system was an asymmetrical one: the doctor had authority over his/her patient and was permitted to control his/her behaviour. In turn, the latter was exempted from his/her regular social activities, beginning with work. Both doctors and patients had to conform to their respective 'roles', an active one for the doctor, a passive one for the patient.[9] Parsons's model was soon criticised for being based on a doctor–patient relationship characteristic of acute diseases. Critics insisted that patients suffering from chronic diseases acquired some knowledge of their illness and became capable of some kind of judgement. Furthermore, sociologists as well as doctors themselves came to admit that, even in the case of acute diseases, patients did not always follow their doctor's advice. After the 'protest' years of the early 1970s, 'medical power' was criticised more and more. Among the critics, the sociologist and historian David Armstrong wrote an article on 'the patient's view' that highlighted the main shifts in the way in which the medical profession questioned and, above all, heard the patient.[10] Armstrong described the appearance of a 'new configuration of illness', which included 'the shifting social spaces between bodies'.[11] Arney and Bergen, both sociologists, referred to 'the return of the experiencing person' around the mid-1950s and the incorporation of the patient's subjective experience in medical practices and know-how.[12] Recently, the social historian John Pickstone has proposed a model of historical analysis inspired partly by Foucault and partly by Jewson, although he does not, strictly speaking, consider the doctor–patient relationship. What is interesting in Pickstone's model of the development of medicine is that, while he sees four socio-cognitive ideal types as having appeared successively, those types can still coexist and continue to be reproduced today.[13]

Commenting on Pickstone's model, Isabelle Baszanger, a sociologist who has studied various physicians in their daily activities, wrote:

> I should like to add a more flexible sociological vision of medicine, one in which all these cognitive forms in constant interaction are continually available rather than recurrent, in a game in which all the cards are used rather than classified in a closed manner and can be mobilized over time.[14]

Drawing on these historical and sociological conceptions of the relationship between doctors and patients, my aim in this chapter is to attempt to disentangle the different components of the construction of medical norms by both patients and doctors. I use the history of the 'management' of diabetes mellitus (DM), a chronic disease that is largely monitored and controlled by the patient him/herself, as a magnifying glass that allows me to identify the part played by both patient and doctor in the construction of those norms. More precisely, I seek to ascertain 'whether the return of the experiencing person' in the relationship between patients and their doctors can be identified during the twentieth century in the case of DM. Further, I will study more closely the complex entanglement of biological, sociological and ethical norms in the daily management of the disease by patients and

228 *Christiane Sinding*

their doctors. I will use the term 'norm' as a generic term that includes medical standards as well as patients' values.

Diabetes mellitus is a disease characterised by so-called cardinal signs: thirst (polydipsia), hunger (polyphagia), excessive urine (polyuria), and the presence of sugar in urine (glycosuria). At the end of the nineteenth century DM was viewed as a disturbance of metabolism. Around 1920 the major biological tests highlighted glucose and ketonic bodies in urine. During the nineteenth century the aim of physicians who were confronted with this disease was always to reduce or even eliminate sugar in the urine (glycosuria). Once it became possible to demonstrate the high level of sugar in the blood (glycaemia), the aim was to reduce that, too. From that point onwards, the severity of DM seemed to be connected with the level of glycaemia – hence the idea that this level had to be reduced at all costs. For a long time the only way even to begin to control the level of glycaemia was to force strict diets on diabetics. Nowadays DM is considered to be an endocrine disease due to the lack of insulin, and is contained by daily injections of this hormone.

DM lends itself particularly well to an exploration of the complex relationship between biological norms, doctors' standards and patients' values. Doctors develop individual therapeutic regimes with their patients and regularly adjust them as the disease develops, and depending on changes in patients' lifestyle and circumstances. But patients can modify their medical prescriptions. They evaluate the state of their health on the basis of subjective feelings (fatigue, discomfort, signs of hypoglycaemia) and blood and urine tests that they can do themselves, owing to a range of increasingly efficient technical tools. Thus, by combining knowledge built up from their own experiences with that provided by health professionals (doctor, diabetes specialist, paediatrician, general practitioner, dietician, nurse), they decide on their treatment on a day-to-day basis, adjusting insulin doses, food and physical activity.

As Prestley has shown in his history of DM, from the beginning of the twentieth century medical practitioners were increasingly averse to accepting patients' autonomy in regard to treatment, considering it to be regrettable but inevitable because patients tended to bend the rules of what was considered a 'good diabetic's' lifestyle. For these practitioners, whom I have called 'disciplinarians', a 'good diabetic' had to be judged on the basis of the objective (i.e. measurable) results he/she obtained.[15] For a minority of physicians whom I have called 'liberals', patients were allowed to have their say, although for them, too, concern for patients' well-being – which inevitably involved the 'rule-bending' criticised by the 'disciplinarians' – was an important issue. Disagreement between doctors adds an additional dimension to the norms issue, showing that the simple opposition between the 'patient's view' and the doctor's view is insufficient to render its complexity. Moreover, medical norms also change over time.

I roughly distinguish between two phases in my exploration of biological norms, doctors' standards and patients' values. During the first, which lasted until the end of the 1970s, conflicting views concerning diabetics' treatment regimes could not be settled by clinical or physiological studies. Physiologists and physicians focused on experimental results that fitted in best with their own preconceptions. They also mobilised strong moral arguments to fight their opponents. The second period started around 1980 and has been characterised by the proliferation of technologies intended to help patients and doctors to contain the disease, and new technical devices, such as self-blood glucose monitoring and measurement of glycosylated haemoglobin, as well as large randomised clinical trials.

Medical norms in cases of uncertainty: the management of DM between quantification and morality, 1900–50

From the late nineteenth century, DM was considered to be a disease of the metabolism, in which the excess of sugar in the blood could not be metabolised normally in cells.[16] This 'excess' of sugar in the blood implicitly referred to a biological norm and a quantitative definition of disease such as the one put forward by Claude Bernard, who used the example of diabetes to illustrate this conception.[17] Having observed higher rates of sugar in the blood and urine of diabetics, he referred to 'normal' and 'abnormal' levels that could be differentiated quantitatively. This suggestion was used to identify health and normality translated into statistical averages, and turned the disease into an object of science that in principle could be remedied by means of appropriate techniques. Doctors confronted with DM consequently aimed at reducing or even eliminating sugar in the urine (glycosuria) and, eventually, sugar in the blood (glycaemia), too. For a long time the only way of ensuring this was to force strict diets on diabetics.

The 'starvation diet': treat, monitor, punish

The prescribed diets varied considerably, depending on practitioners' therapeutic training and preferences. In 1909 Frederik Madison Allen (1879–1964), a doctor on a fellowship at the Harvard Medical School Department of Public Health, undertook a three-year experimental trial on animals, with the aim of developing a scientifically grounded diet for diabetics.[18] He caused DM of varying degrees of severity in these animals by removing all or part of their pancreas, and tested various diets on them. He found that only a very strict low-calorie diet could reduce these animals' glycosuria and glycaemia. Allen affirmed that patients put on what was soon known as a 'starvation diet' avoided certain infectious complications and ketoacidosis, felt better, and could thus live for a few months or even a few years longer.[19] Unfortunately, famished patients frequently tried to break their diets, and hospital staff had to police them to find those who 'cheated', by searching for hidden food often brought in by relatives.[20]

230   *Christiane Sinding*

In a book published in 1919 Allen commented on the difficulty of obtaining strict observance of this diet and cited the case of a child who went so far as eating his toothpaste and birdseed that he happened to have on him. 'These facts', wrote Allen, 'were obtained by confession after long and plausible denials.'[21] The word 'confession' reflects the moral nature of the approach. In an article published shortly before the discovery of insulin (1922), Allen stigmatised 'bad' diabetics whom he held responsible for any complications they suffered. He analysed the causes of death observed in a series of patients subjected to his diet, and concluded that a number of them were due to 'various degrees of infidelity to treatment' – although he tended to blame the doctors even more than the patients for the failure to enforce treatment.[22] Prestley suggests that Allen promoted his view that 'doctors should be responsible, most of the time, for the patient's decline, which he did not consider inevitable'.[23] In Allen's view, doctors tended to sacrifice the patient's future for the facility of a more pleasant present:

> The physician who ignores diabetes in its early or mild form, or who imposes diet only to the extent of restraining glycosuria within moderate percentages, or who advocates treatment directed to the immediate comfort of the patient instead of his future safety, merely betrays ignorance and needs instruction.[24]

This quotation shows that not all physicians shared Allen's views – far from it. However, they were echoed by one of the most respected DM specialists in the United States at the time, Elliot P. Joslin. Since 1915 Joslin had been treating diabetics at the Massachusetts General Hospital, putting them on Allen's 'starvation diet'. Just like Allen, he, too, tended to 'moralise' treatment, although both justified the new therapeutic method in terms of scientific order.[25] In 1919 Joslin wrote a manual intended for doctors and diabetic patients, in which some recommendations took the form of a veritable catechism, as in the following passage:

QUESTION: What can a diabetic patient do for himself besides keeping the urine sugar-free?
ANSWER: Be cheerful and also be thankful that his disease is not of a hopeless character, but a disease which his brains will help him to conquer.[26]

A strong will and discipline were thus integral parts of programmes aimed at controlling DM. Chris Feudtner, a physician and historian of medicine, suggests that Joslin was, for his patients, a 'moral manager' as much as a scientific expert.[27] He identifies a mix of idiosyncrasy – Joslin's strong religious convictions and a taste for biblical citations – and conceptions shared by doctors at the time, who saw the struggle against disease as a personal moral combat rather than a technical matter. Joslin wrote that patients ought to know their disease as well as possible, adding that it was an opportunity to test the patient's character, honesty, self-control and courage.[28]

Morality was a dimension of medical practice. It cannot be separated from the quasi-mathematical scientific rigour that diabetes specialists implemented in their monitoring and treatment regimes. Measurement and quantification were keywords of medical intervention. Patients regularly had to monitor their urine, and measure glycosuria and glycaemia levels. They had to weigh their food and control the composition of meals taken at fixed times, and engage in physical exercise, exhibiting neither excess nor sluggishness. In short, the ideal treatment aimed at disciplining and disciplined bodies. In *Discipline and Punish*, Foucault defined disciplinary methods: 'These methods in which the functions of the body are painstakingly controlled, to which its forces are constantly subjected, and which imposes on it a docility–utility relationship, are what can be called discipline.'[29]

Although Foucault always stressed the constraining power of norms, thus encouraging an interpretation that he sometimes regretted, we should not forget that he also highlighted the fact that medicine could not be considered only in terms of its disciplinary effects. To him, norms are powerful in both a positive and a negative way: they create individuals subjected to power but also able to resist constraints.[30] Foucault emphasised the fecundity and positive effects of medicine.

> What enables medicine to function with such force is the fact that, unlike religion, it is inscribed in the scientific institution. We cannot be content simply to point out the disciplinary effects of medicine. Medicine can function as a mechanism of social control, but it also has other, technical and scientific, functions.[31]

In the case of DM, most of us will have more sympathy for the 'liberals' than for the 'disciplinarians'. Yet the latter's position carried weight, even without an anachronistic examination based on current knowledge. To justify their therapeutic attitude, Joslin and Allen mobilised moral arguments, but they also stressed the apparent scientific fact that their drastic diet led to the disappearance of biological markers of the disease (such as the presence of sugar and acetone in the patient's urine); a decrease of clinical symptoms (such as hunger, thirst and polyuria); better control of infections; and an increased life expectancy.

But was the starvation diet applied on a large scale? To judge from articles published at the time, it seems that this was indeed the case in the United States and probably also in British hospitals. For example, a British doctor wrote: 'The "Allen" dietetic treatment was well known and widely used.' But he added: 'It was a tedious business, many patients would not stand it, and the ultimate results were often far from satisfactory.'[32] Furthermore, many doctors and lay people severely criticised these methods, and the sight of emaciated, starving children moved people and caused profound

232 *Christiane Sinding*

indignation. Opponents accused advocates of the starvation diet of futilely prolonging their patients' lives for a result that was known in advance, since everyone knew that DM patients would die sooner or later. Some physicians defended alternatives to the starvation diet that were far easier to bear and, in their opinion, as effective as Allen's treatment. However, the treatment of DM was soon to be changed drastically with the discovery of insulin.

A new world for diabetics: insulin as a liberating tool

In 1922, while working in the Department of Physiology at the University of Toronto, then headed by John James Rickard Macleod, Frederick Banting and Charles Best first demonstrated the existence in the pancreas of dogs of an 'anti-diabetes principle', soon called insulin.[33] In the same year, Bertram Collip, a Canadian biochemist, who had joined the Toronto team, manufactured a bovine pancreas extract that was effective on human diabetes. This event was celebrated at the time as a medical miracle, and some even believed that the new drug would completely cure the disease. For the time being, diabetics' lives were drastically changed. Patients close to death were 'resurrected', and nearly 80 years later insulin remains one of the great success stories of therapeutic invention. However, as time went by it progressively became clear that by no means all the problems posed by the disease had been solved, and that dreadful complications still threatened diabetics.[34]

Reconfiguring therapeutic practices: new norms of life

With the discovery of insulin, Allen and Joslin relaxed their position as far as diet was concerned and increased the number of calories allowed per day so that patients put on a satisfactory amount of weight. But for them, diet remained the primary element in the therapeutic 'trivet' they prescribed (diet, insulin and exercise).[35] Allen defended his strict position on diabetics' diet through to the end and vilified those who 'took advantage' of the miracle drug to slacken their diet: the use of insulin for the sake of 'gluttony' was inexcusable and dangerous, he asserted.[36] Although more moderate, Joslin was convinced that an excess of sugar in the blood was poisonous for the organism.[37] He pointed out that there was a correlation between the severity of DM and prolonged high levels of glycaemia.[38] Like others, he was well aware of dreadful complications as the disease developed, although it was not known whether these were inevitable. Nor was it established whether the prolongation of patients' lives necessarily led to a considerable protraction and increasing severity of the disease, to the extent that no organ in the patient's body was spared.[39]

Following the discovery of insulin some doctors warned that it would lead not only to the disappearance of the organic ailments caused by DM, but also to a level of well-being to which patients were no longer accustomed.[40] Rollin T. Woodyatt, a diabetes specialist, insisted that the aim of treatment was to keep the patient 'as strong as a normal individual' with the least effort and cost. On diabetic children he wrote, 'I think it is important with these youngsters in school or college to interfere as little as possible with their free physical, social and psychological development.'[41] The argument here reflects a conception of 'normal' that already incorporates a psycho-social dimension. Paediatricians subsequently tended to adopt this liberal attitude, so that their standards differed more and more from those of adult specialists.

The moral component of the diet controversy, easy enough to discern in medical texts from the early 1920s, seems to have been all the stronger since knowledge on diabetes and its development under the new treatment was just starting to be established. This knowledge not only did improve clinical treatments, but also led to the emergence of new experimental methodologies. It was therefore above all clinical data that were put forward to settle the diet issue 'scientifically'. But these data changed with time, both because complications became evident only after several years of observation of patients treated with insulin, and because the treatment itself progressively improved. Not only was insulin treatment becoming increasingly effective and reliable, but from 1936 the first long-acting insulin, which was to change patients' lives and therapeutic protocols considerably, became available.[42] Furthermore, an improved system of technological monitoring and treatment was progressively set up: better syringes, more suitable needles and efficient monitoring. In short, the situation remained in flux as the disease continually changed its appearance, instruments to measure glycaemia or other biological constants were steadily improved, professionals received training, and specialist hospital services were set up.[43] And, of course, doctors' and patients' ideas and practices varied. Although in the early 1950s experimental methods for studying DM improved further, and the demand for patients' autonomy became seen as more legitimate by some doctors, the regimen controversy was still raging.

In brief, until the mid-1950s physicians managed DM in a rather authoritative way, to a greater or lesser degree in line with what Talcott Parsons suggested in his sociological analysis of the 'patient role' – that is, the doctor was 'active' and the patient 'passive'. However, even at the beginning of the twentieth century some physicians had encouraged alternative forms of diabetes care that left more 'freedom' to the patient. Insulin was to further facilitate such an approach. Therefore, social and professional, as well as techno-scientific, factors made the doctor–patient relationship more complex and flexible at various periods.

The return of the experiencing person: taking patients' values into account

From the 1950s most DM specialists began to refer explicitly to the psycho-affective and psychosocial dimensions of the disease in their publications.

234 *Christiane Sinding*

Many of them, especially paediatricians, emphasised the necessity of leaving the patient a degree of autonomy and rejected the idea of too much medical authoritarianism. Edward Tolstoi was one of the most controversial practitioners, as he favoured a regime of relaxed control of DM, so that patients were able to live 'a normal life'.[44] Another 'liberal' suggested in 1950:

> By a liberal or free diet we do not mean that the patient might have an 'unlimited diet' but that he *is* allowed a free choice of food, asked to eat in moderation and to eliminate sugar, pastry and soft drinks. This gives him a responsibility and participation in his treatment and requires a self-imposed discipline which has quite a different effect than that created by a rigid discipline imposed on him by his physician. . . . Such a regimen requires no special planning of menus, no special cooking for the diabetic, and does not set him apart as an invalid.[45]

He emphasised further the importance of adapting treatment to the lifestyle of the patient:

> Another factor to be considered in favour of such a regimen is that it allows within reasonable limits for the continuance of individual and group preferences in food. In our large cities, we deal with patients of many different nationalities which have their own peculiar habits.

He cites the case of a woman of Italian origin who was forced in hospital to follow a strict diet with an English breakfast (grapefruit, eggs and bacon, toast and coffee), and comments:

> Is she happy about it? Hardly! Will she adhere to it when she goes home? Hardly! . . . It is better to find out about her eating habits and to duplicate this as nearly as possible and then to adjust insulin to this, in place of doing the opposite by adjusting a new and complicated diet to insulin.[46]

What is particularly relevant here is that this doctor suggested adapting insulin to the patient's lifestyle, rather than the other way round. This is in line with the approach adopted by most patients undergoing insulin therapy – even if they do not necessarily tell their doctor about it. The scope of this chapter does not allow a detailed analysis of therapeutic methods in Western countries other than the United States. It can, however, be pointed out that similar principles were expressed by French paediatricians, for example, during the same period. In 1958 P. Royer, paediatrician, and H. Lestradet, paediatrician and diabetes specialist, wrote:

> We cannot clearly see justification for a so-called normal diet for the diabetic child. Probably, what is really to be criticized in this method is

the fact that it focuses the patient's and doctor's attention on the patient's consumption of food, thus all too often turning it away from the essential problem, which is the adaptation of insulin therapy as closely as possible to the needs of the diabetic child.[47]

Here again we find the principle of adaptation of insulin therapy to the needs of the patient, a principle that favours patients' autonomy and the preservation of their choices in life.

However, even by 1950 not all physicians were converted to taking patients' values into account. Non-paediatric specialists were particularly reluctant to adopt this new approach, so that disciplinarians and liberals continued to be divided over questions of diet, now increasingly related to the issue of complications. For example, in 1950 a specialist explained the contrasting positions of the two camps in the following way:

> Practices in diabetes care among different clinics of the country are at present following more or less closely the precepts of the two main schools of thought, sharply divided and frankly opposed on some of the basic propositions to which each subscribes: one favouring a 'prescribed-diet–aglycosuric regimen' and the other a 'free-diet–glycosuric regimen'. Adherents of the first school believe that hyperglycaemia with attendant glycosuria is unphysiologic, harmful and responsible for severe complications of the disease.... Adherents of the other school maintain that hyperglycaemia per se, with constant glycosuria ... but without ketosis, is not necessarily harmful if growth and development occur in a child at a normal rate or if normal weight is maintained in adults.[48]

The question that was more and more clearly at the centre of this controversy was the causal link between chronically high levels of glycaemia and the appearance of complications. But how could this link be proved, since clinicians kept throwing contradictory data at one another? The 'disciplinarians' brandished the threat of complications, which seemed more serious and frequent in 'badly controlled' patients – that is, those who had high levels of glycaemia over long periods.[49] Complications were the main issue on which the 'disciplinarians' constantly harped, accusing the 'liberals' of compromising their patients' future with the pretext of favouring their immediate well-being. The 'liberals' retaliated by pointing out the absence of substantial scientific arguments to confirm the glucose hypothesis. Paediatricians, who were practically all 'liberals', tended increasingly to justify their position by using arguments from physiology, such as the energy needs of a growing organism. They noted that the only factor that seemed persistently linked to the appearance of complications was the length of the disease, and that nothing could be proved as to the harmfulness of glycaemia.[50]

Around the same period – that is, the 1950s – new experimental devices on animals were developed that helped to fuel the controversy with a new

236 *Christiane Sinding*

type of argument. Scientists had learned to use toxic substances that selectively attacked the endocrine pancreas; this enabled them to set off in experimental situations kinds of DM closer to those found in humans.[51] However, the animal trials did not provide decisive evidence about the alleged link between chronic high levels of glycaemia and the appearance of complications. One major problem was that, as with humans, scientists could not agree on satisfactory control criteria. Were they to take measurements based on healthy subjects as the ideal yardstick for comparison, or were they to establish different norms? These were central questions in regard to all chronic diseases, not just for the case of DM. All diabetes specialists knew that it was impossible to normalise glycaemia levels completely with insulin injections, especially in the long term, in both humans and animals. Furthermore, what should be considered as an acceptable upper limit? Even in healthy subjects, glycaemia levels vary throughout the day, especially after the person has eaten, for the rate of insulin excreted by the pancreas is constantly adjusted depending on dietary intake and physical state.

In such a situation it was easy for advocates in both camps to select whatever experimental results best supported their own respective positions. With hindsight, it could be said that caution and the principle of *primum non nocere* ('above all do no harm') demand that the patient's future should not be compromised— by exposing him/her to chronically high levels of glycaemia – and that the 'disciplinarian' position was preferable. But if we refrain from retrospective judgements, we have to consider also that the clinician's position at the time was not easy. Were patients' desires to 'live well' here and now, and paediatricians' concerns that children who had sometimes never tasted certain foods be able to eat as they wished, not as legitimate as the will to preserve a future about which there was no certainty anyway?

The apparent correlation between chronically high levels of glycaemia and the appearance of complications was therefore the most difficult physiopathological problem that everyone had to try to solve. Right until the 1980s it was impossible to settle the issue without information on patients' glycaemia levels in their daily lives. Moreover, patients were often suspected of living their lives according to their own standards and 'fiddling' their health cards, not always indicating the worst results of the occasional measurements they took. Mistrust and technical factors combined to make the main issue insoluble until a set of new technologies appeared to improve the quality of monitoring DM and the conditions of patients' treatment administration.

New technologies of truth: patients' versus doctors' norms

Crucially, the new technologies provided for the first time accurate information on patients' management of the disease over long periods of time.

Flexible norms? 237

A new liberating tool for the patient: self-blood glucose monitoring (SBGM)

The invention considered to be the most important by patients and doctors alike was reagents that allowed diabetics to measure their own glycaemia level whenever they wanted to.[52] This innovation afforded them the possibility of modulating their treatment and daily activities in accordance with the test results by instantly dosing their glycaemia in the event of prodromes. It also enabled patients to better assess the effect of diet and exercise. Patients' knowledge about their own state improved, and dependence on biological laboratories and doctors declined. SBGM provided better information about glycaemia levels throughout the day, thus enabling patients to adjust their insulin doses.[53]

For doctors, SBGM was to afford more effective control of hypoglycaemia. Many of them proposed changes in therapeutic methods, advocating 'intensive' or 'physiological' therapy – that is, more frequent, smaller doses of insulin, especially before meals, and attention to diet and exercise. Ordinary insulin was effective only for a short period, hence the necessity to administer injections throughout the day. This also implied that nature could to a certain extent be imitated – hence the term 'physiological therapy'.[54] The drawbacks of this method for the patient were considerable: the inconvenience of repeated monitoring and multiple injections throughout the day. However, self-injection was made easier with the development of insulin pens and new syringes with fine disposable needles.

On the whole, these new methods enabled patients to manage their disease far better and to gain greater autonomy. But the controversy about patients' *chronic* glycaemia levels remained unsolved until the discovery of an effective tool to monitor glycaemia levels.

A disciplining tool for the doctors

In the late 1970s it was shown that an 'abnormal' haemoglobin was present in the red blood cells of diabetics.[55] This haemoglobin linked glucose molecules by means of a stable chemical link and was called glycosylated haemoglobin. Red blood cells containing haemoglobin have an average lifespan of 120 days, after which all forms of haemoglobin, including glycosylated haemoglobin, are 'recycled'. The more that glycosylated haemoglobin has been exposed to high glucose levels for long periods during those 120 days, the higher its level will be. Importantly, it was found that the level of glycosylated haemoglobin represented the average level of glucose to which the organism had been exposed during the three months preceding the measurement. Glycosylated haemoglobin therefore provided an indicator for glycaemia rates over the preceding three months, which from 1980 onwards came to be seen as the key to controlling the disease.[56] This veritable 'spy molecule', as I call it, enabled doctors to know what patients partly knew

238   *Christiane Sinding*

from tests carried out at home but sometimes tried to hide from their doctor: glycaemia levels over long periods.[57] Glycosylated haemoglobin was to have at least two uses: in daily life it became a device for monitoring and managing the disease, and for clinicians and researchers (biologists and epidemiologists) it provided a window on DM complications. High glycosylated haemoglobin levels meant either insufficient insulin doses, bad distribution of those doses throughout the day or, lastly, unsuitable diet and physical activity. Whereas measurement of glycaemia was more useful for patients than for doctors and in any case more liberating for the former, glycosylated haemoglobin was more at the service of doctors, who could measure both the quality of the treatment and the patient's compliance.[58] The latter constituted at once a technical device that provided information on the level of glucose in a diabetic's blood, a normative monitoring device that enabled doctors to discipline 'bad patients' and, lastly, a research tool for large-scale clinical surveys, which were, after a century of controversy, to allow for consensus to be reached on the treatment regimen issue. At the same time, the moral dimension of diabetology became embodied in a technical molecular device rather than being espoused in a 'catechism' as in the early 1920s.

Randomised clinical trials: closure of a controversy?

For a long time it had not been possible to confirm the glycosylated haemoglobin–glycaemia rate link because there was no way of continuously checking patients' glycaemia. It was not until the end of the 1970s that surveys carried out in Belgium and France seemed to confirm the existence of such a link.[59] The Belgian survey showed a correlation between chronically high glycaemia levels and complications, while French surveys spearheaded comparative trials between patients treated by either conventional therapy or intensive therapy. These studies were sufficiently conclusive to encourage experimental practice of intensive therapy. From the 1980s, new surveys were launched, particularly in the United Kingdom and Scandinavia, which paved the way for a large-scale experiment over a ten-year period conducted in the United States by the Diabetes Control and Complications Trial Research Group (DCCTRG). Its aim was to determine whether rigorous control of glycaemia could help to reduce the rate and severity of DM complications. Two groups of patients were studied: one followed their regular treatment with no change whatsoever, and the second group consisted of carefully selected and motivated patients who had agreed to the practical constraints of intensive therapy. When the results were published in 1993, the Diabetes Control and Complications Trial was celebrated as having definitively confirmed the link between chronic high levels of glycaemia and the appearance of complications.[60] Moreover, those who had designed and carried out the study had no doubt that diabetes specialists would feel encouraged to base their practice on strict control of glycaemia.

However, a major difficulty, mentioned from the outset by the designers of the survey and regularly commented on in the medical press, still existed – that is, the difficulty of translating the results of the survey into practice. An editorial in the issue of the *New England Journal of Medicine* that presented the survey results pointed out the necessity for supervision of intensive therapy by a multidisciplinary team, and stressed the importance of the patient's motivation and compliance, and specialist training of the doctors concerned. These kinds of conditions are very difficult to implement in daily practice, not to mention the accruing costs. Therefore, the controversy has never really been closed, since in practice the daily management of DM still poses the same question as in the early twentieth century: how far should one go to meet the standard of a healthy subject?

Possibly the most important progress reported in publications by the DCCTRG was the confirmation of the need to involve patients in therapeutic decisions, to individualise therapeutic protocols as much as possible, and not to let patients feel threatened by the idea of the causal link between chronically high levels of glycaemia and the appearance of complications. This shows just how much doctor–patient relations have changed since the 1920s. It is also important to acknowledge the contribution made by the patients who participated in the trials and employ the innovation despite the apparent restrictions it imposes. Patients readjusted their perception of the disease they suffered from, paying attention even to the slightest changes in their condition on a round-the-clock basis, recording hypoglycaemic episodes (one of the major complications of intensive treatment) and keeping invaluable daily self-evaluation diaries.

Finally, the work of the DCCTRG revealed the plurality of the norms – sometimes congruent and sometimes divergent – that govern the medical world.

Conclusion: a plurality of flexible norms

The story of DM, as analysed above, seems to confirm a historical 'shift' in the doctor–patient relationship – from the constitution of the patient as an object of science to the return of the 'experiencing person'. In the first phase of the modern history of DM (1900–50), rigid cultural and moral values of the medical profession weighed heavily on practices. In the United States those values were widely shared by society as a whole, as pointed out by Chris Feudtner:

> Joslin embodied an ethos widely prevalent in twentieth-century American medicine and society: the desire to control disease and death. His achievements as both architect and spokesman for intensive diabetic management paralleled treatment strategies developed by other physicians in other specialities, evident from intensive care units to high-risk obstetrical practices to trauma surgical services.[61]

240 *Christiane Sinding*

In a period of great medical uncertainty, those values – that is, the desire to control disease at all costs and the active role of the doctor over a 'passive' patient – probably carried even more weight. However, even at the beginning of the twentieth century, divergent voices and values could be heard in the medical world, ranging from a smoother style in the management of the disease to clear opposition by the 'liberals' to the 'disciplinarian' treatment prescriptions. Individual practitioners also adapted the doctrines of academics in their own way, not hesitating to distinguish between what seemed to have practical value and what seemed to be useless complications, thus leading to local diversity of practices. This does not mean that 'moral' values had no bearing on diabetic care; rather, there existed a variety of values, and some of these allowed the patients' values to be taken into account, too.

Furthermore, apart from different professional norms of practice, the objects of inquiry and, above all, the disease itself were constantly redefined during the twentieth century. DM was initially defined as a single, relatively homogeneous, pathological entity – despite differences depending on age, weight and severity. Subsequently it was split into two distinct diseases, initially identified by their different response to treatment.[62] Above all, DM, when treated, took on new forms unknown before.[63] Dosage adjustment for glucose improved steadily. Clinicians, physiologists, biochemists, epidemiologists and statisticians cooperated with or succeeded one another in reformulating extant controversies in their own terms. Statisticians of the DCCTRG declared that the controversy on the management of DM was closed, in theory, recognising that it was difficult to translate the survey results into day-to-day practice. In a sense the controversy persists, because it is still difficult to maintain satisfactory levels of glycaemia in patients. The patients themselves have a variety of ways of coping with the disease: some agree to exercise tight control over their glycaemia, at the price of some of their freedom, while others prefer to preserve more freedom at the price of some control over their disease.

Finally, the question of norms is posed differently in medicine, in contrast to other sciences. Medicine is above all a normative practice aimed at restoring the living standards valued by doctors and patients. It is therefore not surprising that this aim changes with time and place. While the medical 'disciplinarianism' of the 1920s seems particularly shocking to us today, we need to remember that the figure of the 'moral manager' also corresponded to the social mores of the time. We may need to consider that while we may find fault with *how* the 'disciplinarians' tried to control their patients, they appear to have been correct in *what* they wanted to achieve, as the control of glycaemia levels has become seen as vital in the management of DM.

This does not mean that medical 'disciplinarianism' has disappeared and that the norms governing the doctor–patient relationship have changed completely. It might be legitimate to encourage patients to group together and defend themselves against abuses of 'medical power'. It nevertheless seems equally important to avoid simple reactive criticism of medical theo-

Flexible norms? 241

ries and treatment suggestions, as they may be correct and true, not in the sense of universal truth, but in the sense of practical truth as confirmed by patients. It is important for critics of medicine and medical 'power' to consider that medical theories and practices are intrinsically situated in time and space. The object of medicine – the ill human being – is doubly complex: biologically and socially, each individual is different from others and has different expectations and perceptions in regard to their health. Georges Canguilhem believed that medicine was a badly united set of knowledge and practices. More precisely, he considered that medicine was an evolving sum of applied knowledge, constantly reconstituted for each patient in view of a specific therapeutic project. For him, the term 'sum' was more than the simple result of an addition: a unit of operation.[64] This kind of individualised medicine may be more of an aspiration than reality, but it seems that more recently there has been a tendency towards more 'flexible' norms in medicine.

Notes

1 G. Canguilhem, *The Normal and the Pathological* [1978], trans. Carolyn B. Fawcett, New York, Zone Books, 1991, p. 115. See also C. Sinding, 'The Power of Norms: Georges Canguilhem, Michel Foucault and the History of Medicine', in F. Huisman and J. Harley Warner, eds, *Locating Medical History: The Stories and Their Meanings*, Johns Hopkins University Press, 2004, pp. 262–84.
2 Canguilhem, *The Normal*, pp. 92–3. Emphasis in the original.
3 R. Porter, 'The Patient's View: Doing Medical History from Below', *Theory and Society*, 1985, 14, pp. 167–74. See also C. Rosenberg and J. Golden, eds, *Framing Disease: Studies in Cultural History*, New Brunswick, NJ, Rutgers University Press, 1992; S. M. Rothman, *Living in the Shadow of Death: Tuberculosis and the Social Experience of Illness in American History*, New York, Basic Books, 1994, and G. Grob, 'The Social History of Medicine and Disease in America: Problems and Possibilities', *Journal of Social History*, 1977, 10, pp. 391–409.
4 S. Reverby and D. Rosner, 'Beyond the Great Doctors', in S. Reverby and D. Rosner, eds, *Health Care in America: Essays in Social History*, Philadelphia, Temple University Press, 1979, p. 4.
5 N. D. Jewson, 'The Disappearance of the Sick Man from Medical Cosmology, 1770–1870', *Sociology*, 1976, 10, pp. 225–44. Jewson quoted Foucault, but did not really discuss his theses. Despite a few reviews, the publication of *Naissance de la clinique* went virtually unnoticed even in France. After its translation into English, and especially after Foucault gave his Brazilian lectures on the medical institution and 'medicalisation' of our societies, *Birth of the Clinic* gained more readers, but never attained the kind of success of *Discipline and Punish* or *The Order of Things*.
6 M. Foucault, *Naissance de la clinique: une archéologie du regard médical*, Paris, Presses Universitaires de France, 1963, pp. 200–1. Transl. A. M. Sheridan, *The Birth of the Clinic: An Archaeology of Medical Perception*, London, Tavistock, 1973.
7 Foucault, *Birth of the Clinic*, p. 196.
8 Later, in the mid-nineteenth century, these standards would increasingly be based on biological and numerical parameters.
9 T. Parsons, 'The Sick Role and the Role of the Physician Reconsidered', *Milbank Memorial Fund Quarterly/Health and Society*, 1975, 53, 3, pp. 257–78.

242 *Christiane Sinding*

10 D. Armstrong, 'The Patient's View', *Social Science and Medicine*, 1984, 18, pp. 737–44 at p. 740.
11 Ibid., p. 740.
12 W. R. Arney and B. J. Bergen, *Medicine and the Management of Living: Taming the Last Great Beast*, Chicago, University of Chicago Press, 1984. Armstrong, like Arney and Bergen, worked mostly from a Foucauldian perspective and, loyal to Foucault in that respect, they rejected the idea that these transformations took place on grounds of a humanistic concern. They insisted that they were due to epistemic necessity.
13 J. Pickstone, 'The Biographical and the Analytical: Towards a Historical Model of Science and Practice in Modern Medicine', in I. Lowy, O. Amsterdamska, J. Pickstone and P. Pinell, eds, *Medical Innovations: Historical and Sociological Aspects*, Paris, J. Libbey, 1993, pp. 23–47. The four types are the 'biographical–bedside', the 'analytical–hospital', the 'experimental–laboratory' and 'techno-medicine'.
14 I. Baszanger, *Inventing Pain Medicine: From the Laboratory to the Clinic*, New Brunswick, NJ, Rutgers University Press, 1998, p. 188.
15 C. Sinding, 'The Construction of Medical Facts According to Ludwick Fleck', *History and Philosophy of Biology and Biomedical Sciences*, 2004, 35, pp. 545–59.
16 J. W. Prestley, 'A History of Diabetes Mellitus in the United States, 1880–1990', PhD dissertation, University of Texas at Austin, 1991.
17 C. Bernard, 'De l'origine du sucre dans l'économie animale', *Archives générales de médecine*, 1848, 18, pp. 303–19.
18 F. M. Allen, *Studies concerning Glycosuria and Diabetes*, Cambridge, MA, Harvard University Press, 1913.
19 M. Bliss, *The Discovery of Insulin*, Chicago, University of Chicago Press, 1982, pp. 33–9.
20 F. M. Allen, E. Stillman and R. Fitz, *Total Dietary Regulation in the Treatment of Diabetes*, New York, Rockefeller Institute for Medical Research, 1919; quoted by Bliss, *Discovery of Insulin*, p. 37.
21 F. M. Allen and W. Sherill, 'Clinical Observations on Treatment and Progress in Diabetes', *Journal of Metabolic Research*, 1922, 2, pp. 378–455.
22 Ibid., p. 379.
23 Prestley, *History of Diabetes Mellitus*.
24 Allen and Sherill, 'Clinical Observations', p. 378.
25 That is to say, in terms of nutritional theories or theories drawn from research by specialists on intermediary metabolism.
26 E. P. Joslin, *A Diabetic Manual for the Mutual Use of Doctor and Patient*, 2nd edn, Philadelphia, Lea & Febiger, 1919, p. 32. Cited by C. Feudtner, *Bittersweet: Diabetes, Insulin, and the Transformation of Illness*, Chapel Hill, University of North Carolina Press, 2003, p. 115. Emphasis on the importance of a diabetic's being intelligent appears frequently in medical writings of the time.
27 C. Feudtner, *Bittersweet*, p. 314.
28 Joslin, *Manual*, 1918, p. 17.
29 M. Foucault, 'Crise de la médecine ou crise de l'antimédecine?', text reproduced in Daniel Defert and François Ewald, eds, with the collaboration of J. Lagrange, *Dits et Écrits: 1954–1988 Michel Foucault*, vol. 3, Paris, Gallimard, 1994, pp. 40–58 (author's translation). In particular, Foucault criticised 'the radical and bucolic rejection of medicine in favour of a non-technical reconciliation with nature', p. 48.
30 M. Foucault, 'L'Extension sociale de la norme', interview with P. Werner, 1976, reproduced in *Dits et Écrits*, vol. 3, pp. 74–9 at p. 76.
31 M. Foucault, 'L'Extension', p. 76.
32 A. Clarke Begg, *Insulin in General Practice: A Concise Guide for Practitioners*,

London, Medical Books, 1924, p. 44. Illustrating the scepticism and practical attitude of many clinicians, as well as the tension between them and the physiologists whom he accused of an inability to define a 'normal' diet, this author also criticised diabetes specialists' mania for quantification: 'Elsewhere I give reasons for thinking that elaborate calculations based on height, weight, age etc., to determine the exact amount of calories required, are of little practical value' (p. 48).

33 Oskar Minkowski and Joseph von Mering had highlighted the role of the pancreas in sugar diabetes in 1889 and paved the way for the production of pancreatic extracts. See M. Bliss, *The Discovery of Insulin*, Chicago, University of Chicago Press, 1982; C. Sinding 'Making the Unit of Insulin: Standards, Clinical Work and Industry', *Bulletin of the History of Medicine*, 2002, 76, pp. 231–70.

34 The history of the disappointments that followed the discovery and therapeutic use of insulin and the observation of the inevitable appearance of serious complications has been recounted convincingly and often poignantly by Feudtner, *Bittersweet*.

35 Joslin, *Manual*.

36 Prestley, *History of Diabetes*, pp. 127–99.

37 Joslin, *Manual*.

38 Ibid.

39 Ibid.

40 Bliss, *Discovery of Insulin*.

41 R. T. Woodyatt to Elmer L. Sevringhaus, 26 December 1926, The Sevringhaus Papers 1920–1945, The American Philosophical Library, quoted by Feudtner, *Bittersweet*, p. 136.

42 H. C. Hagedorn, B. N. Jensen, N. B. Kraup and L. Wodstrup, 'Protamine Insulinate', *Journal of the American Medical Association*, 1936, 106, pp. 177–80.

43 H. J. John, 'Treatment of Diabetes Mellitus', in S. Soskin, ed., *Progress in Clinical Endocrinology*, New York, Grune & Stratton, 1950, p. 274.

44 E. Tolstoi, 'Treatment of Diabetes Mellitus: The Controversy of the Past Decade', *Cincinnati Journal of Medicine*, 1949, 30, pp. 1–7.

45 John, 'Treatment of Diabetes Mellitus', p. 275.

46 Ibid.

47 P. Royer and H. Lestradet, *Traitement du diabète infantile en régime libre*, Paris, Flammarion, 1958, p. 41.

48 G. M. Guest, 'Treatment of Diabetes Mellitus in Infants and Children', in Soskin, *Progress*, pp. 286–7.

49 Renal insufficiency, cardiovascular complications, gangrene in the lower limbs due to lesions of the arteries or small blood vessels, leading to amputation, local or general wounds that did not heal, recurrent infections, neurological complications and, finally, almost inevitable retinitis that could lead to blindness, were all common.

50 In the introduction to his contribution a physician announced, 'It will be shown that the only definitive factor established as yet is the duration of the disease.' See H. Dolger, 'Factors Influencing Premature Cardiovascular Degeneration in Diabetes Mellitus', in Soskin, *Progress*, pp. 303–6.

51 The pancreas is a double gland with both an exocrine function (secretion in the digestive tract of digestive enzymes) and an endocrine function (secretion of hormones, including insulin).

52 P. Sönksen, S. Judd and C. Lowy, 'Home Monitoring of Blood-Glucose: Method for Improving Diabetic Control', *Lancet*, 1978, i, pp. 729–32; R. Tattersall, 'Home Blood Glucose Monitoring', *Diabetologia*, 1979, 16, pp. 71–4. At the time, one had to compare the change in the colour of tablets or reactive strips under the effect of a drop of blood, with a colorimetric scale. Today's miniaturised measurement devices give the numeric result directly.

244 *Christiane Sinding*

53 It is of interest to observe that while SBGM seems to have been readily accepted and used by patients, not all doctors showed the same enthusiasm from the outset, at least not in France. See Anouchka Coussaert, 'Perdre ou gérer la santé. Une maladie écran, le diabète insulino-dépendant', PhD thesis, Université de Paris V, 1988, pp. 111–13. Coussaert attributes this scepticism to the loss of medical power that went along with patients' increased autonomy.

54 D. S. Schade, J. V. Santiago, J. S. Skyker and R. Riozza, *Intensive Insulin Therapy*, Princeton, NJ, Excerpta Medica, 1983; R. L. Jackson and R. Guthrie, *The Physiological Management of Diabetes in Children*, New Hyde Park, NY, Medical Examination Publishing Company, 1986; I. B. Hirsch, 'Intensive Treatment of Type I Diabetes', *Medical Clinics of North America*, 1998, 82, pp. 689–719. It is interesting to note that Joslin often employed the term 'intensive treatment'.

55 S. Rahbar, 'An Abnormal Hemoglobin in Red Cells of Diabetics', *Clinica Chimica Acta*, 1968, 22, pp. 296–8.

56 K. H. Gabbay, D. N. Haney, K. Hasty *et al.*, 'Glycosylation of Hemoglobin In Vivo: A Monitor of Diabetic Control?', *Diabetes*, 1977, 25, pp. 335–46; G. B. Rubenstein, H. Rochman, S. P. Tanega and D. L. Horwitz, 'Hemoglobin A1c: An Indicator of the Metabolic Control of Diabetic Patients', *Lancet*, 1976, 8041, 2, pp. 734–7.

57 C. Sinding, 'Une molécule espion pour les diabétologues. L'innovation médicale entre science et morale', *Sciences Sociales et Santé*, 2000, 18: 2, pp. 95–120.

58 These distinctions are of course a little sketchy, for both sides took advantage of information obtained in both ways. Yet glycosylated haemoglobin levels were like a punishment or reward for the patient. While doctors compared both types of result, it was glycosylated haemoglobin that they used to 'measure' the quality of control over a long period.

59 J. Pirart, 'Diabetes Mellitus and Its Degenerative Complications: A Prospective Study of 4,400 Patients Observed between 1947 and 1973', *Diabetes Care*, 1978, 15, pp. 143–52; D. Job, E. Eschwege, C. Guyot-Argenton, J. P. Aubry and G. Tchobrousky, 'Effect of Multiple Daily Injections on the Course of Diabetic Retinopathy', *Diabetes*, 1976, 25, pp. 463–9.

60 Editorial, 'The Diabetes Control and Complications Trial', *New England Journal of Medicine*, 1993, 329: 14, pp. 1035–6.

61 Feudtner, *Bittersweet*, p. 141.

62 They were called insulino-dependent diabetes (DID) and non-insulino-dependent diabetes (NIDM), then Type-1 and Type-2 diabetes when the boundary between the two was seen to be less distinct than it had been thought to be.

63 According to Feudtner, medical intervention on DM would simply replace one set of problems by another. He called these medical transformations of the disease 'transmutations'. For instance, a patient saved from diabetic coma could later develop renal failure or retinopathy, which in turn had to be treated, and so on. He highlights the fact that these new forms of the disease are very difficult to cope with, for doctors and especially for patients.

64 G. Canguilhem, 'Le Statut épistémologique de la médecine', *History and Philosophy of Life Sciences*, 1988, 10, Suppl., pp. 15–29.

12 A matter of degree
The normalisation of hypertension, c. 1940–2000

Carsten Timmermann

High blood pressure is a peculiar disorder. In most cases it is without symptoms, and patients are often diagnosed with hypertension, curiously, when they have no idea that they are ill. A quick series of easy measurements with the sphygmomanometer, a piece of laboratory technology that has become part of routine medical practice, delivers the diagnosis. Even though mild or moderate hypertension itself causes hardly any symptoms, most doctors and medical administrators agree that the disorder is 'one of the most important preventable causes of premature death worldwide', and treatment is advisable.[1] High blood pressure is framed today generally not as a disease that causes direct suffering, but as a 'risk factor' in stroke and heart disease, a quantifiable marker of potential disease.[2] However, the boundary that separates normal and pathological blood pressure remains disputed. A recent review article on the pathophysiology of hypertension avoids questions of classification and does not mention any such boundaries.[3] The general consensus, based on a number of long-term epidemiological studies, is that in terms of risk the lowest is the best possible blood pressure. Medical authors tend to be careful not to draw a clear line between physiological and pathological blood pressures, but government-appointed committees are willing to recommend thresholds for treatment, and these thresholds are becoming increasingly lower. In recent US guidelines on hypertension, 'high normal blood pressure' (above 120/80 mm Hg) has been reclassified as 'pre-hypertension' and treatment is recommended.[4]

Well into the 1950s, hypertension was quite a different matter from what we take it to be today. Hypertension was conceived of as a disease, and a pressure reading of, say, 140/80 mm Hg alone (classified as stage 1 hypertension in the new US guidelines) would definitely not have raised a doctor's eyebrows. With only very few, drastic treatment options available, whether a patient was to receive treatment or not was a matter of judgement for the physician rather than the expected (and officially sanctioned) response to a series of sphygmomanometer readings. In general, the hypertensives who received treatment had malignant hypertension, severely increased blood pressure with manifest pathological effects, a disease that not only posed a long-term risk but led to clearly distinguishable, acute symptoms and

246   Carsten Timmermann

possibly the death of the patient. According to one of the pioneers of hypertension research in Britain, Sir Colin Dollery, malignant hypertension has all but disappeared from the industrialised world since effective drug treatments became available in the 1950s.[5] Simultaneously, hypertension was redefined as a quantitative disease, the upper end of a bell-shaped normal distribution. In the absence of symptoms, hypertension has come to be framed by epidemiological data, notions of risk, and a succession of new drug treatments.

The transition from an acute, life-threatening disease into a matter of degree and the difficulty of defining boundaries make hypertension an ideal test case for Georges Canguilhem's classic essay, *The Normal and the Pathological*. Hypertension is a disorder that is defined by modern medical science. In this chapter, after introducing Canguilhem's main arguments I will turn to the role that clinical science has played in the transition of high blood pressure. I will conclude by discussing the wider context of this transition during a time that has often been characterised as the 'golden age' of modern biomedicine, and some of its implications.

The normal and the pathological

Georges Canguilhem's book *The Normal and the Pathological*, first conceived in 1943 and revised in the mid-1960s, has received much attention recently, not least from cultural theorists, after being reissued in 1991 in the fashionable 'Zone' cultural studies series, with an introduction by Michel Foucault.[6] The philosopher and physician Canguilhem owes much of this revived interest in the English-speaking world to the fact that Foucault named him as one of his major influences.[7] It should not be forgotten, though, that *The Normal and the Pathological* was initially above all a book about physiology and its role in the epistemology of medicine. Canguilhem's book is an expression of long-standing concerns, not only in France, about the meanings of the scientific in medicine. He challenges the notion (which he traces to Claude Bernard) that medicine can only be scientific if it is reduced to the application of physiology, with its positivist assumption that life is governed by laws identical in kind to those that govern the world of inanimate objects. He points to the problems associated with Bernard's attempts to identify the normal with a – quantifiable – ideal of organic function that can be assessed by way of rigorous experimentation. Physiology is where the laboratory and the clinic meet, and this leads to tensions. If the body is merely a complicated mechanism whose functions and dysfunctions can be evaluated by way of laboratory technologies (such as the sphygmomanometer), there can be no qualitative difference between normal and pathological states. If, on the other hand, the normal is more or less identical with the 'healthy', and therefore linked with qualitative values, there can be no continuity between normal and pathological states.

The normalisatin of hypertension   247

Canguilhem not only questions the uncritical use of physiological concepts in practical medicine, but also rejects the other common approach to normality, that of statistics. Statistically obtained averages cannot provide a doctor with clear guidelines for judging the health of individuals. While the distinction between normal and pathological is clear for every individual, boundaries between normal and pathological on the level of populations are fuzzy. Furthermore, the real opposite of the normal is the abnormal and not the pathological, and an anomaly does not automatically lead to illness but may merely be a (potentially useful) variation.

Health, according to Canguilhem, depends on the ability of individuals to respond to different environments by adaptation, by adopting new norms, which in certain circumstances can lead to physiological parameters very different from those measured under the ideal laboratory conditions that Bernard aimed for (and these parameters may therefore well be abnormal). Disease, in turn, is caused by the inability to adapt. Malignant hypertension fulfils these requirements: it severely restricts patients' abilities to adapt to new situations, and they know that they are not well. Malignant hypertension in the 1940s and 50s, according to Colin Dollery, was a 'death dealing disease', and most of the patients he encountered before effective drugs became available felt seriously ill.[8] They often had difficulties with breathing at night, were woken in the morning by a headache and troubled during the day by blurred vision.[9] Canguilhem's book emphasises the role of individual experience as the root of all medical science. Perceived illness is the basis of the science of pathology and of all meaningful knowledge on physiological processes, but physiology in turn does not provide us with reliable information on what is pathological. An increased blood pressure may be merely the attempt of the body to adapt to a special situation.

Canguilhem locates the origins of the notions he analyses (and criticises), of the pathological as merely a quantitative variation of health, in the nineteenth century. While well established in physiology, however, these concepts were implemented in medical practice only in the twentieth century. In the following sections of this chapter I will look at the role that the establishment of an infrastructure for clinical research played in this process (in Britain roughly between the end of the First World War and the 1950s), along with the development of new, 'physiological' means of medical intervention: biological and chemical therapeutic agents that were highly visible symbols of medical progress. I will offer possible explanations for the success of the concept of a quantitative disease in a medical landscape shaped by the new clinical sciences as well as new administrative concerns, by contextualising a well-publicised debate over the reframing of high blood pressure in Britain in the mid-twentieth century. The dispute between two influential British clinicians, George White Pickering and Robert Platt, over the nature of essential hypertension provides me with a lens through which to study this transition.[10]

248 *Carsten Timmermann*

Platt, Pickering and clinical science in Britain

Both Platt and Pickering were prominent clinical scientists, but, as we will see, they represented slightly different traditions. Compared to France and Germany, Britain was late to establish an infrastructure for clinical science. Christopher Lawrence has argued in two important articles that until well into the twentieth century the British medical élite were rather sceptical about the new institutions of clinical science.[11] Established British clinicians were not opposed to medical innovations *per se*. However, wedded firmly to a medical marketplace where the part-time affiliation with a medical school provided them with competitive advantages, élite doctors felt uneasy about the growing state intervention in medicine. As Christopher Booth has shown, prior to the First World War England had no clinical science tradition to speak of. There were no full-time professors in clinical subjects, for example, and the London medical schools had no clinical laboratories, hardly any links with the universities, and no paid staff.[12] This changed after the war, not least as a result of activities of the new Medical Research Council (MRC).[13]

To establish an infrastructure for medical research to the Council meant both the training of young researchers and the provision of posts at MRC units in hospitals around the country. Initially, in the absence of an existing clinical research landscape, this was partly an export of Cambridge physiology into clinical settings, and partly an attempt to copy German and US models.[14] The research units of Thomas Lewis and Thomas Renton Elliot at University College Hospital (UCH) were dedicated to the translation of themes such as cardiovascular regulation, pioneered by Cambridge physiologists, into clinical research.[15] The colleague of Platt and Pickering and professor at the Postgraduate Medical School at Hammersmith Hospital, John McMichael, highlighted this in 1952: 'Progress in understanding disease processes is determined by the availability and applicability of laboratory techniques. Clinical investigation closely follows physiology, while surgery and pharmacology provide its therapeutic "experiments".'[16]

George Pickering's work, like McMichael's, was initially informed by the research schools of Lewis and Elliot. Much of Pickering's training was geared towards a career in full-time medical research, and he never worked in private practice. Throughout his career he was based in the 'Golden Triangle' of Oxford, Cambridge and London. He studied at Pembroke College, Cambridge, and pursued his clinical studies at St Thomas's Medical School in London, from where he graduated in 1930. After taking up resident appointments at St Thomas's he entered Thomas Lewis's clinical research unit at University College London.[17] In 1939 Pickering was appointed professor of medicine at St Mary's Hospital, London, where he assembled a group of clinicians and scientists working on the study of blood pressure, employing a wide range of approaches, from biochemistry to epidemiology. In 1956 Oxford University appointed Pickering as Regius Professor of Medicine.

The normalisatin of hypertension 249

Robert Platt's career unfolded in the provinces and was initially not as focused on research as Pickering's. Platt studied medicine in Sheffield and began his teaching career as a part-time lecturer at the University of Sheffield, also running a successful private practice.[18] After the Second World War he accepted an offer to become the first full-time, salaried Professor of Medicine at the University of Manchester, appointed to the first chair of this kind outside the capital.[19] Under his leadership the Manchester department specialised in nephrology, the physiology and pathology of the kidney.[20] Platt's career and his move from part-time university appointment and a flourishing private practice in Sheffield to a full-time university chair in post-war Manchester is representative of the larger changes in British twentieth-century academic medicine, namely the move from part-time to full-time clinical research posts.

In the following section we will examine how their different backgrounds, with Platt more wedded to an older, individualist model of clinical practice than Pickering, found their reflections in different concepts of the nature of high blood pressure.

Hypertensive disease

How was high blood pressure framed when Platt and Pickering started their careers? In the 1930s and 40s, high blood pressure – if no other obvious causes could be found – marked a distinct and specific disease, essential hypertension or hypertensive disease. According to this paradigm, which Platt continued to defend, there was also a distinct group of people, the hypertensives. While they may not know this when young, their blood pressure would inevitably go up later in life if not treated in time. In younger years these hypertensives would not even necessarily have high blood pressure.

Platt and his co-workers in their work on high blood pressure followed up patients who were treated at the Manchester Royal Infirmary for malignant hypertension. Significant for Platt's approach, and distinguishing it from Pickering's, as we will hear, was that he studied patients who were undergoing treatment in his hypertension clinic, and their relatives. In Canguilhem's terms, Platt's patients had already lost their innocence and lived their lives under the new, narrower conditions that the disease was imposing on them. The treatment, in many cases surgical sympathectomies with their serious side effects, kept patients alive but would never return them to the state that Canguilhem calls normative.[21] Platt was looking for family links, and believed he had found the cause of the hypertensive disease of his patients in their genes.

The paper in which Platt summarised the results of his study on heredity and hypertension was published in the *Quarterly Journal of Medicine* in 1947.[22] Drawing on his work with the Manchester patients, Platt suggested that 'essential hypertension is the heterozygous (or occasionally homozygous)

250 *Carsten Timmermann*

expression of a dominant Mendelian characteristic'; in other words, he proposed the existence of a specific hypertension gene.[23] This suggestion was in line with much of the contemporary literature. Platt's article does not explicitly state where he expected the genetic defect to be located, but it is likely that he was thinking about a gene associated with aspects of kidney function. Platt argued for the necessity of long-term follow-up studies into the natural history of hypertension.[24] He hypothesised that these studies were going to reveal that with regard to blood pressure the population was divided into two distinct groups: a normal majority, and a distinct group of hypertensives, whose blood pressure was going to reach pathological levels in middle age.

In the 1940s, Pickering may have agreed with Platt. On the basis of a review he published in 1952 it is quite plausible to assume that Pickering expected the results of a study he and his co-workers were then undertaking at St Mary's Hospital to be in line with Platt's suggestions and the dominant hypotheses regarding the nature of essential hypertension (although he already discusses the difficulty of determining upper limits of normal blood pressure).[25] The debate between the two began two years later when Pickering and his co-authors, Michael Hamilton, John Alexander Fraser Roberts and Clive Sowry, published the results of this study in a series of articles in the journal *Clinical Science*, entitled 'The Ætiology of Essential Hypertension'.[26] The conclusions of Pickering and his co-authors were different from Platt's in a number of significant points. Above all, they disputed his evidence for the existence of two distinct groups, one normal and one hypertensive. Hypertension to Pickering was now merely a quantitative phenomenon, the upper end of a normal distribution of blood pressures. The distinction between physiological and pathological was unclear, and where two groups seemed to show in the data, this was an artefact of measurement. 'Hypertension is,' Pickering wrote in 1974, 'as I pointed out in 1955, a new type of disease in which the deviation from the norm is one of degree and not of kind. It is a quantitative disease.'[27]

Pickering and his colleagues, in contrast to Platt, did not study a group of hypertensives but surveyed the blood pressures of outpatients at St Mary's Hospital who were treated for conditions, mostly surgical, that had nothing to do with hypertension. In regard to blood pressure, they were studying apparently healthy people. The study was the attempt to find the normal distribution of the markers of a potential disease in a healthy population. This approach was subsequently taken much further by large epidemiological studies such as the Framingham Heart Study and the smaller-scale follow-up studies undertaken by the MRC Epidemiological Research Unit in South Wales (for which Pickering acted as an adviser).[28] These studies were designed not only to establish distributions in normal populations, but also to look at the emergence of pathological problems over time. They aimed at calculating the statistical links between physiological parameters in healthy people and subsequent illness, statistical entities that today we call risk factors.[29]

The normalisatin of hypertension   251

Pickering's quantitative concept of hypertension was the product of surveys, and the difference between Platt and Pickering could also be interpreted as an expression of the transition proposed by David Armstrong, from 'hospital medicine' to 'surveillance medicine'.[30] In Platt's eyes, hypertension was an essential reality: either you had it or you did not. According to Pickering, blood pressure was distributed along a continuum. Everybody was to be considered normal, but that did not mean that they were necessarily also healthy. While treatment might be appropriate, this had to be decided for every individual patient, taking into account other parameters. A clear distinction between hypertensives and non-hypertensives was impossible.

Surveys, statistics and genetics

The main factor shaping Pickering's new outlook was his wholehearted embrace of surveys and statistical methods, brought about by his collaboration with John Alexander Fraser Roberts, an expert on statistics and human genetics.[31] Fraser Roberts, the son of a Welsh farmer, had started his career in agricultural genetics in the 1920s, studying inherited characteristics in Welsh mountain sheep. In the 1930s he turned to human biology, and in 1943 he obtained his MD. At the time of the collaboration with Pickering he held three different posts. He was Director of the Burdon Mental Research Department at Stoke Park Colony, Bristol; Director of Research at the Royal Eastern Counties Institution in Colchester (site of Lionel Penrose's work on phenylketoneuria); and Lecturer in Medical Genetics at the London School of Hygiene and Tropical Medicine (home institution of the pioneering biostatisticians and epidemiologists Sir Austin Bradford Hill and Major Greenwood). Fraser Roberts had also established a genetic counselling clinic at the Great Ormond Street Children's Hospital. He was Pickering's link to reformed eugenics, new thinking in psychology, and an increasingly sophisticated body of knowledge in medical statistics and population genetics.[32]

Platt nurtured what he himself called an 'amateur interest' in genetics, and his knowledge of statistics was limited.[33] Statistics was not, strictly speaking, Pickering's specialty either, but he could draw on the expertise of Fraser Roberts. Increasingly central to the debate was the question of whether Pickering's bell curve was really a bell curve, or a composite curve with humps that moved towards higher blood pressures in older populations and represented the carriers of one, or several, hypertension genes.[34] Pickering compared the distribution of blood pressures to Francis Galton's (the pioneer of eugenics) findings on height distribution in Britain, and the distribution of intelligence, which was one of Fraser Roberts's main fields of expertise. The Platt camp, in contrast, compared hypertension with phenylketonuria, a disorder caused by a mutation in a single gene.

The debate between Platt and Pickering triggered a series of letters to the *Lancet* and informed much British research on high blood pressure and the epidemiology of cardiovascular disease in the 1950s and 60s. Well-known

252 Carsten Timmermann

examples were the studies by Morrison and Morris on London bus drivers and conductors, and those already mentioned, by William Miall and his co-workers, on the inhabitants of mining villages in south Wales, both conducted within MRC research units.[35] Miall and his colleagues designed their study in collaboration with Pickering and Fraser Roberts, while Morris and Morrison supported Platt's hypotheses.[36] A team of epidemiologists at the London School of Hygiene and Tropical Medicine, meanwhile, worked on ways of achieving non-biased blood pressure measurements.[37] The debate died down in the mid-1960s, when Platt moved away from his single gene hypothesis, while Pickering conceded that the bell curve may well accommodate pathologies caused by single gene mutations. After all, nobody challenged the statistical distribution of intelligence or body height, despite the existence of disorders such as phenylketonuria which caused mental deficiencies and others that affected body height.

Physiological norms and administrative change

It is comparatively easy to explain what shaped Pickering's new approach to the nature of high blood pressure, but it is difficult to analyse the changing attitudes to what counted as the medical mainstream within the changing social and moral economies of modern medicine. Steve Sturdy and Roger Cooter have attempted to do this for laboratory medicine, arguing that the increasingly central role of the laboratory in modern medicine since the late nineteenth century in Britain was closely associated with new administrative demands growing out of the rationalisation of health systems.[38] They suggest that

> the academicization of leading sectors of hospital medicine, and the introduction of laboratories and other scientific investigative techniques into clinical research, teaching and practice, did much to favour the growth of an administrative as opposed to an individualized way of knowing in medicine. This way of knowing was well suited to the demands of administering a corporate system of mass health care organized around a hierarchical division of medical labour. Shaped by the need to regulate and standardize diagnostic and therapeutic practice, it was closely linked to the pursuit of efficiency both in hospital medicine and in the health care system as a whole.[39]

Sturdy and Cooter do not discuss the central roles of statistics and genetics, which, as we have seen, complemented laboratory approaches in Pickering's new take on high blood pressure. It seems that the implementation of physiological concepts in clinical practice in Britain went along with another epistemic transition in medicine, associated with the rise of the welfare state.

Since the late nineteenth century, as David Armstrong has pointed out,

The *normalisatin* of *hypertension* 253

the dispensary has played an increasingly central role in medical epistemology. Similarly, the survey became a crucial tool in medicine, and Armstrong suggests that this paved the way for a new epistemic system, which he calls 'surveillance medicine'.[40] The objects of surveillance medicine are not individual bodies, as in hospital medicine, but populations. The normal came to be located not in the individual body (as for Bernard) but in the social body. In the course of the transition from hospital medicine to a preventive paradigm organised around the results of surveys, statisticians and geneticists felt that they had something to offer to clinicians. Population genetics combined the survey with the laboratory and, by way of genetic counselling, even with the individual clinical encounter. Fraser Roberts, in the 1940 edition of his textbook, saw the main significance of genetic analysis in its scientific forecasting ability that could potentially help to meet the emerging need for focused prophylaxis in medicine: 'A clear recognition of genetic susceptibility', he argued, 'might be the best approach to the identification of controllable factors.' And, well within the paradigms of reformed eugenics, the 'knowledge that a special hereditary susceptibility existed might sometimes lead to the institution of earlier treatment than would otherwise be the case'.[41] It may hardly be necessary to point out (as Cooter and Sturdy argued for the laboratory) that academic epidemiology, too, had its roots in administrative concerns. The MRC Units for Social Medicine and for Epidemiology had conceptual and institutional links with welfare administration and occupational medicine. The south Wales Unit, was initially dedicated to pneumoconiosis, miner's disease. Jerry Morris, the founder of the Social Medicine Unit was drawn to social medicine through his friendship with Richard Titmuss, the statistician and pioneer of the post-war welfare state.[42]

The late 1940s and 1950s was a time when infectious disease seemed to be defeated and epidemiologists turned to chronic and degenerative diseases, the ailments of middle and old age such as cardiovascular disorders and cancer. The risk factor concept was born in the life insurance industry in the early twentieth century and found its way into mainstream medical science and practice in the 1950s.[43] Epidemiological studies pointed to the association of high blood pressure with cardiac heart disease and turned risk factors into a serious scientific concept.[44] Platt's single gene hypothesis matched the older clinical paradigm of hospital medicine, which looked at specific patients that could be identified and treated. Pickering's quantitative concept was informed by a focus on populations rather than individual patients, and ultimately allowed the treatment of a risk, a potential problem, rather than an identifiable, specific disease.

Therapy defines disease

The post-Second World War period saw not only the rise of administrative concerns in medicine, but also an increasingly central role for the

254   *Carsten Timmermann*

pharmaceutical industry. New therapies for chronic diseases confronted Western health bureaucracies with new cost pressures. Today, drugs for high blood pressure are big sellers. The cost of antihypertensive drugs in the United States, for example, amounts to currently about $15 billion, accounting for 10 per cent of the country's total spending on drugs.[45]

Drug treatments for hypertension were developed around the same time as the debate between Platt and Pickering was enlivening the pages of the *Lancet* and informing much British research on high blood pressure. The new drugs led to the disappearance of malignant hypertension, but, as side effects became less drastic, they also led to continuing debates over the treatment of mild and moderate hypertension, imposing greatly increased costs on the health system.[46] In the absence of clear notions of where the physiological ended and the pathological started, therapy was no longer just reactive. Rather, the availability and expected success of a therapy began to determine the diagnosis.[47] 'While there is no natural dividing line between what is normal and what is abnormal,' Pickering argued in 1974, 'something is known about the levels of arterial pressure above which treatment is beneficial.'[48]

In the 1940s, high blood pressure was treated surgically by sympathectomy in a minority of patients suffering from life-threatening malignant hypertension. Both Platt and Pickering treated patients in this way.[49] The side effects of the operation could be drastic, and it went out of fashion in the 1950s. Surgical sympathectomy was replaced by a class of drugs, the ganglion blockers, which were thought to block the nerve endings of the sympathetic nerve system in what resembled a chemical sympathectomy and whose side effects were almost as drastic as those of the surgical procedure.[50] Pickering studied the effects of these drugs in the early 1950s.[51] Other drugs followed, which all lowered blood pressures but in many cases caused what resembled a new disease in turn.

In 1948 a low-salt rice diet promoted by the émigré Walter Kempner at Duke University (inspired by the teachings of the German lifestyle reform movement) showed an unexpected antihypertensive effect and was tested by an MRC working group that included Platt.[52] It also led to the work on the thiazide diuretics in the laboratories of Sharp & Dohme, drugs that make patients urinate more and lead to a reduction of the amount of fluid and salt in the body. The thiazide diuretics, first marketed by Merck Sharp & Dohme in 1959, had few side effects and were the first drugs that allowed the mass treatment of patients with high blood pressure, even for milder forms of hypertension.[53] It was now justifiable to treat a mere risk factor, a blood pressure at the upper end of a normal distribution, without first having to identify a distinct and specific pathology.

There are parallels with psychiatric disorders, which also became normalised as a result of the growing influence of what Armstrong calls the 'community gaze' and the availability of new drug treatments in the postwar period. According to Armstrong,

In essence, the post-war psychiatric perception was a normalizing gaze: not, as in the Panopticon, a normalizing gaze over an enclosed and inherently 'abnormal' population, but over an entire domain. This normalizing gaze over the whole tended to obliterate the legitimacy of the distinction between normal and abnormal and tended to create one community where before there had been two.[54]

Normalisation had consequences for members of both former 'communities'. The boundaries between healthy and ill, between normal and abnormal (and also between somatic and psychological), became blurred.

Conclusion

Armstrong's approach helps us to understand where the quantitative approach to high blood pressure and the risk factor approach had their origins and why they were so successful in the context of post-war medicine, but this does not automatically mean that Canguilhem's concerns have lost their validity. Surveillance medicine may be part of medical reality today, but it is not the whole story. Medical encounters still take place between individuals, and it is difficult to argue that there is not some essential reality to illness. What Armstrong calls surveillance medicine is merely an additional layer of medical reality, and, as John Pickstone has argued, the history of medicine is not ideally told as a story of successions, in which the new completely replaces older layers.[55] In fact, the hospital medicine of Foucault's *The Birth of the Clinic* (Pickstone calls this analytical medicine) and the older, individualist model of patronage medicine (Pickstone identifies it as biographical medicine) both continue to play important roles in certain realms of modern medical practice.[56]

Canguilhem's book *The Normal and the Pathological* was conceived at the beginning of the rise of the risk factor model. His criticism is mostly directed towards the growing influence of physiological concepts in medical practice. *The Normal and the Pathological* was partly a contribution to the debate over the old question of whether medicine is more of an art or a science. There are clear links and continuities between Canguilhem's thinking and the holist criticism of mainstream medicine that flourished in the interwar period: Canguilhem cites Kurt Goldstein, for example, as a major influence.[57] Another influence was Henry Sigerist, who is best known in the English-speaking world as a historian of medicine, but who also wrote extensively on the theory of medicine and was among the more outspoken participants in debates over a crisis of modern medicine in Weimar Germany.[58] This chapter has focused on Britain, and here criticisms analogous to those voiced by Canguilhem found their expression in long-standing concerns over the incommunicability of clinical knowledge, as analysed by Christopher Lawrence.[59]

The debate between Platt and Pickering partly had its origins in the different meanings that the notions of the 'normal' and the 'pathological' have

256   *Carsten Timmermann*

acquired in the different realms of clinical science, medical practice and health administration. The relatively new field of geriatrics, as Armstrong shows, is one where the blurring of the boundary between normal and pathological is especially noticeable. The variation of physiological parameters becomes broader with age, and may pass into abnormality. This can (but does not necessarily) lead to states that are best described as pathological. But what makes these states pathological? Here we are back with Canguilhem. It depends on the living subject and his or her environment whether a variation is perceived as unbearable. We know when we feel ill (and when we don't). According to the geriatrician Bernard Isaacs, 'the ability to define the "normal" becomes neither a matter of semantics nor statistics, but a burning issue to be decided afresh at every clinical intervention'.[60]

The notion of a risk factor has added a new dimension to the question of what is healthy and what pathological. Being identified as 'at higher than average risk' (of suffering a stroke, for example) reconfigures a subject as not quite healthy, but not quite ill either. A risk factor is not automatically a disease, neither is it a clearly identifiable cause of disease. It is, for example, a behavioural pattern (such as smoking) or a physiological parameter (such as blood pressure) associated statistically with the development over time of disease in a population. But what does this mean for individuals? If, as Canguilhem argues, disease is 'not merely the disappearance of a physiological order but the appearance of a new vital order', so is the assurance that an individual may be at risk of premature death or disability.[61] Whether blood pressure is normal or not is a fairly theoretical question. But when an individual, who may feel perfectly healthy at the time, is told that his or her high blood pressure may affect his or her life expectancy or quality of life, and when that individual is advised to undergo treatment to lower this blood pressure, this affects what Canguilhem calls normativity and turns the individual into a patient.

Sociological studies have shown that in individual clinical encounters both medical staff and patients tend to translate statistical risk into binary categories of normal or abnormal, sick or healthy, which are more easily grasped.[62] While people with high blood pressure may not feel ill, they are nevertheless entering a new stage in their lives when they are told that they are 'at risk' and are prescribed drugs to treat this risk. Being treated provides them with a new identity. If the side effects of the drugs are worse than the symptoms caused by the increased blood pressure, they inevitably have to accept the new 'patient' identity. Ironically, experts and textbook authors such as Pickering have been very aware of this, warning their readers not to frighten their patients unnecessarily or bother them with unnecessary treatments. However, in practice things often look different. The increasing costs that chronic diseases impose on the welfare system have politicised risk factors and created an incentive to turn physiological into political norms. The regulation of physiological functions has become an important issue for

The *normalisatin of hypertension*   257

the regulation of the economy, and the population approach of surveillance medicine provides a means of mediation between individual bodies, the physiological laboratory, and the administrative bodies of the welfare state.

Acknowledgements

I am grateful to the participants in the Manchester workshop and the editor of this volume for useful criticism, and to several of my colleagues, especially John Pickstone, Ed Ramsden and Elizabeth Toon, for stimulating discussions and references I would not have found without them. The research leading to this chapter was supported by a Wellcome Trust postdoctoral fellowship.

Notes

1 Bryan Williams, 'Drug Treatment of Hypertension: Most Patients Will Need a Treatment Cocktail – Including a Thiazide Diuretic', *British Medical Journal*, 2003, 326, pp. 61–2.
2 On the history of risk factors, see William G. Rothstein, *Public Health and the Risk Factor: A History of an Uneven Medical Revolution*, Rochester, NY, University of Rochester Press, 2003, and Robert A. Aronowitz, *Making Sense of Illness: Science, Society, and Disease*, Cambridge, Cambridge University Press, 1998.
3 Gareth Beevers, Gregory Y. H. Lip and Eoin O'Brian, 'ABC of Hypertension: The Pathophysiology of Hypertension', *British Medical Journal*, 2001, 322, pp. 912–16.
4 The guidelines issued in 2003 in the seventh report of the Joint National Committee on Prevention, Detection, Evaluation, and Treatment of High Blood Pressure distinguish between normal blood pressure (<120/80 mm Hg), pre-hypertension (120/80 to 139/89), stage 1 hypertension (140/90 to 159/99) and stage 2 hypertension (160/100 and higher). See Aram V. Chobanian *et al.*, 'The Seventh Report of the Joint National Committee on Prevention, Detection, Evaluation, and Treatment of High Blood Pressure: The JNC 7 Report', *Journal of the American Medical Association*, 2003, 289, pp. 2560–72. See also Janice Hopkins Tanne, 'US Guidelines Say Blood Pressure of 120/80 mm HG is not "normal"', *British Medical Journal*, 2003, 326, p. 1104.
5 C. T. Dollery, 'A Clinician Looks at the Future', *British Journal of Clinical Pharmacology*, 1982, 13, pp. 127–32; interview with Professor Sir Colin Dollery, conducted by the author on 3 July 2002.
6 Georges Canguilhem, *The Normal and the Pathological*, New York, Zone Books, 1991. A useful summary and critical evaluation of the main arguments can be found in Mary Tiles, 'The Normal and Pathological: The Concept of a Scientific Medicine', *British Journal for the Philosophy of Science*, 1993, 44, pp. 729–42. For a discussion of the book in the context of contemporary debates over the social construction of scientific knowledge, see Malcolm Nicolson, 'The Social and the Cognitive: Resources for the Sociology of Scientific Knowledge', *Studies in the History and Philosophy of Science*, 1991, 22, pp. 347–69.
7 For a recent appraisal and a discussion of the links in their work, see Christiane Sinding, 'The Power of Norms: Georges Canguilhem, Michel Foucault, and the History of Medicine', in Frank Huisman and John Harley Warner, eds, *Locating Medical History: The Stories and Their Meanings*, Baltimore, Johns Hopkins University Press, 2004, pp. 262–84. Some of the links are discussed by Tiles,

258 *Carsten Timmermann*

'The Normal and Pathological'. See also Gary Gutting, *Michel Foucault's Archaeology of Scientific Reason*, Cambridge, Cambridge University Press, 1989. For further appraisals, see the papers in a double issue of *Economy and Society* dedicated to Canguilhem's work (vol. 27, 1998, issues 2 and 3, pp. 151–331).

8 Dollery, 'A Clinician Looks at the Future', p. 127.

9 For the clinical symptoms, see also George W. Pickering, *High Blood Pressure*, London, Churchill, 1955, pp. 241–312, and Frederick H. Smirk, *High Arterial Pressure*, Oxford, Blackwell, 1957, pp. 83–116.

10 The dispute is documented in J. D. Swales, ed., *Platt versus Pickering: An Episode in Recent Medical History*, London, The Keynes Press and British Medical Association, 1985.

11 Christopher Lawrence, 'Incommunicable Knowledge: Science, Technology and the Clinical Art in Britain, 1850–1914', *Journal of Contemporary History*, 1985, 20, pp. 503–20; Christopher Lawrence, 'Still Incommunicable: Clinical Holists and Medical Knowledge in Interwar Britain', in Christopher Lawrence and George Weisz, eds, *Greater than the Parts: Holism in Biomedicine 1920–1950*, New York, Oxford University Press, 1998, pp. 94–111.

12 Christopher C. Booth, 'Clinical Research', in Joan Austoker and Linda Bryder, eds, *Historical Perspectives on the Role of the MRC*, Oxford, Oxford University Press, 1989, pp. 205–41. For the rise of laboratory medicine see also Steve Sturdy and Roger Cooter, 'Science, Scientific Management and the Transformation of Medicine in Britain, c.1870–1950', *History of Science*, 1998, 36, pp. 421–66.

13 On the history of the MRC, see Austoker and Bryder, eds, *Historical Perspectives*, and A. Landsborough Thomson, *Half a Century of Medical Research*, vol. 1: *Origins and Policy of the Medical Research Council (UK)*, London, HMSO, 1973, and vol. 2: *The Programme of the Medical Research Council (UK)*, London, HMSO, 1975.

14 In the United States this was above all the successful model of Johns Hopkins Medical School, which in itself was an attempt to adapt German models for the United States.

15 Cf. Booth, 'Clinical Research'; Henry Dale, 'Thomas Renton Elliot, 1877–1961', *Biographical Memoirs of Fellows of the Royal Society*, 1961, 7, pp. 53–74; Arthur Hollman, *Sir Thomas Lewis: Pioneer Cardiologist and Clinical Scientist*, London, Springer, 1997; Helen Valier, 'The Politics of Scientific Medicine in Manchester', unpublished PhD dissertation, University of Manchester, 2002. Lewis, who had been on the payroll of the Medical Research Committee since 1916 was also greatly influenced by James MacKenzie. See also Joel D. Howell, ' "Soldier's Heart": The Redefinition of Heart Disease and Speciality Formation in Early Twentieth Century Great Britain', *Medical History*, Supplement 5, 1985, pp. 34–52.

16 John McMichael, 'Cardiovascular Research: Introduction', *British Medical Bulletin*, 1952, 8, pp. 301–3.

17 John McMichael and W. Stanley Peart, 'George White Pickering 26 June 1904–3 September 1980', *Biographical Memoirs of Fellows of the Royal Society*, 1982, 28, pp. 431–49.

18 See Platt's memoirs: Robert Platt, *Private and Controversial*, London, Cassell, 1972; and the obituary: 'Lord Platt of Grindleford, Bt, M.D. Sheff., M.Sc. Manc., F.R.C.P.', *Lancet*, 1978, i, pp. 114–15.

19 For the significance of this development, see Valier, 'The Politics of Scientific Medicine in Manchester'.

20 Cf. ibid., pp. 294–303.

21 Robert Platt and S. W. Stanbury, 'Sympathectomy in Hypertension', *Lancet*, 1950, i, pp. 651–9. In this class of operations, surgeons removed sections of the

The normalisatin of hypertension   259

so-called sympathetic ganglia, nerves that run on both sides of the vertebral column and that control the automatic responses of the body to all sorts of environmental stimuli. See F. H. Smirk, *High Arterial Pressure*, Oxford, Blackwell, 1957, pp. 401–28.

22 Robert Platt, 'Heredity in Hypertension', *Quarterly Journal of Medicine*, 1947, 16, pp. 111–33. We should beware of the temptation to see molecular genetics as the main origin of medical genetics, as many authors on modern medicine seem to do. See Peter A. Coventry and John V. Pickstone, 'From What and Why Did Genetics Emerge as a Medical Specialism in the 1970s in the UK? A Case History of Research, Policy and Services in the Manchester Region of the NHS', *Social Science and Medicine*, 1999, 49, pp. 1227–38.

23 Platt, 'Heredity in Hypertension', quoted in Swales, *Platt versus Pickering*, p. 8.

24 Ibid., p. 15.

25 George W. Pickering, 'The Natural History of Hypertension', *British Medical Bulletin*, 1952, 8, pp. 305–9.

26 M. Hamilton, George W. Pickering, J. A. Fraser Roberts and G. S. C. Sowry, 'The Ætiology of Essential Hypertension. 1. The Arterial Pressure in the General Population', *Clinical Science*, 1954, 13, pp. 11–35; M. Hamilton, George W. Pickering, J. A. Fraser Roberts and G. S. C. Sowry, 'The Ætiology of Essential Hypertension. 2. Scores for Arterial Blood Pressures Adjusted for Differences in Age and Sex', *Clinical Science*, 1954, 13, pp. 37–49; George W. Pickering, J. A. Fraser Roberts and G. S. C. Sowry, 'The Ætiology of Essential Hypertension. 3. The Effect of Correcting for Arm Circumference on the Growth Rate of Arterial Pressure with Age', *Clinical Science*, 13, 1954, pp. 267–71; M. Hamilton, George White Pickering, J. A. Fraser Roberts and G. S. C. Sowry, 'The Ætiology of Essential Hypertension. 4. The Role of Inheritance', *Clinical Science*, 1954, 13, pp. 273–304.

27 George W. Pickering, *Hypertension: Causes, Consequences and Management*, Edinburgh, Churchill Livingstone, 1974, p. 33.

28 Thomas R. Dawber, *The Framingham Study: The Epidemiology of Atherosclerotic Disease*, Cambridge, MA, Harvard University Press, 1980; W. E. Miall, 'Follow-Up Study of Arterial Pressure in the Population of a Welsh Mining Valley', *British Medical Journal*, 1959, ii, pp. 1204–10.

29 William B. Kannel, Thomas R. Dawber, Abraham Kagan, Nicholas Revotskie and Joseph Stokes, 'Factors of Risk in the Development of Coronary Heart Disease: Six-Year Follow-Up Experience', *Annals of Internal Medicine*, 1961, 55, pp. 33–50.

30 David Armstrong, 'The Rise of Surveillance Medicine', *Sociology of Health and Illness*, 1995, 17, pp. 393–404; David Armstrong, *Political Anatomy of the Body: Medical Knowledge in Britain in the Twentieth Century*, Cambridge, MA, Cambridge University Press, 1983.

31 This is indicated in a lecture draft by Pickering called 'The Genetic Factor in Essential Hypertension', Wellcome Library, PP/GWP/D.2. For the history of medical genetics in Britain and the important role of Fraser Roberts, see Coventry and Pickstone, 'From What and Why Did Genetics Emerge as a Medical Specialism?', and Peter A. Coventry, 'The Dynamics of Medical Genetics: The Development and Articulation of Clinical and Technical Services under the NHS, especially at Manchester', unpublished PhD dissertation, University of Manchester, 2000. On Fraser Roberts, see also P. E. Polani, 'John Alexander Fraser Roberts, 8 September 1899–15 January 1987', *Biographical Memoirs of Fellows of the Royal Society*, 1992, 38, pp. 306–22. On the rise of statistical thinking and its implications, see Ian Hacking, *The Taming of Chance*, Cambridge, Cambridge University Press, 1990.

32 On eugenics and its transformations in the light of the Nazi atrocities in

260   *Carsten Timmermann*

Germany, see Daniel J. Kevles, 'Out of Eugenics: The Historical Politics of the Human Genome', in Daniel J. Kevles and Leroy Hood, *The Code of Codes: Scientific and Social Issues in the Human Genome Project*, Cambridge, MA, Harvard University Press, 1992, pp. 3–36, and Diane Paul, *The Politics of Heredity: Essays on Eugenics, Biomedicine, and the Nature–Nurture Debate*, Albany, State University of New York Press, 1998.

33 Letter, R. Platt to H. Harris, quoted after Coventry and Pickstone, 'From What and Why Did Genetics Emerge as a medical specialism?', p. 1232.

34 On the normalising power of graphical representations, see David Gugerli and Barbara Orland, eds, *Ganz normale Bilder: Historische Beiträge zur visuellen Herstellung von Selbstverständlichkeit*, Zurich, Chronos, 2002.

35 S. L. Morrison and Jerry N. Morris, 'Epidemiological Observations on High Blood-Pressure without Evident Causes', *Lancet*, 1959, ii, 864–70; William E. Miall, 'Follow-Up Study of Arterial Pressure in the Population of a Welsh Mining Valley', *British Medical Journal*, 1959, ii, pp. 1204–10. For the history of these units, see A. R. Ness, L. A. Reynolds and E. M. Tansey, eds, *Population-Based Research in South Wales: The MRC Pneumoconiosis Research Unit and the MRC Epidemiology Unit*, London, Wellcome Trust, 2002; Shaun Murphy, 'The Early Days of the MRC Social Medicine Unit', *Social History of Medicine*, 1999, 12, pp. 389–406; and Virginia Berridge, 'Celebration: Jerry Morris', *International Journal of Epidemiology*, 2001, 30, pp. 1141–5.

36 For correspondence on the preparation for the south Wales study, see George W. Pickering papers, Wellcome Library London, PP/GWP/C.6/51.

37 Interview with Professor Walter Holland, London, 15 April 2002.

38 Sturdy and Cooter, 'Science, Scientific Management and the Transformation of Medicine in Britain'.

39 Ibid., p. 446.

40 Armstrong, 'The Rise of Surveillance Medicine'; Armstrong, *Political Anatomy of the Body*.

41 Quoted after Polani, 'John Alexander Fraser Roberts', p. 319.

42 See Ness, Reynolds and Tansey, eds, *Population-Based Research in South Wales*; Murphy, 'The Early Days of the MRC Social Medicine Unit'; and Berridge, 'Celebration: Jerry Morris'.

43 Rothstein, *Public Health and the Risk Factor*.

44 See *Measuring the Risk of Coronary Heart Disease: A Symposium*, Supplement to *American Journal of Public Health*, April 1957, p. 47.

45 David Spurgeon, 'NIH Promotes Use of Lower Cost Drugs for Hypertension', *British Medical Journal*, 2004, 328, p. 539.

46 W. S. Peart, 'The Problem of Treatment in Mild Hypertension', *British Journal of Clinical Pharmacology*, 1982, 13, pp. 82–90; Medical Research Council Working Party, 'MRC Trial of Treatment of Mild Hypertension: Principal Results', *British Medical Journal*, 291, 1985, pp. 97–104.

47 For an insightful analysis of the links between technological innovation and the framing of disease, see Keith Wailoo, *Drawing Blood: Technology and Disease Identity in Twentieth-Century America*, Baltimore, Johns Hopkins University Press, 1997.

48 Pickering, *Hypertension: Causes, Consequences and Management*, p. 33.

49 Platt and Stanbury, 'Sympathectomy in Hypertension'; George W. Pickering, A. Dickson Wright and R. H. Heptinstall, 'The Reversibility of Malignant Hypertension', *Lancet*, 1952, ii, pp. 952–6.

50 Austin E. Doyle, 'The Introduction of Ganglion Blocking Drugs for the Treatment of Hypertension', *British Journal of Clinical Pharmacology*, 1982, 13, pp. 63–5; William D. M. Paton, 'Hexamethonium', *British Journal of Clinical Pharmacology*, 1982, 13, pp. 7–14; F. H. Smirk, 'Hypotensive Actions of Hexa-

The normalisatin of hypertension   261

methonium Bromide and Some of Its Homologues: Their Use in High Blood-Pressure', *Lancet*, 1952, ii, 1002–5; Edward D. Freis, 'Recent Developments in the Treatment of Hypertension', *Medical Clinics of North America*, 1954, 38, pp. 363–74.

51 George W. Pickering papers, Wellcome Library, London, PP/GWP/C.6/69.
52 'Hypertension, Food Rationing Advisory Committee: Rice Diet; 1948–1950', MRC Papers, UK National Archives, FD1/396.
53 Robert M. Kaiser, 'The Introduction of the Thiazides: A Case Study in Twenti-eth-Century Therapeutics', in Gregory J. Higby and Elaine C. Stroud, eds, *The Inside Story of Medicines: A Symposium*, Madison, WI, American Institute of the History of Pharmacy, 1997, pp. 121–37; Karl H. Beyer, 'Discovery of the Thi-azides: Where Biology and Chemistry Meet', *Perspectives in Biology and Medicine*, 1977, 20, pp. 410–20; Karl H. Beyer, 'Chlorothiazide', *British Journal of Clini-cal Pharmacology*, 13, 1982, pp. 15–24.
54 Armstrong, *Political Anatomy of the Body*, p. 67.
55 John V. Pickstone, 'The Biographical and the Analytical: Towards a Historical Model of Science and Practice in Modern Medicine', in Ilana Löwy, ed., *Medicine and Change: Historical and Sociological Studies of Medical Innovation*, Paris, Les Édi-tions INSERM – John Libbey, 1993, pp. 23–46. For the displacement model, see N. D. Jewson, 'The Disappearance of the Sick Man from Medical Cosmol-ogy, 1770–1870', *Sociology*, 1976, 10, pp. 225–44.
56 Michel Foucault, *The Birth of the Clinic*, London, Tavistock, 1973.
57 In the index to *The Normal and the Pathological* we find nine references to Gold-stein. For more on Goldstein and holism in interwar Germany, see Anne Har-rington, *Reenchanted Science: Holism in German Culture from Wilhelm II to Hitler*, Princeton, NJ, Princeton University Press, 1996. See also Lawrence and Weisz, eds, *Greater than the Parts*; Carsten Timmermann, 'Constitutional Medicine, Neo-romanticism, and the Politics of Anti-mechanism in Interwar Germany', *Bulletin of the History of Medicine*, 2001, 75, 717–39.
58 There are also nine references to Sigerist's work in *The Normal and the Pathologi-cal*. On Sigerist, see Elizabeth Fee and Theodore M. Brown, eds, *Making Medical History: The Life and Times of Henry E. Sigerist*, Baltimore, Johns Hopkins Uni-versity Press, 1997. See also Carsten Timmermann, 'Weimar Medical Culture: Doctors, Healers and the Crisis of Medicine in Interwar Germany, 1918–1933', unpublished PhD dissertation, University of Manchester, 1999.
59 Lawrence, 'Incommunicable Knowledge'; Christopher Lawrence, 'Still Incom-municable'.
60 Bernard Isaacs, 'Has Geriatrics Advanced?' in Bernard Isaacs, ed., *Recent Advances in Geriatrics*, London, Churchill Livingstone, 1978, pp. 1–5 at p. 2.
61 Canguilhem, *The Normal and the Pathological*, p. 193.
62 Sonja Olin Lauritzen and Lisbeth Sachs, 'Normality, Risk and the Future: Implicit Communication of Threat in Health Surveillance', *Sociology of Health and Illness*, 2001, 23, pp. 497–516.

13 Deviant roles, normal lives

Why every piazza needs its own 'madman'

Sara Bergstresser

> Once upon a time, there was the *manicomio* (madhouse) of Bergamo, today it is no more.
> Because we, the last crazies, have left.
> Finally a normal life...
> Today let's have a party: another story has begun...
> > (Advertisement for a festival sponsored by a cooperative of ex-psychiatric patients, Bergamo, June, 2000[1])

> It is a beautiful, hot, sunny day, and when I pass under the *Sentierone*, I see a young man alone on the wooden walkway underneath the *Quatriportico*. He sleeps peacefully; he is dirty and in rags. In the city, everyone knows who he is ... I think that this person represents the total marginalization, more or less voluntary, of a man who could (should) be reintroduced into society...
> > (Letter to the editor, *L'Eco di Bergamo*, 27 June 2000)

In this chapter I will address a particular paradox: the existence of deviant social roles that are so widespread and culturally salient as to become normal. I will look at the significance of a particular Italian social role: that of the local 'piazza madman'. I will argue that, far from being outside of society, any individual who enacts this role actually plays an essential part in the performance of expected social interaction. In fact, if the familiar 'madman' were to fail to appear one day, local residents would notice his absence, and the piazza would take on a sense of unfamiliarity.

This role becomes relevant in conjunction with Italian psychiatric reform and the legally mandated closure of the *manicomi* (psychiatric hospitals; but more literally, madhouses) after 1978. This had two results within the realms of everyday behaviour and social interaction in public spaces. First, individuals who had never had a choice of role, having been given that of 'institutionalised patient', suddenly had the opportunity to choose, if only within a small range of potential roles. Second, following the psychiatric reform law, involuntary commitment was legally limited and ideologically discouraged, which reduced the instance of taking socially disruptive people out of the piazza and into the institution. This resulted in the invention of a

Deviant roles, normal lives 263

Figure 13.1 Advertisement for a festival sponsored by a cooperative of ex-psychiatric patients, Bergamo, June 2000. (Photo by author.)

new lived role based on a theoretical piazza madman figure culled from the past.[2]

This way it becomes possible to discuss Erving Goffman's idea of the 'normal deviant', which applies to everyday social roles, lived experiences, and interaction, rather than theoretical or uncommon characters.[3] While the conceptual categories of deviance and abnormality remain, the profusion of 'mad' individuals consistently visible within public spaces has the result of normalising the role to the point of its becoming predictable, mundane and fundamentally non-threatening within the progression of everyday life. Additionally, the performance of the deviant role is a necessity within the

264 *Sara Bergstresser*

social field because it provides the foil necessary for the definition and maintenance of 'normal' roles. Furthermore, individuals who enact the role of the 'piazza madman' as part of their becoming predictable simultaneously become part of the local landscape and add to the local sense of place, both affirming the comfortable predictability of home and providing a subtle distinctiveness.[4]

Italian mental health reform: psychiatry and territory

In the late 1960s the seeds of Italian psychiatric reform and Democratic Psychiatry emerged from a picture of the institution as a place of violence and suffering. The underlying philosophy, elaborated by Franco Basaglia, hinged upon the classification of mental illness as a *socio-political problem* in which the ill were segregated because of their potential disruption to society.[5] By 1978 this idea of Democratic Psychiatry had also taken on the characteristics of a social movement. In contrast to anti-psychiatry movements in the United States and Britain, the Italian movement quickly gained momentum, and Italy became known for its radical mental health reform and for *Law 180*, which closed all public psychiatric hospitals in the country.[6]

Today, over 20 years after psychiatric reform and deinstitutionalisation in Italy, the principles of Democratic Psychiatry are increasingly overshadowed by medical models of mental illness. The current prestige of scientific and medical knowledge as powerful explanatory models represents an enormous barrier to psychiatric practitioners who hope to retain a social approach to mental health care; they can no longer look to the 1970s climate of social movements for help. The focus of biomedical psychiatry on mental illness as an individual and biomedical problem contrasts with the Basaglian ideology of mental illness as a social problem that can be cured within the larger social group. At stake is the central definition of the role of the mentally ill in society: if mental illness is considered a social problem, this implies that curative responsibility is placed on the social group rather than on pharmacological substances.

Following reforms, the territorial model of psychiatric services has been the predominant goal within Italian mental health care. In current practice this model entails a mental health-care system that is integrated into the national health-care programme yet implemented locally. The impetus for this model came in the early days of reform as an experiment in community-based therapy whereby the existing hospital structures would no longer be used for services.[7] The goal was to move mental health care into the 'normal' world and out of institutional settings.

The Italian word for territory, *territorio*, actually holds much more meaning than the English word reveals. The concept of *territorio* in Italy lies close to daily life as a sense of place, history and belonging. A similar concept is found in the French *terroir*. The 'Translator's Note' to Michel de Certeau's *The Practice of Everyday Life*, vol. 2: *Living and Cooking* describes the difficulty of translating this concept for an English-language readership:

What the American publisher found to be 'too closely linked to some-thing specifically French' can in part be explained in light of the French concept of *terroir*, the difficult translation of which itself illustrates one difficulty in translating *Living and Cooking*.[8]

The translator goes on to explain how *terroir* is an essential component of French life, particularly illustrated through regional cuisine, where the regional *terroir* can literally be tasted in the regional cheeses from the 'tang of its soil', and where 'the danger in . . . uprooting is that the results become "pale copies" of the original'.[9]

There is ample evidence that the concepts of *territorio* and *terra* are also salient within Italian life, particularly within theoretical discussions of the relationship between institutions and geographic locales:

> This connection *terra*–language–culture perpetuates itself in time pre-cisely because our land (*terra*) wasn't unified, and therefore only lan-guage and culture were able to express these connections and the aspects of valour to be found in our communal life. It's a matter, above else, of a language essentially written and rarely spoken, therefore a cultured lan-guage, aligned principally with intellectual reflection. The ties to the *terra* were expressed, therefore, in two somewhat abnormal ways. As a diffuse popular bond, it was anchored to the restriction of physical place – the town, the neighbourhood, the city – and in a certain limited way, weighed us down (*zavorrava*) and held us back.[10]

Psichiatria e Territorio (Psychiatry and Territory) is a widely used concept within the mental health system to indicate work related to community centres and integration.[11] A concern with the role of territory is also present in other planning and policy contexts, including that of public education.

The Italian tendency for families to stay in the same locale from generation to generation shows how territory can hold an implication of permanence, giving distinctive flavour not only to regional foods but also to regional life and inhabitants. The historical continuity of Italian spaces, where history can often be traced back for thousands of years, imbues the concept of soil with a continuity, permanence and non-interchangeability, the importance of which should not be underestimated in any study of the quotidian in Italy. Even small villages can trace their history back for hundreds or thousands of years; the archaeological museum of Bergamo, for example, displays Roman arte-facts found in many small towns of the province, including the town of my research. The concept of local territory is an essential factor in the practice of mundane everyday life; for this reason it is also an idea that pervades local political discourse, where competing parties claim that they, rather than their opponents, are the true defenders of the *territorio*.

By the 1960s, as the Democratic Psychiatry movement gained momen-tum, and other mental health trends gained attention in Italy and France, an

266   *Sara Bergstresser*

important change was taking place in the organisation of the Bergamo *manicomio*. In an interview conducted with Armando Testa, an administrator of the community centre, he described his time working in the psychiatric hospital in the 1960s and 1970s up to its closure.[12] During this period he witnessed a shift in the physical grouping of hospital patients as one of the key moments in the transition from an institutional, diagnosis-based model to the emerging model of *territorio*. Testa remembers this trend as originating in France and subsequently gaining popularity in Italy, a general phenomenon also noted in other accounts.[13] Up to this point, patients had been organised into groups depending on diagnosis, with those labelled 'schizophrenic' being physically grouped together by diagnostic subtype. The organising scheme changed to groupings based on geographic origin, for example specific mountain valleys, the city or the plains. The doctor for each group was also from the designated geographic area. This shift marks an important transition in social role, when the concept of local territory rather than psychiatric diagnosis became the primary marker of social role and personal identity within the context of institutional life. Where once an individual's primary social category might have been 'paranoid schizophrenic', at this point it could have shifted to, for example, 'individual from the Val Taleggio'.

These shifts from territorial to diagnostic categorisations and back again add further complexities to the identity management tasks faced by the individual throughout his or her history of institutionalisation, labelling, relabelling and subsequent deinstitutionalisation. Schur[14] and Garfinkel[15] describe 'status degradation ceremonies' that occur with the labelling of an individual, often at hospital admittance. They describe how this labelling has subsequent implications for self-labelling, where the new identity takes on the definition of truth, and the past identity becomes either a façade or something entirely inconsequential. In this way the person's status is completely changed, and, with this change, his or her past is also redefined to fit the current status. Schur names this process 'retrospective interpretation'. In the case of admittance to the *manicomio*, this process would have involved shift *from* local inhabitant *to* member of diagnostic category. A reversal of this labelling process would indicate the possibility of reappropriating a lost identity associated with pre-commitment life, but with the added necessity to either redefine the past once again or to remember and reappropriate earlier versions of the past.

The 'piazza madman' as social role: performing Italianness and local distinctiveness

Giuseppe Tornatore, in his internationally recognised film *Cinema Paradiso*, chose to include a piazza madman character in his story of a young boy's love of film.[16] This film is successful at recreating a sense of place of mid-1900s southern Italy through the story of a boy and his relationship to films. At one point a movie is being projected outward on to a building so that it can be watched by a crowd in the piazza. In one memorable scene a face pops up yelling, 'La piazza è mia!' ('The piazza is mine!'). The 'madman' proceeds to flush the film audience out of the piazza because it is his bedtime. In this way he asserts his ownership of the piazza as his home – a space simultaneously public and private. When the main character returns to the little village as an adult after the passing of many years, we see that the madman character remembered from his childhood is still there. This phenomenon in media portrayal exemplifies the way in which the existence of a 'piazza madman' is consciously used as a feature meant to suggest not only authentically Italian space but also local specificity and distinctiveness. The appearance of the madman in the first place defines the distinctive character of the village, and through his reappearance he demonstrates that, though time has passed, the village is still the same place: home.

Another famous film, Ermanno Olmi's *L'Albero degli Zoccoli*[17] (Tree of the Wooden Clogs), illustrates a very local sense of place in the late 1800s in the northern Province of Bergamo,[18] where a local 'madman' is accepted within the rural community. In one scene, Giopa, portrayed as a simple yet harmless man wearing tattered clothes, travels to different family homes to ask for food.[19] As he arrives, the children call his name in delight. The procession continues within a religious context, where Giopa enters the house and makes the sign of the cross while looking at the crucifix on the wall. At this point the family members also cross themselves and thank the Lord, saying: 'May he always give us work and good health.' Finally, the family gives the man a piece of bread; the overtones of charity and Catholicism mark this scene. This pattern is repeated in a different home. In this case the children laugh at him, and their mother responds: 'No, children, don't laugh. Poor souls like that who have nothing are closer to God.' The appearance of this character reaffirms the historical imagination of the local madman as harmless and integrated into a special social role within the community and the religious worldview.[20]

In sum, the image of the foolish yet endearing madman can be found both in the South and in the North of Italy, but it occurs as situated within locally specific contexts. References to place and history not only show how the representation of Italy and the performance of Italianness both frequently include the role of the 'piazza madman', but also suggest that this role is associated with the past as well as with the present. The local madman is already a known character in the cast, and he has been for some time.

The central role of the piazza both in physical performance of the role of 'madman' and in Italian social life is particularly illustrative of the ways in which deviant roles actually exemplify cultural norms. Localism, a strong attachment to home and a heightened 'sense of place' are key components of Italian culture. In the same way, because particular individuals are associated with a single area or piazza, the role of 'madman' is localist in a particularly

268   *Sara Bergstresser*

Italian way. As Basso states: 'The experience of sensing places, then, is thus both roundly reciprocal and incorrigibly dynamic'; individuals need the locality to set the stage for the social performance, just as the locality itself depends on inhabitants in order to retain its distinctive character.[21] The post-deinstitutionalisation role of the 'piazza madman' would emerge as a recognisable role because of its fundamental compatibility with Italian history, cultural expectations and practices.

Some public spaces can take on the role of home, imbued with personal meaning and sense of place. Public space as home is particularly central to a consideration of homelessness, where a railway station or public square may be both literally and figuratively home.[22] Even in cases where an individual has a family home or community shelter in which to sleep, a public space may be a figurative home, such as in the case of the 'piazza madman' role. Following psychiatric reform in the 1970s, severe restrictions were placed on involuntary commitment, limiting the practice of clearing the mentally ill from public view. Among the mentally ill themselves this reform opened the possibility of choosing between social roles, rather than being constrained to the single role of mental hospital resident. Many individuals aspired to mainstream social roles, and community mental health centres were set up as tools of social reintegration. On the other hand, other individuals, perhaps experiencing the concept of personal choice for the first time, opted for another path: 'marginal' life as lived literally in the centre of society.

Nadel-Klein defines localism as:

> the representation of a group identity as defined primarily by a sense of commitment to a particular place and to a set of cultural practices that are self-consciously articulated and to some degree separated and directed away from the surrounding social world.[23]

This type of localism can be constructed and used by groups within a locality in order to designate a frame for the experience of identity, as an expression of class structure, or as a strategy for cultural survival. On the other hand, localism can be defined from the 'outside' to serve the categorisation of a marginal group marked by 'backward' practices and provincialism. In sum, Nadel-Klein shows not only how localism is a term whose value varies according to the viewpoint of the speaker, but also how it is a problematic concept for ethnography because of its inherent assumption of bounded communities and uniformly experienced tradition.

My field area, though only about an hour's train ride from Milan, is considered both by Milanese and by local inhabitants to be provincial and at least metaphorically distant. Localism and the valorisation of local traditions are very important aspects of current social and political life. For example, the province in which my research took place is the stronghold of the *Lega Nord*, a political party that emphasises regional and local control and the reduction or elimination of centralised governmental power. In the recent past this party even publicly called for the secession of the northern third of the country, envisioning the formation of a new country named 'Padania'.[24]

Because northern Italy has grown wealthy only within the past two generations, there is also a recent emerging emphasis on the agricultural past and remaining agricultural products of the current day. This trend has arrived in conjunction with the rapidly increasing economic prosperity in this area. While initially dismissed as evidence of poverty, the idea of agriculture and the figure of the artisan/craftsman are now increasingly valorised as aspects of the locality to be preserved at all costs. Peasant ancestors are now described proudly as an essential aspect of individual self-descriptions. This valorisation is evidenced in the meanings attributed to such things as local landscape, locally produced foods and local language forms. This trend has arrived as the European Union is gaining more visibility and power over Europe; local and national identities may shift as the unifying concept of 'Europe' becomes more prominent. Paradoxically, this shift may result in an emphasis of local and European identities rather than national identities.[25] For example, regional foods in Italy have long served as markers of difference, where particular meats, cheeses, wines and pasta dishes are tightly bound to their geographic origins.[26] Distinctive dishes are also connected to a sense of local pride, where gastronomic superiority and historical authenticity are coveted designations, which are now often defined in terms of EU origin control status.[27]

Finally, following the valorisation of aspects of life that are considered local, rivalry with neighbouring zones, a discourse of local autonomy as a desirable outcome, and a local self-image as closed and essentially different from other provinces in Lombardy, it would follow to describe the concept of localism as itself a local tradition. The performance of local belonging may include an ability to speak the local dialect, an encyclopedic knowledge of local features, both natural and built, an enthusiasm for local foods, sports and figures, and a denigration of rival groups in culturally dictated contexts. Though it may be ethnographically problematic, localism nevertheless frames and gives meaning to local life.

Normal deviants

Goffman states that any role that is stigmatised or considered deviant is actually part of a complex and complementary system of norms and counterparts. In other words, the concept of deviance not only allows the norm to exist, but also allows individuals to manage identities by switching between stigmatised and normalised roles, depending on the social context.[28] The deviant role is in fact normative, resulting in stigma management as a 'general feature of society'.[29] In this section I apply this idea particularly to the role of local 'madman' as a re-emerging social role in Italy.

270   *Sara Bergstresser*

As in the example of *Cinema Paradiso*, the assertion that 'La piazza è mia!' marks the piazza not only as a centre of public interaction but also as claimed in certain ways by certain individuals, even to the point of becoming a normalised yet 'deviant' version of a home. This process of investiture with individual and collective meanings progressively builds a social sense of place, constituting an interweaving of culture and landscape. The ability of public space to be homelike also reaffirms its significance as the place of familiar social interactions. Physical spaces, as stages for the enactment of social roles, remain essential pieces of the lived social landscape.

Public space can also be a form of workplace that conforms to expected norms in an ambivalent fashion. Street performers and street vendors work in a semi-official capacity in public spaces.[30] Immigrant street vendors in Italy sell handbags, CDs and other merchandise in piazzas and on main streets. Though police periodically appear to chase them away, their presence is accepted by the many Italians buying products from them daily. Members of Roma groups, commonly known as gypsies, beg for money in highly structured and almost professionalised ways. One day on the Milan underground, for example, a Roma woman recited a speech asking for money and walked through the carriage asking each individual for change. When the train stopped, she got out and sat on a bench at the platform, calmly waiting for the next train. Rather than asking for money at this point, she appeared to be taking the equivalent of a coffee break. A 'co-worker' stopped by and they had a brief discussion. When the next train arrived, she got on, recited the same plea and went through the carriage just as she had on the first occasion.

The Roma and other transient individuals may have a workplace-like relationship to public space, spending the same hours each day consistently performing the same tasks, even if these tasks are not generally considered 'work'. As an essential feature of life in urban, industrialised cities, work is structured as specifically scheduled time and distinct from leisure or home time. For those without fixed employment, often the scheduling of time around a consistent work-like activity each day in the same place provides an approximation of social participation and a way to pass the time as well as a means of subsistence and economic survival.

An example was Carlos, a young man frequently found juggling in public spaces in Bergamo. Though he would ask for money, his presence in the city transcended that of street performer. For one thing, his appearance was distinctive, his face covered in many piercings. He was also well known among high school students for his participation in a communist social forum and for his Spanish/Basque origin. During my fieldwork I learned that Carlos had died. His death became a topic of discussion among residents of the city. An article in the local paper announced his funeral:

> *Tomorrow the funeral of Carlos, the Basque juggler*... The youngster had become a familiar figure for whoever frequented the city centre: he

juggled outside the most notable restaurants and outside supermarkets to gather a bit of money ... he took the path of desperation: homeless, drug dependent, illness ... his burial will be paid from public funds.[31]

Shortly after his death, sites of commemoration were visible throughout the city, especially in one particular space where he was typically found juggling. This space was at the entrance to a department store and centrally located near the city's primary bus-route layover stop. Flowers and poems were affixed to a concrete column outside of the store, and 'Ciao Carlos' was spray-painted both there and throughout the city (Figure 13.2).

For some, a work-like schedule can also be constructed out of movement; the existence of perpetual transit as 'work' shows how city streets, buses and subways become primary space. Just as an individual with a job passes many hours at the workplace, those who spend their days moving through the city follow prescribed routes in the same spaces at the same times day after day. For example, one older man in Bergamo's high city was notable for wandering the streets on a daily basis yelling to himself or to an unseen companion in the local dialect. Most probably living with family members, he was known to begin yelling promptly at five in the morning below a particular apartment building, disturbing the residents. Though certainly annoying to some, this man was also clearly a local and his shouting behaviour had become a part of the normal and expected routines of the day.

Figure 13.2 A spray-painted homage to Carlos, the Basque juggler, after his death, located in the area where he would most often appear to perform his juggling act for passers-by. (Photo by author.)

272 *Sara Bergstresser*

Another older man, whom I call 'the number 6 bus man', would often arrive at the main bus stop around 8.30 in the morning and board the number 6 bus. His commuting schedule corresponded to my own, so I had the chance to see him frequently. Upon boarding the bus, he would ask the occupants, 'Is this the number 6 bus?', sometimes multiple times. During the ride he would often start conversations with bus occupants, themselves commuting regulars. Conversations included traffic delays and Italy's participation in the World Cup. This man would exit the bus at the same piazza as I, and he would spend some time there, while I continued on to my anthropological workplace. At other times of the day he would appear at other city piazzas, indicating that his daily schedules involved more than one commuting trip.

Finally, it is important to note that, though the majority of individuals who perform the 'piazza madman' role become familiar and predictable, there are also those who remain unpredictable. This sustained unpredictability becomes tied to the idea of threat and danger. For example, there was one individual in Bergamo who was quite distinctive; he had a faded black tattoo on his forehead, and he emerged periodically throughout the city. He would appear neither in any consistent place nor at any consistent time, and he would often yell obscenities and approach individuals and groups on the street. People would often run away from him and display extreme discomfort at his approach. One day he appeared in the main square of the high city yelling, and it became apparent that he was wearing a garment generally worn by clergy. He wore a priest's amice (the oblong cloth worn around the neck and shoulders); the garment looked authentic, if tattered, and it was of unknown origin. Individuals in the piazza reacted with shock and discomfort both at his dress and at his obscene words. He also climbed into the central fountain, an action that was met with murmurs of discomfort and disapproval. This demonstration of unpredictability or danger, particularly in the display of sacred and secular in a configuration severely out of place, shows the ways in which the 'piazza madman' can also represent a threat, and a container of ongoing stigma.[32] In spite of many instances of familiarisation and standardisation, the aspects of uncertainty and risk can still remain, and the 'piazza madman' role retains the subtle possibility of danger.

Non-places for non-persons? Spaces of contestation and social performance

In this section I discuss the relationship between physical place and social role, considering public spaces as a kind of stage for the performance of particular types of roles. In fact, the roles I discuss as being examples of normal deviance also tend to take place in a certain type of public space, with the primary example being the piazza. In order to frame this discussion I start with particular theories of space that relegate public areas such as the

Deviant roles, normal lives   273

piazza or railway stations into the category of 'non-places', or places of no social significance. Non-persons, similarly, are defined as individuals treated as if they were of no social significance. Nevertheless, though 'non-persons' are treated as though they are socially irrelevant, they are actually 'persons' playing a particular kind of social role, frequently that of 'piazza madman'. In this way, public spaces are related to normal deviance as the stage upon which these social performances take place.

This section not only offers a specific critique of Marc Augé's theory of 'non-places',[33] but is also intended to provide a general caution to theories of globalisation and conceptions of transnational spaces.[34] Some recent theories of spatial distribution of inequality, whether it be North versus South, East versus West or centre versus periphery, render invisible the daily complexities of mundane urban life in the industrialised world. Meta-descriptions of modernity, post-modernity or Augé's supermodernity, while leaving room for collective social contestation or revolution, risk ignoring the day-to-day contestations of marginalised individuals in the form of alternative uses of public space. Furthermore, public space provides a stage for a performance of normalised deviance, where social norms are broken publicly and with enough predictable consistency to become taken for granted. Where are non-places? According to Augé, non-places are spaces without history, identity or relations, where people are always in transit. Non-places 'do not contain any organic society'.[35] Examples of non-places include airports, railway stations, underground trains, commercial areas such as mega-markets and leisure parks, and the invisibly connected space of wireless and other technological communications. A route through city streets may pass through places even if the route itself is not a place.

Next, it is appropriate to ask: who are non-persons? Goffman speaks of the non-person as playing a discrepant role, neither performer, audience, nor complete outsider.[36] The non-person, unlike the outsider, has some information about the situation and some access to front and back stages. Most importantly, non-persons are treated as if they were not there. Goffman used the example of the servant: an individual noticed only when requests are given and otherwise ignored as unimportant.[37] Young children, the very old, the sick, and those in professions playing unscripted background roles are also examples. Frederickson and Rooney expand the concept of non-persons by making a case for the inclusion of freelance musicians due to their lack of belonging to established groups and because they are typically defined as not present.[38]

I would like to propose a further expanded definition, where the category of non-persons can be extended to anyone treated as socially invisible yet at the same time seen as part of the Gestalt. Non-persons may be individuals performing hierarchically disadvantaged roles, or members of devalued groups. Non-persons can also be individuals in particular contexts or places where they are not recognised as members of predominant social groups or social worlds or are performing actions that deviate from social norms. Here

274   *Sara Bergstresser*

specifically, I use the term 'non-persons' to refer to those who enact particular stigmatised roles and inhabit particular marginalised social realms.

I will illustrate with an anecdote from my own fieldwork period. During a six-month stay in Bergamo in 2000 I noticed a young man who habitually spent the day sitting in the lower city's main piazza, the *Sentierone*. The letter to a local newspaper quoted at the beginning of this chapter refers to this very young man. He would arrive in the morning and sit quietly or sleep for the day, leaving at night. I never saw him speak to anyone, but he would place a dish nearby to collect money from passers-by and would sometimes nod in appreciation for 1,000 lire (now equivalent to about 50 euro cents). His appearance did not change, with a beard, dreadlocks, sandals, and the same clothes day after day. His presence in the piazza was very well known and often remarked upon by passers-by or in general conversation. Upon my return a year later he was no longer present, and I began to ask people if they knew his whereabouts. In response to my inquiries, a local newspaper-stand owner replied that he did not remember him in particular. Then he said: 'You notice them at first, but as time passes they become part of the landscape,[39] and that's sad but it's reality. They rotate in, appear, stay for a period of time, then disappear and nobody knows where they went.'

This expanded definition also comes with the assertion that the performance of non-person or normal deviant roles often takes place in public spaces, even to the point of conflation of people and landscape. For example, Fanon describes the colonisation of Algeria: 'The Algerians, the veiled women, the palm trees and the camels make up the landscape, the *natural* background to the human presence of the French.'[40] Prakash explains a similar example in India: 'During the early part of the nineteenth century, the British treated Indians as part of the landscape, as creatures of its soil, drainage, water, climate, and diseases.'[41] Even the anthropologist can find him- or herself in the role of non-person. Clifford Geertz, in his famous chapter on the Balinese cockfight, recounts the time before his serendipitous brush with the illegal cockfight:

> We were intruders, professional ones, and the villagers dealt with us as Balinese seem always to deal with people not part of their life who yet press themselves upon them: as though we were not there. For them, and to a degree for ourselves, we were nonpersons, specters, invisible men.[42]

These examples make it clear that non-persons are not individuals of no social consequence. Quite the contrary: in the cases of Algeria and India, both colonised and colonisers were profoundly impacted by their hierarchical interaction and coexistence. Also, Geertz explains how his ignored movement through the Balinese social landscape was the subject of intense interest and silent scrutiny. Though he certainly made an impression, he was

Deviant roles, normal lives   275

not yet an accepted member of the social sphere – in a state of social pre-existence. The non-person may be semi-invisible or blindingly visible, ignored and repudiated, but never socially irrelevant.

As common public spaces emerge and change, rather than becoming non-places they take on varying levels of familiarity with a hint of danger, where boundary maintenance can sometimes be observed. In Italy the piazza has long been a primary social gathering place. Typically associated with a church, piazzas have been used as gathering places for political rallies or speeches, sites of mass protest or celebration, and locales of informal inter-action and weekly mass strolls known as the *passeggiata*. The piazza is still a typical site of political protest of every kind, an incarnation that would cer-tainly meet Augé's criteria for placehood.[43] The recent increase in foreign immigration to Italy has also made the piazza a social space for groups of immigrants whose presence is nationally and locally contested. The visibility of the piazza as social space makes the immigrant use of this locale a magnet for social discussion and disagreement about the future of immigration in Italy.[44]

The railway station, similarly, is a favourite location for the homeless, drug users and drug sellers. Groups of young anarchists frequent station car parks in the summer, living in their cars, playing loud music and walking about in various states of undress. By claiming these public spaces, these individuals contest the role of the railway station as just a place of transit. This contestation does not go unnoticed: for example, one day an older woman waiting for the bus outside the station began spontaneously telling me that the young anarchists were shameful drug addicts who had no right to live their naked lives there in the parking lot. In this way, widespread behaviour considered socially deviant or illegal becomes normalised to the point that it is commented upon merely as an everyday type of annoyance.

Sometimes public spaces are the site of active boundary maintenance between social groups. The supermarket, for example, is not just the realm of nondescript shoppers. Augé describes large supermarkets in this way:

> The customer wanders round in silence, reads labels, weighs fruit and vegetables on a machine that gives the price along with the weight, then hands his credit card to a young woman as silent as himself – anyway not very chatty – who runs each article past the sensor of a decoding machine before checking the validity of the customer's credit card.[45]

The next quotation, from a letter to the editor of Bergamo's newspaper, describes a situation dramatically unlike Augé's:

> *Poverty and solitude: we should not let indifference win.* I would like to recount ... an anecdote of everyday life lived in these recent days. Tuesday ... in a city supermarket. The aisles of the supermarket are semi-deserted, the lines empty. I go to pay for my groceries when in the

vicinity of the cash registers a noxious odour reaches my nostrils. Perhaps something has spilled over? An incontinent old person soiled himself? I then notice a hint of irony in the tones of voice of the clerks and observe smiles mixed with embarrassment. I see a clerk busy spraying a deodorant or perhaps a perfumed disinfectant to cover up this terrible odour. Then I hear from the aisles a voice saying: 'Out, go outside, what a stench!' I then think that it's a question of a stray dog that has slipped into the supermarket. I turn to see the animal and to my great surprise I see that, yes, it has fur, but that it's not an animal! An old woman with a shabby old fur coat, slippers and 'modern' black leggings prepares, with her head lowered, to pay for her groceries, among which appears a large bottle of red wine. This scene is probably repeated often, if not daily, seeing the reaction of the clerks and supermarket staff, who, understandably disturbed by the odour, hope that the woman will leave as soon as possible. The scene could be seen as comic, but I only succeed in seeing it as tragedy. I felt a pang at my heart . . . how can it be that in our modern, progress-oriented, technological society that there are people who still live in this way? I am ashamed to be a human being, impotent in front of this misery; I hope only that social services are following the case so they are able, in some way to alleviate the suffering of this woman, otherwise I don't know what to think. I exit a little shaken up and see life, the same as always: city traffic, cell-phones ringing, people in a hurry. Had it perhaps been an apparition?[46]

It is clear that the letter-writer had expected a nondescript trip to the supermarket, but instead she was profoundly, if silently, influenced by the existence of another human being. Furthermore, though non-places are defined as places where individuals move in anonymous solitude, it is important to note that solitude and anonymity are not synonymous. Another article in this local paper describes the same homeless woman in another context:

Homeless and vagrant, when distress lives in the city centre. Vagrant, homeless . . . without any more social or affective ties, those who make the street their only refuge, their only place to live. . . . Yesterday . . . in the nice part of the city, she was the only one sleeping in the sun, one of the best-known 'vagrants' in the city: everyone calls her Anna, in reality, not even she remembers anything about herself. Yesterday afternoon she was sleeping, in full view of passers-by, in front of the windows of boutiques a few steps from the *Sentierone*, a bottle of wine by that point already empty by her legs. The bottle: often the last companion of these people, alcohol as the only resource for alleviating the distress. And the solitude.[47]

It is clear that not only is this individual's life in the city normalised to the point that many already know her and have nicknamed her 'Anna', but also

Deviant roles, normal lives   277

her presence marks a site of moral contestation. The appearance of a home-less drunk in public spaces, while silently noticed by passers-by, can also lead to discussion of the public responsibility to people at risk, as well as identifying undercurrents of disgust and pity for those of particular social categories, including individuals sleeping on public streets with empty bottles at their feet. What is acceptable in a 'modern' society is not clear, and social norms are examined and contested.

In sum, individuals playing roles associated with normalised deviance are often found doing so in 'non-places', and in so far as normal deviants can be ignored and treated as 'non-persons', public spaces themselves become imag-ined as special manifestations of normalised deviation. The public place itself is a space of deviant activity, representing places that are not fully under control. Yet public places are ubiquitous, continuously frequented in passing, and thus familiar. In this way, as the particular 'madman' becomes associated with a particular piazza, the piazza itself becomes characterised by its association with the particular 'madman', and by others who habitually perform social roles within its boundaries. Finally, as described earlier, this can result in struggles and contestations for control of the space and the behaviour of individuals who exist within it.

Conclusions

The social role of 'piazza madman' is an example of how conceptions of nor-mality and abnormality can represent social ascriptions of qualitative value rather than any kind of quantitative mean. The idea of normal, as conflated with ideal or desirable, appears to leave only potential for stigma or for hilarity. Nevertheless, upon closer examination it is apparent that essential social value is drawn from the performances of deviant roles, both in terms of defining hypothetical deviations from the norm and in terms of ensuring the continuing dynamism of social life in public spaces.

In addition, anthropologists and historians can gain valuable insight through an awareness of non-persons and their roles in daily life. Far from being unimportant, these 'normal deviants' act as catalysts for social inter-action. By performing atypical actions, often in an individually predictable and consistent manner, these individuals contest the notion of homogenised public behaviour. It is also valuable not only to recognise the underlying social personhood of non-persons, but also to acknowledge the placehood of 'non-places'.

Finally, the social landscape cannot exist without the intermeshing of social performance and physical space as stage; the ongoing existence and repetition of this dynamic landscape leads to a sense of place as well as feeling of comfort and local familiarity. It is within this multifaceted arena that norms are defined, contested, refined and maintained. In fact, the maintenance of locality not only depends on the repetition of local norms, but also necessitates periodic reminders of what constitutes locally salient

278 *Sara Bergstresser*

abnormal action. Local distinction is achieved through deviance as effectively as it is defined through consistency or reiteration of norms. In this way, it is not only possible but also necessary for some individuals to construct normal lives based on abnormal roles.

Notes

1 Unless otherwise noted, translations from the Italian are my own.
2 See M. Foucault, *Madness and Civilization: A History of Insanity in the Age of Reason*, New York, Pantheon Books, 1965.
3 E. Goffman, *Stigma: Notes on the Management of Spoiled Identity*, New York, Simon & Schuster, 1963.
4 See S. Bergstresser, 'Therapies of the Mundane: Community Mental Health Care and Everyday Life in an Italian Town', Doctoral Dissertation, Brown University, 2004. This research addressed community mental health care and the perceptions of mental illness in Italy. My focus is contemporary within a historical context, and I primarily address the cultural construction of social roles and their everyday performance. My evidence comes from over 12 months of anthropological ethnographic fieldwork conducted at a community mental health facility and surrounding town in the Province of Bergamo, northern Italy, in 2000 and 2001–2. The name of the town is not specified, for reasons of confidentiality. The centre was managed by a non-profit foundation, *Fondazione Emilia Bosis*, but was accredited within the public system.
5 F. Basaglia, ed., *L'istituzione negata* (The Institution Denied), Milan, Tascabili Baldini & Castoldi, 1998. Originally published in 1968.
6 M. Donnelly, *The Politics of Mental Health in Italy*, New York, Tavistock/Routledge, 1992.
7 Ibid.
8 T. J. Tomasik, 'Translator's note', in M. De Certeau, L. Giard and P. Mayol, eds, *The Practice of Everyday Life*, vol. 2: *Living and Cooking*, Minneapolis, University of Minnesota Press, 1998, p. ix.
9 Ibid., p. x.
10 U. Cerroni, *Precocità e ritardo nell'identità italiana*, Rome, Meltemi, 2000, pp. 117–18.
11 *Psichiatria e Territorio* is a frequently encountered name for groups, conferences, or publications related to community mental health in Italy, and the concept is typically expanded within. Each particular example tends to include similar yet somewhat individualised definitions of this concept. An example can be found by reading the internet portion of an international journal dedicated to issues of community psychiatry and 'Bridging Western and Eastern [European] Psychiatry', named *Psichiatria e Territorio*, based in Italy and Ukraine (found at www.psyter.org). The English portion offers a translation: '*Which is the meaning of 'territory' in Italian psychiatry?* Territory is a term employed in Italy, after the more utopistic and radical reform law, in order to define a critical attitude toward the tradition of clinical psychiatry. We have meant territory like country or fatherland, the concrete resources of a socio-cultural context, with the historical roots.' (Please note that grammatical errors appear in the original.)
12 Real names of administrators are used as per their request. All mental health centre programme participants, town residents and non-administrative staff have been given pseudonyms when applicable.
13 N. Scheper-Hughes and A. Lovell, 'Breaking the Circuit of Social Control: Lessons in Public Psychiatry from Italy and Franco Basaglia', *Social Science and*

Deviant roles, normal lives 279

Medicine, 1986, 23, 2, pp. 159–78; A. Cohen and B. Saraceno, 'The Risk of Freedom: Mental Health Services in Trieste', in A. Cohen, A. Kleinman and B. Saraceno, eds, *The World Mental Health Casebook: Social and Mental Health Programs in Low-Income Countries*, New York, Kluwer Academic/Plenum Press, 2002, pp. 191–220.

14 E. M. Schur, *Interpreting Deviance: A Sociological Introduction*, New York, Harper & Row, 1979.

15 H. Garfinkel, 'Conditions of Successful Degradation Ceremonies', *American Journal of Sociology*, 1956, 61, pp. 420–4.

16 G. Tornatore, *Il Nuovo Cinema Paradiso*, 1988.

17 E. Olmi, *L'albero degli zoccoli*, Rome, 1978.

18 This particular province is also the area of my research, and the landscapes in the film are visually consistent with the landscapes I frequently encountered during my research period.

19 Also known as *Gioppino* or *Ol Giopì*, this name is associated with a theatrical and puppeteering character tied to Bergamo. The valleys of Bergamo are famous for their puppet theatres, which have a long history in the area. While there are numerous recurring characters, the most widely recognised is that of the Gioppino, who never fails to appear in a puppet show. He is a caricature that has come to symbolise the stereotypical Bergamasco: an uneducated, simple, hard-working man who always speaks in dialect. He is a large man whose body reflects the hard work he carries out on his farm. He is usually pictured with an enlarged neck that reflects the goitre that was common when the only food available was polenta. The Gioppino is a good-natured character who plays dumb, but in the end he turns out to be more *furbo* (clever) than all the other characters. A local puppeteer probably created the character in the mid-nineteenth century to entertain Austrian troops who liked to laugh at the locals. In the subtext of the original performances, however, the Gioppino outsmarts and ridicules the Austrians. See also L. Ebalginelli and P. Ghidoli, 'Bigio, burattinaio bergamasco', in R. Leydi, ed., *Bergamo e il suo territorio*, Milan, Silvana Editoriale d'Arte, 1977; C. Francia and E. Bambarini, eds, *Dizionario italiano–bergamasco*, Bergamo, Edizioni Grafital, 2001.

20 It is plausible to theorise that many historically grounded social roles, including those of 'village idiot', 'local madman' and even 'holy fool', have a large amount of overlap in their manifestations throughout Europe and European history. In the case of holiness and particular forms of deviance, the ties between innocence (or lack of practical, worldly intelligence), sainthood and madness are still a topic of discussion today in many forms of discourse. For example, some recent writers in Italy and elsewhere have hoped to diagnose St Francis and other religious figures posthumously with mental illness, particularly in reference to historical accounts of stigmata. One article attributes to St Francis a 'crucifixion complex': J. Nickell, 'Stigmata: In Imitation of Christ', *Skeptical Inquirer*, July 2000. Another example involves Padre Pio, a figure from the early twentieth century. He currently has an enormous following in Italy, and his birthplace and churches have become one of the most frequent sites of pilgrimage. Padre Pio wanted to emulate St Francis from an early age. He was often ill, reportedly having visions, and he quite famously was found to have stigmata. For this reason, much like the modern reinterpretations of St Francis as delusional, Padre Pio was also suspected of having *'imitatio Chrisi'*, and he was diagnosed with 'dissociative trance coupled with obsession and loss of identity, and a histrionic personality disorder': P. J. Margry, 'Merchandising and Sanctity: The Invasive Cult of Padre Pio', *Journal of Modern Italian Studies*, 2002, 7, 1, pp. 90–1.

21 K. H. Basso, 'Wisdom Sits in Places', in S. Field and K. H. Basso, eds, *Senses of Place*, Santa Fe, School of American Research Press, 1996, p. 55.

22 See A. Lovell, ' "The City Is My Mother": Narratives of Schizophrenia and Homelessness', *American Anthropologist*, 1997, 99, 2, pp. 355–68.

23 J. Nadel-Klein, 'Reweaving the Fringe: Localism, Tradition, and Representation in British Ethnography', *American Ethnologist*, 1991, 18, 3, p. 502.

24 E. Castellanos, 'Il campanile, la Nutella e l'Europa: Bolognese identity in the face of immigration', MA paper, Brown University, 1998.

25 E. Castellanos, 'Where Do They Fit In? The Impact of Immigrants on the Definition of Community and Society in Bergamo, Italy', Doctoral Dissertation, Brown University, Providence, RI, 2004.

26 C. Counihan, *The Anthropology of Food and Body: Gender, Meaning, and Power*, New York, Routledge, 1999; F. La Cecla, *La pasta e la pizza*, Bologna, Il Mulino, 1998.

27 E. K. Paik, 'Homogenized Planet: Cheese vs. Cheesefood, and the Dilemma of Global Standard', *World Watch*, 2001, 14, 2, pp. 20–9; E. Castellanos and S. Bergstresser, 'Food Fights at the EU Table: The Gastronomic Assertion of Italian Distinctiveness', paper presented at the Annual Meeting of the American Anthropological Association, New Orleans, Louisiana, 2002.

28 Goffman, *Stigma*.

29 Ibid., p. 130.

30 See also M. Duneier, *Sidewalk*, New York, Farrar, Straus & Giroux, 2001.

31 L'Eco di Bergamo, 'Domani i funerali di Carlos il giocoliere basco', *L'Eco di Bergamo*, 7 April 2002.

32 This is particularly important in reference to the continued social relevance of Catholicism and its symbolic representations within Italy. In particular, this is also relevant to M. Douglas, *Purity and Danger: An Analysis of the Concepts of Pollution and Taboo*, New York, Routledge, 1966.

33 M. Augé, *Non-places: Introduction to an Anthropology of Supermodernity*, New York, Verso, 1995.

34 For example, see A. Gupta and J. Ferguson, 'Beyond "Culture": Space, Identity, and the Politics of Difference', *Cultural Anthropology*, 1992, 7, pp. 6–23; S. Low and D. Lawrence-Zúñiga, 'Locating Culture', in S. Low and D. Lawrence-Zúñiga, eds, *The Anthropology of Space and Place*, Malden, MA, Blackwell, 2003, pp. 70–89; J. Friedman, 'Global Crises, the Struggle for Cultural Identity and Intellectual Porkbarreling: Cosmopolitans versus Locals, Ethnics and Nationals in an Era of De-hegemonisation', in P. Werbner and T. Modood, eds, *Debating Cultural Hybridity: Multi-cultural Identities and the Politics of Anti-racism*, London, Zed Books, 1997.

35 Augé, *Non-places*, p. 112.

36 E. Goffman, *The Presentation of Self in Everyday Life*, New York, Doubleday, 1959.

37 Ibid., p.152.

38 J. Frederickson and J. F. Rooney, 'The Free-lance Musician as a Type of Nonperson: An Extension of the Concept of Non-personhood', *Sociological Quarterly*, 1988, 29, 2, pp. 221–39.

39 'diventono parte del paessaggio'.

40 F. Fanon, *The Wretched of the Earth*, trans. C. Farrington, New York, Grove Press, 1963, p. 250. Emphasis in the original.

41 G. Prakash, 'Body Politic in Colonial India', in T. Mitchell, ed., *Questions of Modernity*, Minneapolis, University of Minnesota Press, 2000, p. 216 n. 13.

42 C. Geertz, *The Interpretation of Cultures*, New York, Basic Books, 1973, p. 412.

43 See also S. Low, *On the Plaza*, Austin, University of Texas Press, 2000, for discussion of similar phenomena in Latin America.

44 Castellanos, 'Where Do They Fit In?'

45 Augé, *Non-Places*.

Deviant roles, normal lives 281

46 E. Melocchi, 'Povertà e solitudine: non lasciamo vincere l'indifferenza', *L'Eco di Bergamo*, 8 October 2001.

47 L 'Eco di Bergamo, 'Senza tetto e clochard, quando il disago abita in centro', *L'Eco di Bergamo*, 26 March 2002. It may also be of interest that this local newspaper is owned by the Catholic Church. The tone of some articles reflects a corresponding point of view.

Subject index

abnormality: as complementary to the normal 117–18; different senses of 83; localisation of 89; necessity for 83–4; *see also more specific headings*
abortion 176
adoption: procedures for 15–16, 205–18; therapeutic 211–12
aesthetic judgements 12, 122, 137
Algeria 274
Al-Qaeda 118
anecdote books 74
anthropometry 146, 148, 156, 159
art and art criticism 7–9, 82, 84, 91, 137
'average man' concept 142–4, 150

Bali 274
Bergamo 265–7, 270–4
bespoke garments 144, 147, 150, 158
Biographical History of England 74
blood pressure 17–18, 245–56
bodies, 'ideal' or 'normal' 5–7, 9, 12–14, 26–32, 47, 103, 142, 150–2
bourgeois society 126–7, 135–7
Brewer's Eccentrics, Rogues and Villains 73
British Association 112
British Medical Journal 60

Cambridge Metaphysical Club 187
caricature 12–13, 125–37
character 74, 77–8, 81, 84–6, 91, 126, 128, 215, 230–1
character books 88
Child Welfare League of America 210, 213–14
Cinema Paradiso 266–7, 270
citizenship 103
clinical trials 166
'common type' concept 102–4, 113–18

conjoined twins 8–10, 26, 28, 53–68
conjugal rights 174, 178–9
Contagious Diseases Acts 14, 167–8
contraception 173–7
criminality 32, 101–2, 116
cultural norms 267; *see also* social norms

'democratic psychiatry' movement 264–5
deviance 115, 269, 272–3, 277–8; *see also* 'normal deviants'
diabetes 16, 19, 227–40
Diabetes Control and Comp-lications Trial Research Group 238–40
disability, attitudes to 34
doctor–patient relationships 16–17, 226–7, 233, 239–40
double standard of sexual morality 14–15, 167–8, 171
Down's syndrome 60
dwarfs at court 7–8, 26–47

'eccentric biography' 10–11, 73–91; origins, history and reader-ship of 73–81; themes in 82–90
Eccentric Magazine 77–8, 84–8
École Supérieure des Arts et Techniques de la Mode (ESMOD) 155
Enlightenment thinking 4, 6, 11, 13
ethics 4
eugenics 11–12, 109–12, 117–18, 170, 212–13; reformed 251, 253
European Union 269

family relationships 15–16
fashion 142, 150–1
feminism 165–80 *passim*
foot-binding 58
freaks and freak shows 36–9, 58, 84, 91

Subject index   283

free will 186
French Revolution 146–7

ganglion blockers 254
genetics 253
geriatrics 256
globalisation 273
glycosylated haemoglobin 237–8
gypsies 270; *see also* Roma
  communities

health, definition of 247
heredity 112, 117
homosexuality 4–5
hospital medicine 226, 251
human nature 111, 117
hypertension 18, 245–51, 254

infertility, causes of 216–17
insulin 228, 232–8
intelligence testing 112
Italy 264–70, 275

jesters 33, 38–9

kinship 10, 15–16, 205–18

'labelling' processes 266
L'Albero degli Zoccoli 267
Le Dandy 151, 158
Lega Nord 268–9
lepers 116, 124
localism 267–9
London School of Hygiene and Tropical
  Medicine 252
Louise Wise Services 215–17

Malthusian League 173, 176
mannequins 156–8
medical norms 225–8, 239–41
Medical Research Council (MRC)
  248–54 *passim*
mental illness 20–1, 264
metric system 146–7
midgets 34–5
misers 86–7
mongolism 60
monstrosity 27–9, 36, 53–6, 59–68, 74,
  124–5, 135; degrees of 64–7;
  meanings of 61–4
moral standards 4–6

natural selection 110–11

natural/unnatural binary 3–4, 7–8, 12,
  26–31, 38, 76, 109, 254
naturalistic fallacy 3
nephrology 249
New England Journal of Medicine 239
New Wonderful Magazine 76–80
New York Times 53
'non-places' and 'non-persons' 273–7
'normal deviants' 7, 20, 73, 88, 263–4,
  269–74, 277
normal distribution 3
normalisation: Foucault's theory of 6,
  11, 16, 73, 90, 115–16, 124; in
  nineteenth-century Paris 125–8
normality, definitions of 2, 101–4, 109,
  118, 124
normative statements 2, 5
'normativity' (Canguilhem) 6, 225
norms: creation of 127; as a source of
  power 206; *see also* cultural norms;
  medical norms; social norms;
  statistical norms

ontological statements 5
orthopaedics 152–6
ostracism 134–5
Oxford English Dictionary 101–4

Paris, nineteenth-century normalisation
  in 125–8
'pathological' conditions 2, 6–7,
  17–19, 29, 62, 64, 83, 101, 103,
  123, 183–4, 225, 240, 245–7, 250,
  254–6
patient involvement and the patient role
  233, 239
patients' values and the patient's view
  225–9, 235, 240
pharmakos ceremony 133
philosophy, nature of 186, 201
physiognomy 11–12, 103–12, 117–18,
  126–8
'physiological' concepts in medical
  practice 237, 247, 252–7
'piazza madman' role 20–1, 262–73
  passim, 277
plague victims 116, 124
portraiture, composite 113–15
Prado, the 33
prostitution 167–73 *passim*, 176, 179
psychology, abnormal 183–7, 190,
  199–201
public spaces 272–7

284 *Subject index*

religious experience, empirical approach
  to 183, 201
representation: of human bodies 159,
  165; of national or group identity
  267–8; of normality 14, 54
republicanism 136
rickets 152–3
risk factors 250, 253–6
Roma communities 270
Romanticism 11, 128
Royal Society 58, 74

scapegoat role 133
self-blood glucose monitor-ing (SBGM)
  237
September 11th 2001 attacks 118
sexuality, male and female 14–15,
  166–8, 173–80
Siam 8–9, 56–60
Siamese twins *see* conjoined twins
social class 34
social norms 2–3, 6, 126–8, 225, 273
Society for Psychic Research 183
sociological studies 256; *see also*
  Armstrong, David; Durkheim, Emile;
  Goffman, Erving;
'starvation diet' treatment 229–32
statistical norms 2–3, 5

statistics, use of 142–3, 152, 247, 251
stereotyping 11, 34, 102–3, 123–4
stigmatisation and stigma management
  34, 123, 217, 269, 272, 274, 277
stream of thought 19, 200, 204
Street Offences Act (1959) 179
supermarkets 275–6
surveillance medicine 253–7
Sweden 179
sympathectomy 254

tailoring 13–14, 142–59
teratology 61–2, 65–7
terror attacks 6
The Freewoman 175–6
The Times 57
thiazide diuretics 254

'ubuesque' character 125
ugliness 122–5, 136–7
utilitarianism 111

venereal disease 167–73

Wasserman test 170
Western civilization 14
Wolfenden Committee (1954–6) 179
Wonderful Magazine 74–82 passim

Name index

Acton, William 188
'Aesop of Eton' 86
Allen, Frederik Madison 229–32
Allen, Gay Wilson 194–5
Anderson, James William 188–91
Aristotle 104
Armstrong, David 3, 18, 227, 251–6
Arney, W. R. 227
Arnheim, Rudolf 123, 125
Ashbee, Henry 81
Asquín, Mari-Bárbola 46
Augé, Marc 273, 275
Austen, Jane 80

Bacon, Francis 74, 76
Bain, Alexander 104, 195–6
Bakhtin, Mikhail 30
Baldock, John 84
Ballantyne, J. W. 62, 66–7
Balzac, Honoré de 126
Bancroft, John 180
Banting, Frederick 232
Barde, F. A. 148
Basaglia, Franco 264
Basso, K. H. 268
Baszanger, Isabelle 227
Baudelaire, Charles 136–8
Baynton, Douglas 60
Bazin, Anaïs 133
Beardsley, Aubrey 137
Beck, Christian 147–8, 156, 158
Belen, J. A. Sánchez 32
Bendixen, Kate 165
Benedict, Ruth 15, 206
Bentley, Nathaniel 87
Bergen, B. J. 227
Bernard, Claude 229, 246–7, 253
Bernard, Viola 211, 216
Bertillon, Alphonse 159

Besant, Annie 173–4
Best, Charles 232
Binet, Alfred 183
Bjork, Daniel 196–7
Blackwell, Elizabeth 168–9, 173–5
Blumenbach, J. F. 55
Boas, Franz 1, 15, 206
Bogdan, Robert 91
Bolton, George Buckley 54–6
Booth, Christopher 248
Boruwlaski, Count 84
Boscán, Juan 30
Bourdieu, Pierre 125–7
Bouza Álvarez, Fernando 33
Breward, Christopher 150
Brilliant, Richard 27
Britton, Thomas 86
Brooks, Joshua 55
Browne, Stella 172–3, 176–8
Browning, Robert 80
Buffon, Georges 65
Bunyan, John 198
Burnett, James 85
Butler, Josephine 167–8, 173

Camelford, Lord 85
Campbell, Lorne 38–9
Canghuilhem, Georges 1–2, 7–8,
16–18, 29–30, 124, 225–6, 241,
246–9, 255–6
Carlos, Don 39–40
Carpenter, W. B. 104
Castiglione, Balthasar 30–1
Caulfield, James 74–81, 84, 87–90
Céard, Jean 28
Ceriol, Furió 31
Chamorro, Eduardo 39, 46
Champfleury 128, 131
Chang and Eng 8–9, 54–62, 68

286 Name index

Charcot, Jean Martin 67
Charles V, Emperor 32, 38–9
Charteris, Francis 87
Checa, Fernando 32
Clapperton, Jane 173–4
Clothier, Florence 211
Collip, Bertram 232
Comte, Auguste 20, 184–5
Condorcet, Marquis de 147
Cooper, Bransby Blake 58
Cooper, Sir Astley 58
Cooter, Roger 252–3
Corban, Josephine Myrtle 65
Cousins, Mark 122
Covarrubias, Sebastián de 28–31, 39, 42–5
Cox, Virginia 30
Crawfurd, John 58–9
Cuvier, Georges 55, 104

d'Aguilar, Baron 77
da Vinci, Leonardo 13, 142
Dancer, Daniel 86
Darwin, Charles 80, 104, 110–11, 183–4, 192
Daumier, Honoré 153
Davies, David 42–3
Delas, George 148–9, 152, 156, 158
Deleito y Piñuela, José 33–4, 46
Dempsey, John 81–2
Devereux, Georges 1
Dickens, Charles 80–1, 86, 108
Dollery, Sir Colin 246–7
Douglas, Mary 12, 122
Dürer, Albrecht 123
Durkheim, Emile 1–2, 6–7, 11, 20, 32, 83, 101–2, 116–17, 185

Elliot, Thomas Renton 248
Ellis, Havelock 166–7
Elwes, John 86–7
Eng see Chang and Eng
Éon, Chevalier 87
Erikson, Erik 187–8
Estanislao 29, 39–40
Eve, Paul F. 65
Ewald, François 123, 126–7
Eyles, Leonora 178–9

Fairholt, F. W. 77, 80
Falomir Faus, Miguel 40
Fanon, F. 274
Feinstein, Howard M. 195–6

Feudtner, Chris 230, 239
Fiedler, Leslie 34–5
Flaubert, Gustave 137
Foucault, Michel 1–2, 6, 11, 16–17, 73–4, 90, 115–17, 124–5, 133–6, 226–7, 231, 246, 255
Franklin, Helen 217
Fraser Roberts, John Alexander 250–3
Frederickson, J. 273
Fuller, Margaret 87

Galton, Francis 11–12, 102–3, 109–18, 159, 185, 192, 251
Garfinkel, H. 266
Garsault, François de 145–8
Gaskell, Ivan 26, 40
Gautier, Théophile 151
Geertz, Clifford 274–5
Gesell, Arnold 212–13
Gilman, Sander 12, 59, 101, 103
Goddard, Henry Herbert 213
Goffman, Erving 7–8, 20, 29–32, 46, 73, 91, 123–4, 128, 263, 269, 273
Goldstein, Kurt 255
Goodrich, S. G. 78
Grahn, Theodora 87
Granger, James 74, 81
Granger, William 76, 82, 86, 90
Gudiol, José Maria 46
Guys, Constantin 136

Habermas, Jürgen 3, 6
Hacking, Ian 3, 13, 142, 184, 206
Hall, Stuart 8, 34
Hamilton, Michael 250
Harris, Robert 68
Havens, Kate 193
Hernstein, Richard 3
Hobbes, Thomas 6
Hogarth, William 90
Holanda, Francesco 27
Holcroft, Thomas 104
Hollander, Anne 146
Holmes, Oliver Wendell 80, 194
Holt, Edmund 82
Hood, Thomas 80
Hopkins, Jane Ellice 169, 174
Hotten, J. C. 80–1
Howitt, William 80
Hubert, R. 143
Hudson, Jeffery 84
Hugo, Victor 136, 153
Hume, David 5

Name index

Hunter, Henry 104
Hunter, Robert 55
Hutchinson, Dorothy 205, 211
Hymans, Henri 39

Isaacs, Bernard 256
Isabel Clara Eugenia, Infanta of Spain 40–3

James, Henry 191, 197
James, William 19–20, 122, 183–201
Janet, Pierre 183, 200
Jarry, Alfred 125
Jewson, Nicholas 226–7
João of Portugal, Prince 43
Jones, Joseph 65
Joslin, Elliot P. 230–2, 239
Juana of Portugal 43–4

Kant, Immanuel 12, 122
Kempner, Walter 254
Ketch, Jack 89
King, Edmund 80
Kitto, John 80
Kohut, H. 189
Kuklick, Bruce 187
Kusche, Maria 40–2

Laloo 60
Lambert, Daniel 81
Laqueur, T. 165
Latour, Bruno 5
Lavater, Johann Caspar 11, 102–13, 117, 126
Lavigne, Alexis 154–8
Lavoisier, Antoine Laurent 147
Lawrence, Christopher 248, 255
Lawrence, Susan 165
Lemoine, Henry 77
Lestrader, H. 234–5
Lewis, Thomas 248
Liebault, A. A. 192
Louis XVI 124
Louis-Philippe, King 127, 135–6
Luchet, Auguste 144
Lyell, Charles 55, 104

MacIntyre, Alasdair 2
Mackenzie, P. 80
McMichael, John 248
Margarita María, Infanta of Spain 46
Marianna of Austria 32, 46
Marías, Fernando 45

Maribarbola 46
Marsden, Dora 175
Martin, Charles 86
Martindale, Louisa 171–2
Mathieu-Castellani, Gisèle 27–8
Mayeux, Monsieur 12–13, 128–38
Mead, Margaret 15, 206
Melchiore-Bonnet, Sabine 42
Mena Marqués, Manuela B. 42
Menand, Louis 198–9
Miall, William 252
Michel, Edouard 38
Mill, John Stuart 11, 83–4
Miller, H. V. N. 61
Monboddo, Lord 85
Monnier, Henry 127
Montgomery, W. F. 63
Mor, Anthonis 36–40, 43
Moreno Villa, José 32–3, 39, 44
Morris, Jerry N. 251–3
Morrison, S. L. 251–2
Murdoch, Rupert 10
Murray, Charles 3
Musset, Alfred de 128
Myers, F. W. H. 183, 200

Nadel-Klein, J. 268
Noble, Mark 82
North, John 61

O'Connell, Helen 166
O'Connor, Erin 84–5
O'Donovan, R. W. 63
Olmi, Ermanno 267
Oviedo, Gonzalo Fernández 32–3
Owen, Griffith 84
Owen, Richard 61

Pankhurst, Christabel 171–2
Paré, Ambroise 27–8
Parker, Ida 210
Parsons, Talcott 17, 226–7, 233
Pendleton, James 63
Pérez Sánchez, Alfonso 33
Perrenot de Granvelle, Antoine 36
Perry, Ralph Barton 185–95 *passim*, 198–9
Pertusato, Nicolasito 46
Philip II of Spain 29, 32, 36, 39–40, 43–4, 47
Philip III of Spain 28–9
Philip IV of Spain 32–3, 38, 45–7
Philipon, Charles 128

288 *Name index*

Pickering, George White 18, 247–56
Pickstone, John 227, 255
Pitt, Thomas 85
Platt, Robert 18, 247–55
Pope, Alexander 77, 88
Porter, Roy 27, 36, 43
Porter, Theodore 206
Pound, Ezra 137
Prakash, G. 274
Prest, Thomas 82
Prestley, J. W. 228, 230
Purcell, Rosamond 35
Purvis, William 81

Quetelet, Adolphe 13, 142–3, 150, 152

Ramsbotham, Francis 65
Redworth, Glyn 32
Renouvier, Charles 186–7, 191–9 *passim*
Richards, Robert J. 192, 194
Rivilla Bonet y Pueyo, José de 29
Robinson, Virginia 211
Rochester, Earl of 90
Rooney, J. F. 273
Royden, Maude 172, 178
Royer, P. 234–5
Ruiz, Leticia 42
Ruiz, Magdalena 40–4
Russell, William 77–8, 86–7

Sade, Marquis de 125
Saint-Hilaire, Isidore Geoffroy 61, 65–7
Sánchez Coello, Alonso 37, 43, 46
Scharlieb, Mary 173
Schur, E. M. 266
Schwehn, Mark 190–3
Scott, James 208
Sekula, Alan 115–17
Senden Theis, Sophie van 214
Sentenach, Narciso 38
Serrera, Juan Miguel 44
Serres, Étienne 55
Shepherd, Francis J. 60
Shuger, Debora 42
Sigerist, Henry 255
Sigismond of Poland 39
Simon, Linda 197–8
Sinclair, J. 82
Singerland, W. H. 213–14
Sitwell, Edith 90
Smith, Roger 105
Southworth, John 35
Sowry, Clive 250

Spencer, Herbert 110, 192–4
Stewart, Susan 35–6
Stopes, Charlotte Carmichael 165
Stopes, Marie 177–8
Strout, Cushing 187–91, 196
Sturdy, Steve 252–3
Swedenborg, Emanuel 184
Swift, Jonathan 85, 90
Swiney, Frances 170–1

Taft, Jessie 205–6, 211
Talbot, Mary Anne 87–8
Tavener, Henry 81
Taylor, Eugene 184, 187, 192, 195
Tegg, Thomas 77, 82, 85–7
Temple, Minny 195
Testa, Armando 266
Thackeray, W. M. 80
Thompson, D'Arcy 123
Tiefer, Leonore 180
Tietze-Conrat, Erica 38
Tiles, Mary 54
Timbs, John 77–8, 84
Titian 38–42
Titmuss, Richard 253
Tolstoi, Edward 234
Topham, Thomas 84
Tornatore, Giuseppe 266
Towle, Charlotte 211
Townshend, Chauncey 80
Traviès, Charles-Joseph 128, 131–2
Tristán, Luis 43–4

Velázquez, Diego 33, 38, 45–7
Vernant, J. P. 133–5
Villamanrique, Andrés de 32
Vrolik, Willem 65

Wallace, Russel 104
Wanley, Nathaniel 74, 78, 85–8
Ward, Tom 188, 194
Wesley, John 87
West, Rebecca 175–6
Whipple, L. E. 200
Williams, David 35–6
Wilson, Henry 77–82, 86–9
Winnicott, D. W. 189
Woodall, Joanna 40
Woodyatt, Rollin T. 232–3
Woolf, Virginia 165
Worboys, Michael 170
Wordsworth, William 192
Wozniac, Robert 184
Wright, Chauncey 187